Research and Development in Expert Systems VI

THE BRITISH COMPUTER SOCIETY WORKSHOP SERIES

Editor: P. HAMMERSLEY

The BCS Workshop Series aims to report developments of an advanced technical standard undertaken by members of The British Computer Society through the Society's study groups and conference organizations. The series should be compulsive reading for all whose work or interest involves computing technology and for both undergraduate and post-graduate students. Volumes in this Series will mirror the quality of papers published in the BCS's technical periodical *The Computer Journal* and range widely across topics in computer hardware, software, applications and management.

Some current titles:

Current Perspectives in Health Computing
Ed. B. Kostrewski

Proceedings of the 3rd British National Conference on Databases (BNCOD3)
Ed. J. Longstaff

Proceedings of the 4th British National Conference on Databases (BNCOD4)
Ed. A. F. Grundy

People and Computers: Designing the Interface
Eds. P. Johnson and S. Cook

Text Processing and Information Retrieval
Ed. J. C. van Vliet

Proceedings of the 5th British National Conference on Databases (BNCOD5)
Ed. E. A. Oxborrow

People and Computers: Designing for Usability
Eds. M. D. Harrison and A. F. Monk

Research and Development in Expert Systems III
Ed. M. A. Bramer

People and Computers III
Ed. D. Diaper and R. Winder

People and Computers IV
Ed. D. Jones and R. Winder

CONPAR 88
Ed. C. Jesshope and K. D. Reinhartz

ECOOP 89
Ed. S. Cook

Proceedings of the 7th British National Conference on Databases (BNCOD7)
Ed. M. H. Williams

Graphics Tools for Software Engineers
Ed. A. C. Kilgour and R. A. Earnshaw

People and Computers V
Ed. A. Sutcliffe and L. Macaulay

Research and Development in Expert Systems VI

Proceedings of Expert Systems 89, the Ninth Annual
Technical Conference of the British Computer Society
Specialist Group on Expert Systems
London, 20-22 September 1989

Edited by

Nigel Shadbolt
Artificial Intelligence Group, Department of Psychology
University of Nottingham

Published by
CAMBRIDGE UNIVERSITY PRESS
on behalf of
THE BRITISH COMPUTER SOCIETY
Cambridge
New York   Port Chester   Melbourne   Sydney

Published by the Press Syndicate of the University of Cambridge
The Pitt Building, Trumpington Street, Cambridge CB2 1RP
40 West 20th Street, New York, NY 10011, USA
10 Stamford Road, Oakleigh, Melbourne, Australia

© British Informatics Society Ltd 1989

First published 1989

Printed in Great Britain at the University Press, Cambridge

Library of Congress cataloging in publication data available

British Library cataloguing in publication data available

ISBN 0 521 38477 X

Contents

Preface

Expert systems - a natural history 1
Nigel Shadbolt

Using qualitative reasoning to build diagnostic expert systems 12
Chris Price and John Hunt

Qualitative modelling for industrial applications 24
Hiro Sugaya

Reconciling problem-solving and instructions in one knowledge decomposition framework 34
Benita Cox

DLGMS: A dependency-based lemma generation and maintenance system 43
David E. Wolstenholme

Using meta-level information for expert system control: a "blending" transformer approach 54
Yannis Cosmadopoulos and Richard Southwick

Verification of rule-based expert systems in wide domains 66
Alun Preece

The normalized model and expert systems maintenance 78
John Debenham

Developing cooperative knowledge-based systems 90
Lise Land and Tim Mulhall

An environment for experimentation with interactive cooperating knowledge-based systems 104
L. Sommaruga, N. Avouris and M. H. Van Liedekerke

Invited Lecture
Expertext : Hypertext-Expert system theory, synergy and potential applications 116
Judith Barlow, Martin Beer, Trevor Bench-Capon, Dan Diaper, Paul Dunne and Roy Rada

LUST for life: developing expert systems for life assurance underwriting 128
Fergus Bolger, George Wright, Gene Rowe, John Gammack and Bob Wood

PORTAFOGLIO: A portfolio advisor application 140
Andrea Chierici, Maria Grazia Filippini and Marco Minati

TULIP: Life underwriting expert system 153
Gary Chamberlin, Ian Neale and Mustafa Khan

A knowledge-based approach to telecommunications network alarm monitoring 165
Robin Khan

A knowledge-based system for exchange maintenance 177
J. Butler, W. Stein, J. Shepherdson, K. Beard and J. Bigham

Problems of diagnostic knowledge processing: design and implementation 188
of the system DIGS
Gennady Agre and Danail Dochey

Expert systems, expert tutors and training in elementary statistics 195
Michael Wood

MEEPLES - an expert system for scheduling meetings 207
C. N. Cadas

A parallel expert system for real-time applications 220
Haihong Dai, Terry Anderson and Fabian Monds

Concurrent refinement of structured objects: a language for distributed 235
knowledge programming using specifications and annotations
Mihai Barbuceanu, Stefan Trausan-Matu and Balint Molnar

A graphical expert system for microfossil identification 240
Peter Swaby

FADES: a tool for automated fault analysis of complex systems 253
C. L. Wood

A knowledge-based system approach to the synthesis of distillation sequences 263
Vijay Vadhwana

An expert system for the control of the activated sludge process 276
R. Williams, B. Knight, P. Watts and J. Burns

Keynote Lecture
Future directions in knowledge acquisition 288
Professor Bob Wielinga and Guus Schreiber

Preface

The papers in this volume were presented at the ninth Expert Systems conference organised by the British Computer Society Specialist Group on Expert Systems.

Both the venue and the date of the conference was changed from previous years. this imposed heavy demands on already busy people. I would like to thank all those who helped in putting together the programme for this conference: in particular the members of the Programme Committee, and all those who refereed papers.

The successful production of these proceedings - and the conference itself - is due in large measure to the professionalism and assistance provided by Fiona Pearson and her colleagues at Clearway International.

Expert systems - a natural history

Nigel Shadbolt
Artificial Intelligence Group
Department of Psychology
University of Nottingham
Nottingham NG7 2RD

Abstract

This paper examines the origins, current state and future prospects for expert systems. The origins are traced from the schism with classic Artificial Intelligence. The characteristics of early expert systems are described and contrasted with more recent developments. A number of influential forces operating on present day systems are reviewed. The future trends in the evolution of expert systems are discussed.

1 Introduction

It has always seemed an interesting thought - can we talk about the *natural history* of a machine? In particular, can we use analogies from the natural world when thinking about the computer? There are similarities. We can see more complex computing devices developing from simpler ones. Computers occupy habitats, ecological niches to which they are more or less suited. Various forces operate to select the best of these. Some change, others find a role and remain unchanged, others perish. One can carry the analogy some way. Although it is interesting to note that there are those who suggest it is computing that offers insights into the natural world (Dawkins 1986). The genetic substrate, DNA, is after all an information encoding mechanism *par excellence.*

This paper presents a natural history for one evolving species of computing systems, namely - expert systems. What can we say of their origins, present condition and future prospects?

2 Origins

An important part of the natural historian's work is to establish the lineage or *phylogenetic* history of any species. To which *genus* does it belong? What closely related species are there? When did it become clearly distinct from these related species?

In the case of expert systems, there is agreement that they developed out of a branch of the computing genus known as artificial intelligence (A.I.). The early origins of A.I. systems can themselves be traced back to the mid '50's. Expert systems appeared as a distinct line around the late '70's. However, there is considerable argument about just when and where the divergence took place.

Many would regard MYCIN (Shortliffe et al 1973, 1976) as the first and original expert system. In part, this is because it made evident to the rest of the world the fact that something new had evolved. MYCIN came out of work conducted on the Stanford Heuristic Programming Project. The system assisted doctors in the selection of an appropriate course of treatment for patients with bacteremia, meningitis and cystitis.

It is not the only contender for the accolade *first expert system*. Some would argue in favour of the DENDRAL system (Buchanan et al 1978). It too was developed at Stanford and its function was to infer the molecular structure of unknown compounds from mass spectral and nuclear magnetic response data. Another contender is MIT's MACSYMA system (Martin et al 1971). This system, which is today in widespread commercial use by engineers and scientists, assists in a range of mathematical tasks. It uses mathematical expertise to recognise a user's problem and then selects appropriate methods and techniques of mathematical analysis. The foundation for MACSYMA was the MATHLAB 68 system (Engelman 1971) which originated in the late '60's.

Whichever one is accorded the title all these early systems share strong similarities. They were large, they incorporated substantial amounts of heuristic knowledge. They were built with applications in mind. They were American, programmed in LISP and many people saw them as the new wave in A.I.

Research on other large expert systems continued through the late '70's across a range of application domains. These are now regarded as landmarks in the development of expert systems. CASNET (Szolovits et al 1978, Weiss et al 1978) was a large medical expert system that diagnosed and proposed treatments for disease states related to glaucoma. One of the distinctive features of CASNET was that knowledge was represented in a semantic network that attempted to provide a causal-association model of symptoms, disease processes and treatments. The PROSPECTOR system (Gaschnig 1982) helped in the interpretation of geological data and attempted to assess the likelihood of finding various types of mineral deposits. Its knowledge representation was rule and network based. It used certainty factors and probability propagation methods to encode the idea of confidence in evidence and certainty in conclusions. XCON/R1 (McDermott 1980) configures DEC VAX computer systems. It decides upon the components needed to produce an operational system given a customer's order. It is a constraint driven system - it has knowledge about what components can go together, what the constraints at the installation site are etc. It uses this knowledge, expressed in a rule-based format, to reason forward from the constraint data to a configuration that satisfies the constraints. This commercial system is still in use and is considered one of the most successful in the history of expert systems.

It is interesting to note that early versions of these systems shared many of the characteristics of the progenitor systems discussed earlier. They had large knowledge bases, ran on large computers, consumed man years of research development, were American built and they all received a lot of publicity. It is also interesting to note that they employed a wide range of techniques to represent knowledge and reason with it. In some of the earliest systems we see mixed representation methods; rules, nets and frames. However, it is also salutary to note that four out of the six named systems only reached what is termed the *prototype* stage. Clearly this was not yet a completely mature and exploitable technology.

A new direction in the evolution of expert systems was provided by the work done on EMYCIN (van Melle et al 1979, 1984). The acronym which stands for *essential MYCIN* indicates the skeletal nature of the system, which was MYCIN stripped of its domain knowledge. What one is left with is a rule-based representation language which uses a backward chaining control regime, certainty handling methods, and automatic explanation facilities. This abstraction away from the problem domain left a clean kernel system. The system was restricted to representing and reasoning with knowledge in a particular way. However, it provided an uncomplicated tool with which to build applications. In particular, it could be used to build diagnostic and classification systems. The age of the expert system *shell* had dawned.

Once the template for such shells became apparent they proliferated. Early shells tended to be primarily rule-based. They also began to migrate from costly hardware to PCs, and from LISP to a variety of other programming languages. The simplicity of a kernel rule-based shell made this process straightforward.

The history of some of these early shells illustrates some interesting differences in respect of how expert systems technology developed on either side of the atlantic during the first part of this decade. The original EMYCIN was written in INTERLISP and ran on DEC mini computers. Another early shell was KAS (Reboh 1981). The concept was very close to EMYCIN, the difference was that KAS was the PROSPECTOR system stripped of its geological domain knowledge. Again the system was written in INTERLISP and ran on mini computers.

The development of early US *purpose built* shells is exemplified by Teknowledge's products S.1 and M.1. The S.1 shell was an expert system building tool based on rule-based representations. Its basic control mechanism was backward chaining. However, it also supported alternative representational methods, including frames and a procedural language. The cost of such added functionality in the first part of this decade was that its original INTERLISP implementation ran only on specialised Xerox workstations. The more modest M.1 system was capable of running on IBM PC hardware, it was rule-based and built using a PROLOG backward chaining architecture. It had no other representational capabilities. In fact, for the US M.1 was rather an exception. A survey of US products in the early '80's shows that the main preoccupation was the provision of quite specialised knowledge engineering software which offered a wide range of capabilities. However, one paid a high price both for the software and the hardware.

The UK scene was characterised by the appearance of a number of inexpensive, PC-based shells. Many of these owed much to the effort that had gone into producing PC PROLOGS. These implementations offered a natural vehicle for shells. PROLOG requires little augmentation to function as a shell. In fact, one of the first products APES (Augmented PROLOG for expert systems, Hammond 1982) was just such a shell.

Other shells appearing at or around this time attempted to hide their PROLOG internals from the user. The recurrent feature of these systems was rule-based representations, backward chaining control of reasoning, and often an add-on which provided a means of representing and reasoning about uncertainty.

A great deal of interest was shown in this *first generation* of shells. In the UK A.I. had been progressing steadily during the late '50's and '60's. Unlike the US it never received much governmental support, but by the early '70's a number of centres of excellence and had made significant contributions to A.I. in fields as diverse as theorem proving and robotics. The UK A.I. scene suffered something of a reverse with the publication of the Lighthill report in 1973. For a while there was a real chance we would lose our research groups completely. However, the groups hung tenaciously on, and by the beginning of the '80's the environment was changing. One of the first signs of this changing environment was the founding by Professor Donald Michie in 1980 of the BCS SGES. This specialist group's goal was to bring together a community of individuals interested in the potential of expert and knowledge based systems. The 1982 Alvey Report led to the 350 million pound Alvey programme, the EEC was also getting its ESPRIT programme underway. These initiatives released large amounts of funds into IKBS and its supporting technologies. This largesse was prompted in large part by the inception of the 1981 ICOT or Japanese Fifth Generation initiative. Suddenly it seemed everyone regarded A.I. as the key to future economic success.

As awareness increased and money poured in, more and more companies and academic sites became active in the area. As momentum gathered and expectations rose perhaps it is not surprising that a sense of what the technology could realistically achieve was not always retained.

Nevertheless, this interest together with the emergence of an expert system shell technology led to real progress. Only a few years later Professor Alan Bundy (1987) in a key note lecture at ES87 was able to observe

> the UK expert system community has been very successful in the development of small scale, commercial, rule-based, expert systems. A typical example is a fault diagnosis system for a piece of specialised hardware, consisting of a set of less than 100 rules, running on a PC, in one of the many commercial shells. Part of the success consists in the unexpected (to me anyway) discovery of a large number of commercially interesting problems which yield to such a simple mechanism.

What Bundy was describing in terms of our natural history analogy is equivalent to the *speciation* of simple but effective forms - an explosion of simple systems to fill the many niches that exist.

He also referred to a preoccupation with diagnostic systems. So distinguishing one particular generic class of expert systems. There are in fact a range of types of problem solving we could imagine expert systems performing. A number of classifications have been proposed, the one below derives from Waterman[1] 1986. Each of these different types is proposed to have a different underlying problem solving structure. This is sometimes called the *inference level*. And can be regarded as a type of knowledge in its own right. It is knowledge about how components of expertise are to be organised and used in the overall problem solving system.

Type	Description
Diagnosis	Inferring system malfunctions from observables
Interpretation	Inferring situation descriptions from sensor data
Prediction	Inferring likely consequences of given situations
Design	Configuring objects under constraints
Planning	Designing and sequencing actions
Monitoring	Comparing observations to plan vulnerabilities
Debugging	Prescribing remedies to malfunctions
Repair	Executing a plan to administer a prescribed remedy
Instruction	Teaching of any knowledge level component
Control	Governing overall systems behaviour

Table 1: Generic Problem Solving Categories

Inference level knowledge is, of course, only one variety of knowledge one is likely to find in expertise. Using a classification due to Weilinga and Breuker (1986) we can distinguish three other general sorts of knowledge; strategic, task and domain level knowledge.

Strategic knowledge monitors and controls the overall problem solving. This can have to do with the way resources are used. What to do if the proposed solution fails or is found to be inappropriate in some way. What to do when faced with incomplete or insufficient data. Task level knowledge is sometimes called *procedural* knowledge. This is knowledge to do with how goals and sub-goals, tasks and sub-tasks should be performed. Thus in a classification task there may exist a number of tasks to perform in a particular order so as to utilise the domain level knowledge

---

[1] This is in fact a rather coarse characterisation and if we take just the category of diagnosis it can be further analysed into sub-types; heuristic diagnosis, systematic diagnosis through causal tracing, systematic diagnosis through localisation.

appropriately. By domain level here we mean its narrow sense - knowledge that *describes* the concepts and elements in the domain and relations between them. This sort of knowledge is sometimes called *declarative*, it describes what is known *about* things in the domain.

Any field of expertise is likely to contain, to greater or lesser extents, elements of domain, task, strategic and inference knowledge. At any particular knowledge level the information may be explicit or implicit in an experts' behaviour. Thus in some domains the experts may have no real notion of the strategic knowledge they are following whilst in others this knowledge is very much in the forefront of their deliberations. Also, of course, the requirements on a system about how far it needs to implement these various levels will vary. But they can become evident even in *modest* first generation applications. Moreover, it is acknowledged that significant reasoning about problem domains requires more than just modelling simple relationships between concepts in the domains - it requires causal models of how objects influence and affect one another, models of the processes in which objects participate. This is a hard problem. And often the limitations of first generation expert systems means that sophisticated domain models cannot be supported. It was this point that Bundy went on to discuss in his ES87 address.

> UK knowledge engineers have also been active in building much larger expert systems, with hundreds or even thousands of rules. In addition, they have experimented with alternative knowledge representation and reasoning techniques, e.g frames, objects, semantic nets, etc. This use of large scale expert systems and of alternative and/or multiple knowledge representations has been more typical in the US market, but both are becoming more important here.

In a lecture delivered to the previous years conference, Steels (1986), had also pointed out the need for us to look beyond first generation systems. He pointed out some of the limitations of first generation systems. First generation systems tend to rely on behavioural heuristics, *if X is observed do Y*. These are *surface* models of *performance*, with no *deep* model of *competence*. A second generation system would have an additional component in the form of a deep model which gives the system an understanding of the domain over which the heuristics operate. In fact Steels argues that an important source of inspiration for this second generation component is to be found in A.I. work in areas such as qualitative reasoning (Price and Hunt 1989 this volume, Suguya 1989 this volume). This enhances the problem solving of any system by modelling the domain principles, its causal and functional properties. Associated with the need to provide deep models Steels remarked on the need for powerful methods of building KBSs. One category of tools would help in the knowledge acquisition process - a process that needs to be more sophisticated than ever if deep models are to be implemented.

We can discern then a number of recurrent themes leading up to the present; a substantial number of modest rule-based applications in place, a concern to provide a methodology for the knowledge engineer, the emergence of more powerful shells, the recognition of an impending second generation of expert systems. The questions now relate to the current well-being of the expert system species. Will the dissemination of small expert systems and shells continue? Are knowledge engineering methods available? Can the technology be scaled up to large applications? When will commercial second generation expert systems arrive?

3 Current conditions

The Alvey programme for all its faults, real and imagined, was a great catalyst. It succeeded in forging a bridge between academe and industry. And although as Bramer (1986) remarked many of the best researchers were led into endless rounds of grant writing and administration, there was real disappointment when the Bide report, which suggested a comprehensive follow on to Alvey, was largely ignored. In its place the DTI's Information Engineering Directorate (IED) has attempted to continue what Alvey began. For all its efforts it is hamstrung by the funding conditions it has to work by. Usually a number of partners, commercial and academic, will get together to form a consortium to carry out a programme of work. The consortium can apply for up to 50% of its total eligible costs, academic partners however receive 100% of their costs and this is taken from the 50% of costs the IED will pay to the consortium. The industrials then receive the remaining amount of money in proportion to their original costs. The effect of these rules is to make academic participation unattractive to industrial partners. Moreover, the absolute proportions awarded tend to mitigate against small to medium sized company participation.

The SERC is the other source of funding for academics. However, money is so tight that the SERC only manages to fund a minority of its alpha rated (technically excellent) research proposals in computer science.

Meanwhile the infrastructure that was so painfully built-up in Alvey is gradually coming apart. As yet, we have no definite commitment to funding for community Clubs, Special Interest Groups, mailshots, awareness and training.

Problems of awareness and training are still widespread in the UK scene. The awareness problem manifests itself, in part, in a perception of expert systems as a risky and esoteric technology. Too many institutions only maintain a watching brief. But watching briefs can lead to problems when, for example, management decides to sample the technology. The person maintaining the watching brief is expected to produce a compelling technology demonstrator. Often, there are simply insufficient resources in house to produce a convincing demonstration. The demonstrator fails, the technology is seen to be immature, the management remains unconvinced, the company maintains its watching brief.

At the other extreme, there are those who argue that building expert system is now all routine. They deprive the technology of its success. The achievements disappear under the moving tide of IT advances. In promoting awareness and interest in a technology, it is always important to enumerate the successes and spin offs.

Problems of awareness crop up in another way. The Alvey programme, although beneficial in many ways, fostered a rather introverted community. The consequence of this was that those inside the community were made very aware of the technology, and soon came to think that everyone else must be too. In fact, the technology has not really succeeded in getting outside of the Financial Times top 100 listed companies. There is still a substantial job of awareness to tackle.

There has also been a belief that awareness leads to technical competence. The fact is that acquiring an adequate knowledge engineering competence takes a lot of effort, and a current problem is the provision of trained people. The most comprehensive training is obtained by those who have taken a number of the IKBS M.Sc. conversion courses available and who have computing or a relevant cognitive science background. However many personnel are recruited from general IT conversion courses. The problem here is that these courses are often only marginally relevant to the technologies which comprise IKBS. Training problems are compounded by the fact that we lack an agreed idea of a syllabus or curriculum that might form a minimal requirement for a qualification in knowledge engineering. There are still relatively few Honours undergraduate courses in A.I., and even fewer graduates going on to complete PhDs. Those personnel in post, who are expected to acquire competence in the new technologies face the problem of finding the time and expert help to support their retraining. There is an urgent need to attend to the training requirements in IKBS and A.I.

Moving on to consider the application of expert systems technology, we noted the proliferation of small to medium sized applications. Most of these are rule-based. Most occupy modest but effective niches in a variety of areas from manufacturing to finance, power utilities to medicine. There are, however, a number of areas in which it has proved more difficult to deploy IKBSs. These include real time applications, very large databases applications, and domains where the reasoning is non-standard, where conditions are constantly changing, or where the knowledge base itself needs to be constantly updated. These application areas present technological and methodological problems that are forcing us to apply a richer range of techniques, and develop more powerful methods of IKBS specification and formulation. To some extent, they are setting the agenda for current expert system research.

If we look at current developments in methods and tools for knowledge engineering we find one particularly active area - knowledge acquisition. It is difficult to establish methods and methodologies for conducting acquisition through the life-cycle of KBS construction. The most thorough framework is provided by KADS - Knowledge Acquisition and Domain Structuring (Breuker 1987, Weilinga and Schreiber 1989 this volume). KADS embodies seven principles for the elicitation of knowledge and construction of a system. We will not detail them all here, but one is of particular relevance given the discussion earlier about knowledge levels. It recommends that the analysis should be model-driven as early as possible. This requires that one should bring to bear a model of how the knowledge is structured early on in the process, and use it to interpret subsequent data. This will involve appeal to what we have called inference level knowledge earlier in this paper. It may also include appeal to models of the domain, or devices in the domain (Chandrasekaran, 1988).

An important theme in this and other current approaches to knowledge acquisition is that the enterprise should be viewed under the metaphor of model building, rather than the mining of information. In this regard, we have moved from a transfer view of acquisition to a model view. This recognises that even within first generation expert system construction, a knowledge engineer is engaged in a subtle process. Knowledge engineering is not simply a matter of transferring knowledge from an expert into a knowledge base. The final product is a model of various aspects of an expert's knowledge.

A rather less disciplined methodology and yet one that is almost always associated with expert systems is *rapid prototyping*. The idea is that it is easier for experts to criticise a working system, than it is to specify the system in the first place. Initially, a prototype is built, without much regard to its weaknesses, and the expert makes suggestions about its performance. These suggestions are incorporated into the system by programmers, and at the next session there should be fewer errors. This cycle continues until the expert is satisfied with the behaviour of the system.

There is some debate as to whether rapid prototyping constitutes a methodology or a knowledge acquisition technique. In fact, a growing area of research is concerned to *evaluate* the various claims made about knowledge acquisition methods and techniques (Burton et al 1987, 1988, Shadbolt & Burton 1989).

Tools construction is an important area of current work. Again let us take knowledge acquisition as illustrative. Currently, there four main types of acquisition tool available or under development (Boose 1989 provides a comprehensive review).

Firstly, those systems which are implementations of standard knowledge elicitation techniques, such as repertory grids and concept sorting. Secondly there are those systems which use machine learning techniques to induce rules from sets of worked examples and observed data. In addition to these categories, there are also systems which use knowledge about the structure of a particular domain in order to drive the elicitation. However, these are large-scale systems dedicated to specific projects, and are not generally available. Finally, there are a number of large-scale, generic knowledge acquisition environments under construction. These typically provide a number of automated KE techniques, knowledge base editors, automated transcript analysis and various other support software for the knowledge engineer. These systems are currently at the research stage, and as yet are not generally available. Although they are not yet available they indicate the shape and form of the next generation of knowledge engineering tools.

4 The future

In the last section we mentioned some of the difficult technical problems that must be solved if expert systems are to progress. One of these is expanding the types of reasoning available to systems. Those advancing the cause of second generation systems regard the expansion of reasoning capabilities as crucial. Many applied problems require recourse to non-standard methods of reasoning such as *default* and *abductive* reasoning. Many of these non-standard reasoning methods are *non-monotonic* (Ginsberg 1987 for a review).

Work on non-monotonic reasoning is becoming an important issue in expert systems. Many current expert systems make an implicit assumption of *monotonicity*, facts true at the beginning of a reasoning session are assumed to remain true throughout. If facts subsequently become false then usually the system has to restart inference from the beginning. There is no way of determining what information generated by the system is still valid. Many deductions may have been made on the basis of a fact that is no longer true. There are systems and shells that offer mechanisms to help manage this problem, so-called *truth maintenance* or *belief revision* systems. They tend to incur high computational overheads and complicate problem solving. The provision of more elegant solutions to these problems remains an important area of work (Smith & Kelleher 1988).

Hand in hand with reasoning is the representational component of any expert system. At ES84 Professor Aaron Sloman (1984) made an appeal for the provision of more varied classes of representation to support the kind of complex modelling and reasoning that our second generation systems will require.

He argues that if we look at the notations, formalisms and representational systems used by a wide range of professions, from mathematics to music, programming to cartography, we find a huge variety of types. These have arisen to fulfill requirements imposed by the nature of the domain and the purposes for which they were to be used. Some of the forces that have shaped the development of these *representations* are perceptual and cognitive, and involve problems of parsing and interpreting certain sorts of structure. Some of the forces of development have had to do with the processes that the formalisms are involved in; calculation, planning, searching, and the detailed control of action. Sloman recommended that

> we need to explore the uses of different sorts of formalism for different purposes. We need to understand how an intelligent system can choose between different formalisms, and how it can, on occasions, create new formalisms when doing so would give new insight or heuristic power of some kind

This recommendation still stands. One very radical approach is to be found in the technology of connectionism of neural nets (McClelland & Rummelhart 1985, Rummelhart & McClelland 1985). And is not just the problem of representation that this technology is being applied to. It is also being used to tackle problems in learning and perception, reasoning and information retrieval.

Neural nets consist of a set of processing units. In neural nets all processing is carried out by the units - there is no control or executive program. Units are connected together and each connection has a weight or strength. Unit's receive input and as a function of these inputs compute an output. The system is inherently parallel because many units can carry out their computations at the same time. In a network learning usually occurs due to the modification of the weights of existing connections.

Within such nets the representations are patterns of activation over units. Experience is recorded as changes in the weights of a net. Patterns of activation come and go, what remains are traces when they have passed. A trace is bound to be distributed over many different connections, and each connection is implicated in many different associations. The traces of different experiences are therefore superimposed in the same set of weights. In neural nets one regards the retrieval of a representation as a partial reinstatement of a network state, using a cue which might only be a fragment of the original input.

The whole connectionist research enterprise is generating a great deal of excitement. It is claimed to offer real solutions to very hard problems in representation, perception and learning. Connectionist models seem able to take in large amounts of data and self-organise so as to learn underlying regularities and patterns in the data. They are then able to recognise similar patterns in new data and reinstate previous patterns as appropriate. This makes them an exciting prospect for a whole range of expert system applications.

But such networks are not without their problems (Pinker & Prince 1988). It is often difficult to come up with the right set of inputs. One has to decide how to set the weights on the connections and how they should subsequently modify themselves. Because of the distributed nature of the knowledge in such nets it is virtually impossible to obtain explanations of the net's behaviour. Nevertheless there is no doubt that they will begin to make their presence felt within our subject.

We now move on to a different force which will play a part in how expert systems evolve - hardware developments. We take for granted the remarkable performance now being delivered on lost-cost machines. However, this power is changing both what we can do and how we do it.

The developments in hardware will ameliorate many problems associated, for example, with real time, on-line applications. The emergence of super-PCs will break the constraints imposed by restrictive operating systems and limited memory. A similar breakthrough is occurring in the workstation range - increasing power is offered at falling prices. This will allow quite modest organisations to run networks of powerful machines. These PC-workstations will provide 16 million instructions per second with 32 megabytes of main memory as standard. This sort of power will also support ever more extensive programming environments.

An important secondary feature of this new generation of PC-workstations will be the *routine* provision of large, high resolution displays. Such hardware devices will provide the medium for much more sophisticated Human Computer Interaction (HCI). The incorporation of graphical, video and audio displays into expert system interfaces will provide solutions to some of the problems of information presentation.

A rather different consequence of this raw power may be a move back to *brute force* methods. A major impetus behind early A.I. was the need to produce elegant axiomatisations of problems so as to circumvent hardware limitations. It was simply not possible to imagine building a natural language translation system that operated by recourse to table lookup. When planning or game-playing the search of even quite small problem spaces required intelligent heuristics to guide the search. Increasing computer power allows computationally intensive approaches to become an option. But limitless power and brute force methods can also reduce the motivation to look for principles.

In contrast to technical issues let us consider directions in applications. Whatever field is chosen it is clear that one major development will be the increasing importance of *embedded* expert systems. Such systems will sit within much larger conventional software. Such embedding requires methods and standards if a coherent and consistent design philosophy is to arise that extends from traditional pieces of software through to KBS and expert system programs.

We have already mentioned that more expert systems will be built to tackle a wider range of generic problem solving areas than has been attempted hitherto. As this happens the technology will need to be aware of developments in other branches of A.I. One example is the work that has been steadily progressing in the planning and scheduling sub-fields of A.I. Indeed there are signs that substantial collaboration is occurring in this area between expert system and A.I. researchers.

One set of questions a natural historian would ask, concerns the social life of the species being examined. Whilst it would be a little premature to enquire after the social habits of expert systems, their creators certainly have social ends and ambitions. What of them? There has been within the BCS SGES a long-standing and proper concern for the social consequences and implications of expert systems. There have been a number of conference articles, and now a journal, dedicated to these matters. We will not rework the arguments here save to remind ourselves that expert systems do not exist in a moral vacuum. They raise important issues of responsibility and accountability, matters of judgement and conscience.

5 Concluding remarks

This paper has tried to discern the origins, current state and future directions of the expert system. It has been largely preoccupied with the UK scene, but that reflects the principle interest of our parent professional body the BCS. It has also sought to draw on a somewhat strained and lighthearted analogy with the natural historian's account of the progress of natural forms.

6 References

Boose, J.H. (1989) A survey of knowledge acquisition techniques and tools. Knowledge Acquisition, 1.

Bramer, M.A. (1956). Expert systems in Britain: progress and prospects. In Research and development in Expert systems, ed. M.A. Bramer, III, Cambridge University Press.

Breuker, J. (Ed.) (1987) Model-Drive Knowledge Acquisition Interpretation Models. Deliverable task A1, Esprit Project 1098; University of Amsterdam.

Buchanan, B.G. & Feigenbaum, E.A. (1978). DENDRAL and Meta-DENDRAL: their applications dimension. Artificial Intelligence, 11.

Bundy, A. (1987). How to improve the reliability of expert systems. In Research and development in Expert systems, ed. D.S. Morales, IV, Cambridge University Press

Burton, A. M., Shadbolt, N. R., Hedgecock, A. P. & Rugg, G. (1987) A Formal Evaluation of Knowledge Elicitation Techniques for Expert Systems: Domain 1. In Moralee, D. S. (Ed.) Research and Development in Expert Systems IV. Cambridge University Pres

Burton, A. M., Shadbolt, N. R., Rugg, G. & Hedgecock, A. P. (1988) Knowledge Elicitation Techniques in Classification Domains. ECAI-88: Proceedings of the 8th European Conference on Artificial Intelligence.

Chandrasekaran, B. (1988) Generic tasks as building blocks for knowledge-based systems: the diagnosis and routine design examples. Knowledge Engineering Review.

Dawkins, R. (1986). The blind watchmaker. Longman

Engelman, C. (1971). The legacy of MATHLAB 68. Proceedings: Second Symposium on Symbolic and Algebraic Manipulation, pp. 29-41

Gaschnig, J. (1982). PROSPECTOR: an expert system for mineral exploration. In Introductory Readings in Expert Systems, ed. D. Michie: Gordon & Beach

Ginsberg, M.L. (1987) Readings in non-monotonic reasoning. Morgan Kaufman

Hammond, P. (1982). APES: a detailed description. Report 82/10, Computing Dept., Imperial College, University of London, 150 Queen's Gate, London

Martin, W.A. & Fateman, R.J. (1971). The MACSYMA system. Proceedings: Second Symposium on Symbolic and Algebraic Manipulation, pp. 59-75

McClelland, J. L & Rummelhart, D. E (1985) Parallel Distributed Processing: Explorations in the Microstructure of Cognition Vol 2 Psychological and Biological Models. Cambridge, Mass: MIT Press.

McDermott, J. (1980). RI: an expert in the computer systems domain. Proceedings: AAAI-80

van Melle, W. (1979). A domain-independent production-rule system for consultation programs. Proceedings: IJAI-79, pp. 923-925

van Melle, W, Shortliffe, E.H. & Buchanan, B.G. (1984). EMYCIN: a knowledge engineers tool for constructing rule-based expert systems. In Rule-based Expert Systems, ed. B. Buchanan & E. Shortliffe, pp. 302-328, New York: Addison-Wesley

Pinker, S. & Prince, A. (1988) On language and connectionism: analysis of a parallel distributed processing model of language acquisition. Cognition, 28.

Reboh, R. (1987). Knowledge engineering techniques and tools in the PROSPECTOR environment. SRI Technical Note 243, SRI, 333 Ravenswood Avenue, Menlo Park, California

Rummelhart, D. E & McClelland, J. L (1985) Parallel Distributed Processing: Explorations in the Microstructure of Cognition Vol 1 Foundations. Cambridge, Mass: MIT Press.

Shadbolt, N.R. & Burton A.M (1989) Empirical Studies in Knowledge Elicitation. ACM-SIGART Special Issue on Knowledge Acquisition

Shortliffe, E.H. (1976). Computer-based medical consultations: MYCIN. New York: Elsevier

Shortliffe, E.H., Axline, S.G., Buchanan, B.G., Merigan, T.C. & Cohen, S.N. (1973). An artificial intelligence program to advise physicians regarding antimicrobial therapy. Computers and biomedical Research, Vol.6, pp. 544-560

Sloman, A. (1984) Why we need many knowledge representation formalisms. In Research and development in Expert systems, ed. M.A. Bramer, Cambridge University Press

Smith, B. & Kelleher, G. (1988) Reason maintenance systems and their applications. Ellis Horwood.

Szolovits, P. & Parker, S.G. (1978). Categorical and probabilistic reasoning in medical diagnosis. Artificial Intelligence, 11, pp. 115-144

Steels, L. (1986). Second generation expert systems. In Research and development in Expert systems, ed. M.A. Bramer, III, Cambridge University Press

Wielinga, B.J. & J. Breuker, (1986). Models of expertise. Proceedings: ECAI'86, pp. 306-318

Weiss, S.M., Kulikowski, C.A., Amarel, S. & Safir, A. (1978). A model-based method for computer-aided medical decision-making. Artificial Intelligence, 11, pp. 145-172

Using Qualitative Reasoning to Build Diagnostic Expert Systems

Chris Price and John Hunt
Department of Computer Science
University College of Wales
Aberystwyth
Dyfed
SY23 3BZ
United Kingdom
Email: cjp@uk.ac.aber.cs

Abstract

Qualitative reasoning promises to provide a robust basis for diagnostic expert systems, but its application is limited by ambiguity and the exponential explosion of possible outcomes - hence the simple nature of many of the devices that have been diagnosed so far.

In practice, these limitations can be overcome by adding more knowledge to the qualitative model or to the diagnostic system, but such additions to the system must be made in a principled way, or the diagnostic system will have the same ad hoc nature as most first generation expert systems.

This paper gives a classification of the types of extra knowledge that can be used, and applies the classification to several documented diagnostic systems based on qualitative reasoning.

1. Introduction

Research into qualitative reasoning from the structure and behaviour of systems (Bobrow 1984) promises to overcome some of the problems with heuristic-based diagnostic systems (Merry 1985; Guida 1986; Price & Lee 1988) by providing knowledge-based systems with an underlying understanding of their domain. In theory, this understanding provides a robustness which such systems would otherwise lack, but in practice qualitative reasoning needs to be supported by other domain and diagnostic knowledge in order to make it useful for real applications.

Much of this additional knowledge is often implicitly added to the qualitative reasoning system, and can detract from its robustness without the implementors being aware that this is happening. The solution to this problem is to identify the sorts of knowledge being added to the system, and to be aware of the implications of those additions.

This paper classifies the different sorts of domain and diagnostic knowledge that can be employed in a qualitative diagnostic system. This classification is derived mainly from our research, which concentrates on the qualitative diagnosis of man-made mechanical devices. However, we apply the classification to a wider range of model-based diagnostic systems, only some of which use qualitative modelling techniques.

The paper is structured in the following way:

- *section two* looks at how qualitative reasoning can be used for diagnosis and points out where the problems can occur.

- *section three* describes the different sorts of knowledge that can be used to overcome the problems with qualitative diagnosis.

- *section four* considers several different model-based diagnostic systems, and categorizes the extra knowledge that they employ.

- *section five* presents some initial results obtained by augmenting a simple model-based diagnostic system with appropriate additional knowledge.

2. Qualitative Diagnosis

2.1 Qualitative Simulation

A qualitative model of a device will represent the structure of the device, and the behaviour of each component making up the device. In a mechanical device, for example, the structural description of the device might contain information about how all of the parts relate to one another, and the behavioural description of a component might describe how that component responds to forces acting upon it (Price 1988).

When such a model is used for qualitative simulation, it should reflect the behaviour of a correctly working device. Because the simulation is qualitative, it may be ambiguous where absolute values would be needed to produce a definite result.

2.2 Performing Qualitative Diagnosis

When devices fail, it is because either the structure of the device has changed (something has become disengaged, jammed, fallen out) or the behaviour of a component has changed (because it is broken in some way). Such changes can be reflected by similar changes to the model.

If the correct modelling of components and of the structure only happens when assumptions are true, it is possible to produce models of faulty devices by retracting assumptions (De Kleer & Williams 1987). Given a real device which is faulty, the behaviour of the models of faulty versions of the device can be compared with the symptoms displayed by the actual faulty device. If a faulty model's behaviour matches the real faulty device's behaviour, then the changes to device structure and and component behaviour to produce the faulty model could account for the faults (the actual changes to the structure and behaviour of the actual faulty device).

In this way, it is possible to generate all the possible faults that could have caused the symptoms exhibited by the actual faulty device. This process of candidate fault generation gives a robust, easily maintainable basis for a diagnostic expert system.

2.3 Drawbacks of Qualitative Diagnosis

In order to apply qualitative reasoning to "real tasks" such as diagnosis, some limitations need to be addressed (Kuipers 1985; Schrager et al 1987). Among these are:

Modelling Building a qualitative model usually implies more effort than eliciting heuristics, since it is more information intensive and needs to be more rigorously constructed. The knowledge that underlies heuristics in heuristic-based expert systems has to be made explicit in the model.
If the behaviour of the whole device is made implicit in the description of its structure (rather than synthesized from that structure combined with the behaviour of device independent components), then those implicit simplifications imply classes of possible faults that the diagnostic system will be unable to find.

Ambiguity The qualitative nature of the model sometimes implies ambiguities, where no ambiguity is possible in the real system. The implications of this for diagnosis might be that several plausible hypotheses are generated for a set of symptoms, where only one of those hypotheses would be plausible with a more detailed model.

Complexity For diagnostic problems, qualitative simulation typically generates many possibilities (Bratko 1987). This is because it generates all possible faults. (It should be observed that "all faults" means all faults which can be generated from that particular model - if the model has the wrong level of granularity, faults will be missed). It makes sense to avoid this complexity wherever feasible, as human experts seem to do - first trying out heuristics before falling back on more fundamental knowledge.

Only perfunctory diagnosis can be performed using a qualitative model as the sole source of knowledge about the domain, and about diagnosis in that domain - the generation of possible faults which account for the observed symptoms. Even this generation of candidates may prove impossible to complete because of the ambiguity of the simulations and the large number of possible combinations of candidates.

In order to apply qualitative reasoning techniques to real diagnosis tasks, these limitations need to be overcome through judicious use of domain and task knowledge.

3. Using Extra Knowledge for Qualitative Diagnosis

Adding extra knowledge to the qualitative model and to the diagnostic system which uses that model can overcome all of the limitations that we have explored. The addition of heuristic knowledge which links symptoms to possible causes can allow for rapid handling of frequently occurring cases. The enhancement of the model with more knowledge can resolve apparent ambiguities in the simulation. Information about how to perform diagnosis in the domain can focus the diagnostic system in way that is not possible using just the domain information available in the model.

The main drawback of these additions is that they tend to occur in an ad hoc manner. The easiest way to disambiguate the simulator, for example, is by adding some extra lines of code to deal with every special case that occurs. *If component is a dingle and it is connected to a droggle and current is flowing then... .* By the time this has been done for several "special cases", the qualitative diagnostician has the same nature (and the same problems) as other heuristic systems, and has lost any pretence of robustness.

In order to preserve the advantages of qualitative reasoning when performing diagnosis, it is necessary to recognise enhancements to the basic qualitative diagnostician, to classify them and to be aware of the difference that they can make to the robustness of the diagnostic system.

This section classifies enhancements firstly by which part of the diagnostic task they assist - enhancements to the qualitative model; improvements to the general diagnostic method; knowledge about performing diagnosis for a specific domain; knowledge to assist in deciding what test to perform next. Each of these types of knowledge is then split into subclasses with particular characteristics.

3.1 Additional Knowledge in the Qualitative Model

A qualitative model will normally only reflect the logical structure of the device it is modelling. In the case of a digital circuit, that might be the digital components and the electrical connections between them. In the case of a mechanical device, it might be the components plus a qualitative description of the connections between the components. Extra knowledge is added to the model to reduce model ambiguity or complexity, or because an extra dimension of knowledge is needed for a specific application.

Disambiguation Knowledge This is knowledge that reduces ambiguity by allowing the simulator to decide what might happen in cases where a set of qualitative relationships allow more than one outcome to a situation.

One example of this is adding *order of magnitude* information to a model (Raiman 1986). In effect, this adds extra information to the model that one influence can be disregarded by comparison with another. When the order of magnitude information is about classes of influence, and the order of magnitude relationship is always true (even when the device works incorrectly), then this is very useful knowledge to add to the model.

A more doubtful form of disambiguation knowledge occurs in our own work (Price 1988), as well as many of the systems we examine in section 4. Our models of mechanical devices act at a single level. This means that sometimes there is not enough information to limit the choice of events that can happen in the model to the one which must happen in the real device. *Will the spring be fully compressed before the lever hits the casing?* We add *device qualifications* to the model of a specific device which give the answer to such specific questions about particular states. This type of model enhancement needs to be retractable in order to perform robust diagnosis. The reason that this is a questionable form of model enhancement is because it describes the behaviour of the whole device. Such behaviour must be made explicit and retractable in order for the diagnostic system to reason about faults concerning that behaviour.

Model Simplification In most domains, it is possible to simplify the simulation for particular subclasses of device. De Kleer and Brown (1984) call such simplifications *class assumptions*.

For example, while many mechanical devices rely on the effects of friction for their correct behaviour, there are many others which can be adequately simulated without considering all the friction forces that act when the parts of the device. For such devices, a class assumption that friction is irrelevant reduces significantly the complexity of the simulation.

Application Specific Annotation It is often useful to add features to the domain model which would not normally be part of it, but which is known to be useful for a particular type of application. This is an extension of what happens naturally in modelling - the relevant level of detail is added to the model for a particular domain.

A good example of this is made explicit in Davis' work (Davis 1984), where he adds information about the adjacency of connections on circuit boards, so that he can model bridges between the connections only in places where they are likely to occur.

Each of these types of extra knowledge should be encoded as assumptions that can be retracted, in which the model should display the behaviour it would have displayed if the assumption had never been present. This is for two reasons:

- This enables a diagnostic system to model faults that occur when design assumptions are violated. A simple example of this might be a model of a car engine. A model of the mechanical movement of the parts of the engine might assume that friction can be ignored. That assumption would no longer be true if there was no oil in the engine, so we need to be able to model the engine with friction acting on it.

- Retraction allows the model to be used for different types of application. Diagnosis and most design tasks have different concerns, and so retraction of irrelevant annotations simplifies the model for tasks where those annotations are irrelevant.

3.2 Generic Knowledge about Performing Diagnosis

This is domain-independent knowledge that can be applied to the diagnosis of most man-made devices.

Ordering of choices (single then many) In many diagnostic domains, a single fault is more likely than many faults happening at once. While it would be unwise to limit the diagnostic system to considering only single faults, it is a reasonable strategy to consider possible single faults in some detail before widening the search to multiple faults. By the same token, the system should look at pairs of faults that account for the systems before considering triplets of faults, and so on. The heuristic that all symptoms are caused by a single fault is an extreme example of this more general heuristic, and one that needs to be retractable when the diagnostic system has failed to find a single fault which could account for all symptoms.

Causal chaining In man-made devices, there is usually a link between inputs and the symptoms. This is evident when studying mechanics diagnosing car electrical problems. Having found current at the car battery, and no spark at the spark plug, they look for faults in the components and connections linking the battery to the plugs. Any parts or connections not implicated by such links are assumed not to be responsible. A diagnostic system which reasons from structure and behaviour can apply similar limitations to its search space, although it needs to be analysed before application - for some domains, such assumptions are not valid.

3.3 Domain Dependent Diagnostic Knowledge

Knowledge will be available about the domain, and often about the particular type of device or system that is being diagnosed. Use of this knowledge is always heuristic, and so it should always be used in a "tentative" manner - conclusions that depend on it need to be retractable so that further investigations can be made when those conclusions prove to be false.

Model Focusing For diagnostic applications where a model of the whole device or system would have very many components, breaking the model into several smaller models can reduce the complexity. The problem then is to decide which sub-model contains the symptoms and the fault(s). Lambert et al (1988) use heuristics to choose which sub-area of the domain to model. Another way of doing this is to have a hierarchy of models and apply qualitative diagnosis at each level of the hierarchy. In either case, the diagnostic system needs to be able to recover from the hypothesis that a particular part of the system contains the fault in the case where that hypothesis is proved false.

Use of Device Experience Chandrasekaran (1986) lists several types of heuristic knowledge that come from previous experience with the type of device being diagnosed. Such information can be used in preference to performing modelling when it exists. This is especially the case with classification knowledge, matching symptoms directly to faults.

Association of faults Multiple failures are often much harder to diagnose than single faults. When the diagnostic system has failed to find a single fault which accounts for the symptoms, the search for multiple faults can be ordered by grouping faults which are known to occur together (usually one of the faults is caused by the other, eg. holed cylinder gaskets in a car engine often cause the radiator to empty, giving the symptom of high engine temperature).

Knowledge about the reliability of components Many companies keep reliability records for different components and devices that they manufacture. In other areas, such as process plant design, there is knowledge about where the weak points of the system are. Such information can be used by a diagnostician to order candidate faults according to their likelihood. This ordering can be used both when simulating faulty devices to see whether the faults produce the observed symptoms, and also to prioritise further investigation when several possible faults match the symptoms.

Knowledge of Domain Properties It is also possible to order hypotheses about faults according to the properties of the components. If there are two candidate faults for a symptom, where the first candidate is that a metal bar has snapped, and the second is that a plastic flange has split, and the same force is acting on both components, then we might investigate the split flange first, knowing that plastic is easy to break than steel. This knowledge would be employed when more specific information about reliability of components was not available.

3.4 Test Generation

Test generation attempts to identify tests which will provide information that can be used by the diagnostic process to refine the diagnosis being generated. The knowledge used during the test generation process should be separated from the model as it is heuristic in nature and often represents some higher level testing strategy. It is an intrinsic part of the overall diagnostic process, and needs to be handled in a principled manner.

Candidate Differential Knowledge In many domains, it is possible to state tests which distinguish between two or more candidate faults. *If the fault is in the distributor cap or the HT lead, try replacing the HT lead.* When there are several equally plausible candidates that account for a particular set of symptoms, this type of knowledge can be used to suggest a test to perform next.

Cost of Tests When tests are being generated it is important to know the cost of a test, that is how difficult or time consuming a test will be. If this is not done, then tests will be selected regardless of their complexity. For example, replacing an engine is more expensive than checking an oil level.

Expected Risk or Benefit In any system, there will be a risk associated with the faults being hypothesized. In many systems, eg. a doorlock, the risk factor is negligible, but in others, eg. a process control plant, there may be be a risk to human life through fire or explosion. In such cases, tests which explore high risk hypotheses should be given some priority for investigation.

On the other hand, some tests have the ability to partition the search space by disqualifying large numbers of candidate faults. The benefit of performing such tests means that they should be given high priority.

4. Classifying Published Work

Using the above categories, we have classified the knowledge used by a number of published model-based diagnostic systems. The systems detailed below are representative of all the systems examined. This section shows that all of these systems have enhanced their model-based diagnosis to some extent with information that is not naturally part of their model-based system. Where categories have been left blank, it is not necessarily the case that no such knowledge was used in that system, only that it could not be inferred from the referenced literature on that system.

4.1 Davis

The system presented by Davis (1984) uses knowledge of the structure of a digital circuit and the behaviour of its components to generate a diagnosis. It is able to reason about changes to the behaviour of the components and about changes to the structure of the circuit, for example, bridging connections between tracks of the circuit boards.

Additional model knowledge
Davis uses application specific annotations in his qualitative model, for example, he includes information on the adjacency of components within the device. This allows him to reason efficiently about bridging faults.

Generic Diagnostic Knowledge
Additional diagnostic knowledge forms part of the control strategy of Davis' system. In order to improve the efficiency of the diagnostic process, for example, he uses a

heuristic that states that a single fault is always responsible for the behaviour of the actual faulty device, however it is not possible for the diagnostic system to retract this heuristic in order to reason about multiple faults.

Domain diagnostic knowledge
Davis also implicitly uses additional domain knowledge during the generation of a diagnosis. For example, an ordered list of failure types (generated by an experienced engineer) is used to order the list of plausible candidates.

Test generation knowledge
Davis puts a great deal of emphasis on using the right tests to split the space of possible candidates in half, and encodes empirical test generation knowledge supplied by domain experts in order to select appropriate tests.

4.2 De Kleer and Williams

De Kleer and Williams (1987) describe a system which can diagnose multiple failures in digital circuits.

Generic Diagnostic Knowledge Additional diagnostic knowledge is used to direct the generation of candidate faults. For example, a method similar to the causal chain described in section 3.2 records the dependencies which the inputs use during the simulation of the circuit. These recorded dependencies are then used to generate the possible candidates.

Domain diagnostic knowledge There are a number of areas in which De Kleer augments his system using domain knowledge. For example, the system is given the probability of individual component failures. This knowledge is then used to refine the list of possible candidates.

Test generation knowledge Additional test generation knowledge is used by De Kleer and Williams to generate the appropriate tests. For example, in order to determine which measurement to make next, a cost function is employed which will indicate which measurement will lead to a result in the least number of steps.

4.3 DEDALE

Dague et al (1987) present a system called DEDALE which is a diagnostic expert system which applies qualitative reasoning to analog circuitry.

Additional model knowledge DEDALE adds disambiguation knowledge to the qualitative model by dividing the quantity space into layers. Within each layer all the values have the same order of magnitude, between layers there is an order of magnitude difference. These layers are then used to disregard one influence compared with another by using the order of magnitude information, reducing ambiguity.

Domain diagnostic knowledge Because of the characteristics of the domain (strong interdependence between components), deviations from expected values are treated as a focussing mechanism for the diagnostic system. This focussing down through the device hierarchy can fail, as deviations in one component can be caused by failure of another component. DEDALE has further heuristics to allow it to reason across the same level in order to account for a deviation on a component which is not due to a fault in that component. These heuristics, together with the functional hierarchy which represents the device, give a lot of direction to diagnosis in DEDALE.

4.4 ARIA

Although the system which is described by Schrager et al (1987) is not a diagnostic system, it does generate simulations of both the correctly working device and of a limited set of faulty versions of the device, in this respect it accomplishes part of the task of a qualitative diagnostic system.

Additional model knowledge Schrager et al have made extensive annotations to their qualitative model. For example, they allow processes in one component to know about and to directly alter the qualitative values in another component. Disambiguation knowledge has also been added to the simulation system during what the authors call "tuning sessions". For example, additional qualitative states and processes to manipulate the qualitative values have been added to the simulator which are very dependent on the device being simulated.

4.5 GORDIUS

Simmons and Davis (1987) present a system which combines heuristic rules and qualitative simulation to generate a diagnosis. There are three main steps which are used to generate a diagnosis, these are: generate, test and debug. The generator identifies possible candidates, and the tester checks to see if the candidate passed to it could have generated the actual situation. If the test fails then the debugger either alters the candidate in an attempt to match the actual situation or initiates the search for a new candidate.

Additional model knowledge The qualitative simulation process is not described in detail, and so little can be said about the use of additional model knowledge. However the model does posses some additional knowledge to enable it to handle domain problems such as quantified effects and conditional effects.

Generic Diagnostic Knowledge This system makes extensive use of generic domain knowledge when generating candidates. For example, generic "debugging knowledge" is used to modify (debug) a failed candidate model in an attempt to find a successful candidate model. Generic diagnostic knowledge is also used to control the overall processes of the system.

Domain diagnostic knowledge Domain knowledge is used by all three steps, for example, the generate step uses domain knowledge to associate possible causes with the actual symptoms, and the test and debug steps both use knowledge of certain geological structures.

Test generation knowledge Once the initial situation is described to the system no further information is obtained, thus there is no need for any test generation knowledge.

4.6 IDM

IDM is an architecture built by Fink (1985) which combines both a heuristic representation and a qualitative representation. The architecture contains three expert systems, one for the qualitative system, one for the heuristic system and one to map between the other two. This explicitly separates the additional knowledge and the qualitative knowledge used. However it does not separate the generic diagnostic knowledge form the domain dependent knowledge.

Additional model knowledge In order to successfully simulate her model, Fink has found it necessary to provide additional disambiguation knowledge. For example, a regulator is a basic component of her model, however in the electrical domain it was necessary to break a regulator down into a switch and relay.

Generic Diagnostic Knowledge Generic diagnostic knowledge is used in the diagnostic control system to identify faults. For example: if an output from a functional unit (higher level than a single component) appears incorrect, check its input.

Domain dependent knowledge Most of the knowledge which possesses domain dependent information is held in the heuristic knowledge base, however some of the knowledge is also held in the third expert system and converts values from the heuristic representation into the qualitative representation.

Test generation knowledge This is implicitly referred to by Fink. Her system has some knowledge of the cost of tests but she does not describe this process. It is therefore not possible to identify the use of any additional test generation knowledge.

5. Some preliminary results

We have applied our model-based candidate fault generator to a variety of mechanical devices; a example of which is the simple latch doorlock illustrated in figure 1. In this section, we shall use this device to illustrate the benefits which can be gained from augmenting a model-based system with diagnostic knowledge.

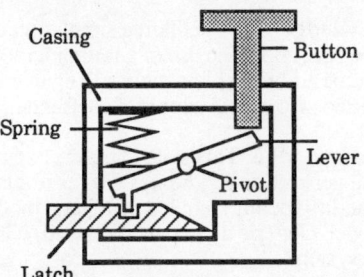

Figure 1: The simple latch doorlock

The model-based candidate fault generator considers all possible combinations of alterations to the sliding device. This would result in $(2^n - 1)$ possible candidate faults where **n** is the number of possible device alterations. In the case of the doorlock, which can generate 19 separate possible alterations, either to the behaviour of components or to the structure of the device. This would result in 524 287 possible combinations of faults.

Several model-based systems have used the single fault assumption to reduce this to 19 possibilities. Experience has shown that quite frequently more than one fault will occur at the same time, which means that dealing only with single faults is unwise, if convenient.

An improvement on the single fault assumption is to order the generation of multiple faults, enabling the system to generate candidate faults in stages; first all single faults are considered, then pairs of faults, then triplets etc. The results of two example diagnostic sessions, illustrated in table 1, are discussed below. Both examples use the simple doorlock, illustrated in figure 1, as the device to be diagnosed. The first example has been provided with the symptoms of a stuck pivot and the second example has to diagnose the symptoms of a multiple fault composed of a broken lever and a broken tooth between the lever and the latch.

5.1 A single fault example: a stuck pivot

The "pure" candidate fault generator must consider all possible alterations to the doorlock in all possible combinations, when generating a diagnosis. As stated above, this results in the generation of **524 287** possible candidate faults which must then be tested.

If *candidate ordering* knowledge is used then the number of possible candidates is reduced to **19**. This occurs because the system first considers all single alterations, and then stops if an appropriate explanation is found for the symptoms. As there are 19 possible alterations, it first considers 19 possible single candidate faults; as the actual fault described by the symptoms is a single fault, an explanation is found and the process terminates.

If *attention focusing* knowledge is used instead of candidate ordering knowledge, then the number of possible candidates considered is reduced to **15**. This reduction is achieved because the system first considers all possible alterations along the causal chain, in this case four, thus giving: $(2^4 - 1) = 15$.

When both candidate ordering and attention focusing knowledge are used, the number of candidates is further reduced, to **4**. This is because there are 4 possible alterations on the causal chain, and these are ordered so that single faults are considered first. As the actual fault is a single fault on the causal chain, a full explanation of the symptoms is found having only considered these four candidates.

	No Augmentation	Attention Focusing	Candidate Ordering	Both
Stuck Pivot	524, 287	15	19	4
Broken Lever & Broken Tooth	524, 287	63	172	21

Table 1: Results of using generic diagnostic knowledge

5.2 A multiple fault example: a broken lever and a broken tooth

Again the pure candidate fault generator must consider **524 287** possible candidate faults when generating the diagnosis.

The use of candidate ordering knowledge reduces this figure down to **172**. This is comprised of the 19 faults represented by single alterations, and the 153 multiple faults represented by pairs of alterations.

Attention focusing can also be used to reduce the number of candidate hypotheses under consideration, for this example, **63** candidate faults have to be considered. This is because there are only six alterations along the causal chain, which are combined in all possible combinations: $(2^6 - 1) = 63$.

By combining both attention focusing and candidate ordering knowledge this figure can be reduced down to only **21** hypotheses considered.

These gains in performance rely on the actual fault being formed of simple alterations to the artifact, and these alterations being on the causal chain. In the worst case, if all the alterations possible in the device were part of the actual device, then no gains in performance would be achieved, however, this is an unlikely fault situation.

This illustrates that even for a very simple device, the use of generic diagnostic knowledge can result in substantial gains in performance.

6. Conclusions

In this paper, we have identified the different sorts of knowledge that can be added to a qualitative diagnostician, and the ways in which these additions can improve the capability of the diagnostician. Most of those improvements come through reducing the large space of possible faults or through searching that space more effectively.

We have applied our classification to many of the more widely known model-based diagnostic systems, and shown that each of them uses the sorts of knowledge that we have identified, although not always explicitly.

The knowledge used to enhance model-based diagnosis is at least as important for efficient, robust diagnosis as is the model on which the diagnosis is based. Given that fact, how do you incorporate all of this knowledge in a domain-independent, device-independent way?

We conclude that the best way to facilitate the easy construction of well-engineered qualitative diagnostic systems is to implement a diagnostic architecture which encourages the diagnostic system builder to explicitly distinguish between the qualitative model and the knowledge that is added to the diagnostic system to improve diagnostic performance. Having identified the sort of knowledge that is needed, we are presently working on such an architecture (Hunt & Price 1989).

Acknowledgements

This research has been carried out as part of Alvey Project IKBS 061. Discussions with Professor Mark Lee and with members of the Alvey DKBS Club prompted a number of the ideas expressed in this paper.

References

Bratko, I. Mozetic, I. Lavrac, N. (1987) *Automatic Synthesis and Compression of Cardiological Knowledge*, in Machine Intelligence 11, Oxford University Press.

Bobrow, D. ed (1984) *Qualitative Reasoning about Physical Systems*, pub. North-Holland.

Chandrasekaran, B. (1986) *Generic Tasks in Knowledge-based Reasoning: High-level Building Blocks for Expert System Design*, in IEEE Expert, pp23-30, Fall 1986.

Davis, R. (1984) *Diagnostic Reasoning based on Structure and Behaviour*, in Artificial Intelligence 24.

De Kleer, J. & Brown, J. S. (1984) *A Qualitative Physics based on Confluences*, in Artificial Intelligence 24.

De Kleer, J. & Williams, B. (1987) *Diagnosing Multiple Faults*, in Artificial Intelligence 32, p97-130.

Fink P. K. (1985) *Control and integration of diverse knowledge in a diagnostic expert system.*, Proceedings IJCAI-85, pp426-431.

Forbus, K. (1984) *Qualitative Process Theory*, in Artificial Intelligence 24, 1984.

Genesereth, M. (1984) *Use of Design Descriptions in Automated Diagnosis*, in Artificial Intelligence 24.

Guida, G. (1986) *Reasoning about Physical Systems: Shallow versus Deep Models*, in

Expert Systems and Optimisation in Process Control, (eds) Mamdani and Efstathiou, Gower Technical Press, England.

Hunt, J. E. & Price, C. J. (1989) *Towards a Generic, Qualitative-based, Diagnostic Architecture*, Proceedings 9th International Workshop on Expert Systems and their Applications, Avignon, pp253-268.

Kuipers, B. (1985) *The Limits of Qualitative Simulation*, in Proc. IJCAI-85, pp128-136.

Kuipers, B. (1986) *Qualitative Simulation*, in Artificial Intelligence vol 29.

Lambert, H. Eshelman, L. Iwasaki, Y. (1988) *Acquiring and Complementing the Model for Diagnostic Tasks*, Proceedings ECAI-88.

Merry, M. (1985) *Expert Systems - Some Problems and Opportunities*, in Expert Systems '85, Cambridge University Press.

Price, C. (1988) *Developing a Qualitative Representation of Mechanical Devices for Use in Diagnosis*, in Engineering Applications of Artificial Intelligence Journal 1(2), July 1988.

Price, C. & Lee, M. (1988) *Applications of Deep Knowledge*, in Artificial Intelligence in Engineering 3(1), pp12-17, January 1988.

Raiman, O. (1986) *Order of Magnitude Reasoning*, Proceedings AAAI-86, pp100-104.

Dague, P. Raiman, O. Devès, P. (1987) *Troubleshooting: when modelling is the trouble*, Proceedings AAAI-87, pp600-605.

Schrager, J. Jordan, D. Moran, T. Kiczales, G. Russell, D. (1987) *Issues in the Pragmatics of Qualitative Modelling: Lessons Learned from a Xerographics Project*, in Comms ACM, pp1036-1047, December 1987.

Simmons, R. & Davis, R. (1987) *Generate, test and debug: Combining associational rules and causal models*, Proceedings IJCAI-87, pp1071-1078.

Xiang, Z. & Srihari, S. N. (1986) *A strategy for diagnosis based on empirical and model knowledge*, Proceedings Avignon-86, pp835-848.

QUALITATIVE MODELING FOR INDUSTRIAL APPLICATIONS

Hiro Sugaya
Asea Brown Boveri Corporate Research
Knowledge Systems Group
CH-5405 Baden, Switzerland

Abstract

The ongoing research on deductive inference, in particular qualitative reasoning, starts demonstrating its usability in various applications. We report our experience with the application of qualitative physics to the modeling and analysis of a cooling circuit used in an electrical power system. While the generation of causal arguments concerning the functionality of the cooling circuit is feasible, the derivation of diagnostic rules out of the generated causal arguments requires much broader knowledge of the domain so as to compete favorably with the conventional shallow approach.

1. Introduction

Design, simulation and analysis of physical processes are typical activities found in industrial applications. The quality of symbolic representation and the processing of domain knowledge about the structure of a plant and the rules that govern the behavior of its component devices are crucial to a successful application of knowledge-based systems. Among the many approaches currently being investigated to the issue of knowledge representation and reasoning, we focus on the role of logic in the context of qualitative reasoning. Since we are concerned with the modeling of technical processes, the basic features of first-order logic are quite natural as a representation formalism. That is, objects of a system can be described by constants, and the properties of each object as well as relations between objects can be represented by predicates.

Qualitative modeling in Artificial Intelligence was first studied by Rieger and Grinberg (1977) in terms of events, states and causal links for reasoning about mechanisms. A new approach to causal reasoning based on the relationship between structure and behavior has been developed by Davis et al (1982) and Genesereth (1982) for modeling digital circuits, and also by De Kleer & Brown (1983), Forbus (1981), and Kuipers (1984) for modeling continuous systems having analog parameters (e.g. mechanical devices). Although the functional model for digital systems is fairly well understood, the one for analog systems requires further works in order to clarify how the structure and components of the system can make up its overall function.

The important advantage of the new approach is its ability to generate causal arguments of a modeled system out of its component behavior. Viewing it in opposite way, the decomposability permits a simpler description of its component function, and at the same time, such functional descriptions can be based on physical laws to ensure the fidelity of causal arguments. The disadvantage is the limitation of modeling itself, i.e., modeling is always incomplete. Sometimes a real world experiment is much simpler than modeling and generating causal arguments. Detecting where a new value is and determining what properties are qualitatively significant is still an open issue and may require some quantitative reasoning. Nevertheless, the qualitative modeling technique has increasingly been applied in various domains to explore its ability for simulation (causal arguments) and analysis (diagnosis) of physical systems: electronic circuits by De Kleer & Williams (1987) and Dague & Raiman (1987); photocopiers by Shrager et al (1987) and mechanical devices by many researchers. This paper describes yet another attempt in the domain of electromechanical devices.

Currently, we are working on a system that supports modeling of physical processes through structure and function descriptions. The input and output behavior of its components is abstracted to a set of discrete states, for each of which a causal analysis is performed. Concepts necessary for modeling an abstract device are organized into a class-subclass taxonomy, and a particular device is modeled through an instance of such generic concepts. This object-based modularization facilitates formalization of component knowledge in physical processes.

In recent years Prolog has been successfully applied to solve many practical applications. Coding of knowledge, especially compiled knowledge, can be well represented by providing an appropriate formalism and inference rules in Prolog. However, acquisition of compiled knowledge in a particular application domain is difficult and often extends over years. Therefore, we investigate an application of qualitative reasoning technique to generating causal arguments and its use as an apprentice to human experts. Furthermore, the possibility of deriving compiled rules out of those causal arguments has also been studied to evaluate the soundness of this approach. Section 2 describes the qualitative modeling technique being used in our work. Section 3 illustrates its application to the causal simulation and analysis of a cooling circuit behavior. A modeling tool is briefly described in Section 4. Experience and problems being encountered with qualitative modeling are described at the end.

2. Qualitative Modeling

Causal analysis of physical systems is an important task for the design and planning of a process plant. Once the overall behavior of a system can be modeled, possible future behaviors can be computed for prediction in trouble-shooting. Causal simulation is a prerequisite since such a technical process cannot simply be brought back from an undesirable state to a previous normal one, instead some corrective steps must be performed to recover from the undesirable state. Typical application of the causal simulation is to answer questions like

"What happens if this valve of a generator cooling circuit gets plugged"
"Can I turn on this breaker of a switchgear station, and why not if I cannot?"

Causal behavior of a technical system can be explained in terms of input-output behavior of its component modules. Specifically, a causal argument consists of a sequence of assertions about the component states each of which is the consequence of previous assertions. Simply put, in a causal argument,

B is the consequence of A if A causes B.

For example, if a valve reduces the area through which water flows, the pressure drop over the valve will increase when the flow rate remains unchanged. The reduction of its flowable area can be considered as an event, and the causal argument is formulated as if a sequence of events is temporally ordered.

In order to construct a causal reasoner of a particular application domain, the following three issues have to be dealt with: the device structure, the device model, and assumptions. In this section we describe the form and logic of qualitative physical laws in the application domain of fluid mechanics, namely the causal model of a cooling circuit (Figure 1). Much of the work in qualitative causal reasoning can be found in the issue edited by Bobrow (1984).

Modules, ports and relations

The structure and function of a technical process can be modeled by means of modules and ports (Davis et al 1982). A module is considered to be a blackbox with ports through which a material, e.g., electrons in eletrical circuits or water in fluid circuits, propagates information as signals. A module may encapsulate components which are again modules. Conversely, modules can be combined together to form a more abstract module. A module with ports defines a syntactical form of a relation (constraint) between inputs and outputs of a component. We write

module(X, I_1, I_2, ..., O_1, O_2, ..., O_n)

where I_i are inputs and O_j are outputs of the module X. A port binds a signal to or from an argument of the relation. The relational description has an advantage over functional description for it permits forward and backward reasoning during a causal simulation.

Device models

So far we have left out the specification of the input-output behavior of a component module. We treat devices such as pipes, valves and a pump as primitive elements of structural descriptions. In a device-centered ontology, each device behavior can be modeled based on a physical law. For example, in a stationary state the fluid law $Q = kAP^{1/2}$ describes the relationship among the three variables Q, A and P, where Q is the flow rate of a valve, k is a constant, A is the flowable area and P is the pressure drop across the valve. The time derivative of the equation yields a confluence equation of the form $\partial Q = \partial A + \partial P$. This confluence provides a basic framework for the behavioral analysis of a hydraulic valve as (De Kleer & Brown 1983). Furthermore, the device topology (different from the structure that describe how devices are connected) is readily reflected in the set of confluences.

The change of variables in a confluence equation is abstracted to either increasing (+), decreasing (-), or steady (0). An algebra of addition and multiplication based on the set of qualitative values {-, 0, +} defines the rule of inference for value propagation satisfying the confluence equation. For example, a steady flow rate $\partial Q = 0$ with decreasing flowable area $\partial A = -$ results in an increase of the pressure $\partial P = +$. Thus, finding a solution in a set of confluences can be considered as a constraint satisfaction problem. Considering device-specific boundary conditions, a different set of confluences can be defined for each qualitative state, e.g., if a valve is open there is no pressure drop across the valve and we have a confluence $\partial P = 0$, whereas if a valve is closed there is no flow and we have a confluence $\partial Q = 0$. This implies that in the modeling of fluid systems a device state concerning the flowable area must be specified so that an appropriate set of confluences will be applied correctly.

We also introduce a notion of quantity spaces and values for symbolic computation, e.g., a quantity space of a flow rate can be specified as a discrete set of zero, low, average, and high. An increase or decrease of a flow rate changes its quantity value from zero to low, from low to average and vice versa. In a causal simulation, the cooling water propagates such quantity values to connected devices.

Causal process

Our primary theme is to construct a causal reasoner which produces causal arguments based on the structure and function descriptions outlined above. We consider each device as a processor appropriately programmed to produce new equilibrium values satisfying the device confluences of its components. Whenever a new value is produced by a device, it is propagated to all connected devices, each of which in turn checks if this new equilibrium value permits to evaluate the final variable of the component's confluence. Information being propagated by a material, i.e., the cooling water, can be modeled as a predicate

material(W, Q, P, T, C, [])

where Q is the flow rate, P the pressure, T the temperature, and C the conductivity of the cooling water W. The last argument is an empty list where foreign materials can be included when they are propagated by the water. In this processor architecture, the qualitative simulation based on confluences is performed within a primitive device, and the causal simulation is performed between devices as if these processors interact with each other.

3. Causal Simulation and Analysis

To illustrate the mechanism of drawing an explanatory causal argument, we apply the above fluid confluence to the generator's cooling circuit as shown in Figure 1.

The cooling water flows through a generator in narrow separated sections called hollow conductors to remove the heat and then through the heat exchanger to give it away. Orifices simply limit the amount of water flow between the main and bypass circuit. We assume that the flowable area of hollow conductors is variable. Given that the differential pressure over generator's winding is increasing and the flow rate of the main circuit is steady, we have the following causal argument:

$\partial P + \partial A - \partial Q = 0$ {given}
diff_pressure of winding is increasing ($\partial P = +$) {premise}
flow_rate of main_circuit is steady ($\partial Q = 0$) {premise}
flowable_area of hollow_conductors is decreasing ($\partial A = -$) {consequence}

The two premises above are obtained from the incoming water, and the consequence is further propagated to its output.

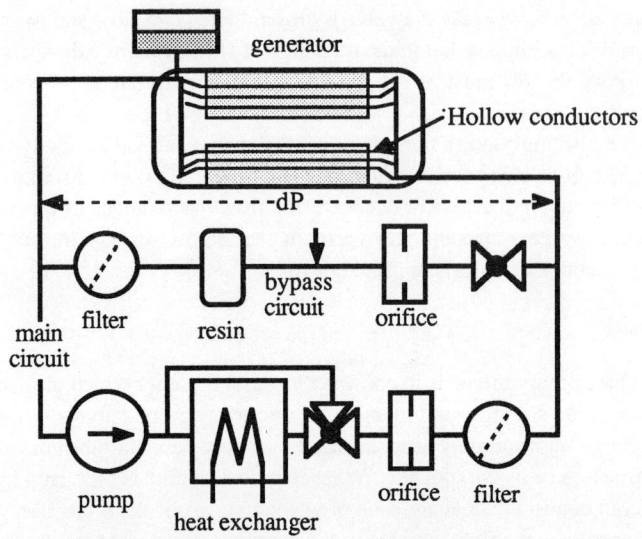

Figure 1. Generator's cooling circuit

In order to compare how our domain expert constructed the diagnostic rules for this application, the following causal rule is depicted from the monitoring example as given by Kriz & Sugaya (1988).

    if   diff_pressure of winding is greater(110) and
           flow_rate of main_circuit is in_range(90, 100)
    then hollow_conductors = plugged .

This reveals that the consequence being derived in the causal argument is different from the rule formulation stated above, i.e., the consequence is a decrease in the flowable area of hollow conductors with no knowledge of whether it is due to plugging or not. And if so, whether plugging is a fault or a correct behavior. De Kleer argues that a teleological assumption will clarify most of such cases being encountered.

        Another application of the causal model is a fault analysis. For example, a leakage in the hollow conductors causes the H_2 gas being filled out in the generator flows into the cooling water. The gas is then further propagated by the cooling water and being collected at the expansion tank. An increase of H_2 gas in the tank causes lowering of the tank level. We have the following causal argument for the tank behavior:

$\partial P - \partial Q = 0$	{given}
flow_rate of H_2_gas is increasing ($\partial Q = +$)	{premise}
pressure of H_2_gas is increasing ($\partial P = +$)	{consequence}

One more interpretation is necessary to reach the assertion that an increase of H_2 gas in the tank causes the tank level lower. This is another function of the tank behavior being viewed as an analog meter.

        Conversely, if the tank level becomes lower after a simulation, the causal reasoner can trace back the causal link to its origin by identifying first the increase of H_2 gas in the tank, then its existence in the cooling water, and its emergence in the hollow conductors of the generator. The causal argument at the generator is

leakage is high	{given}
pressure of H_2_gas is high	{premise}
pressure of cooling_water is average	{premise}
H_2_gas leaks_into cooling_water	{consequence}

Again, the reason why the pressure of H_2 gas is higher than that of the cooling water is simply a design consideration and beyond the scope of the qualitative modeling.

Causal simulation permits in theory a derivation of rules by applying a rule synthesis technique such as ID3 (Quinlan 1983) to causal arguments. For each hydraulic device, a set of foreseeable faults, e.g. plugging, defective device, can be defined and simulated against a single fault to produce cause-effect data. For example, observed indications under normal operation would be that the flow rate of main circuit is average, the cooling water temperature at the generator outlet is low, etc. If hollow conductor is plugged, then average slot temperature and the differential pressure over the stator winding would become high. They are then analyzed to derive decision rules by applying the ID3 algorithm. The result is a classification tree which optimizes a number of decisions for a given set of observed values.

4. Implementation: A Graphical Model Builder

We have developed a tool for knowledge-based modeling and analysis of technical systems in a Prolog-based programming environment ViP (Muller & Sander 1988). Figure 2 shows its application to the modeling of a cooling circuit. The device-centered ontology is particularly suitable for organizing device specific knowledge such as confluences and quantity spaces into a taxonomy of devices where any specialization of such a device automatically inherit its attributes. For example, the two concepts *hollow conductors* and *valve* as depicted in the inheritance lattice share the same fluid confluence being defined at the concept of hydraulic *device*. This inheritance lattice, which can be conveniently represented in frames, permits an efficient storage and retrieval of device specific attributes. The concept of *module* deals with such relations as *composed_of* or *part_of* for a modular description, and *ports* for connections between modules.

The tool supports interactive editing and modification of concepts in the *Concept Space* window. The user may then create instances of generaic concepts (classes) in a separate window and establish connections to build a particular model of a system, say a cooling circuit *scws1*. The expansion tank (surrounded by dotted line segments in Figure 2) is a particular instance of the concept *expansion_tank*, whose slot values are displayed in the topmost window. The concept *expansion_tank* is a specialization of *analog_meter* and *valve*, and inherits the properties from both concepts (mix-in).

The above process architecture fits well to the object-oriented programming technique. Namely, as soon as material arrives at or leaves a component, its behavior can be

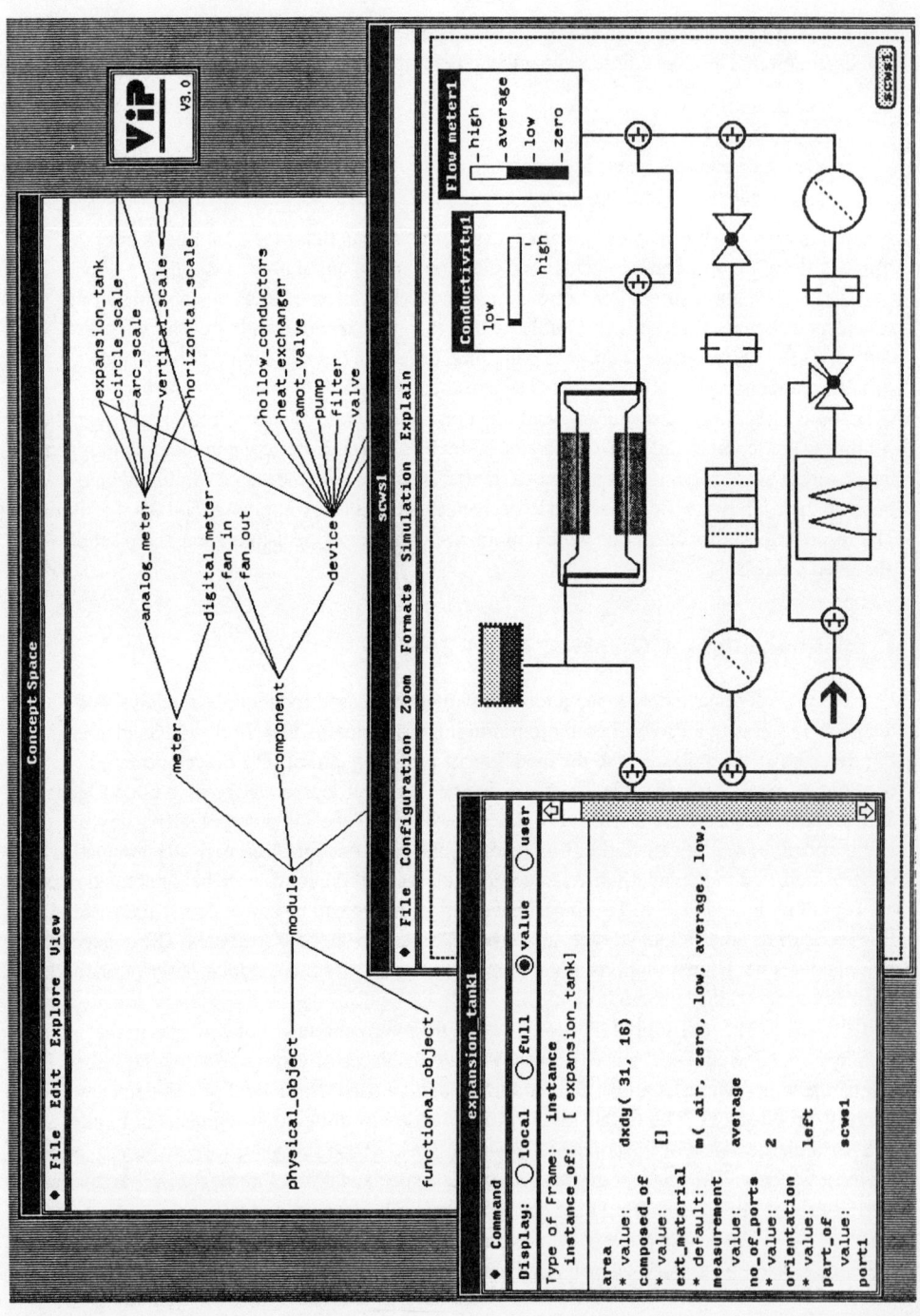

Figure 2. Model of a cooling circuit

evaluated in terms of a demon function. Each device is associated with a Prolog rule having as arguments its device id, state, inputs, outputs and a mode indication (explain or no explain). The simulation (or propagation) continues until no new values can be computed. The result of the causal simulation can be observed either graphically through various meters being attached to the circuit, or can be found separately for each specific observation under the slot *measurment* in the frame window.

5. Discussion

Qualitative causal models

A step from shallow reasoning to model-based reasoning requires not only a description about the device structure and its components, but also fairly thorough understanding of physical laws that govern the underlying device behavior. Specifically, the dynamic behavior of a device can be modeled by introducing higher-order derivatives and treating them as constraints to be satisfied. Since the set of laws to be considered differs from device to device, it is reasonable to construct models that are specialized for each primitive device. Kinds of application where qualitative modeling can practically be applied may be summarized as follows: The overall behavior of a system can be synthesized out of its component modules, for each of which a clear functional definition exists either in the form of an input-output relation as in digital circuits or in the form of a physical law as in electro-mechanical devices. For the analysis of a large complex system, massively parallel computers become necessary to yield causal accounts in a reasonable time. Thus, the qualitative causal simulation, when realized on conventional computers, is usable for analyzing the behavior of a small set of devices of tractable complexity.

In our experiment, we have restricted the use of the qualitative causal simulation within a primitive device to compute its input-output behavior. Outside of a primitive device, the newly computed values are propagated to connected devices as discrete values. This hybrid causal process model, however, has its own drawbacks; namely, it cannot capture a feedback influence (or structural simultaneity) because of the sequential nature of deductions being applied. For example, the cooling water flows through a device to the next one, say an orifice which is actually closed. Consequently, no water flows neither through the orifice nor through the device (contradiction). A new generic component containing these two primitive devices becomes necessary to handle such a case.

Another drawback is the model tuning process that arises during the construction of a device model. The variables expressing parameters of a device model take on a small number of predefined values. Depending on the interaction among primitive devices during causal simulation, a situation may occur where a new parameter value becomes necesssary to distinguish a qualitatively significant point. Accordingly, the value space must be refined further to adequately describe the behavior of the causal process. One possible solution for the automated tuning is to perform numerical analysis to obtain numerical values that are then treated as landmark values for the purposes of explanation as suggested by Shrager et al (1987). The order of magnitude theory permits the handling of numerical values (e.g. comparison, equality) in qualitative reasoning without rendering to quantitatively computing all possible behaviors (Dague & Raiman 1987).

Rule derivation by classification

An obvious advantage of this approach is the avoidance of missing rules that might occur during the rule formation by a human expert. A disadvantage is the limitation of fault covering due to its nature of diagnostic rule derivation according to a set of predetermined faults. The fault-based causal simulation is also risky: One can only be sure with assertions for correct device behaviors and not for misbehaviors. Some problems encountered with this approach are:
- Selection of attribute is random (taken in the order of appearance) and differs from those that the domain expert would select.
- Classification of multiple faults become obscure; the problem of mutiple faults can best be treated by the model-based reasoning as shown by De Kleer & Williams (1987).

Constraint logic programming

In qualitative causal simulation, the behavior of a device is modeled through a set of confluences. The purpose of qualitative simulation is to find values of variables that satisfy the set of confluence equations. The constraint logic programming as shown by Jaffar & Lassez (1987) opens up a new possibility for the application of qualitative modeling and extends the Prolog's unification as a general scheme of constraint solving in the domain of real arithmetic. It is then possible to state the fluid law in a stationary state as a constraint to be satisfied.

```
fluid_law( Q, A, P) :- A = k*A*Psqrt, P = Psqrt*Psqrt.
network_law( Qs) :- sum( Qs, 0).
sum( [], 0).
sum( [Q|Qs], N) :- N = Q+Ns, sum( Qs, Ns).
```

The predicate *fluid_law(Q, A, P)* states the constraint in terms of two arithmetic equations, where the term k is a constant, Q the flow rate, A the flowable area, P the pressure drop across a valve. The network law states the sum of all flows Qs at a node is zero. Constraints expressed in non-linear equations as the one for pressure P above are "hard" problems for the instances of constraint logic scheme based on the simplex algorithm. Ongoing reseach in constraint logic programming focuses on the construction of an efficient constraint solver for linear and non-linear constraints expressed in equations and inequations as shown by Sakai & Aiba (1987).

6. Conclusion

The model-based reasoning provides a sound framework for the design, simulation, and analysis of physical processes. Although the use of qualitative physics for the modeling of device behavior seems appropriate as a methodology, its computational requirement forces its application only to those of tractable complexity. The constraint logic programming seems to offer a promising solution in realizaing such tool functions. The automatic derivation of diagnostic rules out of the generated causal arguments requires much broader knowledge in order to be practically usefull.

Acknowledgement

The author wishes to thank B. Wiederkehr for supplying domain specific knowledge while J. Kriz, C. Muller, S. Hitzig for offering valuable and stipulating discussions to the conception of this work. Comments provided by the conference referees have been beneficial for preparing this manuscript.

References

Bobrow, D.G. (1984). Qualitative Reasoning about Physical Systems. Artificial Intelligence, 24, 1-491. Also from North-Holland.

Dague, Ph., Raiman, O. & Deves, Ph. (1987). Troubleshooting: When Modeling is the Trouble. Proceedings of the National Conference on Artificial Intelligence.

Davis, R., Shrobe, H., Hamscher, W., Wieckert, K., Shirley, M., & Polit, S. (1982). Diagnosis Based on Description of Structure and Function. Proceedings of the National Conference on Artificial Intelligence, 137-142.

De Kleer, J. & Brown, J.S. (1983). The Origin, Form and Logic of Qualitative Physical Laws. Proceedings of the 8-th International Joint Conference on Artificial Intelligence, 1158-1169.

De Kleer, J. & Williams, B.C. (1987). Diagnosing Multiple Faults. Artificial Intelligence, 32, no. 1, 97-130.

Forbus, K.D. (1981). Qualitative Reasonign about Physical Processes. Proceedings of the 7-th International Joint Conference on Artificial Intelligence, Vancouver, BC, 326-330.

Genesereth, M.R. (1982). Diagnosis using hierarchical design models. Proceedings of the National Conference on Artificial Intelligence, Pittsburgh, PA, 278-283.

Jaffar, J. & Lassez, J.L. (1987). Constraint Logic Programming. Proceedings of the Conference on Principles of Programming Languages, Munich.

Kriz, J. & Sugaya, H. (1988). Logic Programming for Industrial Applications. Research Report CRB 88-016 C, Asea Brown Boveri Corporate Research, Baden, Switzerland.

Kuipers, B. (1984). Commonsense Reasoning about Causality: Deriving Behavior from Strucutre. Artificial Intelligence, 24, 169-203.

Muller, C. & Sander, S. (1988). ViP-γ User's Manual, Asea Brown Boveri Corporate Research, Baden, Switzerland.

Quinlan J. R. (1983). Learning Efficient Classification Procedures and Their Application to Chess End Games. In Machine Learning: An Artificial Intelligence Approach, ed. Michalski, R.S., Carbonell, J.G. & Mitchell, T.M., 463-482, Palo Alto: Tioga.

Rieger, C. & Grinberg, M. (1977). The declarative representation and procedural simulation of causality in physical mechanisms. Proceedings of the 5-th International Joint Conference on Artificial Intelligence, Cambridge, MA, 250-256.

Sakai, K. & Aiba, A. (1987). CAL: An Instance of the Constraint Logic Programming and Its Future Extensions. Technical Report, ICOT, Tokyo.

Shrager, J., Jordan, D.S., Moran, T.P., Kiczales, G., & Russell, D.M. (1987). Issues in the Pragmatics of Qualitative Modeling: Lessons Learned from a Xerographics Project. Comm. of the ACM, 30, no. 12, 1036-1047.

RECONCILING PROBLEM-SOLVING AND INSTRUCTION IN ONE KNOWLEDGE DECOMPOSITION FRAMEWORK

Benita Cox,
School of Management,
Imperial College of Science, Technology & Medicine,
53, Prince's Gate,
Exhibition Road,
London SW7 2PG

Abstract

The Explanation-Driven Understanding-Directed (EDUD) User Model is described. The model is based on cognitive principles which provide a method for decomposing knowledge that also may be used for supporting the explanation facilities in an Expert System. Knowledge is decomposed into a hierarchical structure according to EDUD principles and is made operational through the interpretation of the hierarchy. The purpose of the paper is to demonstrate the operationality of the knowledge in relation to a User Model for Intelligent Tutoring Systems and to describe how the principles in question overlap with explanation in Expert Systems. An example of how the framework is used in decomposing a body of knowledge about a domain is provided by analysing knowledge about a car's fuel system.

1. Introduction

To be an effective tutor an Intelligent Tutoring System (ITS) needs to adapt its performance to the user's developmental level at a given cognitive stage. In order to achieve this a profile of the user's current understanding/learning level needs to be constructed. This profile reflects the user's initial knowledge of the domain fragment of an application domain intended for teaching as well as his progress in a learning task brought about by his interaction with the system.

Our objective in designing the Explanation-Driven Understanding-Directed User Model, has been to 'link' explanation with those cognitive processes that may be said to demonstrate a better understanding of a given body of domain-knowledge in the 'learner'. An emulation of these processes could, it was believed, be used for the decomposition of the target-domain knowledge thus providing a systematic way of monitoring progress through the units of the decomposition within the User Model (1,2,3,4,5).

The EDUD approach consists of five evolutionary stages through which the individual progresses in seeking to understand a particular knowledge-domain. These stages provide an efficient and appropriate method for the sub-division of the body of target knowledge into autonomous topic-dependent information structures. Each stage in the process of understanding, has been linked to a previously defined explanation category (6), providing a set of structures, amenable to both computation and human comprehension. The sequencing of the presentation of these categories of explanation is arranged so as to increase the user's understanding of the domain by its incorporation in the User Model.

The EDUD design principles for the User Model have been found to be similar to a knowledge decomposition framework identified by Sembugamoorthy and Chandrasekaran (7) for the purposes of increasing the user's understanding on a problem-solving task. Significantly, they have not adapted this framework for teaching purposes. The contribution of this paper is therefore twofold. On the one hand it offers a demonstration of the operationality of the EDUD framework in relation to the User Model for Intelligent Tutoring purposes and on the other it aims to demonstrate that the EDUD approach can also be used for designing explanation facilities for expert systems.

Whilst the method of decomposition of the pertinent knowledge may be the same for both cases, the sequencing of its presentation is dependent on the application function, that is, whether the decompiled knowledge is required to support explanations of how conclusions are reached on a problem-solving task or for teaching domain-knowledge from first principles.

Accordingly, in this paper we decompose a body of target-knowledge, that concerning a car's fuel system, into a single framework, to demonstrate how the purposes of both explanation facilities for problem solving and instructional requirements may be met by the EDUD approach. In particular, to illustrate how sequencing of the target knowledge effects operationality, we discuss its implications for the design of a dynamic User Model and as explanation facilities.

2. A Link between Problem-Solving and Instruction

Expert system design seeks to construct a knowledge-base capable of representing and supporting the problem-solving methods of a human expert. This frequently means that the knowledge encapsulated in these systems has been tailored specifically for the intended use and as a result it loses transparency and generality (8). The penalty of this approach is that explanation facilities become restricted and are frequently inadequate and inflexible. Improvement of explanation facilities cannot be achieved without making the domain knowledge more articulate. A number of approaches have been proposed as a solution to this problem, including consideration of what types of advice users require in performing a task and how these requirements might be met in an expert system (9), other approaches include examining the meaning and nature of the questions which may be posed by the user during an interactive session with the system (10). Another way of increasing the articulateness of the knowledge is to supplement the compiled knowledge with explicit information about the principles and assumptions used to drive the problem-solving strategy (11). It is the need to supply flexible explanation facilities that provides the bridge between expert systems and intelligent tutoring systems.

An ITS is more concerned with supporting, through the appropriately devised representation, particular learning processes taking place in the user. It is thus approached from the outset from the point of view of providing supportive information in the form of deeper beliefs and justification from first principles.

Whilst an expert system, presents a user with a problem-solution which it may then be required to justify, a teaching system is designed to present supporting information in such a way as to permit the user to achieve problem-solution. The sequencing of the information process is thus different for the two types of system.

This paper identifies the areas where the representational requirements of both problem solving and instructional systems overlap and suggests that this overlap provides a basis for a single representational framework. However, it should be kept in mind, that the framework only applies to certain types of knowledge, that concerned with systems and system-like entities. In addition it identifies how the areas where the two system types do not overlap may still be accommodated within a single representational framework.

3. The EDUD Framework for Knowledge Decomposition

In the EDUD approach knowledge is decomposed into a hierarchically arranged framework. Each node in the framework identifies a stage in the process of understanding and a level of abstraction necessary for representing information about the domain. The decomposition of the target-knowledge consists of providing five major categories of knowledge identifiable with particular types of explanations. The types of explanation in question include:

(i) identity explanations, which are concerned with the definition and classification of objects and fundamental facts,

(ii) functional explanations, which are concerned with the intended functions of objects in the domain,

(iii) causal explanations which are concerned with cause/effect links,

(iv) complex-derivational explanations which are concerned with defining how a domain relates to all other domains with which it is functionally linked, and

(v) hypothetico-deductive explanations which consider relationships both actual and potential.

Because the nodes in the hierarchy are represented at an abstract level, decomposition of the target knowledge to fill each category is arrived at by addressing the following questions:

What is X?
What does X do?
How does X achieve this function?
Why does X achieve this function?
If......then

The information supplied by responding to these queries is then placed in the taxonomical framework and addressed by the node name. A schematic representation of a knowledge decomposition according to these categories for the fuel system of a motor car is shown in Figure 1.

4. Effecting Operationality of Knowledge Through Representation

The basic principle of the EDUD approach is that knowledge is made operational through its sequencing. The ordering of the presentation of the information in the framework will thus be dependent upon the purpose for which the knowledge is being represented, that is whether it is used as a means of explanation for a conclusion reached in a problem-solving function or as a means of increasing understanding in an instructional interaction.

Understanding is viewed as a progression from less to more sophisticated levels through a number of hierarchical stages. Details of these stages are provided elsewhere (1,2,3,4,5). The stages of understanding identified are:
1. The stage of figurative knowing
2. The functional stage
3. The cause/effect stage
4. The complex-derivational stage
5. The stage of hypothetico-deductive reasoning

In understanding each of the stages identified is loosely traversed sequentially 'bottom up', that is, understanding proceeds from the stage of figurative knowing to the stage of hypothetico-deductive reasoning. In explaining how a problem is solved, the order of the reasoning is reversed - 'top-down' (See Figure 2). This is because in problem-solving, a solution is given prior to explanation, whilst in teaching, it is often the case that explanation seeks to encourage solution.

The notion of understanding proposed herein parallels the view that to understand how a device works its function must be seen as related to and arising from its structure (12).

In expert problem-solving reasoning commences in the hypothetico-deductive stage and justification for conclusions is provided by referring to the hierarchy retrospectively. Thus, whilst the learner moves from the stage of figurative knowing, in a step-like sequence through to the stage of hypothetico-deductive reasoning, the expert reasons in the stage of hypothetico-deductive reasoning using the concepts that are already known in the other stages to support his conclusions.

NAME: Fuel System
Def: Part of Engine System
Consists of fuel pump, petrol filter, carburettor, storage tank, flexible hose
Function: Storage, preparation, delivery correct petrol/air mixture
Causes: Mixing of fuel (stored in storage tank, pumped via fuel pump through flexible hose and petrol filter) and air (aspirated from carburettor) to form fine vapour
CD: Engine system requires correct petrol/air mixture to function and prevent spluttering
HD: If engine system spluttering then hypothesise possible fault with fuel system

---

NAME: Fuel Pump (Mechanical)
Def: Part of Fuel System
Consists of diaphragm and one-way valves
Function: pump fuel (from fuel tank) to carburettor (through petrol-filter)
Causes: Movement of diaphragm and one-way valve force petrol from tank to carburettor.
CD: Fuel System requires continuous supply of fuel to be mixed with air to provide explosive mixture
HD: If break in continuous supply of petrol to engine, hypothesise possible fault fuel pump

NAME: Petrol Filter
Def: Part of Fuel System
Consists of paper filter
Function: Filter particulate matter from fuel
Causes: Forces petrol through semi-permeable membrane
CD: Particles in fuel pump or jets in carburettor arrest their functioning
HD: If carburettor or fuel pump not functioning possible cause faulty petrol filter

NAME: Storage Tank
Def: Part of Fuel System
Function: Store Fuel
Causes: holds fuel under atmospheric pressure
CD: to allow engine to run remote from the fuel source
HD: If engine system spluttering then hypothesise no fuel or fuel not under atmospheric pressure

NAME: Carburettor
Def: Part of Fuel System
Consists of Venturi, Needle Valve, Air Filter, Throttle Valve
Function: Mixes air and petrol to explosive mixture
Causes: draws air (via air filter & venturi) and petrol (via float chamber) and mixes to a fine spray. Passed mixture to inlet manifold (via throttle valve)
CD: Engine System requires correct mixture of air and fuel
HD: If engine system spluttering then hypothesise possible fault carburettor

NAME: Throttle Valve
Def: Part of Carburettor
Function: Control amount of petrol entering manifold
Causes: Open & shutting valve results in regulation of amount of vapour
CD: Vapour content determines engine output
HD: If engine output unregulated, hypothesise fault with throttle valve

NAME: Needle Valve
Def: Part of carburettor
Function: Regulate petrol supply to venturi
Causes: supply of narrow head of petrol to venturi
CD: stuck needle valve causes excess supply of petrol to venturi causing flooding
HD: If flooding possible cause stuck needle valve

NAME: Venturi
Def: Part of Carburettor
Function: restrict air intake to carb
Cause: drop in air pressure
CD: because of shape, reduction in air being drawn in and resultant drop in air pressure petrol drawn in
HD: If petrol flooding possible cause venturi malfunction

NAME: Air Filter
Def: Part of Carburettor
Function: Remove dust from air
Causes: forces air through semi-permeable membrane
CD: because dirt particles will choke air, resulting in richer petrol mixture
HD: If petrol flooding, possible cause blocked air filter

Figure 1
Partial Representation of Knowledge about a car fuel system

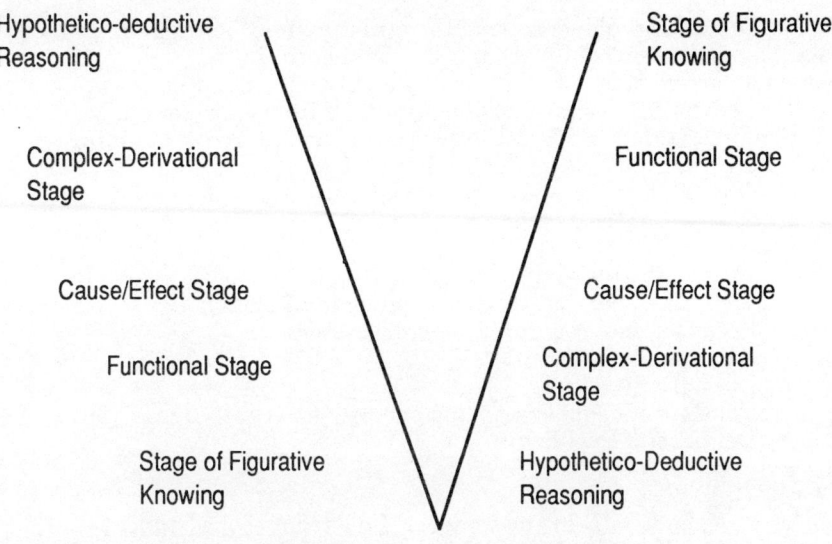

Figure 2
Sequencing of Levels of Reasoning to Justify Problem-Solving Steps or Understanding of the Relevant Knowledge Domain

Consequently, for teaching purposes, the EDUD framework is presented 'bottom up' in order to reflect the direction and development of the user's understanding of how definition (structure) gives rise to function and function is achieved through cause/effect relationships. In addition it provides justification for particular behaviours by linking them to domain-independent phenomena. Finally, understanding of concepts not only at the actual but at the potential level is provided.

Thus, knowledge for teaching purposes may be represented as follows:

Definition: Fuel pump
Is: part of fuel system
Consists of: diaphragm and one way valve
Does: deliver fuel
By: Action 1
Because: fuel required by engine system
If: fuel not supplied to engine system then
    Symptom 1

Action 1
Movement of diaphragm and one way valve

Symptom 1
Spluttering and choking

In expert problem-solving the structure may be used to articulate diagnostic reasoning. Diagnosis commences in the hypothetico-deductive stage of reasoning by setting up a hypothesis for first identifying how an observed behaviour differs from expectation. Confirmation or rejection of a hypothesis is then derived from examining the knowledge in the 'lower levels' of the hierarchy.

Accordingly, knowledge for explaining the problem-solving process may be represented as follows:

> If: Spluttering and choking
> then conclude: (possible) fuel pump malfunction
> Because: fuel required by engine system
> Achieved by: Action1
> Does: Deliver fuel
> Consists of: Diaphragm and one way valves
> Definition: Fuel pump

5. Importance of the EDUD Framework for the Design of the Student Model in Intelligent Tutoring Systems

In the EDUD approach the user's understanding of the material presented to him is assessed at each level in the hierarchy. Based on this assessment a decision is made as to what material should be explained to him next. Because the process of understanding is viewed as sequential, if at any level in the hierarchy the user is functioning successfully all previous levels may be assumed as successfully completed. The levels in the hierarchy thus form the basic framework for monitoring the progress of the user's understanding.

These hierarchies of reasoning have important implications for system design. They allow direct comparison of the user's responses with the steps in the hierarchical structure. In this way, detailed inference models of the processes taking place within the user and the associated cumbersome computational overheads can be avoided.

The goal is to pinpoint the abstract relations which are understood at a specific phase of understanding and consequently 'predict' those relations which still need to be tutored and those which must have already been mastered in order to achieve the present level of understanding.

6. Conclusion

The notion of achieving understanding through sequencing of information has important implications for intelligent tutoring system design, especially for the design of the Student Model. In the EDUD program, which is based on the above principles, the Student Model has been implemented so as to reflect the progression of the student through the knowledge domain.

The method of knowledge decomposition described in this paper affords the opportunity for knowledge for both problem-solving and instructional purposes to be represented within a single structure.

Attention has been focussed on the sequencing of the knowledge to achieve operationality. Interpretation of the hierarchy is thus effected by the order in which each of the abstract nodes are addressed.

An aspect of the framework which has not been hitherto mentioned is that it is relatively domain independent. As such it makes a contribution to the need for tutoring systems to move away from individually hand-crafted applications to the use of general purpose tools.

Acknowledgement

I would like to thank Elizabeth Pollitzer for her insightful comments and suggestions during the course of this work

The author is funded by the SERC

References

1. Cox, B., Jenkins, J. and Pollitzer, E. (1988). Understanding and Concept Acquisition in Adaptive Intelligent Tutoring Systems. In Proceedings of The Fifth International Conference on Technology and Education, Edinburgh.

2. Cox, B., Jenkins, J. and Pollitzer, E. (1987). Explanation-Driven and Understanding-Directed Approach to Knowledge Transfer. In Alvey IKBS Research Workshop on Tutoring Systems, University of Exeter.

3. Cox, B., Jenkins, J. and Pollitzer, E. (1988). An Explanation-Driven Understanding-Directed Approach to Intelligent Tutoring Systems. In IEE Colloquium on Intelligent Tutorial Systems, London.

4. Cox, B. Jenkins, J. and Pollitzer, E. (1988). An Organisation of Domain Knowledge for Tutoring Systems. In Proceedings of the Fifth International Conference on Knowledge Engineering, Madrid.

5. Cox, B., Jenkins, J. and Pollitzer, E. (1988). Explaining and Understanding Engineering Problems - An Intelligent Tutoring Approach. In Artificial Intelligence and Engineering: Diagnosis and Learning, ed. J.S. Gero, Elsevier with Computational Mechanics Publications.

6. Achinstein, P. (1983). The Nature of Explanation. Oxford University Press, Inc.

7. Sembugamoorthy, V., & Chandrasekaran, B. (1986). Functional Representation of Devices and Compilation of Diagnostic Problem-Solving Systems. In Experience, Memory, And Reasoning,

eds. J.L. Kolodner & C.K. Riesbeck, pp.47-74. Hillsdale, New Jersey : Lawrence Erlbaum Associates.

8. Wenger, E. (1987). Artificial Intelligence and Tutoring Systems. Morgan Kaufmann Publishers, Inc.

9. Kidd, A.L. (1986). Explanation for Expert Systems - Some Data and an Initial Categorisation. In Alvey IKBS Expert Systems Theme,Workshop on 'Explanation', Report and Proceedings ,pp.120-122. University of Surrey, Department of Sociology.

10. Hughes, Sheila. (1986). HOW and WHY: HOW far will they take us, and WHY should we need any more? In Alvey IKBS Expert Systems Theme,Workshop on 'Explanation', Report and Proceedings, pp.69-83. University of Surrey, Department of Sociology.

11. Clancey, W.J. (1983). The Epistemology of a Rule-Based Expert System - A framework for Explanation'. Artificial Intelligence, 20, pp.215-251.

12. de Kleer, J., and Brown, J.S. (1982). Foundations of envisioning. In Proceedings of the AAAI-82, pp.434-437, Pittsburgh, PA.

DLGMS: A DEPENDENCY-BASED LEMMA GENERATION AND MAINTENANCE SYSTEM

David E Wolstenholme

BP Research International
Information Technology Research Unit
Chertsey Road,
Sunbury-on-Thames
Middlesex, TW16 7LN
U.K.

Abstract

Many expert systems employ backward-reasoning inference mechanisms. Such systems generally suffer from the fact that whenever a goal is to be proved, the full proof mechanism is employed even when the goal has been encountered before and has already been proved or shown to fail. This wasteful re-computation can be avoided by storing lemmas, i.e. recording solutions, which may be used later. If, however, the data or rules used in a proof are liable to change, the lemmas may become unreliable; lemma maintenance is therefore required to ensure that, following a change, no unreliable lemmas are used.

This paper describes an interactive Dependency-based Lemma Generation and Maintenance System (DLGMS) for use with expert systems employing logic programs; this system generates lemmas for certain checkpoint relationships, as declared by the programmer, and maintains the lemmas by removing any whose support is invalidated by a change to the program or answers supplied by the user. The system is fully able to handle negation-as-failure through its explicit recording of the conclusion that all solutions to a particular query have been found; the support for this may include assumptions that the sets of clauses for relevant relations are complete. The system is designed to be flexible, and allows the developer to explore, through simple meta-level declarations, the benefits of lemma generation and of making certain clause sets stable.

The DLGMS should allow backward-reasoning expert systems to run more efficiently; in some cases, the increased efficiency will be significant. Because the problem of re-computation is alleviated, knowledge representation should also be improved, by being more natural, since there will be less need to pass results as arguments simply to avoid re-computation.

1. Introduction

A major problem associated with pure backward-reasoning logic programming systems is that whenever a goal is to be proved, the full backward-reasoning proof mechanism is employed even when the goal has been encountered before and has already been proved, or shown to fail. Clearly, records of the solutions found to goals could be used to avoid such inefficient, wasteful re-computation. These records are generally called *proof lemmas*, or, more simply, *lemmas*.

If the program from which lemmas are derived is complete and stable, i.e. no changes to the rules or facts are permitted, the only process required is *lemma generation*; any lemmas generated can safely be used at some later time to avoid re-computation. However, in expert systems the program is frequently incomplete, thus necessitating the acquisition of data from some external source such as the user. Now, users frequently wish to change an answer given, e.g. because they know that they made an error or because they simply wish to explore the effect of some different answer. Such a change may mean that a solution found previously may no longer hold since it depended on this answer; if this solution has been recorded as a lemma, this lemma is no longer reliable. Lemmas may also become unreliable if the program itself is unstable, that is, if clauses are liable to be retracted or added, since the solution may depend on the existence or absence of one of these clauses. A process of *lemma maintenance*, a form of truth maintenance, is therefore required, so that lemmas dependent on such changes are not used later if a relevant solution is sought; instead, re-computation should be carried out which can take the changes into account.

This paper firstly discusses both the need for lemma generation, including the possible adverse effects on knowledge representation if lemma generation is not available, and also various approaches to lemma maintenance. Then, a *dependency-based lemma generation and maintenance system (DLGMS)* for use with PROLOG-based expert systems is described. The key features of the system are:

- the recording of solutions found for certain predicates, together with the supports required to justify the solutions; these supports show what the solutions depend on in terms both of other recorded solutions, i.e. lemmas, and of assumptions concerning the unstable or incomplete parts of the program, e.g. the continued existence of a rule used or an answer given;

- the explicit recording of the assumption that all solutions to a particular query have been found, together with the support required for this. In particular, the support may include assumptions that the sets of clauses for relevant relations are complete, i.e. that no more clauses for these relations come into existence;

- full handling of negation-as-failure, using the above feature;

- the use of meta-level declarations to allow the developer to state for which relations lemmas should be generated; we term such relations *checkpoints*. For all other relations, re-computation is carried out as required. This allows the developer to weigh the advantages of avoiding re-computation, through lemmas, against the overheads associated with lemma generation, and to store lemmas only for those relations considered to be sufficiently computationally expensive;

- the use of further simple meta-level declarations that enable the user to improve efficiency, for example, by allowing certain relations to be evaluated directly in PROLOG or by informing the system that certain clause sets are stable, so need not be included in supports.

- lemma maintenance that can handle withdrawal of answers by the user and changes to the rulebase.

The DLGMS is a flexible system, designed to allow the developer to explore the benefits of lemma generation freely, without any need to change the object-level logic program.

2. Lemma Generation and Maintenance in Backward-Reasoning Systems

2.1 Lemma Generation

The problem of wasteful re-computation in a backward-reasoning system can be demonstrated by the following program, written in standard Edinburgh-style PROLOG syntax, with words beginning with upper-case letters denoting variables:

```
net_income(Person, Amount) :-         tax(Person, T) :-
    income(Person, Salary),               income(Person, Salary),
    tax(Person, T),                       allowance(Person, A),
    Amount is Salary - T.                 T is 0.25 * (Salary - A).
```

where the definitions for income and allowance are not shown but are complex and computationally expensive. To evaluate the net income for a given individual, using the first rule, the individual's income must be computed and then tax must be calculated. The calculation of tax, using the second rule, again requires that the individual's income be computed. If the result of the first computation of income were recorded, as a lemma, it could be used when calculating tax instead of re-computing.

The logical status of lemmas is considered in some detail by Hogger (1984), who also considers methods of generating them. In outline, these methods involve the explicit handling of the lemmas at the object level, through direct calls to assert in the rules; this ruins the strictly declarative reading of the program. An alternative approach, using a meta-level interpreter and simple declarations, was taken in sigma-APES (Wolstenholme and Hammond, 1988), in which the developer indicated through meta-level declarations which relations should have their results recorded as lemmas by the interpreter. The declarative reading of the object-level rules thus remained intact. This approach, which handled negation-as-failure (Clark 1978), but did not record dependencies, was also used in the knowledge-based front end, GLIMPSE (Wolstenholme and O'Brien 1987); the use of an interpreter with lemma generation was found, in places, to reduce computation time from over 30 minutes for direct evaluation in PROLOG to about 10 seconds.

An important effect of the lack of lemma generation is that program developers may resort to unnatural knowledge representation in order to avoid the recognized problem of re-computation; in particular, results may be passed as arguments, leading to a plethora of arguments. A simple example is that the above net_income program might be re-written, possibly unnaturally, as:

```
net_income(Person, Amount) :-           tax(Person, Salary, T) :-
    income(Person, Salary),                 allowance(Person, A),
    tax(Person, Salary, T),                 T is 0.25 * (Salary - A).
    Amount is Salary - T.
```

where Salary is passed as an argument to the tax program. Lemma generation should allow improved, more natural, knowledge representation.

2.2 Lemma Maintenance

There seem to be three general approaches that might be taken to ensure the integrity of lemmas when the underlying data, i.e. the program or the user's answers to questions, are altered:

- **invalidate all lemmas**
  This clearly avoids problems of integrity, but is wasteful. With many alterations, the overheads in computing effort incurred by generating lemmas would probably not be compensated for by later savings.

- **invalidate all lemmas possibly affected, but not on a basis of dependencies**
  Such an approach was taken in sigma-APES and GLIMPSE. The times at which all dialogue events and lemma-generations occurred were recorded; when an answer given by the user was withdrawn, all lemmas recorded after this time were also invalidated, even though they might not have been in any way dependent on the answer. Earlier lemmas were left intact, since they could not possibly have been affected by the answer.

- **invalidate lemmas on the basis of dependencies**
  In this general approach, the lemma is stored together with the relationships on which it depends. When a change to some underlying datum is made, only those lemmas dependent on the datum need be invalidated. Clearly, this approach is the most refined, but requires sophisticated mechanisms for implementation. Existing mechanisms include:

ATMS

With the Assumption-based Truth Maintenance System (ATMS) of deKleer (1986), when a proposition is derived it is stored in an ATMS node, together with, amongst other things, the contexts in which it holds; each context is a set of assumptions upon which the derived proposition ultimately depends. Now, if we see information obtained from the user as assumptions, then each derived proposition can be seen as a lemma; it would be trivial to inspect the nodes to see which propositions were valid in a given context, i.e. supported by a given set of answers from the user. The ATMS, however, was developed for use with forward-reasoning systems, and its suitability for use with backward-reasoning systems is unclear; it is also not clear how negation-as-failure could be accommodated.

Incremental Theorem Prover

The incremental theorem prover of Shanahan (1987) was designed for backward-reasoning logic programming systems. In this, a complete record of data dependencies is kept as a structure. If a small change is made to the program, only that part of the dependency structure affected by the change need be altered, leading to fast, incremental changes. The main problems with this system are that the space required is large, since every derivation is essentially treated as a lemma rather than just computationally expensive ones, and that it is not well-suited to systems in which many different queries are posed, since a different structure is constructed for each query, even though these might share sub-structures. This system also cannot cope with negation-as-failure.

Our objective, then, was to develop a lemma generation and maintenance system, able to handle negation-as-failure, that associated supports with lemmas and used these to maintain the lemmas when changes to dialogue and program clauses were made. We also desired that the system should not require that all solutions be stored as lemmas but should, as in sigma-APES, allow a user of the system to specify which relations should generate lemmas. The system developed, the DLGMS, is described next.

3. The DLGMS

We shall firstly describe the meta-level declarations associated with the DLGMS, then outline the basic features of the system, which should provide a basis for understanding the descriptions of the system structures and implementation that follow.

3.1 Meta-level Declarations

Simple meta-level declarations are used to define the characteristics of the program and to control lemma generation and the general method of evaluation. The following meta-level predicates are used, which all take a single argument: a predicate name.

checkpoint: solutions to goals with this predicate name should be stored as lemmas;
stable: the clause set for this predicate name is complete. If such clauses are used in a proof, they need not therefore be recorded as supports, since they are assumed not to be modifiable. Note that a stable clause set for a relation does not mean that the relationship is stable, since the relationships on which it is dependent may themselves be unstable;
interpreted: goals with this predicate name should be evaluated through the DLGMS interpreter;
uninterpreted: goals with this predicate name should be evaluated directly in PROLOG. Such predicates, for example PROLOG primitives, are assumed to be complete and stable, so do not appear in supports;
askable: these are undefined relationships, which should be solved by asking the user, following the Query-the-User model (Sergot 1983).

We shall, loosely, use terms such as *checkpoint goal* or *askable proposition* to mean, respectively, a goal whose predicate name is a checkpoint or a proposition whose predicate name is askable.

3.2 Basic Features

The basic features of the DLGMS system are outlined below; note that here, and elsewhere, we use angle brackets to represent the general type of an argument.

3.2.1 Lemmas and their supports

The support for a given checkpoint proposition, or lemma, is expressed in terms of:

- askable propositions;
- other checkpoint propositions, i.e. lemmas;
- the clauses, both rules and assertions, for unstable, interpreted, relationships used in the proof, expressed as *rule(<rule name>)*;
- completion terms (see 3.2.2).

To demonstrate, consider the following rules, ruleset 1, (rule names precede rules):

r1   a(X) :- b(X), c(r).   r5   c(r) :- h.
r2   a(m).   r6   d :- f, g.
r3   b(m) :- d, e.
r4   b(n) :- c(s).

where a, b, and c are declared as interpreted, but not as stable, d as interpreted and stable, a and b as checkpoints and e, f, g and h as askable. If query a(X) is posed and all askable relations are confirmed, thus yielding a solution a(m) and lemmas for a(m) and b(m), then the direct support for lemma b(m) is the simple conjunction (expressed as a list)

[f, g, e, rule(r3)]

indicating that the confirmations of f, g and e and rule r3, used in the proof, must all continue to exist if the lemma b(m) is to continue to be reliable; note that no assumption about rule r6 for d is included in the support, even though used in the proof, since d is stable, so r6 is deemed to continue in existence. The direct support recorded for lemma a(m) is the disjunction

[b(m), h, rule(r5), rule(r1)] or
[rule(r2)]

indicating that the lemma b(m), confirmation of h, and rules r1 and r5 must all continue to exist, or rule r2 must continue to exist, if lemma a(m) is to continue to be reliable; this reflects the fact that two ways of solving a(m) exist.

Now, the full support for a(m), in terms of *base assumptions* only, i.e. assumptions about askable relations and unstable rules, can, of course, be inferred as

[f, g, e, rule(r3), h, rule(r5), rule(r1)] or
[rule(r2)].

since support is clearly transitive. We do not, however, record the support in this way, preferring, instead, to record intermediate lemmas as supports where appropriate, e.g. b(m) supporting a(m) in the above. This is an important feature of the system, since it facilitates the later process of lemma maintenance.

3.2.2 Handling of all solutions

It is important that we also record when all solutions, if any, to a given checkpoint goal have been found, so that if this goal, or a less general[1] one, is encountered later no attempt will be made to search for further solutions. However, the belief that all solutions have been found is subject to revision, since certain changes to the program or answers given may provide the potential for more solutions; the support for the belief that all solutions have been found must, therefore, also be recorded.

We shall introduce two new terms, comp(G) and all(G), which we call *completion terms*.

comp(G) The term comp(G) is used to represent the assumption that the clause set for goal G is complete, i.e. that future changes will not result in more clauses whose conclusions unify with G, or, if G is askable, in more answers to the question, in addition to those currently given.

all(G) The term all(G) is used to represent the assumption that all solutions to the checkpoint goal, G, have been found and no more will be found.

Ignoring, for now, negation-as-failure, the support for a term all(G) will comprise a conjunction of other completion terms, including, if the definition of G is not stable, the term comp(G). Removal of these supporting terms means that our assumption of all(G) may not be justified, so that re-computation will be required.

Using the above example, the completion terms derived from the query a(X) for a and b, together with their supports, are:

all(b(X)) : [comp(e), comp(c(s)), comp(f), comp(g), comp(b(X))]
all(a(X)) : [all(b(Y)), comp(c(r)), comp(a(X))]

where, again, supports for lower-level checkpoints are not explicitly transferred to higher-level ones.

The above description of the basic features provides a framework within which to describe the data structures used in the system.

3.3 System Structures

The lemma generation and maintenance mechanism generates, modifies, inspects and removes certain data structures in which the lemmas, their dependencies and any answers given by the user are recorded.

The main structure is the DLGMS *node*, used for storing lemmas. Its general form is:

---

[1] p(a, X) is more general than p(a, b)
p(a, b) is less general than p(a, X)
p(a, Y) matches p(a, X)
p(a, X) is unifiable with p(Y, b), but does not match p(Y, b)

Q1 subsumes Q2 if Q1 matches Q2 or if Q1 is more general than Q2

node: <predicate name>
   <lemma>$_1$: <support>$_1$;
   .....
   <lemma>$_m$: <support>$_m$;

where $m \geq 0$; that is, it contains a predicate name and any number of *lemma-support* pairs.

A <lemma> takes either the form, <proposition>, i.e. an instance of the <predicate name> relationship, which may or may not have unbound arguments, or the form all(<proposition>); we refer to the lemma-support pairs formed from these as *positive-lemmas* and *all-lemmas* respectively. Each <support> takes the form:

   <support conjunction>$_1$ or
   ....
   <support conjunction>$_n$

where $n >= 1$; a lemma that has no support does not appear in a DLGMS node.

Each <support conjunction> is represented as a list

   [<term>$_1$, <term>$_2$, ... <term>$_k$], where $k \geq 0$

where <term> is either a <proposition>, a rule term, i.e. rule(<rule name>), or a completion term, i.e. all(<proposition>) or comp(<proposition>).

A lemma-support pair of the form G : Conj$_1$ or Conj$_2$ or ... Conj$_n$; means that G is supported by any of the conjunctions Conj$_1$ .. Conj$_n$. It should be noted that the lemma-support pair G : [] states that G is supported by the empty conjunction, []; this means that G is unconditionally true since no terms, i.e. no assumptions, are required to support G.

As an example, the node for a resulting from the query a(X) for ruleset 1 is as follows:

   node : a
      a(m)   :   [b(m), h, rule(r5), rule(r1)] or
                   [rule(r2)];
      all(a(X)) :   [all(b(Y)), comp(c(r)), comp(a(X))];

The answers given by the user in answer to questions about askable relations are stored in dialogue records. We shall not give details of these; it is, however, important to realize that the records contain both the questions posed and the answers given and include completion terms of the form comp(G), which indicate that all answers to a particular question have been given.

For house-keeping purposes, a *link* of the form

   link(S, D).

is generated for every pair (S, D), such that there is a lemma-support of the form D : L;, where S is a term on one of the support conjunctions of L. We call the first argument, S, the *source*, and the second argument, D, the *destination* of the link. Thus, related to the node for a from ruleset 1 above, the following links will be generated:

   link(b(m), a(m)).   link(all(b(Y)), all(a(X))).
   link(h, a(m)).   link(comp(c(r)), all(a(X))).
   ....   link(comp(a(X)), all(a(X))).
   link(rule(r2)), a(m)).

3.4 Implementation of lemma generation

Evaluation of a query posed to the system is, initially, handled by a simple meta-level interpreter that basically mimics the behaviour of PROLOG, but also provides dialogue through Query-the-User; this hands over evaluation of uninterpreted relations directly to PROLOG. The only overhead related to lemma generation is that each goal is tested to see whether it is a checkpoint goal; if the program contains no checkpoint goals, the efficiency of evaluation is therefore close to that of a simple interpreter. When a checkpoint goal, G, is encountered, the system firstly inspects the appropriate DLGMS node, if any, for the relationship. If this contains lemmas that unify with G, these are used, in turn, as solutions to the goal. When all such existing lemmas have been used, the system checks whether the node supports a term all(G'), where G' subsumes G; if so, this indicates that all solutions to G have already been found and recorded as lemmas, so no further computation is required; if not, further solutions might be available, so re-evaluation of the goal and further lemma generation are carried out using a second, more complex, interpreter.

The key feature of this second interpreter, which also provides dialogue and passes over uninterpreted goals for direct execution in PROLOG, is that the result of evaluation is represented explicitly. It has two arguments: the first is the goal to be evaluated; the second has the form (Result, Support), which represents the result of evaluating the goal. The Result parameter is required because we need to record the reasons for failure to find more solutions to a goal, so such failure must be handled explicitly, rather than implicitly as in normal PROLOG. The Result parameter may be bound either to

succ   indicating a successful solution, i.e. that a proof was found, in which case the Support parameter represents the direct support required for the solution, according to the particular path followed, or to

fail   indicating that, during the search for solutions, an assumption was made concerning the stability or completeness of the program or dialogue that allowed the conclusion that no further solutions were available for the goal following some particular branch of the search tree. The Support parameter states what assumptions were made and thus represents the support for the conclusion of no further solutions. An alternative way of viewing a result of (fail, Support) for a goal G, which fits our handling of negation-as-failure, is that a decision to consider that any successful solutions to G are the only ones, and, hence, if no such solutions exist that G should fail, is dependent on Support.

In outline, the behaviour of the interpreter is that it collects the assumptions used in the proof during the evaluation process; the rules for unstable predicates are also collected. If the evaluation of a checkpoint goal, C, is successful, i.e. the result is (succ, S), where S represents the conjunction of assumptions, including existence of rules, used in the proof of C, then the resulting solution, or lemma, together with its support, S, is stored in the relevant DLGMS node, e.g. as the lemma-support pair C : S.

During evaluation, whenever the search for a further solution, if any, to a particular unstable or incomplete goal, G, is unsuccessful, the result (fail, [comp(G)]) is returned to higher-level goals. This indicates that one reason for a failure to find further solutions to these higher-level goals is the assumption that the clauses (or answers) for G are complete; clearly, additional clauses whose conclusions match G might yield further solutions to the higher-level goals. When evaluating a checkpoint goal, many failure results of the form (fail, [comp(G)]) may be returned, possibly interspersed with successful results. These fail results are stored. When all results, succ or fail, have been found for a checkpoint goal, C, these fail results are collected; together with comp(C), if C is unstable, these form the support for all(C). That is, the necessary support for the conclusion that all solutions to C have been found is the conjunction of all the supports for the fail results found. The result of evaluating C is then returned as (fail, [all(C)]).

To demonstrate, the evaluation of the checkpoint goal a(X) from ruleset 1 yields the following results in the order shown, from which the DLGMS node is constructed:

        X = m   (succ, [f, g, e, rule(r3)])
                 (fail, [comp(c(r))])
                 (fail, [all(b(X))])
        X = m   (succ, [rule(r2)])
                 (fail, [comp(a(X))])

Handling negation-as-failure

Firstly, a check is made to ensure that the negated goal is completely bound, otherwise an error is signalled; this avoids the well-known problem associated with unbound variables in negations (Lloyd 1984).

A search for all solutions, both succ and fail, to the unnegated goal is carried out, as described above. All solutions and associated result arguments found are collected as a list; however, as soon as one succ solution is found, the search is terminated, since clearly the negated goal fails.

If such a successful solution of the unnegated goal is found, where the result is (succ, S), this means that evaluation of the negated goal fails; the result of interpretation of the negated goal is returned as (fail, S). That is, the support for the successful solution to the unnegated goal is also the support for the conclusion that no solution to the negated goal exists. Otherwise, if no succ solutions are found, i.e. the unnegated goal fails so the negated goal succeeds, a result (succ, Supp) is returned, where Supp is the conjunction of all the supports for the fail results found; clearly, each of these supports is necessary for belief in failure of the unnegated goal, and, hence, in the success of the negation. Moreover, the same support must also be returned as a support for a fail solution, since removal of support for belief in the negation should not lead to unquestioning belief in the failure of the negation. To demonstrate, consider the program

a1   a :- not b(p).
b1   b(q).

where a is a checkpoint. If the top-level query, a, is given it will succeed. The result of interpreting b(p) will be simply (fail, [comp(b(p))]). The results of interpreting not b(p) will be (succ, [comp(b(p)]) and (fail, [comp(b(p)]), returned in that order. The DLGMS node for a will therefore include a positive-lemma

> a :   [rule(a1), comp(b(p))];

i.e. a depends on rule a1 and on the assumption that the clause set for b(p) is complete. It will also, however, include an all-lemma whose support includes comp(b(p)), i.e.

> all(a) :   [comp(b(p)), comp(a)];

This means that if we add a new rule, b(X) :- ....., the assumption of comp(b(p)) no longer holds (as discussed later under lemma maintenance); support for a is thus removed, but so is that for all(a). If all(a) were not removed, the goal a would automatically be assumed to fail if encountered later, since there would be a corresponding all-lemma but no positive-lemma, even though the new rule for b(X) might still not yield a solution to b(p).

Example of lemma generation

We shall demonstrate lemma generation by considering the behaviour of the system with the following program, ruleset 2.

a1	a(t) :- b(X), c(X).	g1	g(m, n).
a2	a(X) :- e(X), f(X, Y), g(X, Y).	g2	g(m, X) :- l(X).
b1	b(p) :- not d(m), h(m).	h1	h(m) :- j.
b2	b(q) :- r.	j1	j.
b3	b(s) :- not f(p, p).	l1	l(m).
b4	b(t) :- not g(m, k).	v1	v :- w1.
d1	d(m) :- not v.	v2	v :- w2.
f1	f(p, n).		
f2	f(p, m).		

together with meta-level declarations as summarized below.

checkpoint:	a, b, g	askable:	c, e, r, w1, w2
interpreted:	a, b, d, f, h, j, v	stable:	j
uninterpreted:	g, l		

Suppose the top-level query a(X) is given and the following interaction occurs (user input bold):

	w1?	**yes**	c(s)?	**no**
	c(p)?	**yes**	c(t)?	**no**
=> X = t **more**			e(Y)?	**e(p)**
	r?	**yes**		**no**
	c(q)?	**yes**	=> no (more) answers	
=> X = t **more**				

The DLGMS nodes that result are as follows:

```
node : b
    b(t)        :   [rule(b4)];
    b(s)        :   [rule(b3), comp(f(p, p))];
    b(q)        :   [rule(b2), r];
    b(p)        :   [rule(b1), rule(v1), w1, comp(d(m)), rule(h1)];
    all(b(X))   :   [comp(f(p, p)), comp(r), comp(d(m)), w1, rule(v1),
                     comp(h(m)), comp(b(X))];

node : g
    all(g(p, m))  :   [];
    all(g(p, n))  :   [];
    all(g(m, k))  :   [];

node : a
    a(t)        :   [rule(a1), b(q), c(q)] or
                    [rule(a1), b(p), c(p)];
    all(a(X))   :   [comp(e(Z)), comp(f(p, X1)), all(b(Y1)), comp(c(t)),
                     comp(c(s)), comp(c(q)), comp(c(p)), comp(a(X))];
```

Note that the checkpoint relation name, g, does not appear in the support of any lemma because it is uninterpreted. A DLGMS node for g is, however, generated, with all supports empty, i.e. no assumptions required.

3.5   Lemma Maintenance

The aim of lemma maintenance is to ensure that lemmas that no longer enjoy support following withdrawal of a base assumption (about askable relations and unstable rules) are invalidated and no longer used; our approach is to remove lemmas no longer supported.

We stressed earlier the importance of our representation of supports, whereby the support for a lemma may include other lemmas, so does not necessarily explicitly include all the base assumptions upon which it ultimately depends. The significance of this is that when a base assumption is withdrawn the effect of withdrawal may be considered iteratively, through a process of *propagation*: firstly, its direct effect on lemmas whose support explicitly includes the base assumption is considered; only then, if removal of all support for a particular lemma results, need the effect on other lemmas, dependent on this lemma, be considered. If, in contrast, the supports for lemmas included only base assumptions, the effect of withdrawal of a base assumption on each lemma ultimately supported by it would have to be considered.

Withdrawal of base assumptions occurs due to changes in the rule-base or answers given. We firstly discuss what base assumptions must be withdrawn for relevant changes. We then demonstrate the lemma maintenance procedures, which make use of the links relating assumptions and lemmas, through an example; we do not give details of these procedures or show the resulting links, although, clearly, as DLGMS nodes are modified, links may be removed.

Addition of a new rule for an unstable predicate

If a rule G :- C is added, then the assumption of comp(G'), where G' is unifiable with G, no longer holds. The lack of support for comp(G') must therefore be propagated.

Removal of an existing rule for an unstable predicate

If a rule named R is removed, then the lack of support for rule(R) must be propagated.

Changing an answer to a variable-free question from yes to no, and vice versa

If the answer to the variable-free query, G, is changed from yes to no, G must be removed from the appropriate dialogue record and the lack of support for G propagated; any assumption of comp(G) still holds.

If the answer to the variable-free query, G, is changed from no to yes, G must be inserted into the dialogue record, while terms of the form comp(G'), where G' is more general than G, must be removed from the record and their lack of support propagated.

Changing the solutions given to a question containing variables

Depending on the changes, terms of the form G, comp(G) or both may need to be removed from the dialogue record and their lack of support propagated.

Example of lemma maintenance

To demonstrate lemma maintenance, we shall consider the effect of a certain sequence of operations on the three DLGMS nodes, for a, g, and b, resulting from ruleset 2, used to demonstrate lemma generation.

Operation 1: delete rule b2.

The assumption rule(b2) no longer holds. This removes support for b(q), which, in turn, removes part of the support for a(t); a(t) is still, however, supported through an alternative conjunction. The resulting modified nodes (that for g remains unaltered) are:

    node : b
        b(t)   :   [rule(b4)];
        b(s)   :   [rule(b3), comp(f(p, p))];
        b(p)   :   [rule(b1), rule(v1), w1, comp(d(m)), rule(h1)];
        all(b(X))   :   [comp(f(p, p)), comp(r), comp(d(m)), w1, rule(v1),
                              comp(h(m)), comp(b(X))];

    node : a
        a(t)   :   [rule(a1), b(p), c(p)];
        all(a(X))   :   [comp(e(Z)), comp(f(p, X1)), all(b(Y1)), comp(c(t)),
                              comp(c(s)), comp(c(q)), comp(c(p)), comp(a(X))];

The top-level query b(q) given now would fail immediately, without further computation, since all(b(X)) is still supported. The query a(t) would still succeed, while a(p) would fail, both without further computation.

Operation 2: add new rule, f(p, r) :- l(n).

The assumption comp(f(p, r)), and hence comp(f(p, X1)), no longer holds, so support for all(a(X)) is removed, i.e. we can no longer be sure, without further evaluation, that all solutions to a(X) exist in the node. The nodes for b and g are unaltered, while the node for a becomes

    node : a
        a(t)   :   [rule(a1), b(p), c(p)];

Operation 3: change answer to w1? from yes to no.

The nodes for a and b are altered; g remains unaltered.

    node : b
        b(t)   :   [rule(b4)];
        b(s)   :   [rule(b3), comp(f(p, p))];

    node : a

Removal of assumption w1 removes support for b(p), which, in turn, removes the last support for a(t). Removal of assumption w1 also removes support for all(b(X)). This reflects the fact that we cannot be sure, without further computation, that all solutions to b(X) exist in the node: in fact, if w2 were confirmed, then v would succeed, d(m) would fail and, so, b(p) would still hold.

4. Concluding Remarks

We have shown how, through explicit consideration of assumptions concerning the completeness of rule sets and answers given, a dependency-based lemma generation and maintenance system (DLGMS) able to handle negation-as-failure may be developed. The use of lemmas helps avoid re-computation, but does involve certain, not insignificant, overheads; we have further shown how, through the use of checkpoints, and other simple meta-level declarations, a flexible system may be developed that allows the user of the system to explore the benefits of limiting lemma generation and assumptions concerning completeness in order to optimize performance.

The DLGMS should prove generally useful for logic-based expert systems, where users wish to change answers given or where different, or modified, knowledge bases may be used at various times It should also allow a more natural knowledge representation to be employed, with less need to pass computationally-expensive results as arguments.

Acknowledgements

Thanks to my colleagues at BP Research Centre for their comments and help, especially Rashmi Patel and Alan Heath, and also to my ex-colleagues at Imperial College for earlier discussions on truth maintenance and lemma generation, particularly Murray Shanahan, Richard Southwick and Chris Evans.

References

Clark, K.L. (1978). Negation as failure. In Logic and Data Bases, eds. Gallaire, H. and Lasserre, C. (1978). New York: Plenum Press.

de Kleer, J. (1986). An Assumption-based TMS. AI Journal, 28, pp 127 - 162.

Hogger, C.J. (1984). Introduction to Logic Programming. Academic Press.

Lloyd, J. W. (1984). Foundations of logic programming. Berlin: Springer-Verlag.

Sergot, M.J. (1983). A Query-the-User facility for logic programming. In Integrated Interactive Computing Systems, eds. Degano, P., and Sandewall, E. North-Holland.

Shanahan, M.P. (1987). Exploiting dependencies in search and inference mechanisms. PhD Thesis. Cambridge University.

Wolstenholme, D.E. and Hammond, P. (1988). Sigma-APES User Manual. Richmond, Surrey, U.K: Logic Based Systems.

Wolstenholme, D.E. and O'Brien, C.M. (1987). GLIMPSE: A statistical adventure. Procs. 10th IJCAI, vol 1.

USING META-LEVEL INFORMATION FOR EXPERT SYSTEM CONTROL: A 'BLENDING' TRANSFORMER APPROACH.

Yannis A. Cosmadopoulos and Richard W. Southwick
Logic Programming Group,
Imperial College,
180 Queen's Gate,
London, SW7 2BZ.

Abstract

Clark and McCabe [3] suggest that Prolog be used for expert system construction. They show that the additional functionality required for expert system design may be incorporated into a knowledge base, by adding extra trace arguments, etc., to each clause. This approach has largely been abandoned in favour of a scheme in which this control and environment information is localised in a meta-interpreter. The problem that arises with this meta-interpreter scheme, however, is its lack of efficiency. Partial evaluation has been proposed as a solution, but suffers from its own problems with control and complexity.

In this paper, we argue for a return to the first approach, which we call a *blending* of meta-level information into an object-level database. We present a transformation that produces the blended program automatically, in a way that is transparent to the user. Domain-specific code is written as for a meta-interpreter, and is transformed at compile time. This blended program may be executed directly in Prolog, taking advantage of modern optimization techniques, and resulting in a dramatic increase in efficiency. We show how such a blending transformer may be written from a meta-interpreter, such that the clear specification of the meta-level is used as the basis for the transformation. Finally, we contrast this approach with that of partial evaluation.

1 Introduction

Logic-based knowledge representation is an accepted approach to implementing expert systems. Prolog is the most common practical logic-based representation language currently available. It provides a framework for representing domain knowledge as rules and facts, a practical inference mechanism for object-level execution and a powerful set of meta-level facilities. In general, the simple object-level control strategy offered by Prolog is inadequate because it may prove inefficient, have problems of non-termination and also provides no facilities for explanation or user interaction.

One way of overcoming these difficulties is to augment the clauses with control information at the object-level (Clark and McCabe [3]). Providing an execution trace, for example, would require an additional argument in each clause in the database to hold the trace. But this approach poses problems in that it mixes domain and meta-level knowledge, reducing the modularity and perspicuity of rules in the knowledge base, and decreases the ease of modification of the knowledge base. This approach has largely been abandoned in favour of the use of *meta-interpreters*.

Most system designers do not code directly in raw Prolog. Instead, they use a *shell* which provides an inference engine and a representation language. Control is specified by the inference engine which operates on a *domain program*, written in the representation language, which encodes knowledge specific to the problem domain. This separation of knowledge and control is accepted as an important programming technique, as it improves clarity and modifiability. In logic terms, because it takes a program as data, a shell's inference engine is a meta-interpreter, and the knowledge base the *object-level* program.

The main problem with the use of meta-interpreters is the inefficiency that inevitably occurs when another level of processing has been added. In this paper, we discuss a technique for improving the efficiency of expert system shells, by *blending* meta-level functionality into the object-level program.

The method we propose, a *blending transformer*, combines the advantages of the meta-interpreter approach with the efficiency of the object-level approach. Since it is the meta-interpretation of a program that is inefficient, we blend all meta-level functionality into the object level, producing a program that can be run directly in Prolog, resulting in a dramatic increase in speed. Declarative domain knowledge is represented separately from information for system control. This meta-level knowledge is kept local to the transformer, and is blended with the object-level knowledge at 'compile-time'. The resultant program has the same behaviour as a meta-interpreter acting on the knowledge base, but runs much faster, since not only is an additional layer of evaluation removed, but the transformed program may be compiled for further optimization.

We'll begin by describing meta-interpreters for expert systems, and then show how the functionality of a meta-interpreter may be blended into an object-level program. We then present a method of automating this process, by performing the blending through a transformation process that occurs at compile time. Comparisons are made with partial evaluation, which has been suggested as another solution to the expense of meta-interpretation. Finally, we discuss the implementation of this method, and some applications that have successfully benefited from this approach.

2 Meta-Interpreters for Expert System Shells

The declarative nature of Prolog makes it a useful language for representing domain information for expert systems. While a Prolog database may be queried and solutions found, this is unsatisfactory for expert system use. Expert systems require a richer environment to make them usable.

Prolog-based expert systems are often based around a meta-interpreter that implements standard Prolog execution (Hammond and Sergot [4], Sterling [11]). For use as an expert system shell, the basic interpreter must be extended, both to permit interpretation of the full Prolog language, and to allow non-Prolog operation. Such an extended interpreter may have the following functionality:

- Ability to handle special cases. These include disjunctive goals, negation, and system predicates. In addition, extra-logical features such as the cut operator can be treated.
- It must handle the peculiarities of Prolog implementations, as opposed to pure logic. Certain predicates will not execute correctly if some arguments are insufficiently instantiated; in some Prologs, such calls may cause a system error and should be trapped.
- Additional facilities such as program traces, "why" and "how" explanations, user dialogue, and help can be added.
- Non-standard control and execution strategies may be implemented. Examples are breadth-first search, weighted search strategies, and a user-controlled reasoning process.

Figure 1 shows an interpreter that handles system predicates, negation and records the execution trace (useful for debugging or explanation). User interaction is handled through a query-the-user mechanism (Sergot [9]), whereby the user is asked to supply any missing information.

```
solve(true, true) :- !.
solve((Goal,Rest), (TraceA,TraceB)) :- !,
    solve(Goal,TraceA),
    solve(Rest,TraceB).
solve(\+ Goal, (not(Goal))) :- !,
    \+ solve(Goal).
solve(Goal, (system(Goal))) :- !,
    system(Goal), call(Goal).
solve(Goal, (user(Goal))) :-
    askable(Goal), !,
    query_user(Goal).
solve(Goal, (Goal :- SubTrace)) :-
    clause(Goal,SubGoal),
    solve(SubGoal, SubTrace).
```

Figure 1: A Meta-interpreter

There are several advantages to using a meta-interpreter in an expert system shell. First, there is a distinct separation of control and domain-specific knowledge. The domain may be represented by as set of rules and facts, which may be amended and added to by a knowledge engineer who need not be concerned with the operation of the system. Likewise, the meta-interpreter is also modular – modifications to the system environment and execution are localised. As a result, maintenance is simplified. In addition, a logic-based interpreter has at its base a sound semantics, with all concomitant advantages in specification and verification of programs (Bowen and Kowalski [1]).

For all its advantages, meta-interpretation suffers from a high computational cost. Programs that are executed through meta-interpretation run significantly more slowly than those run directly in Prolog. This additional expense is not due only to the interpreter's extra level of evaluation — there is a hidden cost built into many Prolog implementations. This takes two forms: the high cost of retrieving a clause from the database, and the problems associated with mixing compiled and interpreted ('dynamic') code. Program code that has been optimised (*e.g.* through compilation) cannot be directly interpreted. Prolog implementations account for this by either enforcing a distinction between compiled and interpreted code, or by de-compiling clauses whenever they are retrieved from the database. This is unfortunate, as compiled programs can run at an order of magnitude faster than interpreted ones, let alone meta-interpreted programs.

3 Blending In Meta-Level Functionality

We propose a method that combines the advantages (modularity, perspicuity) of the meta-interpreter approach, but produces a program that can be run directly in Prolog. The domain specific knowledge base is written as usual, as a set of declarative rules and facts that describe the domain. This is done without the knowledge engineer having to worry about the operation and control of the system that will use this knowledge.

Meta-level knowledge, necessary for expert system control, is kept local to a transformer, which is used to blend this information with the object-level knowledge. This is done at compile time, as the knowledge base is consulted. This *blending transformation* process can be so arranged as to be completely transparent to the user. The result is a system whose behaviour is indistinguishable, to a user, from an equivalent meta-interpreter operating on the original, untransformed database.

To illustrate this blending process we shall use an example database defining family relationships. Figure 2 is a simple database defining family relationships. It contains no clauses for relations mother and father, which are intended to be furnished by the user.

```
grandparent(X, Y) :- grandmother(X, Y).
grandparent(X, Y) :- grandfather(X, Y).

grandmother(X, Y) :- mother(X, Z), parent(Z, Y).
grandfather(X, Y) :- father(X, Z), parent(Z, Y).

parent(X, Y) :- mother(X, Y).
parent(X, Y) :- father(X, Y).
```

Figure 2: A family relationship database

Now consider how the functionality of the meta-interpreter of Figure 1 may be blended into this program. An extra argument to hold the execution trace is added to each clause. For example, the first clause for grandparent becomes:

```
grandparent(X, Y, (grandparent(X, Y) :- Trace)) :-
    grandmother(X, Y, Trace).
```

References to predicates which have been designated 'askable' (in this case father and mother) are defined in terms of the meta-level procedure that would have been applied by the meta-interpreter. The goal parent(X,Y), for example, is true if the user supplies an answer for mother:

```
parent(X, Y, user(mother(X, Y))) :- query_user(mother(X, Y)).
```

The full blended program is given in Figure 3. Because the transformed program can be run directly in Prolog, this method yields a significant increase in speed of execution, at the expense of added complexity at the object-level.

The resulting transformed program is equivalent to the meta-interpreter acting on the untransformed database. The nature of the transformation is transparent to the user, though user queries need to be altered to take into account any added arguments. The correct behaviour can be obtained by providing a run-time transformation of queries. This is accomplished by defining a transforming predicate execute_query:

```
execute_query(Goal, Trace) :-
    transform_body(Goal, Trace, NewGoal),
    call(NewGoal).
```

The predicate execute_query could be renamed solve to give a calling syntax and operation identical to the original meta-interpreter. The definition of transform_body will be outlined in the next section on the blending transformer.

```
grandparent(X, Y, (grandparent(X, Y) :- Trace)) :-
    grandmother(X, Y, Trace).
grandparent(X, Y, (grandparent(X, Y) :- Trace)) :-
    grandfather(X, Y, Trace).

grandmother(X, Y, (grandmother(X, Y) :- user(mother(X,Z)), Trace)) :-
    query_user(mother(X, Z)),
    parent(Z, Y, Trace).
grandfather(X, Y, (grandfather(X, Y) :- user(father(X,Z)), Trace)) :-
    query_user(father(X, Z)),
    parent(Z, Y, Trace).

parent(X, Y, user(mother(X, Y))) :- query_user(mother(X, Y)).
parent(X, Y, user(father(X, Y))) :- query_user(father(X, Y)).
```

Figure 3: Blended Object and Meta-Level Program

3.1 A Blending Transformer

Figure 3 illustrates that meta-level information can be embedded in the object-level clauses of a knowledge base, to yield a program which can be run directly in Prolog. As pointed out, however, in both Sterling [11] and Hammond and Sergot [4], this blending of the meta- and object-level makes the database more difficult to read. Even small changes to meta-level functionality may involve substantial modifications to the entire database. This loss of modularity degrades perspicuity and significantly increases maintenance costs of the combined knowledge base. In addition, if the transformation is done manually, this extra complexity at the object-level increases the chance of errors, and is an additional burden on the knowledge engineer. However, these objections are overcome if the transformation process is automated, occurring at compile time. Any subsequent modifications to the knowledge base are performed on the original, untransformed program. We now present such a *blending transform* procedure.

The transform procedure should produce a program that behaves as a meta-interpreter does. A re-examination of the operation of the meta-interpreter shows its relationship to the transformer. The heart of the interpreter is in the recursive step, where solve calls itself with a new goal. All additional clauses handle conditions for special cases and peculiarities of Prolog implementations (*e.g.* the case where the goal is true). Let us rewrite the solve relation to reflect this. In this formulation, solve operates on a list of goals. It selects the first goal from the list, and processes it in some way, returning a new list which is used in the recursive call. The process is complete when the list is empty:

```
solve([]).
solve([Goal|GoalList]) :-
    process(Goal, GoalList, NewList),
    solve(NewList).
```

Now we have a series of definitions of process. In the simplest case, a clause is found whose head matches the goal, and the body of the clause is added to the goal list

```
process(Goal, In, Out) :-
    clause(Goal, Body),
    append(Body, In, Out).
```

All other clauses for process deal with special cases:
```
process(Goal, In, In) :-
    sys(Goal), call(Goal).
process(Goal, In, In) :-
    askable(Goal), query_user(Goal).
```

3.1.1 The Transformer

With this sketch, we can examine the relationship between the meta-interpreter and the blending transformer. This hinges on distinguishing between the recursive part of the interpreter, and the processing part. Since we are transforming clauses, and not executing or expanding them, the recursive part of the process will be left for the Prolog execution. In transforming the program, we are simply applying any possible processing, at compile time. So to transform an interpreted clause, we decompose it into head and body and transform each part, producing a new output clause.

```
transform_clause((Head :- Body), (NewHead :- NewBody)) :-
    interpreted(Head),
    transform_body(Head, (Head:-Trace), NewHead),
    transform_body(Body, Trace, NewBody).
transform_clause((Head :- Body), (Head :- Body)) :-
    \+ interpreted(Head).
```

The predicate transform_body takes a goal and any extra arguments that are to be blended in, and produces a new term. Special cases are treated in much the same way as the meta-interpreter does; this corresponds to the set of clauses for process, above:

```
transform_body((Goal1, Goal2), (Trace1, Trace2), (NG1, NG2)) :- !,
    transform_body(Goal1, Trace1, NG1),
    transform_body(Goal2, Trace2, NG2).
transform_body((\+ Goal), (not(Goal)), (\+ NewGoal)) :- !,
    transform_body(Goal, Trace, NewGoal).
transform_body(Goal, system(Goal), Goal) :-
    builtin(Goal), !.
transform_body(Goal, user(Goal), query_user(Goal)) :-
    askable(Goal), !.
```

The meta-interpreter call to clause serves to prepare the goal list for the recursive step. The corresponding transform definition is the clause that handles interpreted goals. Extra arguments are added to the goal by pulling apart the term into a list, appending the extra arguments, and then reassembling the goal.

```
transform_body(Goal, Trace, NewGoal) :-
    Goal =.. List,
    append(List, [Trace], NewList),
    NewGoal =.. NewList.
```

This transformation can be performed at compile time, as a program is consulted. Many Prologs provide a hook, often called term_expansion, to allow such transformations. This is applied to all program clauses as they are consulted. Alternatively, the transformation can be performed by writing the transformed clauses to a temporary file which is then consulted. In both cases it is necessary for the type declarations (interpreted, askable etc.) to be present at transform time.

Besides the previously mentioned benefits of transformation over meta-interpretation, we have found an added bonus for system designers. Debugging the transformed program, through the use of a Prolog trace facility, is far simpler than the convoluted labyrinth one must follow to trace a meta-interpreter.

3.1.2 Disjunctive Definitions

The clauses for solve in the meta-interpreter of Figure 1 hold for goals of mutually exclusive types, so that solve takes on the procedural appearance of a case statement, similar to that found in procedural programming languages. This fact is mirrored in the transformer, and leads to a one-to-one correspondence between untransformed and transformed clauses. Although this fact makes the transformer simpler to write, it is by no means necessary. For predicates that belong to more than one type, a correct transformation will produce a disjunctive definition in the blended program. This could be written as either multiple clauses for a predicate, or a single clause with the disjunction contained in the body. Suppose, for example, that mother(X,Y) was defined by the clause

```
mother(X,Y) :- female(X), has_child(X,Y).
```

while still being askable. The transformation of

```
parent(X, Y) :- mother(X, Y).
```

could now result in two clauses:

```
parent(X, Y, Trace) :- mother(X, Y, Trace).
parent(X, Y, user(mother(X, Y))) :- query_user(mother(X, Y)).
```

The same information could also be represented more efficiently as a disjunction:

```
parent(X, Y, Trace) :- mother(X, Y, Trace) ;
    (query_user(mother(X, Y)), Trace = user(mother(X, Y))).
```

An alternative approach is to have the transformer *generate* a clause for any askable predicates, which takes the form

```
mother(X, Y, user(mother(X, Y))) :- query_user(mother(X, Y)).
```

Any existing clauses for mother are transformed in the usual way. The additional clauses for askable predicates may be generated by an additional transformer clause, add_askable:

```
add_askable(Pred, (NewPred :- query_user(Pred))) :-
    askable(Pred), !,
    transform_body(Pred, Pred, NewPred).
```

3.1.3 Special Treatment for Meta-level Predicates

Any predicates taking as arguments terms that correspond to object-level goals (*i.e.* meta-level predicates), require special treatment during transformation, as illustrated by the treatment of negation-as-failure (\+). Examples of system meta-level predicates include call and findall, while solve is an instance of a user-defined meta-level predicate.

To illustrate the point, consider the transformation of findall. Because findall takes a goal as an argument, that goal itself must be transformed. So if the goal is instantiated at compile time, it may be transformed directly:

```
transform_body(findall(P,Goal,List),Trace,findall(P,NewGoal,List)) :-
    instantiated(Goal),
    transform_body(Goal, Trace, NewGoal).
```

If, however, the goal is uninstantiated, the transformation must occur at run-time. To accomplish this, we augment the new goal with a call to transform_body.

```
transform_body(findall(Pattern, Goal, List), Trace, NewGoal) :-
    \+ instantiated(Goal),
    NewGoal = (      transform_body(Goal, Trace1, Goal1),
                     findall(Pattern, Goal1, List) ),
    Trace = (Trace1, findall(Pattern, Goal1, List)).
```

To illustrate the effect of this transformation, consider the clause

```
foo(Goal,Y,Out) :- findall(Y, Goal, Out).
```

This will be transformed to

```
foo(Goal,Y,Out,Trace) :-
    transform_body(Goal, Trace, NewGoal),
    findall(Y, NewGoal, Out).
```

3.2 Non-Standard Control

The *blending transformer* we have described in this section is suitable for expert systems using a Prolog-like control and search strategy. This is made explicit in the generalised Prolog interpreter of Figure 4 where the clauses supplied for select_goal, select_clause and add_goal correspond to Prolog's strategy. In this case the transformed program has the advantage of a close correspondence to the original knowledge base, a fact of great use during development and evaluation.

```
interp(Goals) :-
    select_goal(Goal, Goals, RestGoals),
    select_clause((Head:-Body)),
    Head = Goal,
    add_goals(Body, RestGoals, NewGoals),
    interp(NewGoals).

select_goal(Goal, (Goal, RestGoals), RestGoals).
select_clause((Head:-Body)) :- clause(Head, Body).
add_goals(Body, RestGoals, (Body,RestGoals)).
```

Figure 4: Generalised Meta-Interpreter

Implementing transformers for different control strategies is more difficult (as is the case with meta-interpreters), since any alteration to standard Prolog execution must be coded explicitly. In addition, if the required functionality depends on the state of computation (*e.g.* user control of goal ordering), then the blending process is not as straightforward, since these 'dynamic' control strategies require the embedding of tests to be performed at run-time. In particular, a dynamic strategy for select_clause will require clauses to be retrieved from the Prolog database, thus preventing the use of compiled code. Implementing dynamic goal selection does not suffer from this problem.

Note that while Prolog employs a depth-first, backward-reasoning search strategy, we are not restricted to this; a similar transformation process may also be used to implement other forms of reasoning. For an example of this approach applied to produce a forward-reasoning system in Prolog, see (Akira Yamamoto and Hozumi Tanaka) [16]).

3.2.1 Multiple control strategies

In some applications it may be desirable to have a number of different, possibly conflicting, control strategies. In such a case, either a number of different transformed programs may be generated, or alternatively compiled and meta-interpreted execution may be combined. In the latter case, by embedding a trace index that points to clauses in the original, untransformed program, it is possible to use this execution trace to 'guide' the execution of a meta-interpreter acting on the original program. This trace then serves as an 'explanation' of a successful query, and can be generalised to apply to similar queries. This general technique is the basis for explanation-based generalization (Mitchell et al [7]) and has been used in another form for learning rules for search control (Minton and Carbonell [6]).

4 Comparison with Partial Evaluation

There have been other proposals made to deal with the loss of efficiency inherent in meta-interpretation. The most popular of these is partial evaluation (Takeuchi and Furukawa [13], Venken [14]). Partial evaluation is a program optimization and transformation technique, used to obtain efficiency gains in program execution. In this section, we briefly describe partial evaluation for meta-interpreters, and relate this technique to the transformation presented above. We discuss some problems encountered in partial evaluation, and show how these problems are overcome by our transformation method.

Given a program and goal, partial evaluation produces a new program that has been specialised to that goal. Efficiency is improved by eliminating unrelated parts of the program, and performing precomputation on the given goal. Much of the testing and computation can be done once, during the partial evaluation, and so need not be repeated when executing the transformed version of the program.

Partial evaluation in Prolog relies on three techniques: unfolding, clause elimination, and propagation of variable bindings. Unfolding is a program transformation technique (Burstall and Darlington [2]) which consists of replacing a goal being evaluated with the body of a matching clause. If there are several clauses that match the current goal, a new goal clause will be produced for each. If the partial evaluation is done with respect to a goal with some variables bound, we can use this information to eliminate clauses whose heads will not unify, thereby pruning the program space of clauses that do not match. Propagation of variable bindings means that partially instantiated variables are propagated forward from a goal to its subgoals. In a complete program (one in which no predicates are undefined), partial evaluation is the same as finding all solutions to a query.

For expert system shell construction, partial evaluation is applied to a meta-interpreter. Consider a meta-interpreter I, which can determine the validity of some query with respect to a program: $I(P,Q)$. If we partial evaluate this interpreter with respect to some object level program, the result is a specialised meta-interpreter: $peval(I, P, I_P)$. "partial evaluate the interpreter I with respect to the program P, giving a new interpreter I_P". Now I_P is an interpreter specialised to a particular program P. The following equivalence results:

$eval(I,P) \iff eval(I_P,P)$

So applying partial evaluation to our *solve* predicate gives us a new interpreter:

$solve(P,Q) \iff solve_P(Q)$

Partial evaluation, when applied to a meta-interpreter and object program, corresponds to the use of a compiler to produce code that is specialised to a target machine. The result is a meta-interpreter with the object program 'mixed-in' (Sterling and Beer [12]). A meta-interpreter takes a program as data, and computes some result over that data. Partial evaluation folds the data into the interpreter, increasing efficiency and producing a program which can be run directly. Thus partial evaluation of a meta-interpreter with respect to its object-level data can be thought of compiling the program into Prolog.

4.1 Problems with Partial Evaluation

The process of partial evaluation can be seen as 'running' a program with a partially instantiated query. All non-evaluable predicates are collected, comprising the conditions for the success or the original query. Ideally, the program, with respect to a given query, is reduced to a number of atomic literals that correspond to all solutions for that query. Since at this point the problem is completely solved, no further optimization can occur.

There are some problems with partial evaluation, however. The first is that while partial evaluation is a sound and complete transformation when applied to pure logic programs (Lloyd and Shepherdson [5]), the extra-logical features of Prolog are more difficult to handle. Chief amongst these are negation in the bodies of clauses, and the cut operator. Partial evaluating *cut* is difficult, for example, because it has no semantics at the meta-level; a cut interpreted at one place at the meta-level is expected to effect execution at some other place. In addition, problems exist in backward propagation of variable bindings over impure primitives (cut, read, write, etc.). While there have been proposals made that deal with these problems (O'Keefe [8]), they are obviated by our approach. Because we are merely *translating* a program, as opposed to *interpreting* it, any extra-logical features remain local to the clause in which they occur.

Partial evaluation specialises a program to a particular query. This is fine, if only one query is to be posed, but in general one would prefer not to have that restriction. Our program transformation achieves this expectation by translating all clauses of a program – no specialization occurs.

Partial evaluation can be quite difficult to control, especially when deciding whether to unfold a particular goal. The usual method for controlling this process is to annotate the object program, completely specifying how to handle special cases. Typically, one needs to declare that certain goals should be unfolded, while for others, unfolding should be inhibited. Some goals should be unfolded only if certain arguments are bound. In addition, extra control must be added to handle recursive programs. A program that would ordinarily terminate satisfactorily may enter an infinite loop if insufficient arguments are instantiated. This is usually handled by maintaining a list of goals that have been encountered, and terminates the evaluation if the current goal is a member of that list. Again, certain recursive goals should be allowed to be unfolded, and this information is also recorded as annotations to the program.

In practice, partial evaluation is an iterative method. The partial evaluator is run on the program, the system designer notes where it has broken or behaved inappropriately, and makes the necessary annotations. This process is repeated until the desired behaviour is achieved, a sometimes arduous task. If changes are made to the interpreter or the object program it is run on, this process must be repeated. Our system, in contrast, does not need to worry about extra-program annotations. In other words, it operates successfully on whatever information is available to the meta-interpreter.

So although partial evaluation can potentially produce the most efficient program possible (a set of atomic conclusions representing all solutions), in practice it is a procedure that is difficult to design and control. The blending transformer is easy to set up and use, and does not suffer from the same kinds of problems.

5 Conclusions

We have presented a technique for taking the control and environmental features of an expert system shell, and blending them into the object-level knowledge base. We have shown how to construct a blending transformer, given a meta-interpreter. This transformer operates on programs as they are loaded, so as to be transparent to the user. In this way, control specification can be isolated at the meta-level during design and development, and blended into the object-level at run-time. This blending procedure offers the following benefits:

- Substantial increase in speed, since we can execute code directly in Prolog, without the expense of an additional level of evaluation.
- The ability to take advantage of optimizations provided by many Prolog implementations.
- The blending transformation is transparent to both user and knowledge base constructor.
- The transformed program is easier to trace than a meta-interpreter operating on a database.
- Any extra-logical features remain local to the clause and present no difficulties.
- All clauses are translated, resulting in a program that can answer general queries, rather than being specialised to one particular query.
- The large amounts of program annotation required for partial evaluation are not necessary.

The program transformer described in this paper has been implemented in Quintus Prolog. The transformation is done as a program file is consulted, using the term_expansion hook provided as a Prolog primitive.

This technique has been adopted for use in an intelligent front end. The implemented 'shell' handles rule-trace explanations, query-the-user (Sergot [9]), lemma generation, suspended queries (Wolstenholme [15]), user control of search and topic explanations (Southwick [10]). A transformer similar to ours has also been used to implement a version of Apes (Hammond and Sergot [4])[1].

6 Acknowledgements

The authors would like to thank Marek Sergot, for his discussions and inspiration. Thanks are also due to Damian Chu and Kostas Stathis, for their helpful comments on earlier drafts of this paper.

References

[1] K. A. Bowen and R. A. Kowalski. Amalgamating language and metalanguage in logic programming. In K. Clark and S. Tarnlund, editors, *Logic Programming*, pages 153–172, Academic Press, 1982.

[2] R. Burstall and J. Darlington. Transformation for developing recursive programs. *Journal of the ACM*, 24:44–67, 1975.

---

[1]Sergot, private communication.

[3] K. L. Clark and F. G. McCabe. PROLOG: a language for implementing expert systems. *Machine Intelligence*, 10:455–470, 1982.

[4] P. Hammond and M. J. Sergot. A PROLOG shell for logic based expert systems. In *Proceedings of the Third BCS Expert Systems Conference*, Cambridge, 1983.

[5] J. W. Lloyd and J. C. Shepherdson. *Partial Evaluation in Logic Programming*. Technical Report CS-87-09, University of Bristol, 1987.

[6] S. Minton and J. G. Carbonell. Strategies for learning search control rules: an explanation-based approach. In *Proceedings of the 8th International Joint Conference on Artificial Intelligence*, pages 228–235, Milan, 1987.

[7] T. M. Mitchell, R. M. Kellar, and S. T. Kedar-Cabelli. Explanation-based generalization: a unifying view. *Machine Learning*, 1:47–80, 1986.

[8] R. A. O'Keefe. On the treatment of cuts in Prolog source level tools. In *Symposium on Logic Programming*, pages 68–72, Boston, Massachusetts, 1985.

[9] M. J. Sergot. A query-the user facility of logic programming. In P. Degano and E. Sandewall, editors, *Integrated Interactive Computer Systems*, pages 27–41, North Holland, 1983.

[10] R. W. Southwick. Topic explanation in expert systems. In B. Kelly and A. Rector, editors, *Research and Development in Expert Systems V*, Cambridge University Press, 1988.

[11] L. Sterling. *Expert System = Knowledge + Meta-Interpreter*. Technical Report, Department of Applied Mathemathics, The Weizmann Institute of Science, 1984.

[12] L. Sterling and R. D. Beer. *Meta-Interpreters for Expert System Construction*. Technical Report, Case Western Reserve University, 1985.

[13] A. Takeuchi and K. Furukawa. *Partial Evaluation of Prolog Programs and its Application to Meta Programming*. Technical Report TR-126, ICOT, 1985.

[14] R. Venken. A Prolog meta-interpreter for partial evaluation and its application to source to source transformation and query-optimisation. *ECAI 84: Advances in Artificial Intelligence*, 91–101, 1984.

[15] D. E. Wolstenholme. Saying "I don't know" and conditional answers. In D. S. Moralee, editor, *Research and Development in Expert Systems IV*, pages 115–125, Cambridge University Press, 1987.

[16] A. Yamamoto and H. Tanaka. Translating production rules into a forward reasoning Prolog program. *New Generation Computing*, 4(1):97–105, 1986.

VERIFICATION OF RULE-BASED EXPERT SYSTEMS IN WIDE DOMAINS

Alun D. Preece
Artificial Intelligence & Expert Systems Group
Computer Science Division
University College Swansea
Swansea SA2 8PP

Abstract

The importance of expert system testing is highlighted, and the relationship between empirical validation and logical verification is described. A basic set of requirements for a knowledge base verification tool is described, and the rôle of such a tool in the expert system development cycle is indicated. The importance of completeness checking for knowledge bases is emphasised, and it is shown that previous verification tools have failed to address this issue satisfactorily. A completeness checking tool which operates in difficult domains with wide knowledge bounds using heuristics is described, together with its use in two contrasting case studies. The rôle of this tool in knowledge acquisition is discussed.

1. The Rôle of Automated Tools in Checking Expert Systems

The testing of expert systems is possibly more important than the testing of any other kind of software, due to their complexity and the nature of their rôle in decision-making and decision-support tasks. Expert system developers must test their systems as extensively as possible throughout the development process, using methods of *validation* and *verification*.

Validation applies to testing that expert system outcomes resemble the outcomes of the human expertise modeled by the knowledge base. Such testing should be performed both in laboratory trials (Spiegelhalter 1983) and in field trials (Wyatt 1987). *Verification* applies to testing that the knowledge base is logically sound and complete. Since any complex expert system will have a great many possible situation and outcome combinations, empirical validation will rarely test all possibilities exhaustively. However, suitable automated tools can operate upon knowledge bases to perform such tests, referring questions of omissions, conflicts, etc to the design team for revision (Mars 1987).

Validation and verification are complementary, and should be incorporated in a development methodology for expert systems, as shown in Figure 1. The order in which the three assessment methods appear in the cycle relate to the relative costs of the methods: Since automated checking will, in general, be less expensive than tying up human and organisational resources for validation trials it is reasonable from a project-management point-of-view to apply these tests most frequently.

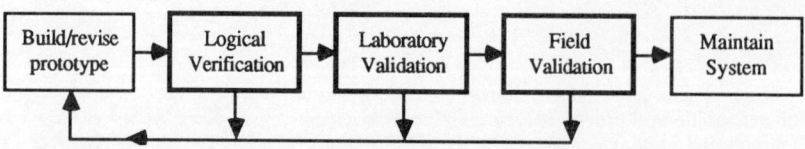

Figure 1: The Expert System Development Cycle

This paper is concerned with the automated verification phase in the above cycle. Since production rule-based expert systems have a basis in formal logic (Bundy 87) we feel that it is vital that this is exploited to provide as much logical testing as possible. Where logical problems are discovered by verification tools, these may be results of either the systems failure to meet its specified goals, or of logical flaws in the specification itself (the goals of the system may not be logically sound). Verification tools therefore have a useful and important rôle within expert system specification, as well as in testing that systems meet their specifications.

2. Techniques Used in Automated Expert System Verification

Automated checking procedures (if used at all) usually form part of a knowledge acquisition or expert system development tool. Although there is work in this area on automated expert system *validation* tools, notably Davis (1979) and Politakis (1984), we will solely concern ourselves here with verification systems. The vast majority of work in this field lies in the area of rule-based expert systems, since the semantics of production systems are better understood than those of frame-based systems, semantic network systems, or hybrid-representation systems. This gives rise to specific notions of completeness, redundancy, and so forth (Bundy 87).

Perhaps surprisingly, this field is relatively small. The two most significant systems developed in this area are due to Suwa *et al* (1982) and Nguyen *et al* (1985). Suwa's verification program was developed as a component of the ONCOCIN system, and Nguyen's CHECK system originated as part of the Lockheed Expert System, LES, but was later generalised somewhat as a tool for checking knowledge bases built using the ART shell (Nguyen 87). ONCOCIN, LES and ART are all essentially goal-directed rule-based systems.

We shall identify the following set of checks which must be performed by a verification tool for rule-based knowledge bases:

- *Redundancy* Two rules conclude the same outcome from the same input data. In practice this may involve inefficient operation and maintenance difficulties.
- *Conflict* Two rules conclude different outcomes from the same input data. In practice this may lead to the system holding inconsistent beliefs during execution.
- *Subsumption* Two rules conclude the same outcome, but one has additional constraints, which may or may not be necessary.
- *Circularity* The knowledge base contains a cyclic inference chain, which may cause a backward-chaining inference engine to enter an endless loop.
- *Unsatisfiable conditions* A rule condition tests a value against a parameter but there is no way that the parameter can hold that value - either by asking the user by firing a rule.
- *Dead-end rules* A rule concludes a value for a parameter which never satisfies any rule condition. If this rule were satisfied it would conclude a subgoal that could not lead to the satisfaction of any higher-level goals. In effect, any reasoning chain employing the rule would not proceed any further. This may not be an error but the system designer should nevertheless be aware of it.
- *Missing rules* There is a set of parameter instantiations that will result in no successful conclusion of the knowledge base goal. In practice this means that there is some real-world situation (represented by values assigned to parameters) that the system has no outcome for.

Note that in the case of missing rules, although situations described by such rules may be logically possible, they may not be *empirically* possible. For example, the situation sex=male and pregnant=yes. Such combinations, discovered by the rule-checker, could be included as *constraints* which the system would employ to validate input data.

Some of the above problems are illustrated in the following example:

Rules:
1 :: g = g1 if a = a1 and b = b1
2 :: g = g2 if c = c2
3 :: g = g1 if b = b1
4 :: g = g3 if a = a1
5 :: c = c2 if g = g2
6 :: g = g3 if a = a1

Problems:
Subsumed by 3, conflict with 4
Circularity with 5
Subsumes 1[1]
Conflict with 1, redundant with 6
Circularity with 2
Redundant with 4

Nguyen's CHECK and ARC (ART Rule Checker) systems each cover most of these cases by using static examination of the rules, and employing a number of graph structures for checking circularity and relationships between rule chains (described in detail in Nguyen 1985 and Nguyen 1987). Their primary weakness lies in the case of missing rules: CHECK only looks for single parameter instantiations that are not covered by any rule ("missing values"), while ARC does not check for completeness.

Completeness is better addressed by Suwa's program, using a tabular method. Checking is made easier in ONCOCIN because each rule has an explicitly-specified context which essentially indicate what data the rule concludes. For each such context, the rule checker constructs a table indicating all data items referred to by the rules applicable in that context, and their values in each rule. The table is inspected by the checking program for conflict, redundancy, subsumption and missing rules[2]. An example of the table based upon the above rules is shown below:

Context: establishing g

Table:	Rule:	Outcome:	a	b	c
	1	g1	a1	b1	*
	2	g2	*	*	c2
	3	g1	*	b1	*
	4	g3	a1	*	*
	6	g3	a1	*	*

Note that "don't care" (*) values can appear in the table, indicating that a parameter does not appear in a particular rule.

Essentially, the ONCOCIN rule-checker checks for completeness by considering all combinations of parameters and values and lists the combinations not appearing in the table. An algorithm for this, employing cardinal numbers, is described by Puuronen (1987), and is more efficient than a symbolic table inspection algorithm. However, this approach, as we shall show later, is only appropriate for contexts involving small sets of parameters.

It should be stressed once again that, pragmatically, these tools need to be used as part of an interactive process involving the human developers and experts. Some apparent logical problems may in fact be empirically valid, especially in cases of semantically impossible "missing" rules and valid "dead-end" rules. However, it the responsibility of the designer to be aware of such potential problems and determine which need correction.

---

[1] Note that the subsumption of rule 1 by rule 3 may indicate that rule 3 is incomplete, needing an additional constraint, or that rule 1 has an unnecessary constraint. This situation may have come about as a result of an error in knowledge base updating, where a rule was modified but its original version was not removed.
[2] No check for cyclic inference chains is performed by Suwa's rule-checking program.

3. Checking Expert Systems in Wide Domains

Many useful expert system applications are in *wide domains*, where typically many more factors have to be considered in the decision-making process than would be needed in a narrow domain (Basden 1983). Expert systems are easier to build in narrow domains, since domain bounds are defined more clearly, knowledge acquisition is more straightforward, and systems operate more efficiently. Unfortunately, many valuable applications lie in wide domains, such as medicine, social work, education, and economics.

For our purposes, because of the wider range of factors (parameters) bearing relevance on an outcome, knowledge bases built in wide domains are harder to verify than their narrow counterparts. However, for exactly the same reason, it is more important that such verification is done, since the resulting combinatorial explosion of possible situations and outcomes make empirical testing less effective. Probably the most important aspect of checking in wide domains is completeness, since missing rules will be harder to spot manually. As we have already seen, this requirement has either been inadequately addressed in previous work, or previous methods lack sufficient power to cope with a wide domain (the failure of the tabular method employed by Suwa will be clearly demonstrated in the following section).

The following sections of this paper develop the core of a knowledge base verification tool for rule-based expert systems, and illustrate its use on a practical application built in a wide domain. In an effort to show the generality of the method, we also present a counter-example in a narrow domain.

4. Completeness Checking in Wide Domains

We first need to define what we mean by "completeness". For this purpose we will assume a simple, generic production rule formalism in which each rule consists of two parts: a *conclusion part,* which concludes an outcome by instantiating some data item with a given value, and a *condition part,* which is a conjunction of individual conditions, each of which is a test to see if some data item has a given value[1]. The data item in the conclusion part is called the rule *subject*. The subject will take the given value if all tests in the condition part succeed. For the time being we will assume that all data items are single-valued *parameters*.

The rules are invoked in a goal-directed, backward-chaining inference strategy. One parameter is selected as the overall *goal* of the system, which it tries to establish by successfully evaluating the condition part of some rule whose subject is the goal. Each parameter in the condition part of this rule is either itself investigated using a rule, in which case it becomes a *subgoal*, or it is asked of the user, provided it is designated as *askable*.

We will define completeness in the context of such a search for a value for some goal G. G has associated with it a *dataset* D_G of all parameters that could be tested in the search for G, and a *ruleset* R_G of all rules that could be invoked in the search for G. D_G includes all subgoals in a search for G, and all items that may be asked of the user in that search. R_G includes all rules with G as a subject, and all rules with a subject in D_G.

Every data item $d_i \in D_G$ has a set of values V_{d_i}. The function vals(d_i) = | V_{d_i} | gives the number of values d_i can take. An *instantiation* of a data item d_i is a tuple $\langle d_i, v_{ij} \rangle$, where $v_{ij} \in V_{d_i}$.

A *path* P_G is a non-empty set of instantiations of data items in D_G, containing no more than one instantiation of each data item. Formally, if $\langle d_i, v_{ij} \rangle \in P_G$,

---

[1]Rule condition parts may also be disjunctions, but for completeness checking they will be transformed into conjunctions. This is described in section 9.

then $\langle d_i, v_{ik} \rangle \notin P_G, j \neq k$. Each $d_i \in D_G$ need not appear at all in a path. Furthermore, an item will only appear in a path if it is askable of the user.

Informally, a path represents a real-world situation that may possibly occur – represented by a set of data that the user could supply the system. Each goal G sought by the system has a potentially huge universe $\mathbf{P_G}$ of paths associated with it, particularly in a wide domain.

One final concept is needed in order to define completeness for a set of rules R_G: The function covered(P_G, R_G) is true if either:
- The instantiations in P_G, when supplied as data to R_G, cause a value to be concluded for G, or:
- There is some path $P_G' \supseteq P_G$, such that covered(P_G', R_G) is true, and *at least one* instantiation in P_G is used by R_G in concluding a value for G.

If covered(P_G, R_G) is true then P_G is *covered* by R_G, otherwise P_G is *null* for R_G [1].

Informally, the first case above represents the notion that the user-supplied data is used by the inference engine to build a valid search tree. The second case says that the user-supplied data in P_G provides part of a valid search tree which is incomplete (more data is needed to complete the proof of G, but the existing data provides part of the solution). Since the path can quite legitimately contain more data than is actually used in the tree, we need the additional constraint that at least one instantiation in the path is used in building the tree. The following example should clarify this:

Consider the following knowledge base fragment:
Goal G = g
Dataset D_G = { a, b, c }
Values V_g = { g1, g2 }, V_a = { a1, a2 }, V_b = { b1, b2 }, V_c = { c1, c2 }
Ruleset R_G= {
    1 :: g = g1 if a = a1 and b = b2,
    2 :: g = g2 if a = a2 and b = b1,
    3 :: g = g1 if b = b1 and c = c1
}

The following are examples of *covered* paths:

    { $\langle$a, a1$\rangle$, $\langle$b, b2$\rangle$ }   covered by rule 1
    { $\langle$a, a1$\rangle$, $\langle$b, b1$\rangle$, $\langle$c, c1$\rangle$ }   covered by rule 3 [2]
    { $\langle$a, a2$\rangle$ }   covered by rule 2 [3]
    { $\langle$b, b2$\rangle$, $\langle$c, c1$\rangle$ }   covered by rule 1 [4]

The following paths are *null* :

    { $\langle$a, a1$\rangle$, $\langle$b, b1$\rangle$ }
    { $\langle$a, a2$\rangle$, $\langle$b, b2$\rangle$ }
    { $\langle$c, c2$\rangle$ }

---

[1] P_G is only null with respect to the ruleset for the designated goal G – it is not necessarily null for all rulesets in the knowledge base.
[2] Note that $\langle$a, a1$\rangle$ is unnecessary additional information - this path would still be covered without it, but its inclusion does not invalidate the coverage of the path.
[3] This is covered because there is a path P_G' { $\langle$a, a2$\rangle$, $\langle$b, b1$\rangle$ } that is covered by rule 2, and the tuple $\langle$a, a2$\rangle$ is used in concluding the value g2 for goal g in this case.
[4] There is a path P_G' { $\langle$a, a1$\rangle$, $\langle$b, b2$\rangle$, $\langle$c, c1$\rangle$ } covered by rule 1, and the instance $\langle$b, b2$\rangle$ is used in concluding the value g1 for g.

Note that if the second requirement of case two for the covered function was not enforced, then the path { ⟨c, c2⟩ } would be covered by the path { ⟨a, a1⟩, ⟨b, b1⟩ }, since { ⟨a, a1⟩, ⟨b, b1⟩, ⟨c, c2⟩ } is covered.

The ruleset R_G is *complete* if covered(P_G, R_G) holds for all $P_G \in \mathbf{P}_G$. Null paths indicate possible missing rules – they are basically "conclusionless rules".

The naïve algorithm for checking completeness of a ruleset associated with a goal G appears below:

> *determine D_G and R_G ;*
> *while there is an untried path P_G {*
>   *generate(P_G, D_G);*
>   *if not covered(P_G, R_G) then*
>   *output(P_G);*
> *}*

The problem with this algorithm lies in the huge number of paths that the generate function creates. This number is given by the formula:

$$\left(\prod_{i=1,n} \text{vals}(d_i) + 1 \right) - 1, \quad \text{where } n = |D_G| \text{ and vals}(d_i) = |V_{d_i}|.$$

For example, a dataset of 3 items, each with 2 possible values (as in the above example) would need 26 paths to be tested. For 16 items, 6 values each there would be 3×10^{12} paths. Because of this formula, the algorithm faces combinatorial explosion on non-trivial tasks. This is why the Suwa and Puuronen techniques described earlier flounder in both wide domains and large narrow domains[1].

Obviously we need heuristics to control the generation of paths, particularly in wide domains, where $|D_G|$ is large.

5. Approach Employed by the COVER Program

The COVER (COmpleteness VERifier) program performs verification of rule-based systems in wide domains. To this end it performs the seven types of checking listed earlier: redundancy, conflict, subsumption, circularity, unsatisfiable conditions, dead-end rules, and missing rules. COVER has been designed to check the knowledge bases of a generic rule-based expert system shell, implemented in Prolog. COVER itself is implemented in Prolog and C.

Redundancy, conflict, subsumption, unsatisfiable conditions, and dead-end rules are checked by a direct symbolic comparison of rules, which is implemented quite efficiently in Prolog. Cyclic inference chains are detected by constructing a dependency graph at the same time as performing the previous checks. Nodes in this graph are rules, arcs link rules which reference one another: a rule-node is linked to all rule-nodes whose condition parts match the conclusion of the rule. For example, the node for rule *a=a1 if c=c1* would be linked to the node for rule *g=g1 if a=a1 and b=b1*, since the test *a=a1* matches the conclusion *a=a1*. A cyclic graph detection algorithm (also implemented in Prolog) traverses this structure to detect all cyclic inference chains and report them.

Completeness checking utilises a heuristic-assisted development of the earlier naïve algorithm to generate and test possible null paths. It is geared to exploit the

---

[1] Remember that Suwa's approach was designed to take advantage of the small datasets and rulesets resulting from the structuring of the knowledge base using contexts. In effect the knowledge base author is explicitly constraining the search space, but this cannot be done easily for all systems.

sparse nature of wide domains, but is also acceptably efficient on narrow domains, as our case studies will show. Two heuristics are employed:

Heuristic 1: Although $|D_G|$ is large for a wide domain, many combinations of data items are irrelevant. For example, in the DISPLAN geriatric discharge planning system used for our first case study the fact *has hearing aid* would be relevant to considering the assessment of the patient's *hearing*, but *has hearing aid* would not be relevant to the assessment of *incontinence* .

We can reduce the search space significantly by only considering the relevant data combinations, provided the system can recognise 'relevant' combinations of data. This can be indicated by checking if data items appear together in the same successful search tree for a goal. That is, if two items appear together in a rule, or if one item can be used to conclude the value of an item in the same rule as the second item. Remember that only items that can be asked of the user are considered. For example, in the rules

$$g=g1 \text{ if } a=a1 \text{ and } b=b1, g=g2 \text{ if } c=c1, b=b1 \text{ if } d=d1$$

a is relevant to b and d, but not to c, since a and c are in different search trees for g.

Heuristic 2: We can further reduce the paths generated by:
- generating smallest paths first; and
- considering most powerful discriminants first within a path. Most powerful discriminants are data items which appear in most rules. This is evaluated from a count of rules in which the data item appears in the condition part.

Then, if a path is null we ignore all paths which are supersets of it. This heuristic works because, in the first case we can eliminate a large number of paths which merely add additional irrelevant items to an already-null path, and in the second case we impose an ordering on the items in the path, which allows for much faster comparison and elimination of covered paths.

A highly-desirable side-effect of the second heuristic is that we always get an ordered listing of the minimal missing rules required to complete the ruleset, with the most important omissions (with most powerful discriminants) presented first. An example of the use of these heuristics appears below, using the previous ruleset and dataset:

Dataset $D_G = \{ a, b, c \}$
Values $V_g = \{ g1, g2 \}, V_a = \{ a1, a2 \}, V_b = \{ b1, b2 \}, V_c = \{ c1, c2 \}$
Ruleset $R_G = \{$
    $g = g1$ if $a = a1$ and $b = b2$,
    $g = g2$ if $a = a2$ and $b = b1$,
    $g = g1$ if $b = b1$ and $c = c1$
$\}$

The following combinations of data items are relevant: $\{a, b\}, \{b, c\}$.
The order of discriminants is: b, a, c [1].

The following paths (only) are generated, in this order:
$\{ \langle b, b1 \rangle \}, \{ \langle b, b2 \rangle \}, \{ \langle a, a1 \rangle \}, \{ \langle a, a2 \rangle \}, \{ \langle c, c1 \rangle \}, \{ \langle c, c2 \rangle \},$
$\{ \langle b, b1 \rangle, \langle a, a1 \rangle \}, \{ \langle b, b2 \rangle, \langle a, a1 \rangle \}, \{ \langle b, b1 \rangle, \langle a, a2 \rangle \},$
$\{ \langle b, b2 \rangle, \langle a, a2 \rangle \}, \{ \langle b, b1 \rangle, \langle c, c1 \rangle \}, \{ \langle b, b2 \rangle, \langle c, c1 \rangle \}$

Of these, the following paths are null:
$\{ \langle b, b1 \rangle, \langle a, a1 \rangle \}, \{ \langle b, b2 \rangle, \langle a, a2 \rangle \}, \{ \langle c, c2 \rangle \}$

---

[1] Since b appears in 3 rules, a in 2, and c in just one.

Note that Heuristic 2 causes smallest paths to be considered first, so single-item paths are considered before pairs. Furthermore, variations on more powerful discriminants are considered before weaker ones, so that item b is considered before a, for example. Note also that the paths { $\langle b, b1 \rangle, \langle c, c2 \rangle$ }, { $\langle b, b2 \rangle, \langle c, c2 \rangle$ } were not generated because { $\langle c, c2 \rangle$ } had already been established as null at that stage.

In this simple example 12 paths were generated, instead of the full 26. As demonstrated by the later case studies, savings are considerably higher in larger domains.

Once the missing rules have been produced the developer can obtain the expert's opinion on whether they should be included as valid rules in the knowledge base, in which case a conclusion needs to be supplied, or whether they should be marked as "unreasonable", as in the case of *sex=male and pregnant=yes*. These cases could be employed by the system to validate input data (in this respect the verification system acts as a constraint generator), and would also eliminate paths containing the "unreasonable" situation in future completeness checks.

7. Case Study One: The DISPLAN System (Wide Domain)

The DISPLAN system is designed to assist a team of health care professionals in planning successful discharges of elderly patients, from hospital to the community. The central task of discharge planning is to identify the needs of the patient and provide a set of support facilities to cover them. Support can include equipment, social and community services, medical services, and the patient's extended family. The discharge planning domain is wide because it is multidisciplinary, overlapping parts of medical, paramedical, nursing, mental, geriatric and social domains (Preece 1989).

An operational version of DISPLAN was implemented using the Crystal expert system shell, and runs on an IBM PC at a local geriatric hospital. It was originally tested using purely empirical means. We wanted to perform a logical verification of the knowledge base for the reasons described earlier: there were potentially so many possible situations that we could hardly hope to cover them all. Unfortunately, the Crystal tool, although ostensibly rule-based, did not offer an ideal structure for verification. This was mainly because there is no means of entirely separating declarative from procedural knowledge in the Crystal knowledge representation (this is a weakness of most commercial UK products). The procedural knowledge had no logical meaning for our verification.

Therefore, the first step was to rewrite the DISPLAN system in a generic Prolog expert system shell to enable proper separation of the different types of knowledge. The COVER system was then run on the revised knowledge base. The following table summarises the results of running COVER on a subset of DISPLAN:

COVER applied to DISPLAN (wide domain):

Number of rules:	144
Size of dataset:	49
Maximum relevant items in a path:	5
Mean relevant items in a path:	3
Mean values per item:	3
Total possible paths in universe:	3×10^{29}
Paths actually generated by COVER:	11,000
Null paths discovered:	59
Time taken (approx):	30 sec.

The main points to observe here are the large dataset, compared to the small number of relevant items in each path. This accounts for the very good performance in this domain. The majority of the nulls discovered were actually single "missing values", most of which were genuine "do nothing" cases. For example, *mobility = manages unaided*. Some were invalid situations, such as *hearing = deaf* and *has hearing aid = yes* (the system need never consider the patient having a hearing aid if they are deaf). The remainder were genuine "missing" cases, for example *mobility = needs physical assistance* and *carer assist mobility = no* (no support can be provided to assist the patient's general mobility if their carer refuses to do it).

Most important was the fact that these genuine missing cases had not been detected in empirical tests on over 100 actual patient cases from the hospital. The other checks performed by COVER uncovered several subtle problems, including some typographic errors and a number of potentially dangerous cycles. For example, a conclusion *general mobility=bedfats* (instead of "bedfast") caused the rule in question to be marked as a dead-end, since this value was (unsurprisingly) not matched by any rule condition. An example cyclic problem concerned rules of the form:

set1 includes [...] if set2 includes [...],
set2 includes [...] if set1 includes [...].

The system, seeking to evaluate set1, would require set2 to be evaluated. Exploring set2 as a subgoal requires set1, and the system enters a loop.

Work on DISPLAN has convincingly demonstrated the effectiveness of the COVER program on a practical application in a wide domain. Future work planned involves the automatic translation of the verified system to Crystal for incorporation in the hospital system.

8. Case Study Two: The TAPES System (Narrow Domain)

The TAPES system is an expert system to select suitable adhesive tapes for a variety of jobs. It was originally implemented as an experimental trial of a rule-induction system, and permitted selection between 30 different tapes, based on factors like choice of substrates (the materials to be stuck together), contact area, exposure to liquid, proximity to food, etc. This system was used for our purposes purely as an experimental test of COVER. It was chosen for a number of reasons:
- It was an example of a narrow domain: most of the different factors were relevant to each other. We therefore expected COVER to perform less well since its heuristics would not be able to reduce the search space so effectively.
- It was of a realistic size for a set of rules concluding a single goal (a tape), and it was about the same size as our DISPLAN subset, in terms of rules.
- It had been generated using an induction algorithm, which had already produced a set of missing rules for it (as "unknown" cases). We therefore had a decent-sized set of test data to compare COVER's results to.

The results of this verification appear below:

COVER applied to TAPES (narrow domain):

Number of rules:	162
Size of dataset:	16
Maximum relevant items in a path:	7
Mean relevant items in a path:	4
Mean values per item:	6
Total possible paths in universe:	3×10^{12}
Paths actually generated by COVER:	168,000
Null paths discovered:	26
Time taken (approx):	20 min.

Note that the smaller dataset results in a smaller universe of paths, but the higher number of relevant groupings means that COVER needs to do more work to check the search space: fifteen times as many paths needed to be generated than for DISPLAN. Even though, for an application that was deliberately chosen as a "hard" task for COVER the resulting time taken is not unacceptable, since the users need not be present while the system runs. This case study demonstrates that COVER is applicable to non-wide domains.

Incidentally, the missing rules indicated by COVER turned out to be more minimal that those from the induction program: 26 as opposed to 58, although both sets of rules were exactly equivalent. The reason for this was that certain missing rules from the induction system had unnecessary additional constraints. For example, there were rules of the form: *a=a1 and b=b1 and c=c1, a=a1 and b=b1 and c=c2*, which could be replaced by the single rule: *a=a1 and b=b1* (assuming c can only take the values c1 and c2).

9. Extensions to COVER for Practical Use

The rule-based representation described earlier in this paper is inadequate for real applications. It can only handle rule condition parts as conjunctions on unnegated conditions, and insists on all data items being single-valued. The COVER algorithm as described also cannot handle numeric or continuous data values, and can only work with discrete, categorical data items. All of these restrictions had to be lifted in order to apply COVER to DISPLAN and TAPES, and these extensions to COVER were implemented as follows:

Disjunctions in rule conditions: Disjunctions of conjunctions were handled by splitting each conjunction off as a separate rule with the same conclusion. Nested disjunctions were handled by introducing a new subgoal and making this the conclusion of the set of rules formed by splitting the nested disjunction. For example, the rule
  g=g1 if a=a1 and b=b1 or a=a2 and (d=d1 or e=e1 and f=f1) or c=c1
would be replaced by the pre-processor with the set of rules:
  g=g1 if a=a1 and b=b1, g=g1 if a=a2 and x=x1, g=g1 if c=c1,
  x=x1 if d=d1, x=x1 if e=e1 and f=f1

Negated rule conditions: A negated askable item was simply represented as a negated tuple, that is $\langle a, \neg a1 \rangle$. A negated subgoal was handled by using DeMorgan's theorem to negate the set of instantiations proving the subgoal. For example, the rules
  g=g1 if not a=a1, a=a1 if b=b1 and c=c1
essentially are converted to (assuming *b* and *c* are askable):
  g=g1 if not b=b1 or not c=c1
This can then be dealt with as for negated askable items and disjunctions within rules, described above.

Numeric items: These were handled by COVER in the same manner as would an induction algorithm such as ID3 (Quinlan 1987). The numeric values tested by the rules were divided into disjoint subranges, and each treated as a discrete value of a categoric item. This was done manually for the examples above, but could easily be performed automatically by COVER.

Set (multi-valued) items: We employed the simplest approach of treating each "set includes value" expression as a separate true/false fact, with one such fact for each value that could be included in the set. For very large sets this would need to be handled more efficiently, using a more compact representation.

10. The Rôle of COVER in Knowledge Acquisition

An integrated shell and verification system provides a powerful vehicle for expert system building since empirical validation and logical verification can both be performed on the same "workbench". It must always be remembered that the automated approach is limited: "completeness", in the sense that we have used the term here, is really "coverage". In the case of the DISPLAN application, we can use COVER to tell us the circumstances in which the patient fails to be offered support, but we cannot tell if all possible support is offered in rule conclusions (or even if the concluded support is correct). In TAPES, COVER will spot situations in which no tape will be offered, but it is powerless to check whether, for example, all situations in which a particular tape would be offered are represented in the rules for concluding that tape. The verification system simply does not have this knowledge – but the human expert does. This is why the verification process is cooperative and a part of knowledge acquisition.

Use of COVER on practical (operational) applications has raised a number of ergonomic questions which have not yet been fully addressed in this work. The presentation of missing rules and other potential problems is rather rudimentary, and it is currently up to the knowledge engineer to add them manually to the system, although this could easily be done automatically by COVER (if the user wished). In addition, the user interface, written in Prolog, is somewhat crude and should be much friendlier.

In general conclusion, COVER needs to be more tightly-coupled to the Prolog shell system, and able to directly operate upon and modify the knowledge base, under the user's guidance. Work is underway to perform this restructuring. The current situation is illustrated in Figure 2(a), whereas the desired improved system is shown in Figure 2(b).

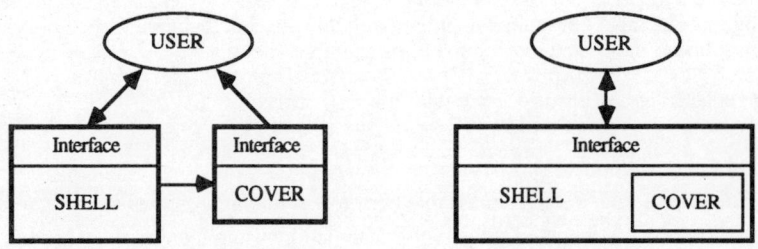

Figure 2(a): Current System   *2(b): Improved System*

11. Automated Verification and Expert System Shells

The most serious limitation in applying automated verification and validation techniques to systems built using current commercial expert system shells was highlighted by the work on DISPLAN: Such shells tend to allow developers considerable "extra-logical" facilities in system construction, permitting free and undisciplined mixing of declarative and procedural knowledge in applications. Common types of procedural knowledge include control knowledge, arithmetic, and user interface screen display information. Declarative and procedural knowledge can usually be mixed in the same rule.

Such systems are not verifiable in a logical sense; the techniques described in this paper cannot be applied to them unless a major knowledge base restructuring is performed to separate the different kinds of knowledge. For example, control knowledge properly belongs in meta-rules, which should be clearly identified as such by the system designer. Similarly, user interface display knowledge should be separated into appropriate constructs (this is done in some systems by the provision of "screen" structures). Control meta-rules, if based upon logical formalisms (non-determinism, for example), can be verified separately from the object-level declarative knowledge. Thus, gaps in the control structure for a system can be identified. These approaches were employed in re-writing the DISPLAN Crystal knowledge base into a generic rule-based representation.

We are investigating the question of to what extent the verification system can automatically partition the different kinds of knowledge in the knowledge bases of commercial shells. Certainly, the problem would be simplified greatly if expert system vendors recognised the importance of verification issues. We believe that tools must be designed with these issues in mind if we are to benefit fully from expert system technology.

References

Basden, A. (1983). *On the application of expert systems*. International Journal of Man-machine Studies, 19, no.5, 461–77.
Bundy, A. (1983). *How to improve the reliability of expert systems*. In Research & Development in Expert Systems IV, ed. D.S.Moralee, pp.3-17. Cambridge: Cambridge University Press.
Davis, R. (1979). *Interactive transfer of expertise: the acquisition of new inference rules.* Artificial Intelligence, 12, 121–57.
Mars, N.J.I. & Miller P.L. (1987). *Knowledge acquisition and verification tools for medical expert systems*. Medical Decision Making, 7, no.1, 6–11.
Nguyen, T.A., Perkins, W.A., Laffrey, T.J. & Pecora, D. (1985). *Checking an expert knowledge base for consistency and completeness*. In Proc. 9th Int. Joint Conference on Artificial Intelligence, pp.375–8.
Nguyen, T.A. (1987). *Verifying consistency of production systems.* In Proc. 3rd IEEE Conference on Aritificial Intelligence Applications, Orlando, Florida, pp.4–8.
Politakis, P.G., & Weiss, S.M. (1983). *Using empirical analysis to refine expert system knowledge bases* Artificial Intelligence, 22, no.1, 23–48.
Preece, A.D. (1989) *DISPLAN: designing a usable medical expert system.* In Expert Systems: Human Issues, ed. D.Berry & A.Hart. London: Kogan-Page.
Puuronen, S. (1987). *A tabular rule-checking method.* In Proc. Expert Systems and their Applications, Avignon, France, pp.257-68.
Quinlan, J.R. (1987). *Inductive knowledge acquisition: a case study.* In Applications of Expert Systems, ed. J.R.Quinlan, pp.157-73. Cambridge, Mass.: Addison-Wesley.
Spiegelhalter, D.J. (1983). *Evaluation of clinical decision aids, with an application to a system for dyspepsia*. Statistics in Medicine, 2, 207–19.
Suwa, W., Scott, A.C. and Shortliffe, E.H. (1982). *An approach to verifying completeness and consistency in a rule-based expert system*. AI Magazine, Fall 1982, 16–21.
Wyatt, J.C. (1987). *The evaluation of medical decision aids; a discussion of the methodology used in the ACORN project*. Lecture Notes in Medical Infomatics, 33, 15–24.

THE NORMALIZED MODEL AND EXPERT SYSTEMS MAINTENANCE

John Debenham

Key Centre for Advanced Computing Sciences
University of Technology, Sydney
Broadway, NSW 2007
Australia

Abstract

An approach to maintaining expert systems, in particular, expert systems within an intelligent database environment, is described. This approach involves the "normalization" of the knowledge in the expert system, and the use of the structure of a device called the "normalized model" to support the maintenance process. In this way, each "atomic" change to the application is effected by pursuing a single linked chain of modifications in the normalized model. The algorithm which drives the maintenance procedure is quoted in full.

1. Introduction

We discuss the maintenance of *expert, knowledge-based systems,* by which we mean expert systems which have been designed so that they could be implemented naturally within an "intelligent database environment". An *intelligent database environment* consists of a relational database together with some knowledge processing module or expert systems shell. Our concern is with the construction of *maintainable* expert systems in this environment; our approach employs a device called the "normalized model". The use of this model has the attractive feature that each "atomic" change in the application can be represented by a single linked chain of modifications to the normalized model.

The kernel of the representation of an expert systems application contains a representation of the *data* (i.e. the individual "data items"), the *information* (i.e. relations constructed from data items) and the *knowledge* (i.e. the rules of the expert system). Intuitively, if an expert system is to be maintainable then it is highly desirable that these representations of data items, information items and knowledge items should each be "independent", (or, should not "overlap"). (We say that two items of data, information or knowledge are not *independent* if it is not possible to modify one without modifying the other if consistency is to be preserved.) The well known normal forms for information (Kent, 1983) ensure that represented information items are independent in this sense. We have proposed (Debenham, 1989) extensive new normal forms for data and for knowledge which should ensure that represented data and knowledge is also independent in this sense.

As far as maintenance is concerned, an ideal expert systems implementation would be one which had the property that if one real "thing" were to change in the application then only one represented "thing" would have to be changed in the implementation. For technical reasons this ideal is not strictly achievable, even if the data, information and knowledge are all normalized in the sense indicated above. However, we propose the use of a *normalized model* as a "management structure" which "sits between" the analyst and the implementation of the expert system. This normalized model has the attractive property that, as long as the data, information and knowledge are all normal, if one real thing changes in the application then one *linked chain* of modifications will have to be effected in the normalized model. This linked chain of modifications to the normalized model will then lead in turn to a complete specification of the precise modifications which should be performed to the actual implementation of the expert system. The technique described here is presently being built into a prototype "Knowledge Analyst's Assistant" in the laboratories of the Commonwealth Scientific and Industrial Research Organization at North Ryde in Sydney, Australia. This prototype will be available for experimentation early in 1990.

Our experiments with design techniques for expert, knowledge-based systems were first reported in (Debenham and McGrath, 1982). Since that time we have come to realize the significance in building Expert Systems which are designed for maintenance (Debenham, 1985). Difficulties with the maintenance of early expert, knowledge-based systems are now well understood (Steels, 1987). However little has been done to promote design techniques which prevent these difficulties from occurring (Walker, et al, 1989). We will discuss here the use of the normalized model as an integral part of the design and maintenance process for expert, knowledge-based systems. The normalized model also receives extensive coverage in the recent text (Debenham, 1989).

2. Foundation for Modelling

As a general preamble to our discussion we first clarify precisely what is meant by the "data", "information" and "knowledge" in an expert systems application. A clear understanding of these three notions, and of the relationships between these three notions, will provide the rationale for the structure of the normalized model.

The fundamental, indivisible real objects in an application are called the *data* in that application. Individual, real data objects are identified by unique, identifying *labels*.

An important structural feature of many relations is the so called "functional dependency" *from* the key domains *to* the non-key domains. For example, in the following relation the number of an item might be sufficient to determine the buying price of that item; i.e.

item/buy-price(item-number, $'s)

Thus a relation can represent a functional dependency between items of data; the details of such a functional dependency are actually represented by associating *tuples* with the relation. Note that we cannot give a succinct definition of the above functional dependency; in fact the only way that we are likely to be able to specify the function is by listing all tuples, concerning the numbers of items and their respective buying prices, which satisfy it.

Consider the simple rule "To convert from degrees Fahrenheit to degrees Celsius, subtract 32 and divide by 1.8.". This rule is also in functional form, in fact it is a function *from* degrees Fahrenheit *to* degrees Celsius. This function is also between two items of data which are "degrees Fahrenheit" and "degrees Celsius". However it differs from the relation just discussed in one important way; this time, we can actually define the function f : (deg F) → (deg C) by:

$$f(x) = (x - 32) \div 1.8$$

Both of the examples just considered concern functions between items of data. The first cannot be defined succinctly as a definition that will "work for all values"; it is thus called an *implicit functional association*. The second can be defined succinctly and "for all values"; it is thus called an *explicit functional association*. Note that we have used the word "association" rather than "dependency" to acknowledge that the context of our discussion is more general than functional dependencies in relations.

Consider the simple rule, "the selling price of an item is the buying price increased by the mark-up rate for that item" which might be represented in Horn clause logic as (Hogger, 1984):

$$\text{item/sell-price:\$}(x , y) \leftarrow \text{item/buy-price:\$}(x, z),$$
$$\text{item/mark-up-rate}(x, w), \quad y = w \times z \qquad [Z]$$

This rule is also in functional form. In fact it represents a function *from* the relations "item/buy-price" and "item/mark-up-rate" *to* the relation "item/sell-price". The nature of this function is quite explicit; it is succinct as it enables a large amount of information about the relation "item/sell-price" to be deduced. Thus it is also an explicit functional association. (Note: we have chosen Horn clause logic to illustrate this discussion solely because it is a comparatively well known formalism; we are not promoting Horn clause logic as a general purpose, knowledge processing formalism.) If clause [Z] in fact enabled *all* the tuples which satisfy "item/sell-price" to be deduced it would be called a "clause group"; a *clause group* is a collection of one or more clauses, all with the same head predicate, which enables all of the information in the head predicate to be deduced from the information in the body predicates. The clause group [Z] is denoted by:

$$\text{item/sell-price} \Leftarrow \text{item/buy-price, item/mark-up-rate}$$

We are now in a position to define what we mean by the "data", "information" and "knowledge" in an expert systems application:
- the *data* is the fundamental, indivisible real objects in that application;
- the *information* is the implicit functional associations between data in that application. See (Stonier, 1987) for an alternative view;
- the *knowledge* is the explicit functional associations between items of information and/or data in that application.

Note that in this categorization there is no reference to implicit functional associations between items of information. It may be shown that this is not in fact an omission.

On many occasions the clauses in a group need to make use of "computational predicates". For example, a group may need to refer to the "sort" predicate which sorts a list into ascending order. In this case, "sort" would not be considered to be a body predicate of the group; the "sort" predicate would be regarded as an *internal predicate* of purely computational significance. In other words, the head and body predicates of a (clause) group are those predicates which are relations, i.e. those predicates which could in principle be stored as a table.

From the above discussion we note the relationship between the data, information and knowledge; we see that, in a very real sense, the data forms the vocabulary in terms of which the information is expressed, and the data and the information together form the vocabulary in terms of which the knowledge is expressed. Thus data, information and knowledge form a hierarchy as shown in Figure 1.

It should be clear that, in practice, a real functional association can occur which is genuinely part explicit and part implicit. In this case the association should be decomposed into its explicit and implicit components. In (Debenham, 1989a) it is shown that sub-typing provides a powerful tool for achieving this decomposition.

The hierarchy shown in Figure 1 determines our basic principle for modelling an expert systems application. The basic principle is:
- all fundamental, indivisible objects are represented in the *data model;*
- all implicit associations between items of data are represented in the *information model;* and
- all explicit associations between items of information and/or data are represented in the *knowledge model.*

It is important to appreciate that this principle for modelling does *not* say, for example, that "anything that *can* be represented in a relation is therefore information".

We are now in a position to introduce our conceptual architecture for implementing an expert system. We assume that there is some repository for the populations, labels and constraints on populations and labels; such a repository is called a *data base* (with all due apologies for our corruption of this otherwise well known term!). We assume that there is some repository for the relations, tuples and constraints on relations and tuples; such a repository is called an *information base.* We assume that there is some repository for the groups, clauses and constraints on the groups and clauses; such a repository is called a *knowledge base.* In practice, the data base, information base and knowledge base facilities may all be provided by an expert systems shell.

things	associate	represented by	grouped in	modelled in	implemented in
data	-	labels	populations	data model	data base
information	data	tuples	relations	information model	information base
knowledge	information/data	clauses	clause groups	knowledge model	knowledge base

Figure 1 The data, information and knowledge hierarchy

We now describe the *roles* that populations, relations and groups play in an implemented expert system. The relations and populations which are naturally associated with updates, that is, those relations and populations into which raw (information) updates may be directly entered, are called *update relations* and *update populations.* Likewise, the relations which are naturally associated with queries, that is, those relations from which information is extracted to satisfy queries, are called *query relations* and *query populations.* Thus, from this perspective, the functional role of the knowledge in an expert system is to enable the query relations and populations to be deduced from the update relations and populations. To achieve this, some of the relations and populations will be stored and some will be deduced. Stored relations and populations are called *real relations* and *real populations;* deduced relations and populations are called *virtual relations* and *virtual populations.* It is important to appreciate that if the operational constraints of the system are to be satisfied, the real relations and populations will not necessarily be the same as the update relations and update populations (Debenham, 1989b). A group is an *update group* if it is used to deduced the values of the real relations or real populations from the update relations and update populations. A group is called a *query group* if it is used to deduce the values of the query relations or query populations from the real relations and real populations. In addition, those relations and populations which are heads of update groups and are not real relations or real populations are called *virtual update relations* and *virtual update populations.* Those relations and populations which are the heads of query groups and are not query relations or query populations are called *virtual query relations* and *virtual query populations*.

3. The Normalized Model

A central feature of our approach to constructing *maintainable* expert systems is the construction of the "application model" and the three "system models". The *application model* is constructed first and contains a representation of the application in quasi-natural language; each statement in the application model is "atomic" in the sense that it corresponds to just one entry in one of the three system models. Each statement of the application model has one of three forms:
- asserts the existence of a population, relation or group;
- attaches a label, tuple, clause or constraint to an existing population, relation or group, or
- attaches an integrity constraint either to an existing population, relation or group, or to their constituent labels, tuples or clauses.

The three *system models* are formal models; they are the "data model", the "information model" and the "knowledge model". The three system models are constructed during (conventional) data analysis, (conventional) information analysis and our knowledge analysis (Debenham 1989). (See Addis 1985 and Twine 1989 for an alternative view.) The *data model* contains details of each population, the labels associated with each population, and the constraints on each population and its associated labels. The *information model* contains details of each relation, the tuples associated with each relation, and the constraints on each relation and its associated tuples. The *knowledge model* contains details of each group, the clauses associated with each group, and the constraints on each group and its associated clauses. The three systems models also contain details of the *role* which each item of data, information and knowledge plays, where the roles are as defined in §2.

In short, the application model provides the documentation for the system, and the three system models together provide a complete formal specification for the system. Once they have been normalized in the sense described in (Debenham, 1989), these four models taken together are referred to as the *normalized model*. See Figure 2 for a representation of the construction sequence for an expert system.

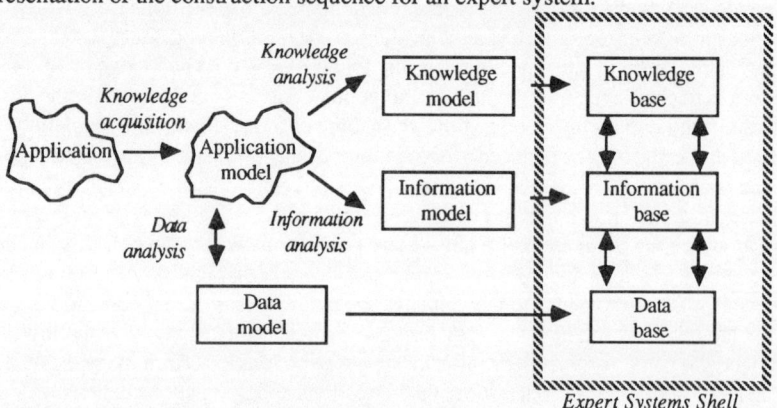

Figure 2 The construction sequence for an expert system

It is important to note that the normalized model, as we have described it, does not necessarily provide a framework for representing every feature of an application. For example, procedural meta-knowledge, which specifies *how* the rules of the expert system should be employed will not be represented in any of the three system models. However, it is our experience that in practice the three system models are capable of representing the greater part of an expert systems application.

In §4 we will describe how the normalized model actually functions in supporting the execution of maintenance operations on an expert system. In that description we will refer to four different kinds of "link" in the normalized model. These four kinds of links are called links of type 1, type 2, type 3 and type 4. They are:
(1) each statement in the application model is linked to a unique corresponding entry in one of the three system models;
(2) each population in the data model is linked to all relations in the information model in which that population is a domain; and each population is linked to all groups in the knowledge model in which that population occurs. Each relation is linked to all groups in the knowledge model in which a relation occurs;
(3) each entry in the three system models is linked to the corresponding statements which implement that entry. If the expert system is implemented in an expert systems shell then these corresponding statements will all be statements expressed in that shell, alternatively, if the expert system is implemented within an intelligent database environment then these corresponding statements will either be represented within the relational database or in the knowledge processing module.
(4) each update or query group is linked to those groups whose head predicates are the body predicates of that update or query group.

The first three types of link are illustrated in Figure 3.

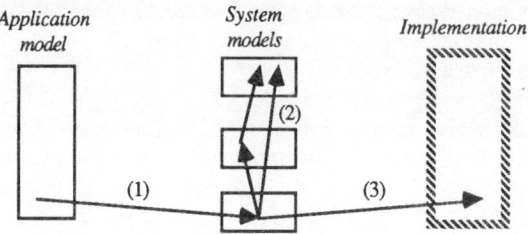

Figure 3 Showing possible link types (1), (2) and (3)

The normalized model should be seen as an integrated and interrelated structure which provides the interface between the domain expert and the programmer as depicted in Figure 4. The normalized model both provides the domain expert with a readable specification of the expert system, and provides the programming staff with a formal specification of the expert system. Thus the normalized model provides the domain expert with a representation of the system in which statements requiring modification can easily be identified. Furthermore, the normalized model, once it has been modified, provides the programmer with a precise specification of the modifications that should be made to the implementation. Thus, the derivation and preservation of this model should be seen as the most vital function of the whole design and maintenance process. It is not possible to over emphasize the importance of ensuring that the normalized model is correct, and that it is, in fact, normal.

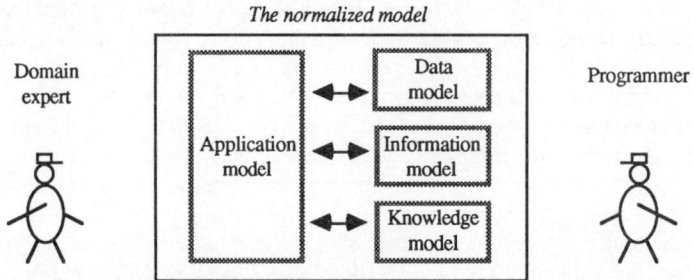

Figure 4 Interface between domain expert and programmer

4. Maintenance and the Normalized Model

We concern ourselves here with "atomic" changes to the application. An *atomic change* is a change in the application which can be represented as either an addition, deletion or modification of a population, relation or group, or an addition, deletion or modification of a label, tuple, clause or constraint attached to an existing population, relation or group. It is important to note that atomic changes are not necessarily trivial changes. For example, suppose that we are advised that "the whole basis for calculating sales tax has been changed"; then if there was a population called "sales-tax" this would be an atomic change in which the starting point for the linked chain of modifications would be a modification to the meaning of the population "sales-tax".

We have seen that the normalized model contains type (1), type (2) and type (4) links. We now describe how, in response to a single atomic change in the application, these links support the maintenance of the expert system. We will see that these links are used to generate a single linked chain of modifications to the normalized model in response to a single atomic change. (Once again, we note that this discussion is *not* complete as it refers to atomic changes only.)

All maintenance operations are executed in five phases. These phases are:
- a statement in the application model is identified as the beginning of the linked chain of modifications; (Note that this may include the addition of a new statement to the application model.)
- the type (1), type (2) and type (4) links are employed to identify all the statements in the application model which are also candidates for modification. This second phase is recursive in that if statements which have been identified as candidates for modification are confirmed by the analyst as actually requiring modification then they will in turn lead to even more candidates for modification and so on;
- the analyst actually modifies all of the statements in the application model which need to be altered;
- the type (1) links are employed to identify all aspects of the three systems models which need to be altered, and
- the modifications to the three systems models are prepared and presented to programming staff together with the type (3) links as a complete specification of the maintenance operation to be performed on the implemented expert system.

The most complex phase is the second phase in which those statements in the application model which have to be modified are identified. This is achieved by navigating the three system models using the type (2) and type (4) links to identify all entries in the system models which have to be altered. Each entry in the three system models that has to be altered will be associated with a unique set of statements in the application model. It is important to note that if this method is implemented then the user need not be aware of the calculations taking place in the three system models, and only need view the corresponding statements in the application model. In other words, the user will be presented with an "intelligent traversal" of the application model.

The type (2) links will group the entries in the three system models into connected components. In practice, we might expect to find the entries in the three system models in just one connected component. A naive strategy for maintenance is to identify an entry that requires modification and then to check every entry connected to that entry by a chain of type (2) links. Such a strategy would be exhaustive but very costly, and, as we have noted, could easily lead to the checking of every statement in the application model. One could argue that this exhaustive process is necessary to ensure that the modification has been fully executed. However we take the view that the design technique itself should attempt to restrict the number of candidate statements to be checked for correctness, especially when the statements originate from maintenance operations which are "expected" to occur. We propose that an effective restriction of the number of candidate statements for modification may be achieved:

- first, by ensuring that the data, information and knowledge models are all normal, and
- second, by employing the notion of a "fixed population", which is described below, the number of type (2) links that have to be investigated during the complex second phase are reduced.

A population occurring in a clause, either directly as a population or as a domain of a relation in that clause, is called a *fixed population in that clause* if, in the expression of the clause, labels of that population occur. If a population is not fixed in a clause it is called *free* in that clause. For example, in the clause:

spare-part/selling-price(x, y) ← spare-part/buying-price(x, z),
spare-part/supplier(x, 'ABC & Co'),
$y = z \times 1.25$

which could be interpreted as "the mark-up rate for spare parts supplied by ABC & Co is 25%", the population "supplier" is fixed and the other populations are free. A population is called *fixed in a group* if it is fixed in any clause in that group. Thus, nominating a population as free in a group is really a constraint on that group which prevents labels from appearing attached to that population in the expression of the clauses in that group. As we will see, the presence of fixed populations in a group complicates the maintenance problem. However this does not imply that labels cannot be referred to by a clause. For example, if it is required to refer to a label representing "today's date" this can be achieved by an implicit occurrence of the label using the "is-a" or "is-the" predicates as follows:

is-the[today's-date](x)

which would set x to the label representing "today's date"; this label would actually be attached to the population "today's date" which would be stored in the data base.

We now describe our strategy for limiting the number of type (2) links used in the second phase. This strategy is activated by the identification, via a type (1) link, of an entry in one of the three system models as requiring modification. In the statement of the algorithm that follows, *all* modifications are made *subject to* the requirement that they do not violate any constraint. In what follows each modification will lead to the identification of a stack of entries in the three system models as "candidates for modification". These candidate entries are checked in turn to see if they do in fact require modification; this is achieved by displaying, for scrutiny, the corresponding statement, or statements, from the application model. Those candidate entries which are thus marked for modification will lead to even more candidates and so on. Thus each modification takes the form of a linked chain. Recall that if this algorithm is implemented then the user need only view the statements in the application model; in other words, the calculations in the three system models as described below, and which guide the process, can be hidden.

1. (Rationale: the introduction of new populations, relations and groups must be compatible with the structure of the system.)
- *if* a modification is to introduce a new population *then* introduce that population together with any constraints on that population.
- *if* a modification is to introduce a new relation *then* introduce that relation together with any constraints which should include the constraint that while the relation exists its domains should exist as populations.
- *if* a modification is to introduce a new group *then* introduce that group together with any constraints on that group which should include both the fixed population constraint, and the constraint that while the group exists the relations and populations in terms of which the group is expressed should exist.
(Note: each group will have attached to it a *fixed population constraint* which will specify the only populations from which labels may be used in the expression of the group and will insist that any labels occurring in the clauses in the group do in fact belong to one of those specified populations in the data model.)

2. (Rationale: the meaning of populations and relations must be consistent within the normalized model.)
- *if* a population is identified as requiring modification and that modification is to delete that population or modify the meaning of that population *then*
  - delete or modify that population *and*
  - use single type (2) links only to identify, as candidates for deletion or modification, all groups and relations containing that population.
- *if* a relation is identified as requiring modification and that modification is to delete that relation or modify the meaning of that relation *then*
  - delete or modify that relation *and*
  - use single type (2) links only to identify, as candidates for deletion or modification, all groups containing that relation.
- *if* a group is identified as requiring modification and that modification involves the modification of the meaning of the populations and relations in terms of which the group is expressed *then:*
  - that group ceases (temporarily) to be a candidate for modification, *and*
  - use single type (2) links only to identify, as candidates for modification, all populations and relations in that group whose meaning is to be modified.

3. (Rationale: the modification of groups must not interfere with the deductive flow of the system.)
- *if* a group is identified as requiring modification and that modification is either the deletion of the group or is a modification which does not involve the modification of the meaning of the populations and relations in terms of which the group is expressed *then:*
  - modify (or delete) that group and its constraints, *and*

- re-identify the query and update groups and re-compute which relations and populations are to be stored *unless* the modification was to replace the original group with a new group which has exactly the same head and body predicates as the original group.

  (Note: a modification to a group is a change to the structure of the whole group; this should be seen in contrast to a simple modification to one of the clauses in the group with the head and body predicates of the group left unchanged.)

4. (Rationale: the values associated with the update populations and relations must, using the knowledge model, imply the values in any population or relation that can be derived from the update populations and relations.)

- *if* a relation (or population) is identified as requiring modification and that modification is to add, delete or modify a tuple (or label) in that relation (or population) *then:*
  - add, delete or modify that tuple (or label) in that relation (or population), *and*
  - *if* the modification introduces a new label in a population *then* use the type (2) links to identify, as candidates for modification, all relations in which that population is the key and all groups in which that population is fixed, *and*
  - *if* the modification is to an input relation (or input population) *then* use the type (4) links to re-compute any real relation (or population) whose tuples (or labels) may be effected by the changes to that input relation (or input population), *and*
  - *if* the modification is to a derived, non-input relation (or derived, non-input population) *then* use the type (4) links to identify, as candidates for modification, all the groups, update relations and update populations involved in the derivation of that tuple (or label) from the update relations and populations.

- *if* a group is identified as a candidate for a modification which is to add, delete or modify a clause in that group *and* the modification does not introduce any new head or body predicates to the group *and* the modification does not involve any modification to the meaning of the populations and relations in terms of which the group is expressed *then:*
  - add, delete or modify the clause in that group *and*
  - *if* that group is an update group *then* use the type (4) links to identify all stored populations or relations whose labels and tuples are calculated using that group from the update populations and relations, and re-compute these populations and relations.

5. (Rationale: the normalized model must remain consistent with the specified constraints.)

- *if* the modification is to add, delete or modify a constraint for a population, relation or group *and if* that modification does not cause the constraint to be violated *then* complete the modification *else* display those values which violate the constraint as candidates for modification.

  (Note: the modification of constraints will require a management strategy. For example, if a modification is made to a constraint attached to a derived relation then, how are we to decide whether the tuples of that relation should be calculated then and there to see if they satisfy the constraint, or whether the constraint should be applied to the tuples derived in the normal course of the operation of the system?)

This completes the exhaustive description of our strategy for all atomic changes. See also (Martens and Bruynooghe, 1989) for an interesting discussion on the management of constraints.

In is instructive to see how the maintenance strategy works. For example, suppose that we have two relations "item/buy-price" and "item/sell-price" and one rule linking them together:
$$\text{item/sell-price}(x, y) \leftarrow \text{item/buy-price}(x, z),$$
$$y = z \times 1.2 \qquad [X]$$
and suppose that the relation "item/buy-price" is stored and the relation "item/sell-price" is calculated on demand. Now suppose that the following modification is presented "item number 246 sells for $33.60". The analyst uses the type (1) links to identify the definition of the relation "item/sell-price" and notes that this relation should contain the tuple (246, 33.60). This relation is a non-input relation. Thus using a type (2) link we identify, as candidates for modification, the group [X] above and the input relation item/buy-price. Suppose that we are advised that the rule [X] is correct then attention passes to the relation "item/buy-price". Here we identify that the tuple (246, 28.00) should be present. This relation is an update relation, and the tuple is simply modified accordingly, and that completes the operation.

5. Conclusion

We have discussed the meaning of data, information and knowledge and seen how the relationships between those three objects are reflected in the structure of the normalized model. Then we have seen that the normalized model may be employed to manage the maintenance process. In this process, an atomic change is implemented by following a linked chain of modifications to the normalized model. In this way a diligent analyst can be sure that each change to the application has been fully represented both in the model and in the implementation of the expert system.

References

ADDIS, T.R., (1985), "Designing Knowledge-Based Systems", Kogan-Page.
DATE, C.J. (1986), "An Introduction to Database Systems" (4th edition) Addison-Wesley.
DEBENHAM, J.K. and McGRATH, G.M. (1982), "The Description in Logic of Large Commercial Data Bases: A Methodology put to the test", Proceedings of the Fifth Australian Computer Science Conference, pp. 12-21.
DEBENHAM, J.K. (1985), "Knowledge Base Design", Australian Computer Journal, Vol 17, No 1, pp 187-196.
DEBENHAM, J.K. (1989), "Knowledge Systems Design", Prentice Hall.
DEBENHAM, J.K. (1989a), "Managing Expert Systems: Four Key Issues", in Proceedings of the Fifth Australian Conference on Applications of Expert Systems, pp 143-188.
DEBENHAM, J.K. (1989b), "The Implementation of Expert, Knowledge-Based Systems", in Proceedings of the Eleventh International Joint Conference on Artificial Intelligence, Detroit, August 1989.
GAINES, B.R. (1987), "Foundations of knowledge engineering", in (M.A. Bramer, Ed.) "Research and Development in Expert Systems III", Cambridge University Press.

GRAY, P.M.D. (1989), "Expert Systems and Object-Oriented Databases: Evolving a New Software Architecture", in "Research and Development in Expert Systems V", Cambridge University Press.

HOGGER, C. (1984), "Introduction to Logic Programming", Academic Press.

KENT, W. (1983), "A Simple Guide to Five Normal Forms in Relational Database Theory", C. ACM, Vol 26, No 2, Feb 1983, pp 120-125.

MARTENS, B. and BRUYNOOGHE, M. (1989), "Integrity Constraint Checking in Deductive Databases using a Rule/Goal Graph", in (L. Kerschberg, Ed.), "Proceedings from the Second International Conference on Expert Database Systems", Benjamin Cummings.

NAPHEYS, B. and HERKIMER, D. (1988), "A Look at Loosely-Coupled Prolog/Database Systems", in Proceedings Second International Conference on Expert Database Systems, George Mason University.

SIBLEY, E.H. (1987), "An Expert Database System Architecture Based on an Active and Extensible Dictionary System", in (L. Kerschberg, Ed.), "Expert Database Systems", Benjamin Cummings.

STEELS, L. (1987), "Second Generation Expert Systems", in (M.A. Bramer, Ed.) "Research and Development in Expert Systems III", Cambridge University Press.

STONIER, T. (1987), "What is Information", in (M.A. Bramer, Ed.) "Research and Development in Expert Systems III", Cambridge University Press.

TWINE, S. (1989) "Towards a Knowledge Engineering Procedure", in "Research and Development in Expert Systems V", Cambridge University Press.

WALKER, A., KOWALSKI, R., LENAT, D., SOLOWAY, E. and STONEBRAKER, M. (1989), "Knowledge Management", in (L. Kerschberg, Ed.), "Proceedings from the Second International Conference on Expert Database Systems", Benjamin Cummings.

DEVELOPING COOPERATIVE KNOWLEDGE-BASED SYSTEMS

Lise Land and Tim Mulhall
Knowledge-Based Systems Centre
Touche Ross Management Consultants
Hill House
1 Little New Street
London EC4A 3TR

Abstract

The KADS methodology has been under development for the last five years under the ESPRIT project P1098. It is based on ideas from conventional systems development and cognitive modelling. One of its most powerful features is an expertise model that enables knowledge engineers to analyse expertise in a coherent way. More recently a *cooperation* model has been developed, which provides the framework for analysing modality or user-related issues. Its existence is a major advance in the development of cooperative knowledge based systems. These systems ensure that the users feel comfortable in using knowledge-based systems. In KADS models drive the system development process in such a way that we can regard development as a model transformation process. This paper describes this model transformation approach to developing cooperative knowledge-based systems. A case study is also presented to illustrate the power of the modality framework.

1. Introduction

The KADS methodology for developing knowledge-based systems (KBS) evolved over the past five years as part of the Esprit Project P1098[1]. It is based upon the phases of conventional systems development namely analysis, design, implementation, testing and maintenance in the given order. The research has concentrated on the first two phases i.e. analysis and design, and models or frameworks are now available for guiding these phases.

The activities of the analysis phase can be divided in three groups: business requirements, expertise and user issues. The framework for making explicit the business requirements bears many similarities with that for conventional systems analysis and this is not surprising given the basis upon which KADS was built. By contrast the activities for analysing the expertise are derived from a four-layer model of expertise which is unique to the project. This model is now well-developed and tested, and has been successfully applied to assist in the development of more than 15 knowledge-based systems both inside and outside P1098 (e.g. Weilemaker & Billault 1988, Hayball et al 1987).

User issues have been under consideration for as long as the expertise issues but efforts within the project have in the past concentrated on providing useful guidelines and techniques for interface design i.e. the 'how' of user-system interaction. This approach is useful and would normally be sufficient for conventional software since in the latter case the task carried out by the system is usually quite clear to the user. In the case of a KBS the problem being solved is typically ill-structured and hence the functionality of the system is not always transparent to the user. The transparency of a KBS cannot be achieved simply

---

[1] The Esprit Project P1098 aims to develop a methodology for KBS. The partners in the project are STC plc, SD-Scicon, Cap Sesa Innovation, University of Amsterdam, KBSC of Touche Ross and NTE GmbH.

by the use of interface design techniques. In order for a KBS to be successful the 'what' of interaction i.e. what kind of interaction the user wishes to have with the system has to be understood and represented in the system. In other words an understanding of how the system and the user should *cooperate* in problem solving must be obtained. A model of cooperation has been developed, which attempts to capture what users may want from a KBS and represents a major advance for knowledge-based systems. It is also a useful tool that enables the knowledge engineer to have a better understanding of the role of the user with regard to the system.

Design activities are derived from three different views of the prospective KBS and result in the production of two models: the functional model which describes functions that will be available in the system to be implemented, and the physical model which describes how these functions will be implemented. The design framework has already been used in several KBS developments (Barthelemy & Simonin 1987, Weilemaker 1988).

Given the model-oriented approach of KADS the production of a KBS can therefore be regarded as a process of model transformation as summarised in Figure 1 (Weilinga 1989).

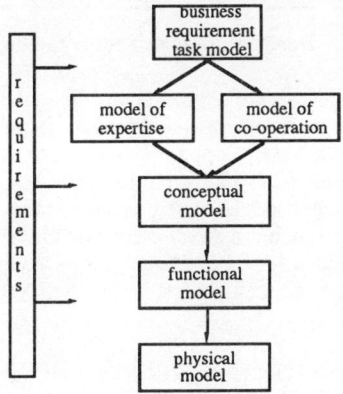

Figure 1: Transformation of KADS models

As indicated earlier the cooperation model is the most recent development of KADS and has therefore not been fully integrated with the other KADS models. This paper is an attempt to present an integrated view of KADS and hence make explicit the transformation process implied in Figure 1. This will provide a means of developing coherent, cooperative knowledge-based systems. The value of the cooperation model is illustrated by a case study (in section 5).

2. KADS analysis models

2.1 Business requirement task model

Business requirements are also referred as 'external' requirements because they are related to the organisational issues which are external to the expertise under consideration. The set of activities identified within KADS are summarised in Figure 2. The framework is not a rigorous one in that the key outputs which would form as inputs to the subsequent activities of the development are not explicit.

```
┌─────────────────────────────────────────────────────────────┐
│ Analysis of the present situation                           │
│                                                             │
│  • Develop model of the present situation                   │
│  • Determine objectives of the organisation                 │
│  • Define problems of the organisation                      │
│  • Define task to be tackled by prospective system          │
├─────────────────────────────────────────────────────────────┤
│ Analysis of objectives and constraints                      │
│                                                             │
│  • Define objectives of prospective system                  │
│  • Define compatibility requirements                        │
│  • Define man-machine interface requirements                │
│  • Determine development and operational environments       │
│  • Define control and security constraints                  │
│  • Determine organisational model                           │
├─────────────────────────────────────────────────────────────┤
│ Determination of functional requirements                    │
│                                                             │
│  • Formulate the functional requirements                    │
│  • Formulate the system structure                           │
│  • Formulate any information requirements                   │
│  • Investigate expected future enhancements                 │
│  • Determine consequences of the system                     │
└─────────────────────────────────────────────────────────────┘
```

Figure 2: Business Requirements Framework

Many of these activities are targetted at enabling the knowledge engineer to understand his client's business environment and objectives in order that a system which would meet the client's needs can be developed. This is essentially the case for the 'analysis of the present situation' set of activities which are principally designed for the benefit of the knowledge engineer, to increase his understanding of the domain. Only the last activity within this first set, task orientation, has a direct impact on the type of system to be built. It defines, in global terms, the boundaries of the business that should be under consideration. It gives the initial business requirement task model to be considered.

2.2 The Expertise Model

In KADS, expertise is represented in four layers:

- *domain* layer, which describes the concepts of the application domain (the business requirement task model) and relations between the concepts. It is also referred as 'static' knowledge;
- *inference* layer, which contains knowledge about the inferences that can be made using the static knowledge. The entities of this layer are 'metaclasses' and 'knowledge sources';
- *task* layer, which describes all ways in which the inference elements described in the inference layer can possibly be combined;
- *strategy* layer, which contains strategic information on the circumstances under which particular task structures would be applicable. In simple KBS, this layer is usually not present.

The four layers correspond to four different types of knowledge. Note that the word 'task' here has a different meaning to that in the business 'task' model. Here it refers to 'expertise task'. In addition to capturing the domain specific elements of expertise they capture 'structures' of knowledge in a form independent of implementable representation techniques. Hence they are characterised as 'epistemological'. By definition the domain layer is application-dependent since it describes concepts of the domain. The task and strategy layers are to a large extent also domain dependent (although less than the domain layer) in that the problem solving approach is specific to the domain under consideration.

The inference layer is the most generally applicable: different business tasks have similar inference features for e.g. medical diagnosis has similar inference procedures to that of car mechanics fault diagnosis. The generic inference structure that describes these two specific tasks is that of 'diagnosis'. This notion of generic description is powerful because it can be used as a model for guiding the analysis of expertise where the business task matches the generic one. KADS provides a library of such generic models. They are also referred as 'interpretation' models because they can be regarded as models for interpreting verbal data (i.e. data that is usually obtained from interviewing experts) on expertise. If an application can be completely represented by one of the generic models, then developing the expertise model is a process of model refinement which is easier than that of model building.

Figure 3 summarises the objects and representation techniques for each level of knowledge.

Layer	Entities	Representation
Domain	concepts, relations	glossary, structure diagrams eg.hierarchies, networks
Inference	metaclasses knowledge sources	inference structure diagram, inference description
Task	goals, control statements	structured language
Strategy	plans, strategies	structured language

Figure 3: Entities and representation of expertise knowledge

2.3 The Cooperation Model

Interaction between the user(s) and the system implies 'division of labour' and 'initiative' taking i.e. which agent does what at which point in time and under what circumstances. KBS that have been built so far cannot adapt to unusual circumstances that may occur when users with different levels of skills and system expectations are involved because the distribution of labour in these systems is fixed or equivalently because only one user model is assumed by the system. In practice there may be more than one type of user and hence different user models may need to be rationalised and represented in a system. Current KBS also assume that the user always understands the intention of the system. In situations when this intention is misunderstood by the user it is desirable that the system should recognise this and take appropriate initiative. Thus where appropriate either agent (system or user) should have the initiative during the problem solving process. In KADS the development of cooperative KBS is characterised by:

- an understanding of the sub-tasks of the business requirements task under consideration (the real-world tasks) and the flow of information between them i.e. the space of all real-world tasks, the agent and ingredients needed for each task;
- an identification of alternative agents and sources of these ingredients and the initiatives of these ingredients i.e the 'space of modalities';

- an understanding of the circumstances under which the modalities are applicable i.e. a cooperation management strategy.

The cooperation model that results from the above set of activities consists of: a labour distribution space, a space of modalities and a cooperation management strategy. Note that, as with the expertise strategy, the cooperation management strategy may not be present for simple systems.

2.4 The Conceptual Model

The expertise and cooperation models together form the conceptual model of the KBS. The expertise and cooperation models also complement each other in that they describe the workings of the same system from two different views, that of the expert and that of the user. There is a strong relationship between the characteristics and nature of the elements of the two models. For example overall strategic information is captured by the strategic layer (from the expertise model) and the cooperation management (from the cooperation model). The correspondence between the levels of each model is summarised in Figure 4.

Expertise	Cooperation
Domain	ingredients
Inference	labour distribution
Task	modalities space
Strategy	cooperation management strategy

Figure 4: Relationship between expertise and cooperation models

There is an important distinction between the way the two models are developed: it is normally easier to develop the expertise model by starting with the domain layer; with the cooperation model, the task analysis (for obtaining the labour distribution space) is first carried out. The latter is a top-down approach whereas the former is bottom-up. This difference in model development procedure ensures that any knowledge needed by the system is not overlooked.

Knowledge Validation

Because of their difference in perspective the models can be regarded as an informal validation tool for each other. It should be possible to match elements or groups of elements from one model to elements of the other model. The elements roughly match according to the correspondence summarised in Figure 4. The correspondence between the two models and the validation process is described briefly below:

Domain ↔ ingredients
The domain layer from the expertise model contains concepts and structures. The concepts should be matched against objects from the ingredients of the cooperation model: If a concept appears in the domain layer but not in the ingredients then it is either internal to problem solving, or an omission in the ingredients list. Similarly if an object is in the ingredients list but not in the domain layer of the expertise model, either it has been

overlooked, or it only contributes to a system task that does not interfere with the problem solving task.

Inference structure ↔ labour distribution
In theory the expertise model captures all information that the system will need for problem-solving and in developing a KBS we aim to encode this problem-solving knowledge in the system. Thus, in terms of 'labour distribution' we can assume that the system would be the initiator of problem-solving knowledge since it has that knowledge. System-initiated tasks in the labour distribution space should correspond to the knowledge sources in the inference structure (of the expertise model). Any task in the labour distribution space which has the system as the agent and which does not correspond to any knowledge source (or set of knowledge sources) should be considered as a potential mistake in the expertise model. Similarly any set of knowledge sources which does not match with any task in the labour distribution space can mean two things: that there is a mistake in the expertise model or that the task space is not complete or not accurate.

Expertise task structures ↔ modalities space
A task structure can be identified as a result of different user needs. Thus a modality (or a group of modalities) may correspond to a task structure. If a modality cannot be associated with any task structure then its validity must be investigated. It may also be the case that an expertise task structure is missing.

Strategy ↔ cooperation management
The cooperation management should be the overall guiding strategic module (de Greef et al 1988). Thus any strategic issues in the strategic layer should be present in the cooperation management.

3. The design models

The design activity considers the system from three views:

- *functional*, which is a transformation of the "conceptual model into a set of functional blocks" (Schreiber at al 1987), taking into consideration the external requirements (see Figure 1). The functional blocks are related to each other by the relations 'consist-of', 'input/output', 'control'. A useful set of function types are available, which can be used as a tool for function formulation. These are: problem solving, explanation, data I/O, data storage and control;
- *behavioural*, which is basically the selection of Artificial Intelligence (AI) methods to support any particular function. These methods may already be present in the description of knowledge sources but clearly, only the problem solving types of functions are likely to be AI related;
- *structural*, which describes the building blocks of the function. These building blocks can then be composed into the system architecture.

The functional viewpoint gives the functional model; the behavioral and structural viewpoints result in the production of the physical model of the system. The related activities are summarised in Figure 5.

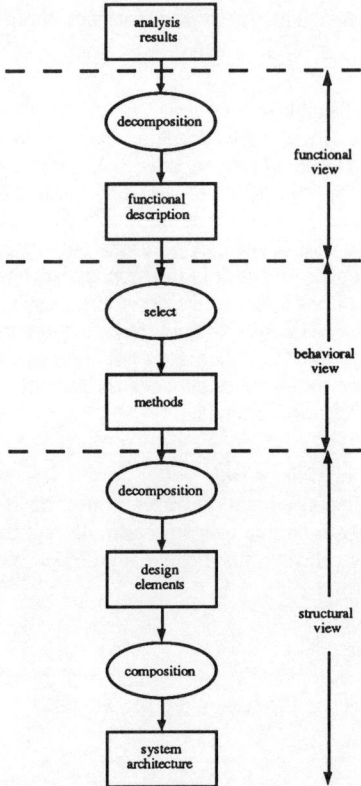

Figure 5: Design viewpoints

4. Mapping analysis onto design

The analysis items that input to the corresponding design view are summarised in Figure 6. It represents a coherent view of the KADS KBS development process.

Design Layer	Business	User	Expert
Functional	Functional requirements Constraints	Cooperation management Modalities Task distribution	Strategy Expertise task structure Inference structure
Behavioral		Modalities Task distribution	Expertise task structure Knowledge sources descriptions
Structural	Constraints	Task distribution Ingredients	Inference structure Domain concepts and structures

Figure 6: Analysis outputs for design viewpoints

The following case study illustrates the impact of the development of the cooperation model – the outcome of the *modality* analysis – on the system being implemented. In other words it illustrates the concept of a cooperative system.

5. Case Study: TRESSA

The system that we consider is called TRESSA (Touche Ross Expert System Selection Advisor, Land & Porter 1989). The system was built using KADS modelling techniques. However the analysis phase of TRESSA did not consider the cooperation model since the latter was not yet developed at the time. Several comments about the system were made by a group of evaluators (Oxby 1988). Here we illustrate how at least one of them could have been avoided had a modality analysis been carried. We do so by first presenting a 'post-hoc' modality analysis of the system.

5.1 The business requirement task model

The functional requirement of the system is to assess the feasibility of proposed knowledge based system development projects.

5.2 The expertise model

The initial inference model (see section 2.2) that was chosen to drive the analysis phase of TRESSA was heuristic classification (Clancey 1985), and the derived inference structure for TRESSA is given in Figure 7 (c.f. Land & Hickman 1989).

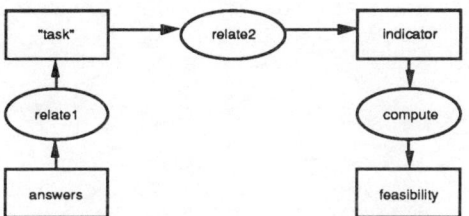

Figure 7: Inference structure in TRESSA

Given 'answers' to questions within a group (a feasibility assessment 'task' in the TRESSA vocabulary), TRESSA uses heuristics to make a numerical assessment (relate1) for that 'task'. It makes a similar numerical assessment (relate2) of the value of feasibility 'indicators', based on the value of relevant feasibility assessment 'tasks'. Finally, indicators aggregate into an overall 'feasibility' assessment by an algorithmic method, which is called 'compute'.

5.3 Implicit modality task model

We can attempt to understand the implicit modality of the existing system by using the inference structure shown in Figure 8. The modality tasks would correspond to the knowledge sources within the inference structure. This is consistent with the cross-validation process described in section 2.4. This gives the following initial modality task model shown in Figure 8.

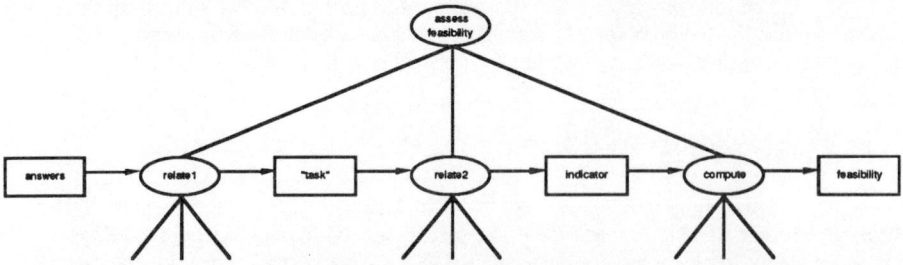

Figure 8: Initial modality task model

On closer look at the functionality of TRESSA we note that it can make other forms of inference that are not represented in the basic inference structure in Figure 7. Firstly, in certain circumstances, it can infer the value of an 'indicator' directly from an item of information provided by the user of TRESSA. We can show this by adding new knowledge source called 'relate3' (because it is the same kind of inference as 'relate1' and 'relate2'). Secondly, the overall feasibility assessment 'computed' from 'indicator' values may be adjusted in cases where items of information provided by the user of TRESSA have extreme values. We can show this by adding a second new knowledge source 'adjust1'. Finally, the overall feasibility assessment 'computed' from 'indicator' values may be adjusted, depending on the value of a feasibility assessment 'task'. We show this by adding another new knowledge source 'adjust2'. These additional tasks to the modality task model are shown in Figure 9. The task 'assess feasibility' has been omitted to aid the clarity of the diagram.

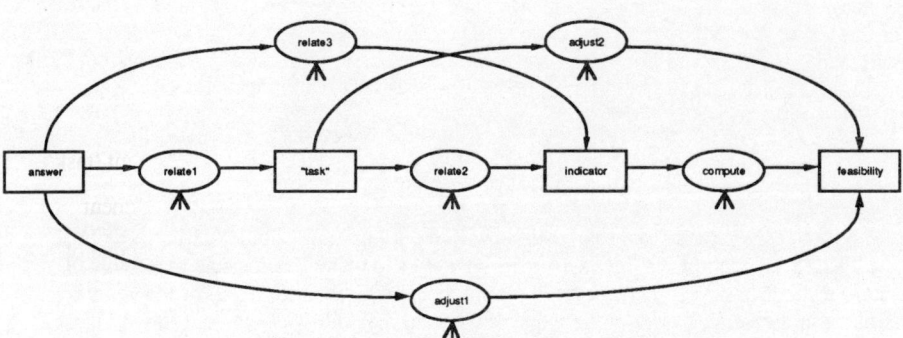

Figure 9: Revised modality task model

Assuming that we decompose the modality task down only to the level of knowledge sources in the inference structure, we can omit the branches to further subtasks stemming from the knowledge sources. The inference structure corresponding to Figure 9 is shown in Figure 10; the objects have been rearranged to give a neater diagram. It provides the framework for our considerations of modality within the TRESSA case study.

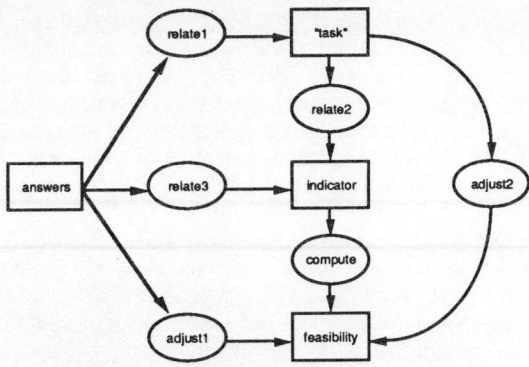

Figure 10: Revised inference structure

5.4 The space of modalities

TRESSA addresses questions to three different user groups or *stakeholders*. These are: the 'knowledge engineer', the 'expert' and the 'user'. The term 'user' is intended to mean the user of the prospective KBS, the feasibility of which is being assessed through the use of TRESSA.

The evaluation of each feasibility assessment 'task' is dependent on information provided by a stakeholder. In the inference structure (shown in Figure 10) there is no distinction between information provided by different stakeholders. We will need to make this distinction because it has modality implications: Since neither the 'user' nor the 'expert' will become knowledge engineers, they will want maximum support from the system. This implies that the system will have the initiative if the stakeholder is the 'expert' or the 'user'. On the other hand, a knowledge engineer conversant with the use of TRESSA will want to take the initiative to query or provide relevant information to the system. Thus the implied or default modality in TRESSA can be illustrated as in Figure 11.

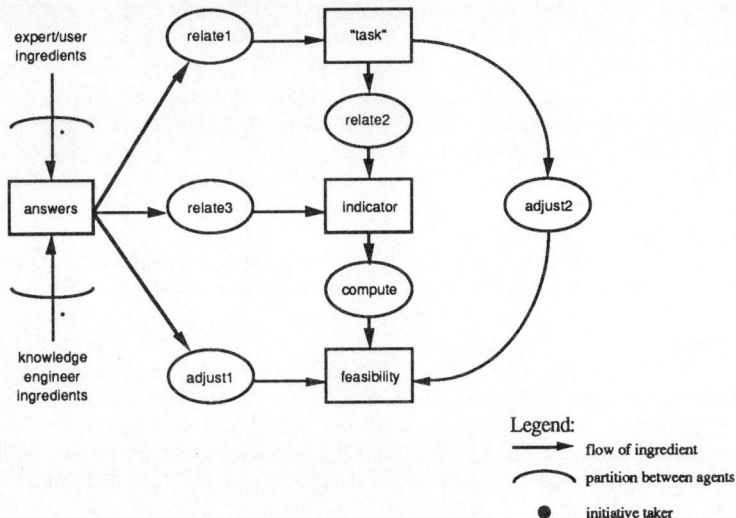

Figure 11: Default modality of TRESSA

5.5 Considering evaluators' comment – Further modality analysis

One of the comments made by the evaluators was that the nature of the 'conclusion' reached by TRESSA was too terse. They suggested they would have found the system much more useful if it gave advice on actions to be taken to enhance feasibility. Then the user of TRESSA could hold another consultation with the system in order to make a renewed assessment of feasibility (Mulhall & Taylor 1989). In this respect, they imply using TRESSA as a kind of 'risk management' advisor, in the early stages of a KBS project.

If TRESSA is to be used in a 'risk management' capacity the 'user' and 'expert' stakeholders may want to alter specific responses given in a previous session. To do this it will be necessary to provide them with the capability of reviewing these previous responses. They may wish to make as few as one alteration, or none at all. In this situation the 'user' and 'expert' user groups should have the initiative.

Assigning agents to modality tasks

To investigate whether a modality other than the default one applies to a situation it is useful to consider each of the modality tasks in turn. In this case this is equivalent to considering the knowledge sources in turn. The three 'relate' knowledge sources are really multiple instances of the same knowledge source. Thus it would make sense to assign these to the same agent and the agent in this case should be the system since it has knowledge about how to operationalise 'relate'.

Upon first inspection there may seem no point allocating 'adjust1' to a stakeholder rather than to the system since this would mean the stakeholder performing the entire feasibility task. In any case, if the stakeholder really did wish to adjust the overall feasibility directly, he need not use the system to do it. He could merely take the result offered by the system and adjust it for his own purposes, outside the province of the system.

The above argument would be true were it not for the fact that there is more than one stakeholder and that it may be used in a kind of 'risk management' capacity. This means that a stakeholder could review the responses to the questions posed by the system provided by another stakeholder and adjust the feasibility assessment accordingly. For example it is very likely that the knowledge engineer may wish to have this privilege, being the only stakeholder with sufficient understanding of knowledge engineering issues. Use of this privilege may be seen as overriding a feasibility assessment which is based in part on the responses of the other users. If the knowledge engineer wishes to exercise it, he should have a good reason to do so, as one way of interpreting this situation could be that knowledge is missing from the knowledge base. Hence, it would be a good idea to ask the knowledge engineer for an explanation of why he made the adjustment. Such information would be helpful in future knowledge base revisions. A similar argument is also true for the 'adjust2' knowledge source.

Assigning responsibility for 'compute' is much more straightforward. Since it is a straightforward algorithmic calculation it should be allocated to the system.

Summary

In some circumstances 'adjust1' and 'adjust2' may be allocated to the knowledge engineer. Theoretically, these allocations may be made separately, resulting in a total set of four modalities (including the default). This is still quite a small number, so we have represented them all in Figure 12. New boundaries, and hence new initiatives are introduced by these new labour distributions. We have assumed that if the knowledge engineer wishes to make an adjustment to the feasibility assessment he will take the initiative to do so. However, the system will take the initiative to ask for an explanation for the adjustment. After all, the other stakeholders will be interested in the explanation in addition to its possible use in the acquisition of missing knowledge.

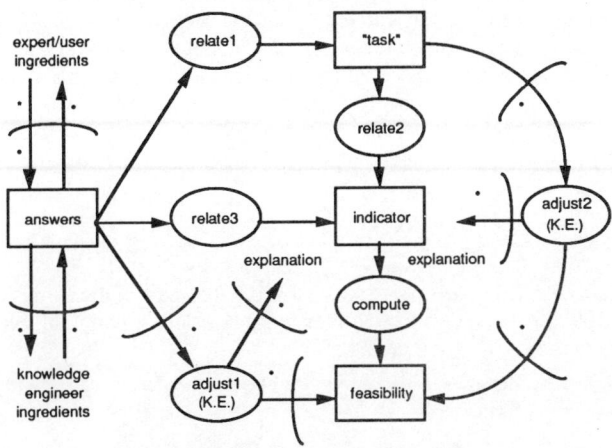

* In uses of the system subsequent to the first, for the same feasibility assessment, the initiative may be reversed.

Figure 12: Set of modalities for TRESSA

A modality analysis of TRESSA as described above would have offered a solution to the 'risk management' function of TRESSA as requested by the evaluators and indeed has provided solutions to other problems highlighted by the evaluators (Mulhall 1989). Re-engineering the system to support the four modalities summarised in Figure 12 (i.e. developing the cooperation management) is relatively simple and in this case can be implemented by altering the existing task structure (as described in Mulhall 1989).

6. Conclusion

In this paper we presented the KADS approach to developing knowledge-based systems. The approach can be regarded as a series of models transformation which form a coherent view for developing cooperative systems. At the root of developing cooperative systems is a cooperation model; we illustrated its importance via the post-hoc modality analysis of a knowledge-based system and discussed the use of the cooperation model derived in the light of the problems as highlighted by the evaluators of the system. The cooperation model also has an important role as an expertise validation tool.

6.1 Role of the Cooperation Model in Analysis

The KADS cooperation model for a KBS was developed independently of the KADS expertise model and for this reason makes it a powerful validation mechanism for expertise, and vice-versa. The information contents of both models correspond to each other in a broad way and information in one model can be checked against the other to ensure completeness and validity.

6.2 Expertise Validation

Knowledge validation is an issue which has been neglected in KBS development. So far the technique for verifying either model is by seeking the opinion of the people from which the model was derived. Thus the expertise model is validated by seeking the expert's comments while the cooperation model is validated by setting up experiments with the user as the subject. Often expertise validation is accompanied by building a prototype and observing the effects of the knowledge. The cross-validation technique outlined here provides us with a validation method which does not require resource in prototype building.

Acknowledgements

Much of the work described in this paper was carried out as part of the B4 task of the ESPRIT Project 1098. Paul de Greef of University of Amsterdam originally formulated many of the ideas of the cooperation model.

References

Barthelemy S, Edin E, Toutain E, Becker S (1987) Requirements Analysis in KBS Development, Esprit Project P1098, Deliverable D3, Cap Sesa Innovation.

Barthelemy S & Simonin N (1987) Experiment F4: design and implementation, CSI-F4-RR-002, Esprit Project P1098, Cap Sesa Innovation.

Brachman RJ (1979) On the Epistemological Status of semantic Networks; In: N.V.Findler (Ed.) Associative Networks, Academic Press, New York.

Breuker J & Weilinga B (1988) Models of expertise in knowledge acquisition, In G.Guida & C.Tasso (eds) Topics in Expert systems design: methodologies and tools, North Holland Publishing Company, The Netherlands.

Breuker J, Ed., (1987) Model Driven Knowledge Acquisition: Interpretation Models, Esprit Project P1098, Deliverable D1, University of Amsterdam and STL.

Clancey WJ (1985) Heuristic classification, Artificial Intelligence 27, pp289-350.

de Greef, Breuker J, de Jong T (1988) Modality: an analysis of functions, user control and communication in knowledge-based systems, Esprit Project P1098, University of Amsterdam.

Hayball C, Land L, Mulhall T, Wright I (1988) F6 Experiment: Evaluation Report, Esprit Project P1098,STL.

Land L & Hickman F, (1989) Assessing the feasibility of a knowledge-based system, to be published in 'KBS Management Review' journal, Vol 1., No. 3.

Land L & Porter D (1989) TRESSA: Analysis, Design and Implementation Notes, Working Paper, Touche Ross Management Consultants.

Mulhall T (1989) TRESSA Case Study: Recommendations for further development, Esprit Project P1098, Working Paper, Task B4, Touche Ross Management Consultants, March 89.

Mulhall T & Taylor R (1989) TRESSA Case Study: Evaluators Comments, Esprit Project P1098, Working Paper, Task B4, Touche Ross Management Consultants, Febuary 89.

Oxby G (1988) Feasibility and Requirements Assessment of a KBS: Evaluation Report, Engineering Industry Training Board.

Schreiber G, Bredeweg B, Davoodi M, Weilinga B (1987) Towards a design for KBS, Esprit Project P1098, Deliverable D8, University of Amsterdam and STL.

Shneiderman B (1987) Designing the User Interface: Strategies for Effective Human-computer Interaction, Addison-Wesley.

Wielemaker J, Billault JP (1988) A KADS analysis for configuration, Esprit Project P1098, Deliverable E5.1, University of Amsterdam.

Weilinga B (1989) Esprit P1098, Phase II Review, April 1989, Touche Ross Management Consultants.

AN ENVIRONMENT FOR EXPERIMENTATION WITH INTERACTIVE COOPERATING KNOWLEDGE BASED SYSTEMS

L. Sommaruga, N.M. Avouris, M.H. Van Liedekerke
Joint Research Center of the CEC,
CITE, KBS Lab, TP 440,
21020 Ispra (VA), Italy

Abstract

The need for complex architectures for distributed expert systems, distributed knowledge bases and data bases is emerging in a series of application areas. The techniques suggested by the Distributed Artificial Intelligence (DAI) area of research, dealing with the description and creation of loosely coupled software systems, that can interact in order to solve problems in a cooperative way, have been applied for the design and implementation of a knowledge based system for chemical emergencies management.
A number of interesting theoretical ideas have been applied in a practical framework, resulting in a working prototype and a shell of Cooperation, called *CooperA* (Cooperating Agents) which is described in this paper.
CooperA has been designed and developed by the authors as a software environment supporting the cooperation of heterogeneous distributed semi-autonomous knowledge based systems presented to the user via a customized user interface. These modules can be incrementally and selectively integrated into the system, with which the user can interact through a special User Interface Agent. Each expert module incorporates a self description mechanism, which allows the shell to integrate them with each other. Finally the user interface incorporates active modelling of the system, so that the user can see the flows of interaction among the agents.

1 Introduction

In the frame of activities of the Knowledge Base Systems Sector of CITE/ JRC, and within a research project involving the design and development of a complex knowledge based system, we have been led towards the investigation of the possibilities that the new subdiscipline of Artificial Intelligence, termed Distributed Artificial Intelligence (DAI), dealing with the description and creation of multiple intelligent systems that can interact, could offer in solving the problems of the particular application area in which we were involved.
Within DAI, distributed problem solving is the cooperative solution of problems by a decentralized and loosely coupled collection of agents, located in a number of distinct processing nodes. The computational elements called *Agents* (also known as actors, knowledge sources or processors nodes) can perform sophisticated problem solving and cooperatively interact. When faced with a problem that could be solved more effectively through cooperation, the agents work together by identifying subproblems each should solve, solving them concurrently and integrating their results (Decker,87). In the case of

our application a set of expert systems, representing different domains of expertise, need to interact in order to manage chemical emergencies. So we were led to the use of a multi-agent approach in order to improve the global efficiency and also by the fact that this particular kind of problem is modelled more naturally in terms of a collection of knowledge bases, corresponding to different domain experts.

Despite the intense activity in the area of DAI worldwide, most of the environments developed so far, are experimental and do not provide the typical knowledge engineering tools, necessary for eliciting, structuring and representing the knowledge required in order to build the various agents of the distributed system. So the approach that we decided to take was to extend an existing commercially available knowledge engineering environment, by building into it the structures and mechanisms for handling a community of interacting expert systems. The result of this effort was a generic testbed for distributed knowledge based applications, called CooperA (Cooperating Agents), which is presented here.

CooperA has also been created for experimentation reasons, were various problem-solving architectures and techniques can be tried. It permits the complete integration of semi-autonomous, heterogeneous knowledge based systems at different levels of granularity and complexity.

Let us first describe some of the terms used in this description. With the term *cooperation* we mean the effect of all actions undertaken by the agents in which they take part and to which they contribute. With *semi-autonomous* we mean that agents are not completely independent with respect to their knowledge (e.g. data and tasks). *Heterogeneous* means that different agents can be based on different knowledge representations. *Intelligent* means that agents can present a certain behaviour, i.e. a rational behaviour dictated by the common human logic in a particular knowledge domain.

A *CooperA version 1.0* release is now running on a Symbolics 3640 lisp-machine, in an extended knowledge engineering environment that allows experimentation with different distributed systems. The CooperA model has been implemented using CRL-Lisp, which is Common Lisp extended with capabilities to represent knowledge under schemata (frame) form. The main reasons for selecting this development platform are:

- it meets the specifications of a fast prototyping environment, integrating various knowledge representation paradigms, that are essential for experimenting with heterogeneous problem solving elements;
- it is based on the object-oriented structure of CRL (schemata), which provides the basic elements and mechanism for data and problem solving;
- it provides facilities like inheritance, context based knowledge structuring and demon functions, which are extensively used by CooperA kernel.

2 General description of CooperA

CooperA is designed as an experimentation testbed for distributed problem solving systems. The building components of CooperA are:

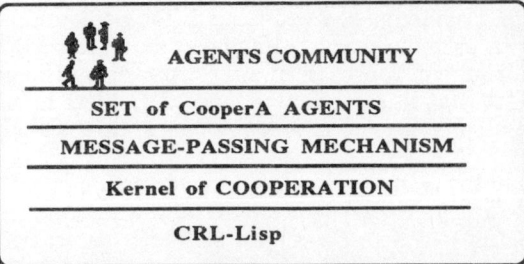

Figure 1 A layered description of CooperA Environment

    1) the *CoKernel* (Cooperation Kernel) represents the cooperation shell and consists of a collection of initialization procedures and system facilities that each agent can use;
    2) the *message-passing mechanism* performs communication between agents; it is built by functions that handle and control messages. Messages play an important role in the cooperation, since it is only through them that information is exchanged and hence communication is possible;
    3) the *collection of CooperA system agents* is a set of agents created by CooperA independently of the application; they perform operations of common interest. An example is the *User Agent* who handles all I/O operations and communication with the external world and represents, within the community, the user of a CooperA application;
    4) the *community of application specific agents*: an agent is the basic computational entity of CooperA. Each agent has the capability and contains the knowledge to fulfill one or more tasks. It also contains knowledge about the external world (other agents, their location and their capabilities).
    On the level of the CooperA kernel layer and with the help of CooperA system agents, the user can define agents, each one representing knowledge in various domains. So a community of agents is created in which the user is inserted through the *User-Agent*, who interacts with the community during problem solving.
    Message-passing has been considered to be the most suitable communication paradigm for the flexible and dynamic creation of distributed systems (Hewitt,84).

3. Description of an Agent

    CooperA agents are active structures that communicate by means of messages. Each agent exists in its own unique environment, structured as a context. In this environment, an agent contains knowledge about the agents in the external world and the information to communicate with them in a sensible way.
    A CooperA agent has a well-defined structure and its characteristics are expressed through a number of attributes. They are:
        context: it is used for representing the agent's address;
        status: it contains the agent-status, changing at run-time;
        goals: the agent current goals, used during problem solving;
        current-message: the message currently being processed;

__has-tables__: it refers to the data-structures that the particular agent contains, used for acquaintance modelling and communication;
__in-q__: the input queue where incoming messages are put, waiting for the attention of the agent;
__out-q__: the output-queue where outgoing messages are put, waiting for being sent by the kernel;
__my-skills__: a list of goals that the agent can satisfy, with corresponding methods to achieve them;
__unsatisfied-goals__: a list of goals that cannot be reached using the local rule base and the knowledge world of the agent;
__activation-method__: the method necessary for the activation of the agent;
__plans__: the plans of the agent for achieving some goals;
__precondition__: a set of conditions necessary for activating the particular agent.

A CooperA agent performs one of the following three actions: receiving a message; sending a message; reasoning within its knowledge world in order to accomplish its tasks.

All messages are sent or received through two queues: the *outgoing-messages queue* (*out-q*) from which the outgoing messages are transmitted, and the *incoming-messages queue* (*in-q*) that receives and handles incoming messages. For each one of these queues a function is preset in order to coordinate respective actions that have to be undertaken according to the message type. For instance when an agent receives a request, it questions accordingly its own local world of knowledge or activates its rule base using its inference engine, trying to fulfill the request. Then returns the information estimated to the agents requesting or interested in it.

In order to facilitate cooperation between agents, each agent contains the attributes *my-skills* and *unsatisfied-goals*. The former contains all the knowledge relative to its own capacities, while the latter contains reference to all information that might be needed, but is not found in its own world and to the sources (if known a priori) that can provide this information.

The attribute *Status* of an agent describes the current status of the agent activity during execution. It can take one of the following values: *new*, *inactive*, *running* and *waiting*. The value is assigned and handled by the appropriate kernel functions. When an agent is created during the initialization phase, it gets the status *new*. It remains in this status until the initialization and creation of the necessary data structures is accomplished; then its status is changed to *inactive* the first time that the agent is invoked. The agent remains in the inactive status until it receives a message for activation. In that case it changes its status to *running* and remains in that status for as long as it is active. When finished, it returns to the inactive status. The *waiting* status is used to put the agent in a condition of temporary suspension of its execution in expectation of an external event.

The *plans* attribute could contain sequences of actions, needed for fulfilling a goal and could be used during the phase of the agent activities planning.

The *preconditions* attribute could contain a series of conditions or minimal set of events that must be verified before the agent can be activated, thus making sure that the agent activation could have some desirable results for the community.

All the information contained in the attributes is added during the phase of creating the agent and is compatible with the formalism used to structure and represent the knowledge locally. The attributes, describing the agent, are not seen and can not be understood directly by the other agents of the community.

Each agent has its own knowledge of the external world that permits cooperation. This information is contained in data structures local to the agent and created dynamically during the initialization of the system, once the community of agents is defined.

During the execution of a task, an agent can be in one of the following situations: a) in need for some information, unknown to its own world, it has to decide to what agent to address a request for that information; b) having calculated some results, it has to decide to what agent to send these.

To solve the first problem, a CooperA agent makes use of a particular structure: the *Yellow-Pages*. In this table, for each unsatisfied-goal, i.e. information it cannot find or compute in its own world, the agent finds a list of agents in the community who could elaborate that information, in other words, satisfy the goal in question.

To solve the second problem, the agent consults its *Interested-in-Table*, where it finds for each *my-skill*, i.e. information it can find or compute by itself, a list of agents in the community who could be interested in this information.

Another information indispensable for the communication is the location of the agents. Each agent has in its world a table called *Modules*, that maps the name of each known agent into a corresponding address. In a real distributed environment, this redundancy of information avoids superfluous exchange of information.

The CooperA message is defined as a data structure containing: an *identity* that is a unique symbol, permitting reference to the message; a *type* that is a qualifier indicating the particular kind of message, i.e. whether it is an information request, an answer, etc.; a *content* that, in accordance with the message-type, refers to the actions it would like to invoke, or any other knowledge or information. E.g. it can contain the name of a goal, eventually followed by a list of parameters or it can contain an answer to a request, knowledge concerning actions, procedures, plans, allocation of tasks, etc.; a *sender* that is the agent identity of the message creator; a *receiver* that is a list of agents to whom the message is addressed.

All messages are instances of a prototype containing these attributes. Appropriate kernel functions have been defined to create and handle these messages.

4. Communication between Agents

A description of the way the communication between the intelligent CooperA agents takes place is included in this paragraph.

As already mentioned, the model of inter-agent communication is based on a mechanism of message-passing (see figure 2). The communicated knowledge reflects the particular structure in the local knowledge base. So a protocol for structuring messages in a uniform way is provided in CooperA. There is also some provision for the communication with the user of CooperA, since CooperA has been designed for heavy interactive flavoured systems.

5. The Communication Protocol CP

The exchange of information between all agents is done through a *Communication Protocol* (CP). The CP addresses the problem of defining a common representation of the intersecting parts of the knowledge bases. A relevant real world metaphor is a common language understood by an international group of experts assembled around a table to solve a particular problem. The sender-agent creates an outgoing message first in its own "local language", e.g. using symbols that have only locally a meaning. During the message sending operation, a translation into a "global language" message takes place. This global language is part of the CP. The inverse translation takes place at the receiving agent. The process of translation from local to global language before, and from global to local language after, is called the message *CP-interpretation*.

The *Communication Protocol (CP)* maps semantically and lexically the requests and replies between heterogeneous agents. This two step transformation takes place according to the scheme:

Agent$_{sender}$ --> Comm. Protocol --> Agent$_{receiver}$

First the message is positioned in the out-q of the sender agent. Then the out-q manager demon takes care of processing the message translating it into the global language (CP) and calling the adequate Cokernel functions. The message passing action is simulated by copying the message schema from the context (address) of the sender into the context of the receiver, translating it into the receiver's local language and finally putting it into its in-q. There the message is ready for being processed by the in-q manager demon.

CooperA uses a data structure called *Dictionary* and some relevant kernel functions during the CP-interpretation phase. Each agent is provided with a Dictionary, in which the part of the agent's local knowledge which could be of interest to the rest of the community is mapped into a global representation. The correct definition of these dictionaries permits communication between heterogeneous agents. This is a necessary (but not sufficient) step towards coherent behaviour of the community of agents.

6. Communication strategies in CooperA

The CooperA user is given the possibility of experimenting with different communication strategies for solving a problem. The community's behaviour can be different, depending on the selections on a set of global switches. The switch *multiple-request* decides whether the set of alternative candidates for satisfying a particular goal could be exhausted before the requesting agent decides about the reply, eventually passing the request directly to the UA. The switch *broadcast-reply* decides how an answer is communicated to the external world of an agent, communicating the result exclusively to the agent who has made the request or to all agents that could be interested in that information, according to the best knowledge of the owner of the result.

Different CooperA agents exchange information including uncertainty in the form of certainty factors. Meta-knowledge about the

Finally there is the possibility to set alternative communication strategies, that can influence the problem solving activity and the overall system convergence to a solution (see section 6).

Agents react upon receiving a message according to their rules of behaviour, expressed as activation methods, and the particular type of the received message. The active part of the agent acts on the local world of knowledge by making inferences on it or modifying it. This world consists of a closed set of knowledge, only locally visible to the agent.

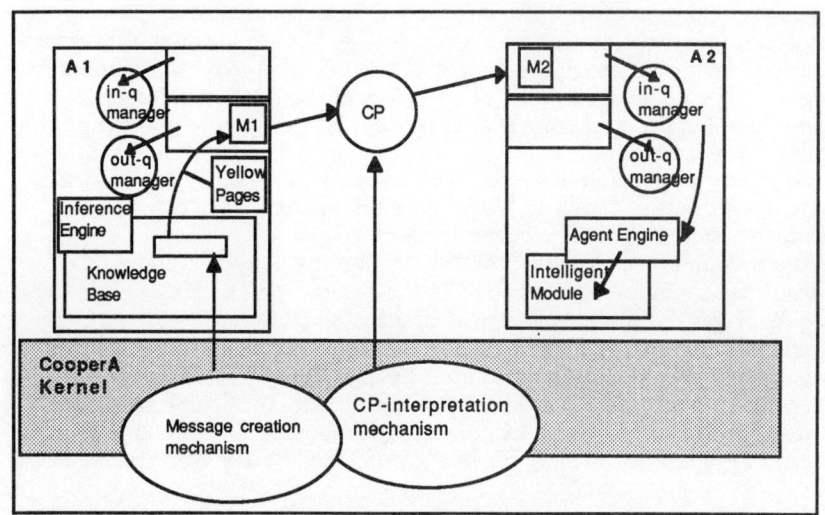

Figure 2. Communication between Agents A1 and A2

Messages are created by a sending-agent, who makes use of appropriate Cokernel functions and the local world of knowledge. The created message is put in the out-q of the sender and a kernel demon (*out-q manager*), monitoring the queue, is activated. This kernel service performs the message transmission by copying the message in the in-q of the receiver, where an appropriate demon (*in-q manager*) monitoring the queue is activated and passes control to the receiving-agent, if it is available and ready for execution (see figure 2). If the message is tagged as an answer to a previous request, the receiver matches the message with the pending request and reasons about the relevance of the supplied answer, which eventually can update the receiver's world of knowledge or begin a new query. If the message is tagged as a request to the receiving agent, the receiver tries to activate the appropriate method in order to satisfy the goal specified by the message. If the message is a request addressed to the user-agent, it contains all the necessary information for specifying the dialogue with the user. The actual interaction with the user is managed by a special CooperA agent, called *User-Agent*, which transmits back the user's reply to the agents interested in it.

The message-receiver will be activated if its status is inactive. If not, the received messages remain in the incoming-messages queue, waiting for the agent to be ready to process them. In general, messages are FIFO processed, but it is possible, in principle, to introduce some kind of priority handling in the queues.

uncertainty handling mechanism is essential for an agent in order to interpret a supplied reply. CooperA provides the switch *ask-for-cf* which decides whether the uncertainty management mechanism is active.

Current version of CooperA is designed as a distributed systems programmer workbench. The system commands and utilities are available through a graphical representation in the so-called Workbench window.

One of the capability of the CooperA user interface is that it can visualize graphically the problem solving activity in the system and that it can let the user to have access to the tools and commands available in a graphical way.

7. Data-structures for acquaintances modelling

The data structures described in this paragraph (see Figure 3) model locally the acquaintances of an agent in a CooperA community.

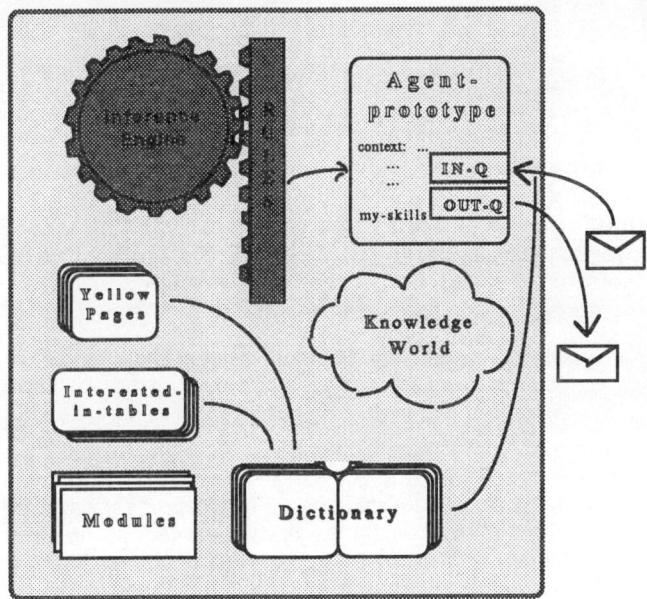

Figure 3: Data structures of a CooperA Agent

The *Yellow-Pages* structure contains a description of all the acquaintances of the agent who are in a position to satisfy goals that the agent is interested in. The metaphor used is that of a yellow pages style directory. This directory is dynamically created during the initialization of the agents, taking into consideration the participants of the particular group of agents attempting to solve a problem and the needs of the particular agent. The yellow-pages schema of *agent-x* have therefore the form:

{ *Yellow-Pages$_x$*
    goal-1: agent-11 agent-12 ...
    goal-2: agent-21 agent-22 ...
    . . .   }

The *Interested-in-table* of some agent contains information about agents who are interested in its skills.

This model is also created dynamically during the phase of the configuration of a community of agents. The form of the interested-in-table for agent-x is:

{ *Interested-in-table$_x$*
    skill-1: interested-agent-11 interested-agent-12 ...
    skill-2: interested-agent-21 interested-agent-22 ...
    .   .   .
}

The kernel function *Create-Yellow-Pages-et-al* takes care of the creation of these two acquaintance modelling structures. Another kernel facility is the *Update-Yellow-Pages-et-al* which takes care of updating the structures in the case that "late comers" join an existing group of agents.

The *Dictionary* data structure contains a directory of associations between concepts, locally defined and used by an agent, and global terms, defined in the frame of the Communication Protocol (CP). The structure of the *Dictionary* for the agent$_x$ is:

{ *Dictionary$_x$*
    .....
    local-concept$_j$: CP-concept$_j$ address$_j$
    ..... }

where local-concept$_j$ is a slot referring to a local symbol, CP-concept$_j$ is the globally known name of the local concept and address$_j$ represent the local address of local-concept$_j$.

If the same CP-concept is related to a local-concept$_k$ of an other agent, the two concepts are considered, as referring to the same symbol in a virtual global name-space of the community of the distributed agents.

The importance of this structure in the case of heterogeneous community of independently built modules is obvious. However the problem that the CooperA programmer is faced with during the development of the Dictionary structure of an agent is not a trivial one. The coherence of the distributed problem solving activity depends a great deal on an accurate semantic and lexical mapping of the concepts defined in the frame of the various knowledge bases. Once this mapping has been completed the operation of developing structures like *dictionary* is straight forward. So far the mapping of the knowledge between agents is entirely left to the CooperA programmers initiative. However the idea of automating this process, in a future version of CooperA, using perhaps hypertext-based tools is an exciting prospect.

8. The User Agent and the CooperA interface

The User-agent (UA) is structured in the same way as all other CooperA agents and communicates with them through the same message passing mechanism described. However this UA, representing the user (considered as a boundless domain of knowledge), is special as far as acquaintance modelling and request message structuring is concerned. There is a special type of message: *user-request* referring to communication with the UA. The reason for specifying this type of message is that since the UA does not contain any application specific knowledge, it needs when requested to satisfy a goal, to be supplied with information on how to establish a dialogue with the user in order to satisfy the requested goal.

The dialogue style selected and tried so far is based on multilevel menus, so the meta-information contained in a user-request message concerns the type of menu, prompt line, possible alternative answers, help etc. There is no reason to assume that other dialogue styles, like command language, iconic etc cannot be used in the future. It is also envisaged that some user modelling could be integrated in the UA, which would mean different dialogue styles for different classes of users.

The knowledge, necessary for building the user-dialogue, is usually owned by the agent making the request. So this should be passed to the UA which takes care of the graphics, windowing system etc for visualizing the request and managing the dialogue. After the interaction phase, the UA will take care of forming the reply message according to the results of the dialogue with the user, and passing it to the requesting agent or the agents interested in it. The User-agent manages also messages supplying information to the user and answering its requests.

A customized user interface has been also developed (the CooperA Workbench, see figure 4), which permits to the user to configure dynamically the system and see the flows of interaction among the agents.

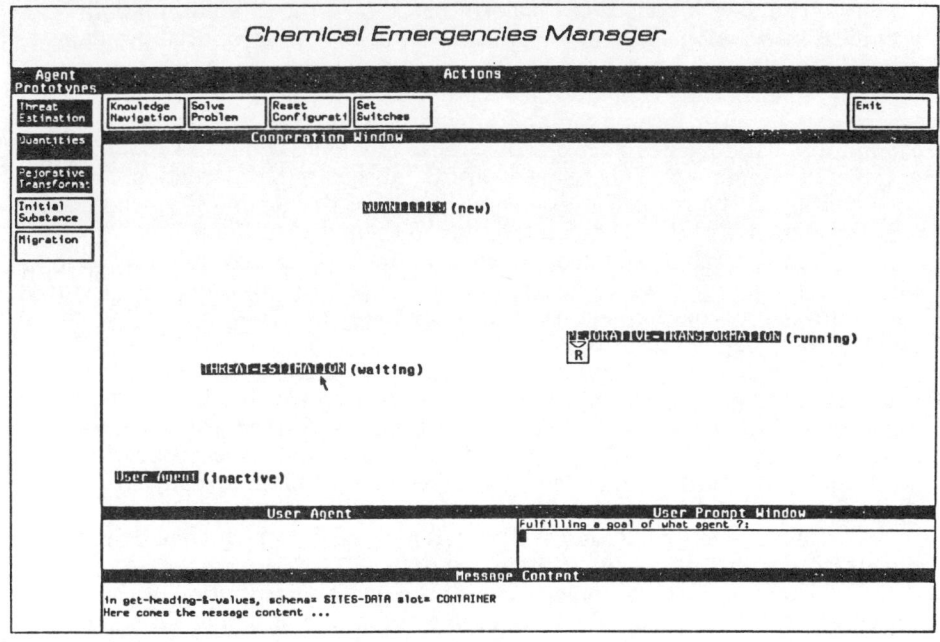

Figure 4 The CooperA Workbench

9. Evaluation and perspectives of CooperA

The CooperA testbed, developed for the cooperation of heterogeneous intelligent agents, has been an attempt to build a software environment that supports distributed problem solving. In order to build CooperA we have borrowed some of the ideas of the current research activity in the area of Distributed A.I., but also introduced some innovative features. The most interesting characteristics of CooperA are:

- The integration of distributed knowledge base and distributed problem solving building tools in a powerful knowledge engineering shell, which permits experimentation with full scale cooperating knowledge based systems developed within the shell.
- CooperA has a strong flavour of experimentation. There is provision for global settings of the environment which permit alternative communication strategies, taking in consideration management of uncertainty etc.
- The concept of knowledge navigation during the problem-solving, a useful debugging tool allowing the user to follow closer the effects of the agents activities.
- Some attempts were made to handle the difficult problem of interaction between the distributed heterogeneous knowledge bases contained in the different agents. So, the Communication Protocol has been introduced, trying to establish a global standard knowledge representation for the community of agents that permits mutual understanding of agents, using their own local formalisms;
- The user interface of CooperA, based on a direct manipulation graphical interaction style, allows visualization of the distributed problem solving activity and direct access to the commands and options of the system.
- The special User interface Agent (UA) in the agents community is responsible for user interaction and for representing the user within the community. This agent has a domain knowledge on I/O devices handling, graphical systems etc.. This "expert" of I/O takes care of interaction with the user, taking off the responsibility from the rest of the community, who need only to interact with the UA in a familiar to them and uniform way.
- The search of an adequate solution for a particular subtask during the cooperative problem solving activity can be performed through an iterative agents invocation mechanism, supported by CooperA. This feature permits a fault-tolerant behaviour of the community.

CooperA has introduced a new line of research in our Laboratory which is expected to produce some more interesting results. In a first phase, some improvements and extensions of the CooperA testbed are envisaged, along the phase of CooperA testing and validation in various application cases (such as in chemical emergencies management) which is already in progress, (VanLiedek,89).

Some of the limitations of the current version, which should suggest the starting points of the future research are:
- There is a lack of concurrency and physical distribution of the agent activities. So far the main effort has been given in the design of a distributed knowledge based system, with a simulated distribution in problem solving. The use of concurrent processes and computer networks based hardware platforms should make CooperA more efficient and capable of handling a new range of applications.
- The acquaintance modelling features of the CooperA language are limited. The models are constructed a priori and cannot be modified dynamically. There is not possibility of reasoning about the skills of the acquaintances and there is no mechanism for some organizational structuring of the community.

- Some mechanism for automating the development of the
Communication Protocol and therefore the mapping of the elements of the
heterogeneous knowledge bases should be introduced. This is a feature which
is missing from the current version of CooperA.
- Extension of the User Agent domain knowledge, by adding some
elements of user modelling and so improving the interaction with the user,
which can be based on dialogues adaptable to different user profiles and
characteristics.

References

(Decker,87) Keith S. Decker; "Distributed Problem Solving Techniques: a survey", IEEE Transactions on Systems, Man and Cybernetics (pag 729-740) v. 17, 1987.

(Durfee,86) E. H. Durfee, V. R. Lesser, D. D. Corkill; "Cooperation through communication in a distributed problem solving network", in Michael N. Huhns Distributed Artificial Intelligence, (chap. 2, pag 29-58) Pitman Publishing, London, Morgan Kaufmann Publishers, 1987.

(Gasser,86) Les Gasser, Carl Braganza, Nava Herman; "MACE: a flexible testbed for Distributed A.I. research," in Michael N. Huhns Distributed artificial intelligence (chap. 5, pag 119-152) Pitman Publishing, London, Morgan Kaufmann Publishers, 1987.

(Grice,75) H. P. Grice; "Logic and conversation", in P.Cole e J.L.Morgan, "Syntax and semantics.III.Speech Acts", New York Academic Press 1975.

(Hewitt,84) Carl E. Hewitt, Henry Lieberman; "Design issues in parallel architectures for Artificial Intelligence," Proceedings 28th IEEE Computer Soc. Int. Conference, San Francisco CA, (pag 418-423) Feb. 1984.

(Hughes,68) G. E. Hughes, M. J. Cresswell; "Introduction to Modal Logic", London 1968.

(Kornfeld,81) William A. Kornfeld, Carl E. Hewitt; "The scientific community metaphor", IEEE Transactions on Systems, Man and Cybernetics (pag 24-33) January 1981.

(Ricci,83) Pio Ricci Bitti, Bruna Zani; "La comunicazione come processo sociale", Il Mulino, cap.7, 1983.

(Sommaruga,89) Lorenzo Sommaruga; "Cooperazione mediante comunicazione fra agenti intelligenti", Degree Thesis, Faculty of Information Science, Università degli studi di Milano, Milan, 1989.

(Sommaruga,89) L. Sommaruga, N. M. Avouris, M. H. Van Liedekerke; "Studies in Distributed Artificial Intelligence: Part I: Development of the testbed environment CooperA", JRC Technical Note I.89.63, CITE, JRC Ispra, Italy, May 1989.

(Sridharan,87) N. Sridharan; "Report on the 1986 Workshop on Distributed Artificial Intelligence", The ai magazine Fall (pag. 75-85), 1987.

(Suchman,87) Lucy Suchman; "Plans and situated actions: the problem of human-machine communication," Cambridge University Press, New York, 1987.

(VanLiedek,89) M. VanLiedekerke, N.M. Avouris, L. Sommaruga; "Development of a distributed Chemical Emergencies Management System, using CooperA" JRC Technical Note, Ispra, 1989 (in preparation).

Expertext: Hypertext-Expert System Theory, Synergy and Potential Applications

Judith Barlow[*], *Martin Beer, Trevor Bench-Capon,
Dan Diaper, Paul E. S. Dunne, and Roy Rada*

Department of Computer Science
University of Liverpool
LIVERPOOL L69 3BX

Formal graph theory representations can describe the underlying semantic net models associated with both expert systems and hypertext. Hypertext and expert systems can contribute synergistically to implementable expertext systems by exploiting the class relationships that form the links between nodes in semantic nets. Possible applications for expertext systems are identified and their potential to solve existing problems is discussed. Considerable emphasis is placed on locating the intelligence in systems that include both users and an expertext system.

1. Introduction

The trend of computer system applications such as expert systems; natural language interfaces; and hypertext can be characterised by the following stages: (i) approximately identify the nature of a computer system that does not currently exist; (ii) implement such a computer system; (iii) start looking in earnest for real world problems that the new style computer system can solve; (iv) develop a whole set of variations on the new system; (v) reassess the utility of the new technology and withdraw some of the more optimistic claims made in the early euphoria. While such a characterisation is admittedly a simplification, it has merit as a cautionary note on our current practices. This paper intends to introduce another new technology, expertext, and, although stage (i) has already been reached (Rada & Barlow, 1988; 1989), stage (ii) has not yet been achieved. However, to break away from the system lead development cycle, this paper will attempt two things. First, after a brief review of expertext's enabling technologies from both expert systems and hypertext, a theory will be espoused that is intended to underpin subsequent expertext developments. Second, possible applications of the technology will be identified. Expertext will not be an 'all singing, all dancing' technological breakthrough, but we believe that it will solve some of the problems that currently exist with both expert systems and with hypertext. It is anticipated that this approach will avoid expertext suffering the major limitations associated with expert systems

---

[*] Visiting researcher from U S WEST Advanced Technologies, 6200 S. Quebec Street, Englewood, Colorado 80111 USA.

while still overcoming navigational and other problems associated with having no intelligence within a hypertext system.

1.1. Locating Intelligence in Systems

One can characterise the difference between traditional databases and expert systems in terms of the location of intelligence in the user-computer part of the system (Diaper, 1989). With traditional databases all the intelligence resides with the user who, when searching for a record or set of records, must solve the problem of specifying the search keys and their logical relationships. In contrast, expert systems internalise much of this intelligence such that with many expert systems the user is merely prompted with requests for data in a manner and order determined by the expert system.

Hypertext systems have a passive nature in contrast to the active intelligence of expert systems. It remains for systems to be developed which can automatically traverse hypertext links for hypertext to become intelligent and like expert systems, the tendency will be to transport intelligence from the user and into the computer system. The expertext proposals outlined in this paper are the basis for the development of intelligent hypertext systems. However, our cautious approach is to suggest that rather than removing the intelligence from the user, as happened with expert systems, what is to be preferred is a sharing of intelligence between the user and the expertext system.

1.2. Expert Systems: Applications and Problems

A goal of expert systems is to provide advice that is consistent with that which a human expert would. An expert system can also *explain* its reasoning process by offering mid-run explanations as to *why* it posed a particular query as well as provide post-run explanations as to *how* it arrived at a particular conclusion. The purpose of these explanation facilities in expert systems is to facilitate a meaningful dialog between the user and the computer system. Users have been critical of the value provided by expert system explanation facilities. Even when good explanation facilities are provided, such facilities seldom allow the user to alter an expert system's processes. The cost of embedding this intelligence in the computer part of the system is reflected in the domain specificity and rigidity of expert systems.

Some of the most famous expert systems have not gone beyond the development stage because they could not be easily integrated in the work place or they did not communicate smoothly with the user. MYCIN, while provably expert within its domains of bacteremia and meningitis, is not routinely used by physicians when a bacteremia or meningitis question arises. MYCIN's developers subsequently shifted their attention to a hypertext information system (Shortliffe, 1981). INTERNIST, an expert system which can handle a wide range of internal medicine problems, has been converted into a teaching tool which allows the user to browse through the knowledge base in hypertext fashion. Other medical expert-information systems are following the hypertext paradigm (Timpka, 1986). The developers of tools for building expert system have seen the value of integrating hypertext features within expert systems. Knowledge Pro, an expert system development tool released in 1988, allows the system developer to embed hypertext links in both the query and explanation facilities. Users who do not understand a query can browse text related to the query. Similarly hypertext browsing is available in both mid-run and post-run explanations.

1.3. Hypertext: Applications and Problems

Text is a body of natural language which conveys a coherent message. People agree that hypertext includes links that are missing in text. Whether these links are between textual units or within a semantic net that points to textual units depends on the application. We favour the approach to hypertext in which a semantic net points to units of text (Rada, 1989). Accordingly, a hypertext system includes a text database, a semantic net which points to text, and an interface for browsing.

When a document is delivered on paper, the reader proceeds by turning pages, but in a hypertext system the reader *browses* across networks. The reader is thus allowed to see a connectivity of ideas within the text. The enthusiasm about hypertext is, however, dampened by the experience that readers tend to get lost when they are presented with complex networks (Raskin, 1987).

Hypertext is a textual analogue of a database and when browsing similar navigational problems arise. Whereas a database may not carry more information than the data within it, the semantic net in hypertext carries knowledge beyond that contained in the text. Creating a hypertext semantic net creates new meaning (Doland, 1989). However, whether the hypertext creator, let alone the hypertext user, understands the impact of this new knowledge is, in many cases, debatable.

One way to lessen the navigation problems with hypertext is to define the semantics of the semantic net. A related strategy is to place more sophisticated help or guide facilities in the semantic net. One of the greatest challenges to the development of successful hypertext systems concerns the insertion of expert procedural guides to browsing (Halasz, 1988).

1.4. The Expertext Solution

Both expert systems and hypertext may be described as networks so that both are open to interpretation in graph-theoretic terms. The expertext framework outlined in the next section is related to the human memory model of Morton and Bekerian (1986) called "headed records". In this model there are two types of nodes: headers and blocks. A block contains natural language text which is readable by a user. Each block of text is connected to a header (see Figure 1). However, given that natural language text can not be fully formalised, the nature of what is linked in the block to the header needs to be at a relatively high level.

The header does not contain a complete specification of the text block, but enough that its major contents are specified. A finer understanding of the text block of each header is thus left to the intelligence of the expertext user. In a production rule system, the header may include rule antecedents or rule consequents. Thus the header nodes contain a computable representation in a standard expert system rule-base representation. The knowledge base representation in the header may be used by an inference engine in the normal expert system manner but may

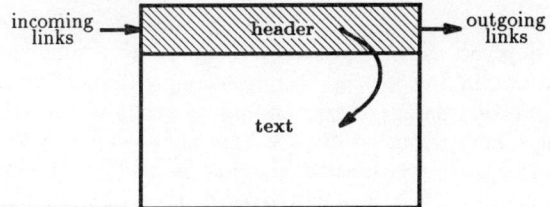

Figure 1: The *outgoing* and *incoming* links are expert system links which can be used for inferencing. The internal link between the *header* and *text* is a hypertext link that can be used for browsing.

also be appreciated by the user. Expertext acquires the properties of hypertext by linking bodies of text via their headers. It contributes to hypertext navigation because links between headed records are well specified.

2. A Framework for Hypertext, Expert Systems and Expertext

Graph-theoretic models are frequently used to represent data in hypertext and expert systems. A directed graph, $G(V, E)$ is defined by two sets: V a finite set of *nodes*; and $E \subseteq V \times V$ a finite set of *edges* (or *links*) between nodes. Formally E specifies a binary relation over nodes of the graph thus if $x, y \in V$ then $(x, y) \in E$ indicates that x 'is-related-to' y. Semantic nets extend this purely structural form by additionally associating a *content* with each node in a graph and by explicitly labelling links with some named relation e.g 'is-a', 'is-the-parent-of' etc. The differences between the use of semantic nets to support knowledge representation in expert systems and as a model of documents in hypertext lie in the nature of what constitutes the node content and in the mathematical properties of the labelling relations. It should be noted that the concepts of *node content* and *labelling relation* are rarely (if ever) specified in a precise manner.

Expert systems utilise precisely defined relations between entities in the knowledge base since their extension can be computed from the system: this is essential if the reasoning process driven by the inference engine is to yield conclusions which are both sound and consistent. Hypertext systems are based on some form of semantic net, but very often the relations represented by the links in this net are not defined with any great precision, rather relying on the subjective connotations of any labelling present to convey the meaning. Thus, for example, a typical net may use a relation *'is-a'* to link nodes without making it clear whether this class-superclass relation is intended to be exhaustive, so that any instance of the superclass must be an instance of, at least, one of the sub-classes, or whether it is intended to be exclusive, so that any instance of a superclass must be an instance of, at most, one of the sub-classes. Other decisions about the relations need to be made, and these are not necessarily taken consistently across the whole net. In a hypertext system this tends not to matter too much, since the user of the system can impart intelligence allowing him to recognise and reconcile any inconsistencies that may occur.

If hypertext and expert systems are to be merged into a single system the lack of precision in relations in the former becomes unacceptable. The expert system will apply its computation-based understanding of relations to the more loosely used relations of the semantic net within the hypertext system, with the inevitable result that some uses of these relations will be inappropriate. Therefore it is essential that at least some of the relations employed in the two systems, namely those on which the systems will interact, should be harmonised through some common model. This means that the use of the relations in the hypertext system must be based on some definition of those relations, and this definition must correspond to the computational behaviour of the expert system. The question thus becomes one of how we are to express the precise definitions of these relations and how such expressions are to be made operational when constructing the systems. An ambiguous relation cannot be used as if it were unambiguous without unwanted conclusions being drawn (or desired conclusions not being drawn), whereas an unambiguous relation can be catered for in a system which uses that relation in other senses also. The sentence "every student uses a computer" is ambiguous in that every student may use a different computer if they all have micros, or they may all use the same computer where they use a mainframe. This distinction must be made if we formalise the sentence into predicate logic, and different conclusions will follow, according to the choice made. In natural language, however, the ambiguity can be allowed to pass, relying on the reader to understand the intended meaning according to the context and his judgement. The first concern, therefore, must be to provide a means for making the relationships within the hypertext system precise, and in such a way that this conformity with the chosen interpretation can be imposed on the system builder.

To facilitate analysis of expertext we present a simple, formal model of *Expertext*, E, as a sextuple:

$$E = (\Sigma; H; B; \pi; \tau_{HH}; \tau_{HB})$$

where

Σ is a finite alphabet of text symbols.

H is a finite set of *headers* (cf. § 1.4).

$B \subseteq \Sigma^*$ is a finite set of text blocks.

$\pi \subseteq H \times B$

$\tau_{HH} \subseteq H \times H \times \Sigma^*$

$\tau_{HB} \subseteq H \times B \times \Sigma^*$.

In the broadest sense a *header* may be viewed as any computable function which can be composed with other functions via the operator specified in the link between two *headers*. To make the interpretation more concrete, we suggest that a *header* be viewed as the antecedent or consequent of a rule. The ordered triple (h_1, h_2, implies) in τ_{HH} means that h_1 implies h_2. $\pi \subseteq H \times B$ is a *pairing relation* which associates with each header in H a *single* text block in B. Note that, although the situation may rarely arise in practice, a single text block can occur with two or more distinct headers. τ_{HH} is the set of header-to-header links each of which is labelled with a (possibly null) relation name. τ_{HB} specifies the set of header-to-block links which are taken to be bidirectional so that an explicit representation of block-to-header links is not required. The sub-structure (H, τ_{HH}), call it *ES*, may be viewed as encoding an expert reasoning process. If this sub-structure *ES* is only browsed by the user, then *E* reduces to a hypertext system.

To construct *ES*, one must focus on what τ_{HH} means and bring ambiguities into the open. When *headers* are not constrained to rule antecedents and consequents and τ_{HH} is not limited to *implies*, inferencing still requires that τ_{HH} is consistent throughout the graph. Furthermore the specification of general properties of τ_{HH}, such as symmetry and transitivity, may allow some links to be added automatically, both relieving some of the burden of constructing the graph and avoiding any unintended oversight of such relationships.

Given precise definitions for the relations used by the hypertext system, an expert system could be constructed using these definitions. It is not necessary that both systems contain precisely the same set of relations, but it is necessary that there be an intersection, and the extension of this intersection known, since relations falling outside of the intersection must be used exclusively by the one system. The possibility of relations appropriate to one system only needs to be allowed since it may well be that imprecise relations are of some utility in the hypertext system, which will make their use desirable, and the expert system may make use of internal relations of little interest to the hypertext system. It is thought also that availability of precise, applicable definitions of a relevant set of relations will help to clarify the thoughts of the expert systems builder, and thus produce a better product. If, however, the systems are to be linked, it must be done on the basis of shared interpretation of the relations used by both systems. This requires that the interpretation be made determinate within the hypertext system and this interpretation employed in the expert system.

The development, modification and extension of classes of expertext nets could be controlled in a natural way by specifying formal systems of graph modification rules. There is a good deal of current interest in using graphs to express a formal model of an electronic document. This line of thought has been extended by Koo (1989) to include the notion of a set of graph modification rules which can be used to express the conditions under which modifications (additions and deletions) to documents can be made. Rules for certain classes of documents have been produced in Bench-Capon and Dunne (1989). These ideas could be fruitfully applied to the construction of hypertext systems. There is no reason why the construction of the graph should not be governed by the use of a set of graph modification rules. Thus each relation used in the semantic net would be associated with a set of rules saying when a link expressing such a relation could be added to the graph, and when deleted. These rules would specify such things as the node types which such a relation could link and whether the relation was one-to many, one-to-one, or many-to-one.

3. Applications of Expertext

The expertext model can be applied to problems which can be modeled using either hypertext or expert systems. Expertext models can also be applied in the many other areas including computer assisted instruction (CAI) and database systems. We now explore how expertext can be applied to electronic directories and document generation.

3.1. Electronic Yellow Pages

Electronic directories, such as the Electronic Yellow Pages (EYP), are becoming increasingly popular media for providing access to large and diverse bodies of information. The purpose of the *Yellow Pages*, whether in electronic or paper form, is to provide the consumer with easy access to information about the availability of products and services. An EYP has the ability to provide many additional features that a paper Yellow Pages can not. Extended features include access to current, up-to-date product and service information; multiple indexing and cross referencing schemes; advertisements which incorporate graphics, sound and animation; and intelligent guides to assist the consumer in locating a supplier of a product or service which can best meet the consumer's needs.

In France, the government has taken a leading role in making electronic information services more readily available. An EYP is accessible to all customers of the French Minitel System (Stoner, 1988). British Telecom has installed an on-line EYP for London. Use of the system requires a personal computer or terminal, a modem and an identification code number. The EYP data is stored in a relational database and includes a menu-driven interface. In another EYP project the consumer to may browse the directory in hypertext or relational database form, as well as view fully-animated colour advertisements backed by stereo sound (Woo, 1989). Consumers can search the directory by locale, hours of operation, specific products or services, specific brand names, method of payment required, available modes of product delivery, accreditation by profession or civic organisations, etc.

An example of the type of dialog that a consumer might have with an EYP is as follows:

Consumer: I want to find a store in the City Centre area which sells Singer sewing machines, is open at 7pm on Thursday and will accept payment by VISA or ACCESS.

EYP: Sorry, there are no businesses available which meet all of your requests. Might I suggest instead:

Machines Inc. in the City Centre sells sewing machines and is open at 7pm; however they do not sell Singer brands or accept any credit cards.

Sewing Unlimited in the City Centre sells Singer sewing machines but is only open from 10am to 5pm Monday through Friday. They accept both VISA and ACCESS.

The Big Store in Huyton sells Singer sewing machines and is open until 10pm. They accept both VISA and ACCESS.

Would you like to view any of these advertisements?

An expertext design of a multimedia EYP using the model presented in § 2 may include a block B for each individual advertisement. Just as it is easy for the user to get "lost" while using a paper *Yellow Pages* directory, without careful planning the navigation problem could be compounded in an electronic version. Expert systems controls can provide an expert navigator which guides the consumer through the relevant portions of the EYP.

Each advertisement *block* will include propositions in its *header* that characterise the advertisement, such as store name, store type, phone number, and address. There need not be explicit links between the *header* of an advertisement block and any other header. But expertise is implicit in the header-header relations. For example a header for "grocery store" might be connected to a header for "store". More generally, a hierarchy of business types could be represented as rules like "grocery store implies store".

The headers may include production rules which are used to narrow the search space of EYP advertisements to a set which meets the consumer's needs. Rules can be used to query the user for information as to which product or service they require, which brand they prefer, whether hours of operation are important, in which locale they prefer to do business, if method of payment is relevant, etc. Once the search space includes only those advertisements which meet the consumer's needs, another level of rules can check to see that the number of advertisers presented to the consumer is a reasonable size (e.g. that there is at least one business, but not more than 20 in the presentation set). If the presentation set is empty, the system may remove some search criteria such as locale or hours of operation and tell the consumer that no business exists which can exactly meet his/her needs; however, a business in another locale is available. The "expert system" part of the expertext system can interact with the user to arrive at a set of advertisement blocks for viewing.

In this example, the expertise has been rather isolated from the text. The expertise can be represented as a set of rules within the framework of E in § 2. In the extreme case, the headers which contain rules about searching have empty text blocks associated with them, and the headers that are directly linked to advertisement blocks may not participate in header-header relations. To further develop the EYP as expertext the rules and text might be more intimately connected.

The EYP can readily be used to illustrate an extension to the model in § 2. Not only can the definition of B be extended to include sound and animation, but the definition of a block can be extended to include more embedded headers pointing to other blocks. In this case a block stores information in hypermedia form. The consumer can browse through different elements in one advertisement block. For example, a block B for an business advertisement may appear as in Figure 2. Such an EYP is made more commercially viable by the availability of readable-writable laser disk devices.

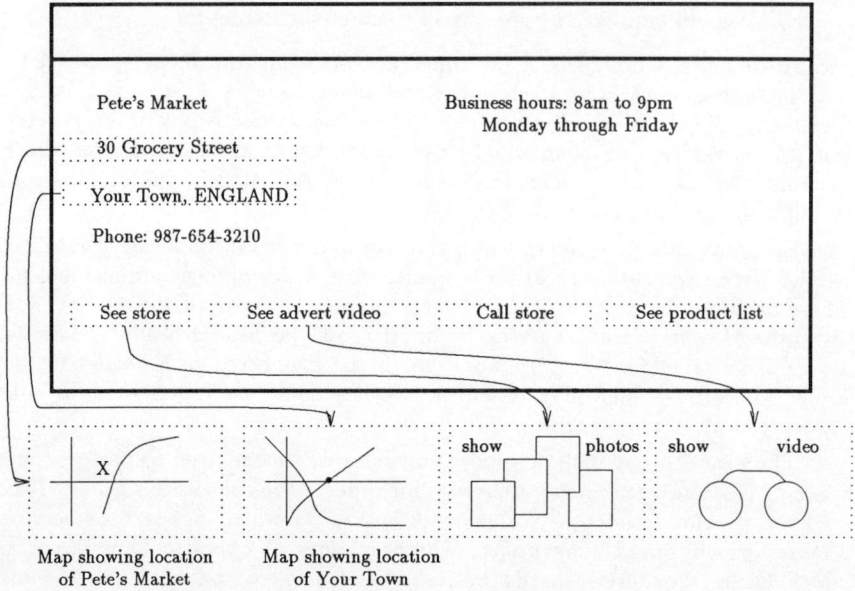

Figure 2: Information within a block *B* may include pointers to other blocks. A block may contain graphics, sound, and video.

3.2. Document Generation

Many of the difficulties with managing large documents are caused by the author having a different conceptual view than that of the reader. This means that tools intended to support authors are usually very difficult for readers to use. The opposite is also true. A number of document management systems (e.g ANDREW from Carnegie-Mellon University Information Technology Center) provide a partial model for overcoming these problems. These systems separate the storage model from the visualisation of the document. This allows the document to be displayed in the most appropriate form for its current use. Several representations include

- an outline of major headings,
- a network representation of the links in the semantic net, and
- part of the actual text.

Any of these can then be displayed on the same, or different screens, and can be automatically updated, in unison. The expertext architecture provides the means by which a author interface can be designed.

There are a number of instances of documents, which need to be customised, depending on which class of reader is to be addressed. An example is an undergraduate project report which consists of:

- the project itself,
- a systems manual,
- a programming manual, and
- a proposed Physics practical.

The last three were generated from the first, with about two thirds of the contents being extracted at least once. Expertext allows these derived documents to be generated from a single document network by following a different set of links through the network (see Figure 3). This can be implemented by providing a different set of rules (forming a document template) to the inference engine.

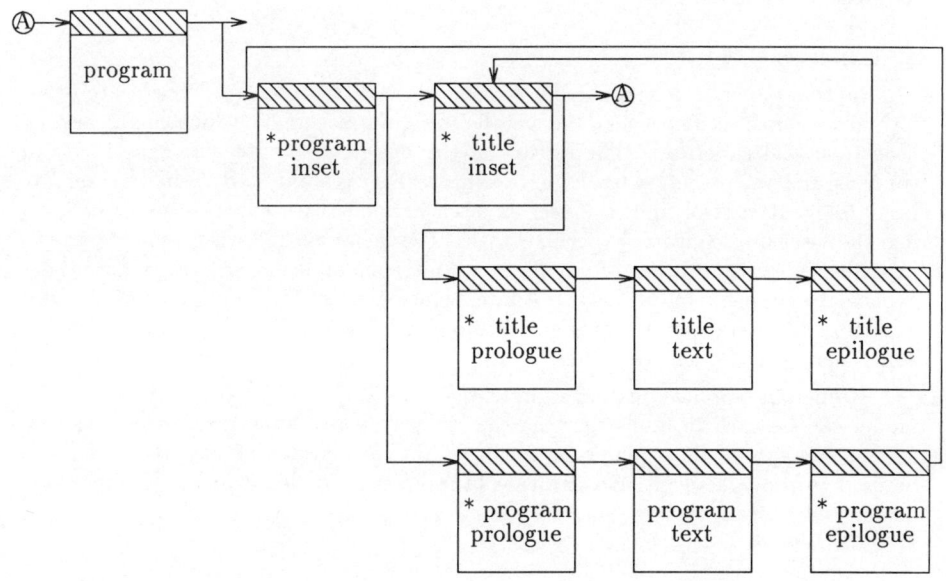

Figure 3: The text blocks whose header is marked with * are automatically generated by the program template.

The links between headers may be interpreted as implication links. Rules embedded in headers, not here pictured, would say that a certain type of search should be followed to produce a certain document. Figure 3 suggests a depth-first search and when the traversal returns to an already visited header, the text block associated with that header is not printed again.

One class of authoring tools that has received considerable attention in recent times involves the work of collaborating authors. The problem is to merge texts from several sources, and to provide the means for version control. An additional requirement is to allow co-authors to maintain both private notes and public comments that will be seen by the other members of the team. All these might be better maintained using expertext methodology, whereas the multiplicity of link types would make such a system difficult to control in a conventional hypertext system.

Other problems in using hypertext methodology for cooperative writing are related to the need to maintain a coherent, permanent representation of the document. It is not adequate to lock the complete document whenever an amendment is to be made, as no advantage over conventional file management techniques is obtained. It is necessary to maintain the document in such a way that only the minimum restrictions on access are required. This can be enforced within expertext by locking only those records that are to be modified and allowing other authors and readers access to the rest of the document. This is similar to conventional database technology.

4. Expertext's Future

In this paper, a formal model for expertext was presented. There are other formalisms such as Petri nets and parallel program schemata which might also be used to model expertext. The essence of the design is to integrate expert system controls and inferencing with hypertext browsing capability. Rather than removing intelligent control from the user as often happens with expert systems or leaving the user to navigate hypertext with little help as happens with hypertext, expertext offers a sharing of intelligence and control between the user and the expertext system. Such a sharing of intelligence and control may allow people and expertext to interact in a synergistic fashion such that they produce work of value which neither could generate alone.

Numerous applications for expertext are yet to be explored. The expertext model can be used to add expert navigation features to hypertext systems as well as to add hypermedia explanation facilities to expert systems. Expertext can also be used to provide an intelligent means of interacting with and manipulating databases.

5. References

Bench-Capon, T.J.M. & Dunne, P.E.D. (1989). Consistent Graph Modification Systems for Some Classes of Electronic Document. *Report CS/CSCW/1/89*, Computer Science Department, University of Liverpool, Liverpool.

Diaper, D. (1989). Designing expert systems: from Dan to Beersheba *Knowledge Elicitation: Principles, Techniques, and Applications*, ed. D. Diaper, pp. 15-46, Chichester: Ellis Horwood.

Doland, V.M. (1989). Hypermedia as an Interpretative Act. *Hypermedia, 1, 1,* 6-19.

Halasz, F.G. (1988). Reflections on Notecards: Seven Issues for the Next Generation of Hypermedia Systems. *Communications of the Association of Computing Machinery, 31, 7,* 836-55.

Koo R. (1989). A Model for Electronic Documents. *ACM SIGOIS Bulletin*, 10, 1, 23-33.

Morton, J. & Bekerian, D. (1986). Three Ways of Looking at Memory. In *Advances in Cognitive Science*, ed. N.E. Sharkey, pp. 43-71, Chichester: Ellis Horwood.

Rada, R. (1989). Writing and Reading Hypertext: An Overview. *Journal American Society Information Science, 40, 3*, 164-171.

Rada, R. & Barlow, J. (1988). Expert Systems and Hypertext. *The Knowledge Engineering Review, 3*, no.4, pp. 285-301.

Rada, R. & Barlow, J. (1989). Expertext: Expert Systems and Hypertext. To appear in *Proceedings of EXSYS 89*, Paris: IITT-International.

Raskin, J. (1987). The Hype in Hypertext. In *Hypertext '87*, pp. 325-30. Chapel Hill: University of North Carolina.

Shortliffe, E., Scott, A., Bishcoff, M., Campbel, A., van Melle, W., & Jacobs, C. (1981). ONCOCIN: Expert System for Oncology Protocol Management. In *Proceedings International Joint Conference Artificial Intelligence*, pp 876-881.

Stoner, M. (1988). French Connections with Minitel: The Future Has Arrived in France. *Online, 12*, no. 2, 67-70.

Timpka, T. (1986). LIMEDS Knowledge-Based Decision Support for General Practitioners: An Integrated Design. In *Proceedings Tenth Annual Symposium on Computer Applications in Medical Care*, pp. 394-402. IEEE Computer Society.

Woo, S. (1989). CD ROM Technology Prototypes Advanced Yellow Pages. *Pioneers of Innovation: The Research Magazine of U S WEST, 3, 1*, 19-23.

LUST FOR LIFE:
DEVELOPING EXPERT SYSTEMS FOR LIFE ASSURANCE UNDERWRITING

Fergus Bolger, George Wright, Gene Rowe, John Gammack and Bob Wood.
Bristol Business School and Bristol Transputer Centre, Coldharbour Lane, Frenchay, BRISTOL BS16 1QY. UK.

Abstract

This paper reports the experience of a business school research team in developing an expert system for life assurance underwriting in collaboration with a major UK insurance company. The current underwriting practice and organization within the company concerned is initially outlined by way of background to the expert system project. Next our progress to date on the LUST underwriting training system is described along with the business case for such a system and development details. Some pros and cons of the approach taken are then discussed, followed by a consideration of possible future extensions to LUST. Suggested enhancements are justified by our assessment of progress on two other underwriting expert sytems, and through analysis of business advantages for the insurance company relative to development costs. Finally we derive some knowledge engineering lessons from our experience, and draw some conclusions regarding future strategy for applied AI.

1. Introduction

This paper summarizes our progress in a collaborative expert system project between a polytechnic business school and a major insurance company. In it we describe the nature and operation of the underwriting training system we have developed, discuss possible future directions, and indicate some of the lessons we have learnt regarding expert system development for insurance.

1.1 Life Underwriting

The New Business A department (NBA) is part of the New Business and Records Division of XX Insurance. Reporting to NBA are two groups of branch offices located in the north of England.
The responsibilities of NBA include those which result from the receipt of life proposals through to issuing policy documents. These responsibilities entail underwriting proposals (ie coming to decisions), transferring policy details onto records, and issuing the policies. NBA do not have contact with clients except through the branches.
Independent Financial Advisors (IFA's) send completed proposal forms from their clients on to the branches. Clerical staff in the branches assess each proposal form and decide whether to accept the proposal as it stands and then send it on to NBA, or make no decision but send it directly to NBA.
The clerical staff in the branches make these underwriting decisions on the basis of a manual provided by NBA which

contains information about unacceptable and acceptable proposals. For example, if the proposal form contains the word 'ulcerative colitis' the manual instructs the clerk as to what medical evidence to collect, if any. In addition, the branches have financial limits on proposals for which the collection of medical evidence is compulsory. Details of proposals are entered into a computer system at the branches by clerks. This system provides a check list to ensure that the clerical staff do not overlook any important details on the proposal forms.

There are approximately 80 people with underwriting capabilities within the New Business departments. Of these, only 10 can evaluate any proposal - irrespective of proposed amount assured or medical evidence. The remaining underwriters are placed in one of 9 discretionary bands determined by size of sum assured and the complexity of the medical evidence required. The basic task of an under-

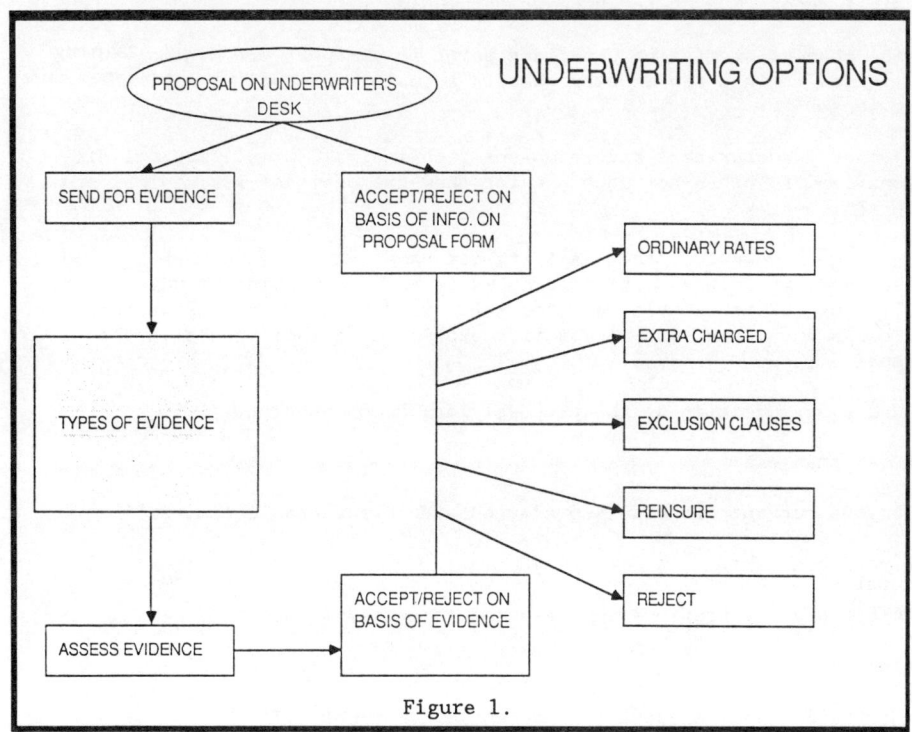

Figure 1.

writer is to decide whether the proposal can be accepted at standard premium rates, can be accepted at increased premium rates, or must be declined (see Figures 1 and 2).

Almost 95% of proposals are accepted at standard rates and 4.5% are accepted at increased premium rates. Of all the proposals received, 60% are currently accepted at standard rates at branch level with no medical evidence. On average, the New Business departments see medical evidence on 20% of all proposals. The underwriters also ask for medical examinations on particular proposers as deemed necessary. Overall 3,500 proposals pass through XX Insurance's New Business departments each week, and over half these proposals involve two lives.

1.2. How is underwriting performed?

The chief underwriter at XX Insurance noted that ''it comes down to feel''. Some rules of thumb that can apply include:

''If the writing on a proposal is shaky and the proposer is young it could be Parkinson's Disease. We'll need medical evidence''.

''If the applicant has an artistic occupation he might be susceptible to lifestyle risks''.

And some other insightful comments:

''A good underwriter will home in on the two key words in the medical report...a junior underwriter wouldn't''.

''The chances of missing a salient point in a report are minimal but I'll find it in a few minutes whereas a junior underwriter will take a lot longer''.

''Junior underwriters have problems with medical terms...medical dictionaries are often not much use for they are designed for medical students''.

However, the majority of the underwriters work is routine and explicitly expressed as rules in underwriting manuals. The following is an example of the sort of rules used by underwriters, although they are not necessarily expressed in this manner in the manuals:

''Has every question on the proposal form been answered?''

If yes then ask:

''Is the current proposal sum assured within acceptable limits?''

If yes then ask:

''Are there any previous sums assured in force?''

If no ask:

''Are height and weight within acceptable parameters?''

etc.

1.3. How do junior underwriters learn their job?

The chief underwriter noted that mostly this occurs in one-to-one conversations between more experienced underwriters and their juniors which are generally instigated when difficulties occur. This learning process is time consuming and inefficient. In addition, evaluations by senior underwriters as to when juniors may be given greater discretion may be relatively arbitrary, since there is no formal assessment of competence and different seniors may disagree (Bolger, Wright and Rowe, 1989). See Figure 2.

1.4. The proposed system.

The proposed system was to model the procedures used by a senior underwriter as s/he makes an underwriting decision. The expert

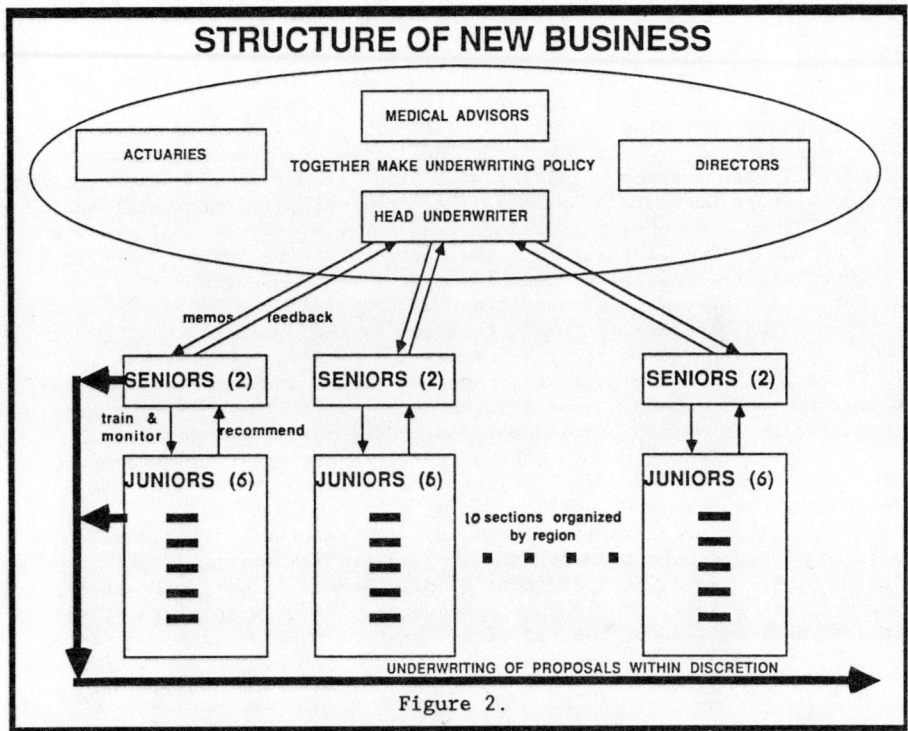

Figure 2.

system will then act as a training device that will be available to junior underwriters. In practice, the system will guide a trainee in a step-by-step fashion as he or she works through proposal information. The trainee will respond to the system's questions via a keyboard and the system will provide explanations of the rationale for each step in the evaluation and the relevance of the particular material that the trainee has entered into the system.

2. The Life Underwriting Training System (LUST)

The overall conception was of a system that would be used by new entrants to XX Insurance who possessed little or no knowledge of life assurance underwriting.

The function of the system is to train underwriters up to a level where they can:
- assess those proposals which can be accepted/rejected at once
- assess when further evidence is required, and what form this evidence should take.

The system was NOT designed to train underwriters in determining the appropriate underwriting action on the basis of evidence returned. It must also be emphasized that the system is NOT capable of automatically making decisions on proposals in its current form.

Trainee underwriters interact with the system which recommends a course, or courses, of action with respect to a particular proposal under consideration by the trainee. The system interrogates the trainee about details on the proposal form, and will finally suggest the action(s) which the trainee should take.

Extensive help screens are provided which the trainee is able to consult in order to establish the rationale for considering particular sections of the proposal form. Rationales for the final recommendation are also given. The system ensures that the trainee will both become familiar with the structure of the proposal form and gain an understanding of XX's ''philosophy of underwriting''. To achieve these outcomes the trainee uses the system to evaluate a series of dummy and live cases. The former are necessary in order to ensure that the trainee becomes familiar with some of the less common, but potentially significant, types of proposal.

The benefits of such a training system include:

i. Increased consistency of underwriting decisions throughout the New Business sections at XX, and to prevent the perpetuation of inconsistencies which occur within the current apprentice-master relationship between novices and senior underwriters.

ii. Reduction in the currently heavy training demands on senior under writers, thereby allowing them more time to concentrate on underwriting the most problematic proposals.

iii. Acceleration of the pace of training so that more, and more highly skilled underwriters become available more quickly.

iv. Saving expenditure by preventing inexperienced staff sending for evidence when it is not required, ie when any form of returned evidence will not substantially alter premium rates. Send-

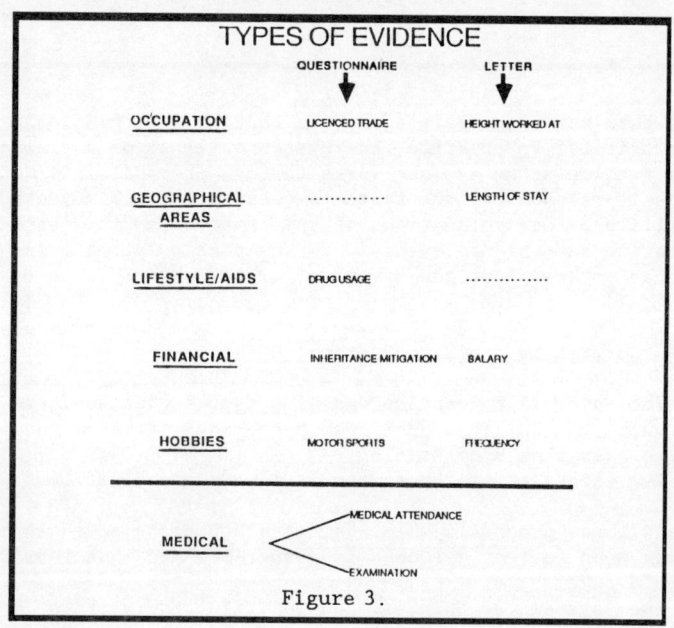

Figure 3.

ing for unnecessary additional evidence costs money and causes unwarranted delays in decision making on some proposals.

v. Increased speed of response to new or changing risks since the expert system can be easily modified or enlarged to allow reliable dissemination of new information.

The training system was written as six separate modules corresponding to the domains identified at an early stage of knowledge elicitation from a senior underwriter. These six modules are listed in Figure 3.

Each module is encoded as a knowledge base written in the KES (Knowledge Engineering System) expert system shell. All the knowledge bases are written as production systems with heirarchical attribute structures. The smallest knowledge base (AIDS) consists of approximately 30 rules whilst the largest (MEDICAL) consists of around 150 rules. The six modules are linked together sequentially in a manner corresponding to the typical approach taken by a senior underwriter when assessing a proposal form. The user front-end is a window environment with separate windows for dialogue with the system, help/ explanations, and recommendations.

The knowledge elicitation was performed by between 1 and 3 (normally two) knowledge engineers at any one time. Participating in the knowledge elicitation was, of course, at least one 'expert'. Usually the expert was the same senior underwriter although other underwriters at lower levels of discretion were also involved. In some instances upto three underwriters participated interactively in a single knowledge elicitation exercise. Knowledge elicitation techniques included structured and unstructured interviews, card sorts, repertory grids, and context focussing (see, for example, Wright and Ayton, 1987).

The knowledge thus elicited was then represented in the forms of decision trees or, in the case of the financial and medical knowledge bases, as matrices (see Gammack, Battle and Stephens, 1989). These intermediate representations were then coded as prototype knowledge bases within KES.

After debugging, the prototype knowledge bases were individually tested by both the 'expert' senior underwriter and by junior underwriters (the latter being the potential users of the system). Both the intermediate representations and the knowledge bases were modified in the light of suggestions arising out of this extensive testing of the prototype modules. The whole system, comprising the linked knowledge bases, is currently (June 1989) being tested by the underwriters and modifications are continuing to be made.

The intermediate representations, cross-referenced to printouts of the knowledge bases, serve as documentation for the system. An example of a dialogue with one of the modules is given in Figure 4, along with the corresponding documentation.

It should be noted that a certain amount of interpretation and judgement is required on the part of the user (e.g. with respect to allocation of occupation, ailment, hobby etc. to particular pre-set categories). This is one reason why the system as it stands cannot be used for automatic underwriting. It was felt that from a training viewpoint it is important to make explicit certain categories relevant to risk assessment. Thus, for example, trainees learn that certain types of occupation which can be described as ''administrative'' entail little or no risk and therefore can be accepted at ordinary rates with no evidence sent for. Conversely, occupa-

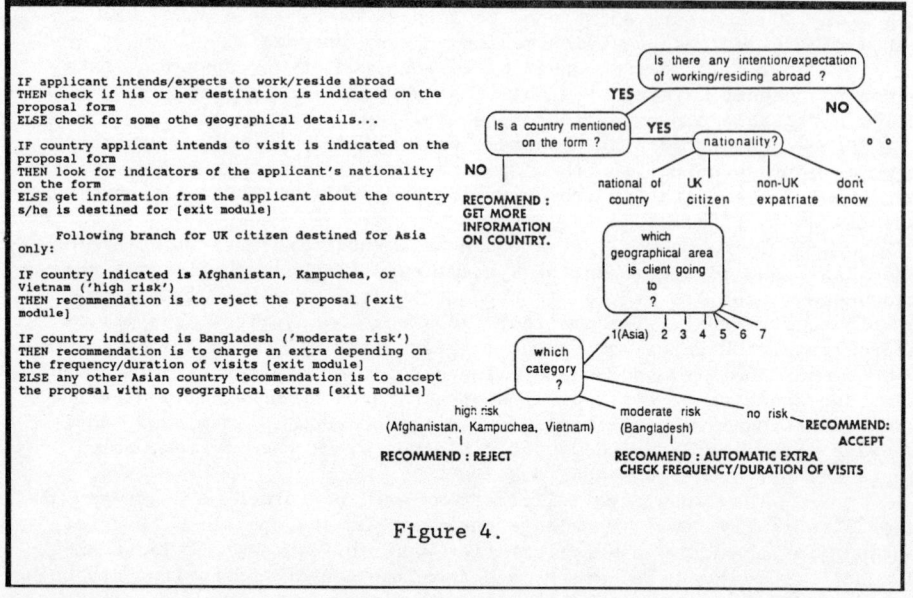

Figure 4.

tions falling in the categories of "sport" or "entertainment" may involve certain lifestyle risks (e.g. travelling abroad, drink and drugs, AIDS etc.) and consequently may require further evidence to be sought depending on other details given on the proposal form. These categories were validated with junior underwriters to ensure a low rate of mis-categorization: lists of examplars of categories are provided on-line to a similar end.

The issue of the feasability of providing the exhaustive lists of occupations, ailments, hobbies etc. required by a fully automatic underwriting system is addressed in the next section.

3. Discussion of LUST

3.1. Why choose underwriting?

From an initial feasability study within XX Insurance where several expert system applications were considered, life underwriting seemed to have the most potential for various reasons:

- Much of underwriting practice is already expressed as rules which are explicitly stated in reference manuals
- As indicated above there is still a subjective or judgemental aspect to underwriting which means that a statistical approach alone would not be feasible (see Bolger, Wright and Rowe, 1989)
- As we have seen there are distinct stages to underwriting as it is currently practised at XX Insurance so it is relatively easy to break up the domain into manageable components
- A good business case exists for the training system and for certain automatic underwriting systems
- There are currently no useable underwriting sytems available as far as we know from the literature.

3.2. Why a training system?

As we have indicated there is currently no formal training system in operation at XX. The existing apprenticeship is expensive and may lead to inconsistencies being perpetuated (op cit). Further, by focussing on the training aspect it is possible to restrict the expert system to coping with some of the less problematic proposals ie those which are normally left to junior underwriters.

As we have seen, the training nature of the system means that it is desirable to leave some of the reasoning to the user. This obviously reduces the amount of data and rules that one must build into the expert system.

3.3. A modular approach

Building an expert system in the modular manner of LUST has both some advantages and disadvantages.

The advantages are that individual modules are essentially small, self-contained expert systems. This makes their development easy and, since they are relatively simple to understand, any modifications to the modules raises few difficulties. Adding additional modules in order to extend the system is also a fairly simple matter.

The disadvantages of the modular approach include difficulties of linking modules so that consitency is maintained within a single session. For example, we found that it was necessary to allow data transfer between modules in order to relieve the user from having to repeatedly enter the same data regarding e.g. age, sum assured, and length of policy. This problem we found easiest to overcome by allowing KES to read from and write to a data file common to all modules. This also proved useful for providing an overall summary of proposal details and recommendations at the end of each session.

A second disadvantage of the modular approach is the difficulty of encoding interactions between modules e.g. if the applicant is a journalist and travelling abroad then an extra might need to be charged whereas either of these factors individually may be acceptable at standard rates. In other words, the present modular approach could mean that a number of small risks which are individually acceptable, but together unacceptable to a senior underwriter, could slip through the system. At the moment LUST avoids this problem by warning the user of these possible connections within each relevant module (ie in the above example warnings would be given in the Occupations and Geographical modules). However, this is not ideal and would be of little use to an automatic system - some superordinate program of, for example, demons might be one solution. However, from our discussions with underwriters the number of interactions at the level of discretion LUST currently trains to are relatively few although they would become a serious issue if the system were to be extended to the assessment of evidence returned.

4. Extensions to LUST

As indicated above, the current expert system is restricted to training underwriters up to the level where they know when to send out for further evidence, and the sort of evidence to be acquired. Various extensions to the current system can be envisaged. We do not believe that a straight extension of the current system, to train in the assessment of all returned medical evidence ie medical attendence and examination reports, is a viable commercial proposition. Our belief is justified by our recent evaluation of the ARIES life underwriting demonstrator system (Chamberlain, Neale and Khan, 1989). This demonstrator took two person-years to develop and only gives advice on underwriting ischaemic heart disease. The on-line demonstration of the system-user interaction we saw took 25 minutes to complete for just one part of one proposal. Therefore, unlike LUST, ARIES does not seem broad enough either to train underwriters up to a particular level of discretion, nor could it be adapted to automatically process proposals without being extended to cover numerous other ailments. We believe that such extensions would take considerable development time extrapolating from the time so far taken.

In view of this we will focus on some alternatives which avoid lengthy interactions with the user by means of automatizing parts of the underwriting process.

One option would be to attempt to automatize the <u>entire</u> underwriting process. Details from proposal forms could be entered to the system by a clerk with no underwriting experience. Evidence would automatically be sent for where required with details from medical reports, questionnaires etc. again entered into the system by a clerk (the system could automatically keep track of proposals as they progressed through the phases of underwriting). Finally, the system could issue policies and keep records of all underwriting business to be checked against future proposals and claims.

From our discussions with underwriters, reading of the literature, and review of other systems it seems that to build such a system would be quite an extensive knowledge-engineering exercise. The example of the Nippon Life expert system (Intellicorp, 1988) suggests that a system capable of handling 90% of cases requiring medical evidence would need in excess of 2,000 rules i.e. over 5 times the number currently utilized by the training system. These new rules would have to be elicited from senior underwriters therefore requiring a substantial investment in terms of their time. It would also take us at least one man year (extrapolating from the time spent developing the training system) to code-up, test, and document such a system.

Although manpower investment from underwriters and developers is not an automatic deterrent to such a system, the cost of following such a course may not be justified by the results. This is partly because the technical success of such a project is uncertain. For example, it is unclear whether the existing hardware (PC's) and software (KES) would be able to cope with a system of this size, and if so whether the system would be fast enough to be usable (the Nippon Life system utilized the much larger and more powerful KEE system running on a VAX 8350). It is possible that in order to achieve satisfactory performance on available hardware a radically different software environment may be needed.

The business case for complete automation of the underwriting process is also controversial. On the one hand increased speed and consistency of processing applications should improve the service to the customer and thereby provide XX Insurance with a competitive edge. On the other hand, in addition to the question of whether full automation is technically realizable, is the issue of maintainability. Who would maintain the system? Who would take over if the system failed? Who would be responsible for making new underwriting policy? In view of these problems it seems that at least some skilled underwriters would have to be employed. This produces a redundancy of underwriting expertise, the expense of which, along with development costs, has to be traded against the advantages of speed and consistency of underwriting.

In sum, it is unlikely that such a system would enable fully automated underwriting in the forseeable future, and the costs of development and maintainance may outweigh the advantages of completely automated underwriting. In view of this we believe that this option is perhaps better regarded as a research project.

Perhaps a more realistic approach would be to convert the current system from a training aid to a system which would automatically assess proposals.

This would be a system which automatically assesses both when evidence is required *and* the type of evidence to send for. Such a system could be responsible for composing personalized letters and questionnaires, and sending them to the customers, IFA's, or branches as appropriate. Assessment of evidence returned from these sources would still be assessed by human underwriters whose task could be assisted by an extended training system or decision aid. The existing training system would still be required in order to train underwriters up to the level where they can learn to assess evidence. Alternatively, or in addition, further non-medical information could be sought by on-line questioning of the proposed life assured or his/her agent.

A further enhancement would be to add modules to enable the evaluation of additional non-medical evidence which would be returned in response to automated dispatch of questionnaires/ letters or in response to on-line questionning of the proposed life/ assured or his/her agent.

This system would be relatively easy to implement, at least from a software development point of view. Little more knowledge elicitation would be required (unless enhancements to the current training system were envisaged), therefore underwriters' time would not be used. The main programming task would be to embed the knowledge bases within existing systems so that the expert system could read proposal information from a data-capture system such as the one already existing in branches, write to the case-management system currently under development, and interface to mail-merge systems so as to send out policies or letters of rejection as appropriate. Some small modifications to the existing knowledge bases would be required but the main burden of programming could be performed in-house by XX Insurance's IS department.

The main additions to the existing expert system would be lists of occupations, ailments, hobbies etc. so that the system could take over the task of making risk categorizations which are currently left to the user. With the possible exception of medical details, this should not be a particularly onerous task. Our discussions with underwriters suggest that lists would not have to be enormous in order to cover the vast majority of cases. Further, our communications with the developers of the KES system make it clear that such lists could be read by the expert system from standard database files which means that the original lists, and any future changes, could easily be entered by secretarial staff with no programming experience.

The system should be able to to deal with approximately 20% of cases <u>above</u> those already underwritten at branch level thereby allowing around 80% of cases to be underwritten automatically (ie those requiring no assessment of medical evidence).

It has been estimated that the proposed automatic system will give substantial savings to XX Insurance purely on the basis of a reduction of unnecessary medical evidence sent for. Of course, the extent of savings will depend on striking the correct balance between being under- and over-cautious with respect to risk retention. However, we are confident that our knowledge engineering techniques coupled with our empirical research into underwriting (see Bolger, Wright and Rowe, 1989; Wright and Ayton, 1987; Gammack, Battle and Stephens, 1989) will allow us to strike this balance correctly. It should be noted that substantial financial benefits should also accrue to XX due to the increased share of business resulting from the virtually immediate assessment of the majority of proposals which this system permits.

5. Knowledge Engineering Lessons

By way of a summary, some of the things we have learnt in the course of the project include:
- pick a do-able domain, think small!
- it is essential to have at least one willing expert
- access to a range of experts with varying degrees of expertise is useful
- it is important to involve the users in the development process
- often it is useful to use two or three knowledge engineers at the same time (one can record/monitor the situation and think of tactics while the other(s) interact with the expert)
- be prepared to try a variety of knowledge elicitation techniques and be inventive (having a 'spare' knowledge engineer helps here too)
- finding the best intermediate representation for the task is highly important (it may be necessary to create a representation 'de novo' if existing methods are unsuitable)
- choose a shell which can grow with you
- taking a modular approach to system development has many benefits which probably outweight the disadvantages.

6. Conclusions

From our experience, the 'knowledge acquisition bottleneck' referred to by Feigenbaum (1979) is not now a major barrier to profitable commercial expert systems because many powerful techniques exist. Rather, the major constraint is the reluctance of executives and DP managers to invest in 'unproven' technology. Applied AI may have regained respectability amongst academia, but deep-seated fears remain in business and industrial communities. Our belief is that the solution to commercial technophobia lies in getting as many viable (profitable and maintainable) expert systems up and running as soon as possible.

Such a goal is unlikely to be opposed in principle, however, one might be led to believe from certain quarters that such a goal is impossible in practice. For example, in a recent newspaper article, Donald Michie (1989) stated:

"To simulate expert skill in industrial strength problems, something in the range 4,000 to 40,000 rules is typically needed".

We maintain that, if these figures are true for existing expert systems, then knowledge engineers have been focussing on inappropriate problems and consequently it is unsurprising that commercially viable systems are few and far between.

Our maxim is to ''go for the low hanging fruit'' with respect to expert systems applications. The shell-based training system we have described in this paper consists of only a few hundred rules but will save our clients considerable expenditure by virtue of releasing hard-pressed senior underwriters from training duties, and by speeding up the training process so as to allow junior underwriters to conduct more business, more quickly.

Another application we have seen, written in the same shell for a major high-street financial house, provides expert advice in the form of a personalized letter regarding offshore financial arrangements. Such a system is proving its worth in terms of providing the institution concerned with a largely increased share of this particular market. Again this system utilizes much fewer than the 4,000 rules Michie stipulates for a commercially viable system.

We have found that the 'small is beautiful' approach is much more acceptable to DP managers and executives than large-scale research projects. Results are attained quickly, planning and budgeting of projects becomes possible, and the resulting system is understandable to users and consequently maintainable.

One might argue that such systems do not require expert systems technology - this is true - but the important aspects of rapid production, understandability, and modifiability would be difficult if not impossible within a traditional DP lifecycle. Also our system is 'expert' in the sense that it captures human expertise, albeit in a very restricted domain. The secret of building powerful systems with very few rules in our view lies with identifying the correct domain from a business standpoint and embedding the rule-base within existing data-capture, database, statistics, and mail-merge packages.

References

Bolger, F., Wright, G., and Rowe, G. (1989). Expertise: theory and data. Paper presented at SPUDM-12, Moscow, August 1989.

Chamberlain, G., Neale, I. and Khan, M. (1989). TULIP: a life underwriting expert system. Paper presented at ES '89, London, September 1989

Feigenbaum, E.A. (1979). Themes and case studies in knowledge engineering. In Expert systems in the microelectronic age, ed. D. Michie. Edinburgh University Press.

Gammack, J., Battle,S. and Stephens, R. (1989). A knowledge acquisition and representation scheme for constraint based and parallel systems. Paper to be presented at IEEE Cambridge, Mass., November 1989.

Intellicorp (1989).Nippon Life System improves underwriting performance.

Michie, D. (1989). A new neural fever to use our noggins. Computer Guardian, 16 March 1989.

Wright, G., and Ayton, P. (1987). Eliciting and modelling expert knowledge. Decision Support Systems, $\underline{3}$, 13-26.

PORTAFOGLIO: A PORTFOLIO ADVISOR APPLICATION

Andrea Chierici [1], Maria Grazia Filippini [2], Marco Minati [2]

(1) Cassa di Risparmio di Parma - Ufficio Marketing - Strada al Ponte Caprazucca, 4 - 43100 Parma - Italy - Tel.: (39) 521 490490 - (39) 521 490493 - Fax.: (39) 521 490424
(2) Artificial Intelligence Software S.p.A. - Via Rombon, 11 - 20134 Milano - Italy - Tel.: (39) 2 2141230 - (39) 2 2640197 - Fax.: (39) 2 26410744

Abstract

The problem of integration between expert systems and databases in financial services offered to clients has been highlighted by recent interest in the utility of these tools in solving specific problems.
This paper presents PORTAFOGLIO, a portfolio advisor integrated with a bank's computing system. It is a non-prototypal realization of an integrated front-office expert system conceived to support a bank's employee in over-the-counter financial consultancy. PORTAFOGLIOhas a special architecture which supports modularity and integrability according to the guide-lines followed during the development of the system: *evolution* instead of revolution, *integration* instead of isolation, *open* instead of closed architecture.
This work describes not only technical choices but also the advantages, disadvantages, and economic implications of the application.

1. Introduction

For many financial domains requiring high-level expertise in problem-solving, there exist applicative and methodological solutions in Artificial Intelligence (AI) which are valid alternatives to traditional computing systems [11]: recent experience in the design and realization of Expert Systems has consolidated this trend, and a market which is constantly expanding has attracted a great deal of research.
Professional fields such as finance and banking already use computer support systems for some everyday tasks. One of the most decisive factors in this trend has been the spread of Personal Computers (PC) as low-cost tools easily connected to networks. Consequently it is important to preserve the existing culture concerning the use of traditional tools on PC, integrating them with new and more powerful technologies: the main environments for the development of AI systems on PC are now available with interfaces to those kinds of tool.
Moreover, user interfaces supported by Expert Systems on PC are often not as sophisticated as traditional packages: for instance, natural language interfaces (the most suitable for AI applications) are either not available for small computers except as prototypes. In any case, existing Expert System interfaces do not conform to standard protocols (financial case sheets, bureaucratic forms, etc.).
The problem of a coherent integration of conventional and AI systems arises from a design strategy oriented to a more general architectural solution: this work presents one of these architectural solutions developed in a banking field and based on the enhancement of the features of a database by techniques for treatment of knowledge, namely Expert Systems.
The fields of application of expert systems, in banking and finance, usually have the following features:
- A large range of products;
- The need to have many experts in different places;
- Problems in which symbolic reasoning is relevant;
- Problems whose hypotheses change very quickly;
- The need to know the reasoning behind the answers given by the system;

- A unique formula to calculate the results does not exist.
In banking the need to free the most qualified activities from the restrictions imposed by simple data elaboration is becoming more and more urgent.
An area which has attracted much interest is the application of expert systems to financial consultancy.[1][3]
In counselling services it is useful to have, as a daily activity support, a "mechanism" which is able to *determine* algorithms to solve a problem instead of one which simply *executes* algorithms according to a fixed schema.[9]
It is for this reason that knowledge-based systems have proved the most suitable advanced technology for dealing with the dynamic and complex problems deriving from the client-bank relationship in financial consultancy services.
A knowledge-based system which is able to reproduce the methodological approach of the expert can be a valid support, guaranteeing high performance and predisposition to any required updating. In this light, PORTAFOGLIO represents a non-prototypal realization of an integrated expert system conceived to support a bank's employee in over-the-counter financial consultancy. This system has arisen from the need, identified in the Cassa di Risparmio di Parma (CRParma), to improve the services offered to clients, by making them automatic and by distributing expert knowledge in each branch.[12]

2. Expert Systems and Databases: representational vs. architectural problem

The problem of integration between Expert Systems and Databases has been highlighted by recent interest in the utility of these tools in solving specific problems [6]. In the general context of this integration we can distinguish two main trends:

. representational, where Database's performance is enhanced by the possibility of representing not only information but also knowledge (incomplete knowledge, negative knowledge, for instance) using formalisms deriving from basic research in AI knowledge representation, and of employing an inference mechanism (to extract and to use implicit information, draw conclusions from them, etc.), or the Expert System's performance is enhanced by the most important characteristics of Databases (effectiveness in terms of speed, security and reliability of shared-data);

. architectural, where besides specific research regarding the realization of mixed systems [5] architectural solutions for the integration between Expert Systems and Databases can be divided into two categories:

a. systems where Databases need data coming from an expert consultation: for instance, data can be the result of a particular treatment involving specific knowledge processed, in the same way that we can have the result of a complex calculation requiring specialistic knowledge in order to store data in some particular place (See Bandini, Doldi, Lattuada, Malacart: «*Expert Systems integration with databases: the example of STREMO*» in [1]);

b. systems where Expert Systems interrogate Databases in the same way that a human expert consults information sources in taking decisions or solving problems: in this case Databases are seen as containers of information.

In the work described here we are mainly interested in this last category, and the design of the system PORTAFOGLIO has been influenced by this. The architectural strategy of the proposed system comes from the realization of an Expert System which consults Databases in order to produce more qualitative information. In fact, the selected financial field concerns the evaluation of clients intending to invest money by acquiring stocks and shares, and the counselling of an adequate portfolio. This task is performed by an advisory activity, which requires interpretation of the client's situation and investment goals, and the analysis of the product classes which best satisfy these needs, by means of specialistic expertise often based on heuristic knowledge.
The design of a support system for investment consultancy must take into account the availability of information concerning financial products on a PC Database (Focus [2]). A database, although able to manage information efficiently and reliably, is inadequate for the

formalization of deductive mechanisms based on logic and heuristics. From this springs the need to integrate the Database with an expert module which can reason in the face of unreliable or incomplete information.
Having looked at the aims behind the PORTAFOGLIO project in terms of integration with Databases, we consider next its significance in the A.I. field with regard to:
* the use for which it has been studied;
* the problems which is able to solve.

As to the position of the system compared to an human expert, we can state that PORTAFOGLIO is a **support** expert system because it has been conceived to help consultants in their work. It is therefore employed as a reference or support instrument in decision making tasks.[9]
The choice of a support rather than a substitution system derives both from the importance that CRParma gives to the training of its employees, who are considered as a primary resource for the bank's activity, and from the personal and fiduciary relationship with customers, who would have been reluctant to accept what appeared to be a 'self_service' system.
With regard to the problems the system is designed to solve, we could classify PORTAFOGLIO as a **configuration** system.
Starting with information gathered during the consultation, and taking into account possible constraints or preferencies voiced by the investor, the system

constructs a complex object
(shares portfolio)
from a set of simple objects
(shares - financial products in general)
while respecting constraints and choices imposed by the customer.

3. Problem and requirements

Cassa di Risparmio di Parma (CRParma) is a medium size interregional credit institute (it has 1300 employees who work in 61 dependences).
As a result of growing competition and the forthcoming internationalization of the banking market, the institute, within the processes of reorganization and rationalization of the productive structure, has identified the activity of consultancy for customers as a critical success factor.
As far as *commercial consultancy* to companies is concerned, the rationalization has taken place through the introduction of the professional figure of *client manager*, to whom the functions of planning, coordination, management and monitoring of contacts with a certain number of clients are referred.
Financial consultancy to private citizens has been rationalized through the introduction of the *Expert System PORTAFOGLIO*, integrated in the computing system of the bank and coherent with institute's orientation.
The general principles followed in developing PORTAFOGLIO can be summarized as following:

- **evolution** instead of revolution: the system represents an enhancement to traditional EDP with the aim of exploiting all opportunities provided by advanced computing technologies;
- **integration** instead of isolation: in addition to traditional automation, we would like to check the effect, impact, and real advantages, in the computing system of the institute, deriving from the introduction of advanced technologies. In this context, the system constitutes a module which communicates (both ways) with the overall computing system of the bank and represents a part of the more specialized marketing information system;
- **open architecture**: the desire to build a system which is easily portable and can be inserted in a different context from the original one has been realized in PORTAFOGLIO which has been built therefore as a system "with standard plugs and sockets".

4. The Expert System PORTAFOGLIO

4.1 Technical and economic implications: advantages and disadvantages of the system

The introduction, with PORTAFOGLIO, of advanced computing technology applications in the traditional EDP world has involved some organizational problems. Although expert system technology offers the possibility of solving problems in a flexible way, there is a risk of creating a device which is isolated from the complex computing system of a bank. The problem is to create a synergy among the functions involved in the project in order to develop a 'virtuous circle' that integrates the expert system into the bank computing structure. This necessity led, in the beginning, to the creation of a pool of different sector experts (financial, marketing, computing) working together, coordinated and supervisionated by CRParma Marketing division in accordance with the market orientation of PORTAFOGLIO Expert System.

The main aim of the project was the development of an expert system which puts at the disposal of branch level consultants all the information necessary for a consultancy, which is customized but which nevertheless fits in with company policy, employing a tool which is easy to use and understand and which is always up to date.

The flow of knowledge to the branch consultant (not necessarily expert), as well as the distribution of know-how, will have as immediate feedback an alignment between the head office and branch level from the operative point of view which will be translated into a controlled decentralization of consultancy. For this reason, during the development of the system, attention was given neither to deep or sophisticated technical-financial notions nor to predefined mathematical models, but to criteria of a logical nature based on common sense and the experience of CRParma technicians. Simplicity and immediacy of use were the requirements made on the system, so as not to bar access to those who do not have specific knowledge (difficult formulas or complex models).

The introduction in CRParma of an expert system for financial consultancy, has brought many advantages and differentation factors which have proved useful for creating a new institute identity in the financial counselling service.

With PORTAFOGLIO we wanted:
* to distribute to sales personnel correct and comprehensible information about the nature and features of various products available while avoiding excessive training and preparation;
* timely updating of this information from a central location;
* to support sales personnel in identifying the types of products that are suitable for any particular client profile or requirement while explaining and justifying the advice;
* to propose, for each product type, the individual products that match the Company's policy;
* to encourage sales personnel to adopt a uniform approach which is compatible with the Company's sales and marketing objectives.

4.2 PORTAFOGLIO architecture

From a logical point of view the system is made up of the following components:[10]
* a **knowledge base** which contains both theoretical objective knowledge concerning financial products, and the personalized judgements of the experts who work in the bank. While theoretical notions can be considered lasting, the expert judgements generally have a dynamic nature because they are influenced by market changes;
* a set of **databases**, external to the knowledge base, which contain information concerning shares and other financial products;
* a **reasoning and explanation mechanism.** The explanations are intended to back up the advice proposed by the system and to provide a better comprehension of the information extracted from databases.

From an analysis of the problems connected with financial consultancy in banks and of their

solution by expert consultants, the system has been divided into three independent and autonomous modules, each of which contains the three components mentioned above. These modules correspond to distinct phases of the line of reasoning taken by the consultant in suggesting a customized portfolio to the client:
* **module of goals/aims identification (Client Analysis);**
* **module of abstract solution (Typologic Mix);**
* **module of final proposal (Detailed Portfolio).**

The first module identifies, by means of a restricted number of questions, the client's requirements and expectations. It outlines a profile of the client, deduced from parameters such as
- personality-psychological profile (disposition towards risk, culture, and so on);
- economic-income profile (type of income, saving);
- providential-insurance profile.

In addition it gives an explanation about the reasons behind the formulation of the questions themselves.

The module of goals/aims identification works in an economic context represented, in the expert system, by the so-called *macroeconomic scenario*. Such a scenario contains economic data concerning forecasts of the trend in interest rates, the structure of rates comparative short term preferencies. It directs the module in the subdivision of the client's investment into amounts and durations. This module then produces, as output, the data of the consultation and the goals which the client intends to achieve with the investment.

When the introduction (through a special interface) of data useful to identify a client's requirements has taken place, the Expert System provides advice at two stages:
1) during the second module:
   identification of a mix of the classes/types of products which may be recommended, distinguished by duration (months) and amounts (millions of Liras) (i.e. the generalized abstract solution);
2) during the third module:
   identification, for each type, of a series of products arranged according to their suitability for the client.

The system delegates to bank's financial consultant or to the client himself the final choice about the kind of purchase which must be carried out, since it is believed that in this way people feel responsible for the purchase itself.

5. Technical choices

During the planning of the system, particular attention was paid to two features which had to be respected, according to the architectural choices made, both conceptually and operatively:
- *modularity*;
- *integrability*

These features were realized by taking inspiration from the reasoning followed by an human expert in financial consultancy and from the optimization and exploitation of existing resources.

5.1 Modularity

The need of verifying, during intermediate steps, the reasoning followed by the expert system and of possibly changing partial solutions led, during the planning, to the structuring of PORTAFOGLIO in three independent modules.

The modules were developed taking into account their independence and autonomy: they are functionally separated both for input and for output, taking data necessary to their functioning from databases realized with the IVth generation language Focus.[2]
PORTAFOGLIO provides in this way the opportunity of using the modules in an independent way: for example, the consultant could begin the consultation starting directly

from the second module, taking the necessary data directly from the Focus databases.
Each module produces a report containing a justification about the conclusions reached: such reports may be analyzed separately or together, and may be considered as a final document to deliver to the client. The modularity gives the system ease of extension and enlargement; moreover, the changes made to a specific module do not imply any alteration to the modules which are logically connected with it: each one can be easily re-executed, independently of the others.

5.2 Integrability

As regards the "principle of coherence", according to which every instrument used in the bank must comply with a uniform plan of development for the institute's computing system, PORTAFOGLIO is perfectly integrated with the Infocenter of which it actually constitutes an important field of application.[10]
Thus another basic decision to ensure the employment of the expert system concerned the choice of the hardware on which to start development. From the beginning, the idea of employing a computer exclusively devoted to development was excluded because of an awareness of the difficulties which could arise at delivery.
The integration considered in this office must not be thought of only in terms of hardware, but above all in terms of applications. In turn, the information derived from the system itself feeds other computing subsystems such as, particularly, the Marketing one.
From experience it has become more and more evident that the fundamental moment which marks the transformation of an expert system from a simple «general purpose» prototype into a program which can be considered really useful for bank employees is represented by the *integration of the expert system into the computing system of the institute*.[12] That means that the expert system must communicate with data already present in the bank, in our case concerning shares and other financial products.
The access, on behalf of the consultants, to the expert system connected with data must be kept simple and it must be able to take place in every branch.
The concept of integration just explained must not only be regarded as a direct connection with data input, but it also applies to the recording of output data. This becomes important if the bank has the ability to extract commercially useful information from input and output data.
By recording on a centralized database the features, needs and purposes which lead each specific client to invest certain amounts, and by combining these elements with the output of the expert system (i.e.the advice about financial products which best satisfy the clients' requirements) it is possible to have continuous and always updated information useful for identifying the preferences and tastes of different kinds of customer. In other words, it means that, given certain characteristics of the client and having defined a set of suggestions proposed by the expert system, it is possible to associate this information with the products effectively sold by the consultant.

6. Implementation choices

In accordance with the two mentioned base requisites, three fundamental requirements immediately arise:
1) to realize a short, simple and immediate interview (detailed only when the clients are also experts);
2) to avoid the detection of standard typologies "client-portfolio";
3) to connect an extra module which analyses the macroeconomic performance.

The realization, in the Client Analysis Module, of an articulate interview with not more than twenty answers, has satisfied not only the requirements of conciseness and reasonable question length in the interactive phase, but also avoids questions which could be perceived by the investor as interference in personal matters (family status, job, ...). Such information, if necessary, will be taken by the system from institute data bases.

The building of the Typological Mix Definition Module, as we will see, respects the second point articulating its reasoning in two phases:
- evaluation of the financial product classes according to single client purposes identified by the Client Analysis Module;
- configuration of the partial solution achieved by "opportunity" rules which build a general, coherent and congruent portfolio.

This splitting up does not lead to an optimal solution, but represents quite well the process of adjustment-balancing by which the expert builds up a portfolio. The choice has been supported by the fact that he uses *heuristics and experience* rather than *deterministic algorithms* to achieve a solution.

The module of the third point is currently just a data base without any inference rules. In fact, in this phase of development, the judgement of the macroeconomic indexes is left totally to the central expert's criterion; in a following project phase, these criteria will be rendered explicit with rules referred to such indices.

6.1 The Modules and their Integration into the Computing System of the bank

From a descriptive point of view, every module of the system can be seen as black box whose input - output - functioning we will analyse.[7]

CLIENT ANALYSIS Module: The requirements of the client

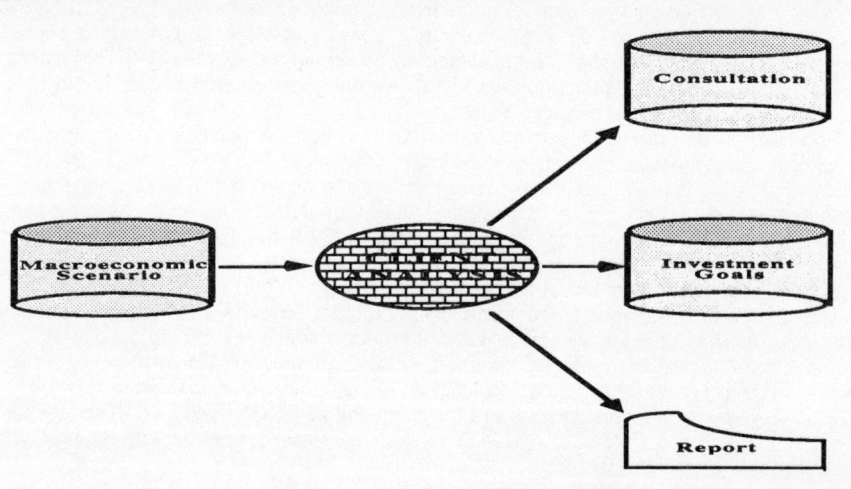

Figure 1 CLIENT ANALYSIS Module

The input to the Client Analysis Module is the information derived by the interview which the system carries out with the client; through the mediation of a financial consultant and the entries present in the data base relative to the macroeconomic scenario.

The use of Savoir [4], for knowledge representation, has meant that the questions put by PORTAFOGLIO are backed up with explanations on why the system has put these questions. The explanations are given to the user, who in this case is the financial consultant. This module, after asking the questions aimed at identifying the requirements, determines from the knowledge base the aims of the investment (in terms of characteristics and relative capital), stores in the data bases the information it receives, uses or obtains, and builds a report containing the explanations of the reasoning used to reach the conclusions.

In particular, the investment purposes can be formalized in classes and for each one it can be useful to know duration (e.g. short term income), destined capital, etc. Among the purposes currently considered by PORTAFOGLIO are capital gain, gradual accumulation, periodic income, liquidity. The system is able to consider an hypothesis where the client has various investment purposes. The splitting up of investment capital according to different purposes considers various factors: riskiness of the client, his general motives, rates and so on.

TYPOLOGIC MIX DEFINITION Module: From client's requirements to the products portfolio

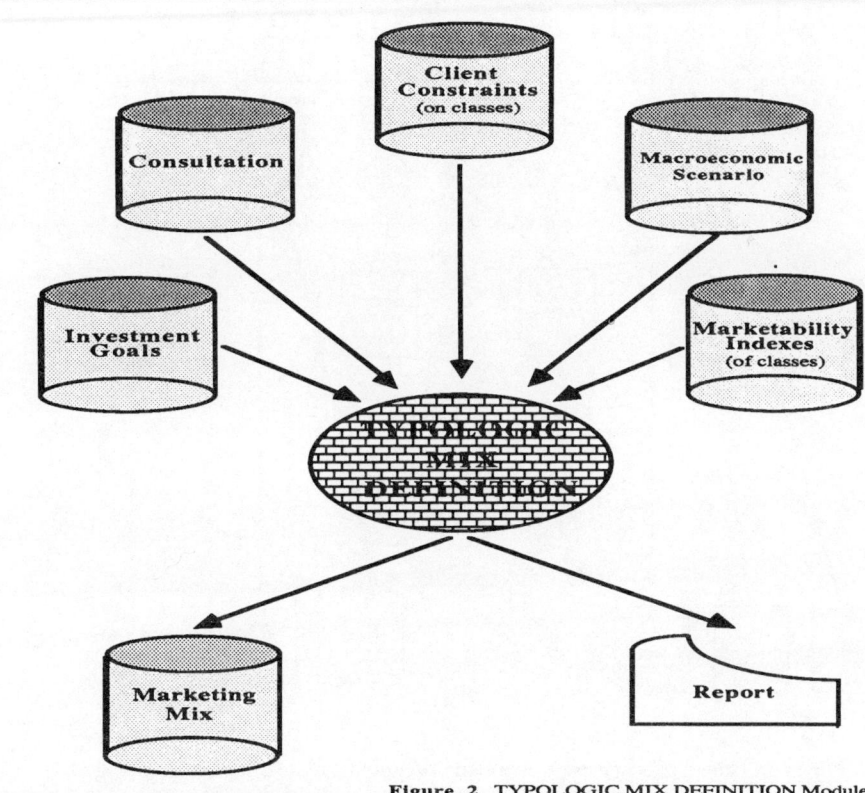

Figure 2 TYPOLOGIC MIX DEFINITION Module

The system uses a subdivision of the financial products in at least 15 classes: liquidity, short term bonds, medium-long term bonds, shares, etc. For each one a 'tree' has been constructed (Figure 4) to represent the relationships among class characteristics and the client's purpose. The tree has the following interpretation: the single product class is evaluated according to the "direct purpose" and the "other conditioning factors", determined in the phase of client analysis.

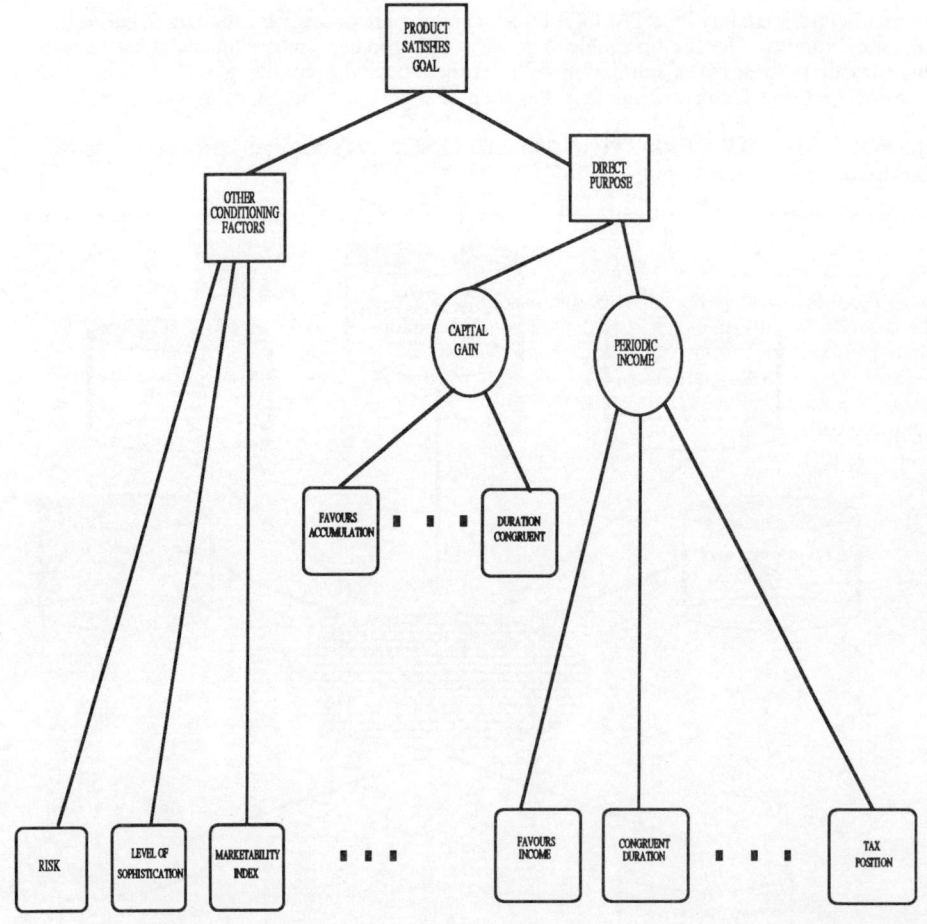

Figure 4 Product classes evaluation tree

If, for example, the direct purpose generically is capital gain, the factors involved in evaluation are the predisposition of the class to capital gain, and the adequacy of the duration of its products to the client's requirements; if the goal is also periodic income, the system also evaluates the periodicity of the income, and so on.

The variable "other conditioning factors" is evaluated by parameters such as risk (matched with the client's desired risk level), sophistication (matched with client's financial culture), etc.

The input of the Typological Mix Definition module comes from the database concerning any constraint imposed by the client on the classes of financial products (if the client intends to lay down constraints), the database concerning to the aims of the investment as identified from the Client Analysis Module, and the consultation database.

This information can be inserted in the data base off-line through Focus procedures available as direct up-dating functions which can be activated from the main menu of PORTAFOGLIO. With this information, the knowledge base first evaluates the general classes of financial product, by matching their characteristics and the goals of the client. For example, the system evaluates the couples "desired risk level - riskiness of the product" and "client's financial culture - sophistication of product" for each class.

In the second phase, a general portfolio is configured using rules which balance the division of the amounts among the classes which are considered more suitable for the client's goals. For example, if "Bond (Closed-end) Investment trusts" and "Capital (Open-end) Investment trusts" have been evaluated as suitable for the client's goals, this stage will optimize the two partial solutions suggesting in the place of one of them an alternative but similar class of shares, or replacing both of them with the more general solution "Balanced Investment trusts" that synthesize the features of the two previously singled out classes.
Outputs of the Typological Mix Definition module are:
- a report in natural language describing the product classes judged, by PORTAFOGLIO, as best meeting the customer's requirements and serving his purposes;
- records of the Marketing Mix database.

The latter will be used by the final counselling module in order to determine the individual bonds and their pertaining amounts for each product class included in the same records.
The solutions of the Typological Mix Definition module can also be shown graphically by means of a specific Focus procedure. This produces a "pie chart" which can be constructed according to:
1) the typology of the classes;
2) the investment duration;
3) both specifications.

Moreover, the implementation of Focus procedures for graphical representation enables the user to modify the databases and to display the outcome of these changes immediately.

FINAL CONSULTANCY Module: The final proposal

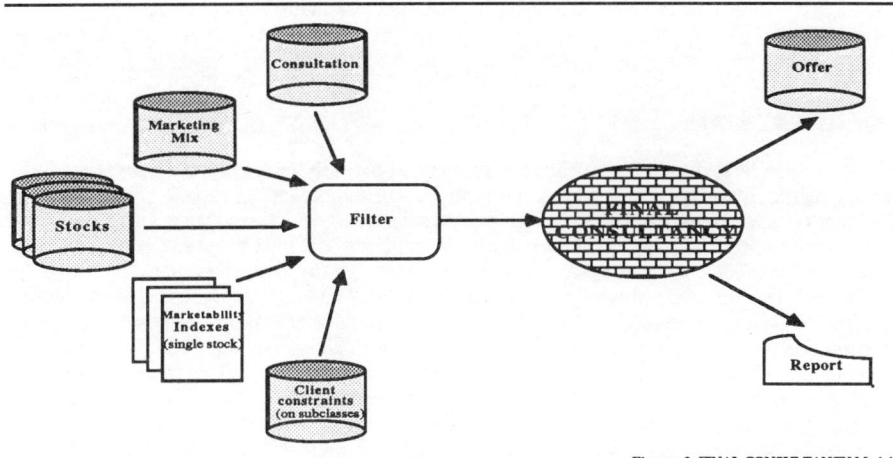

Figure 3 FINAL CONSULTANCY Module

Unlike the modules discussed above, the Final Counselling module operates on input databases by means of an appropriate procedure called 'Filter'. The input of this Filter is, along with Consultation and Marketing Mix databases, a database set comprising information on bonds which the bank intends to sell through its branches. To these databases another is added which contains the client's constraints on subclasses and individual bonds.
The procedure selects the individual bonds, belonging to the classes sorted by the Typological Mix Definition module, which comply with the client's constraints and have a suitable duration, etc.
The input of the third module is thus made up of the Filter's output, i.e. the set of products it has sorted out together with the pertaining parameters. The final counselling module uses

these parameters for an overall evaluation aimed at developing the offer.
The knowledge base is structured by the following parameters: yield, riskiness, sales indexes, etc.
This parameter (a marketability index), fixed by the bank, is particularly important as the Filter selects the shares which the bank wishes to sell within a determined period as long as these choices do not violate the background macroeconomic scenario.
Successively this output is re-read by Savoir, taking into account the subjective indices (fixed by stocks and shares department) which measure the bank's priorities among the products in the portfolio. (*N.B.*: The updating of these indices and of the macroeconomic scenario lies within the province of the head offices; it is automized and completely transparent to the branch consultants whose work, using PORTAFOGLIO, conforms with the company's sales policy and with the latest decisions taken).
As output the Final Consultancy module produces a report in natural language and the so called offer's database.
The former describes the suggested portfolio with the specification of the individual bonds and their pertaining amounts and a detailed account of the system's conclusions.
The suggested advice should not be taken as obligatory, unmodifiable or definite by the consultant (the system user), but rather as matter for an intelligent discussion with the investor; if necessary, the suggested portfolio configuration can be retailored. This is facilitated by PORTAFOGLIO's modular architecture, which enables the consultant to directly intervene at any stage of the counselling, and the re-running of modules whose inputs are altered by such manipulations.
The verification of coherency among the different information used by PORTAFOGLIO (introduced or manipulated by the user) is a task of the system itself.
Each step of the consultation, together with acquired information, is recorded in a file handled by Focus, which, besides allowing rapid and efficent retrieval for the consultation, is also a flexible tool for the statistical sampling and documentation of collected case histories.

7. Status and evolution

PORTAFOGLIO has been implemented partially on a Personal Computer and partially on the mainframe of the bank; currently it is installed and running at some of CRParma's branches for a checking stage using real cases.
It has been developed using, for knowledge representation, the expert system shell Savoir in the version for PC [4], a powerful tool which can handle incomplete and uncertain information. The specific knowledge of the three modules has been represented by derivation trees (Figure 4) and expressed by the representation language of Savoir. The system, which is continuously growing, is made up of about 1000 rules (250 Kbyte). An interface, realized by means of the IVth generation language PC-Focus [2], allows the system modules to have access (to modify, read and write) the databases containing parameters and information concerning the financial products; these databases are present on the bank host system and are accessible through the Focus procedures. In particular the databases concerning
 - macroeconomic scenario,
 - financial products classes,
 - financial products details
are exclusively accessible to read and are periodically transferred from Host to PC. This allows, along with a quickly updating of parameters and information about financial products, a completely transparent 'refreshement' of the situation in the branches.
Pro-Pascal is the language used to interface directly Savoir and Focus [4].
The system is used on IBM PS/2, standard configuration, inter-connected through a local network and linked up with the mainframe. It works on local level with a single workstation accessing both local and central databases, realizing in this way complete integration with the company's computing sytem.

8. Conclusions

The proposed approach should has some major advantages:
. in an environment where there are no users with a grounding in computer science, the proposed architecture allows traditional tools to be employed without specific training for the Expert System consultation;
. the possibility of drawing conclusions in absence of complete data allows decisions to be taken without a new testing procedure, thus saving time and re-testing costs;
. the final report on the obtained data justifies the inferential path followed by the Expert System: this allows the Expert System's suggestions to be checked in order to verify the result.

Two benefits have been gained from this enterprise: first, PORTAFOGLIO allows the institute to supply a qualitatively better consultancy service; second, it produces an image benefit which brings the institute to notice in the national banking system.

Some evaluations may be made about the experience acquired during the development of the system.

The planning of PORTAFOGLIO has allowed us to experiment with advanced and complementary techniques having shorter implementation times compared to those of traditional EDP. In contrast with standard traditional programming procedures, we have seen an incremental conceptual improvement of the system.

During the pilot installation phase, an interfunctional work group, was set up: this produced an operative synergy among central and branch offices, with the effect of strengthening operative integration among different offices.

In terms of informative gain, the Marketing division of the bank, which played the role of main purchaser of the project, has at its own disposition a complete and constantly updated panorama on market preferences which allows client's profiles to be constructed in order to realize market segmentation by building ad hoc specific financial products. As a next step, the enlargement of system's functionalities is under study with the aim of supporting not only the activity of financial product sales, but also the distribution of the bank's different products.

This work has disclosed several new issues to be considered in future. As the bank aims at improving the quality of services offered to customers, in the future the possibility of reaching such a result within other sectors will be assessed. Moreover, the implications of the proposed architecture for other tools both for knowledge representation and other types of Databases are going to be investigated.

Acknowledgements

We would like to thank all the people who helped directly and indirectly with the project PORTAFOGLIO. We thank in particular Dr G.Catellani and Dr A.Mossini for their competent and constant work in developing the system. We are also indebted to all the people of the Information Center CRParma, to the happy staff of Artificial Intelligence Software for their help and support during the development of the project, and particularly to Pauline Raine e Richard Power for their great contribution to the final release of the paper.

References

[1] AA.VV., Les Systemes Experts & Leurs Applications - Avignon, 30 Mai/3 Juin 1988 (8th International Workshop).

[2] AA.VV., PC/FOCUS Information Builders, INC Users Manual 3.0 - New York.

[3] AA.VV., Sistemi Intelligenti a supporto delle decisioni nelle banche e nelle assicurazioni (a cura di E.Bentsik) - Franco Angeli Editore, 1988.

[4] AA.VV., The SAVOIR Expert System Package - User Manual, I.S.I. Limited, Version 1.5, 1988.

[5] Brodie, M.L., J.Mylopulos, Knowledge Bases and Databases: Semantic vs. Computational Theories of Informations, New Directions for Databases Systems, G.Ariav, J.Clifford (eds.), Ablex Pu.Co., 1986.

[6] Cerri, S., V.De Antonellis (eds.), Basi di Conoscenza e Basi di Dati, Proc. A.I.C.A., Milano, Maggio 1987.

[7] Chierici, A., M.G. Filippini, M.Minati, Expert System PORTAFOGLIO: Internal Report (a cura di Artificial Intelligence Software) - Milano, 1988.

[8] De Marco, M., G.Bruschi, E.Manna, G.Giustiniani, C.Rossignoli, Sistemi informativi ed elaboratori elettronici: il computer nella gestione delle imprese , Il Mulino ed, 1987.

[9] Filippazzi, F. - Le frontiere dell'informatica, Sole/24 Ore (ed.) - Milano, 1986.

[10] GDI Tecnology Assessment and Management - Commercial Expert Systems in Banking and Finance...and how to make them run - International Conference Lugano June, 6 - 7 1988.

[11] Hayes-Roth, F., D.B.Lenat, D.A.Waterman, Building Expert Systems, Addison Wesley, Readings, MA, 1983.

[12] Mossini, A., - "Sistema esperto integrato per la consulenza finanziaria al cliente" - Atti Conferenza Annuale G.U.I.D.E. - Vienna, 7 - 10 Giugno 1988.

TULIP:
Life Underwriting Expert System

Gary Chamberlin, Ian Neale & Mustafa Khan
Aries at City
City University, Northampton Square
London EC1V 0HB

Abstract

TULIP stands for 'Training system for Underwriting Life Insurance Proposals'. It was built during 1988 by Aries at City, the follow on of the Alvey Aries Club at City University. No Government money was involved, the work being sponsored by twelve insurance and reinsurance companies, who formed the management Committee. The systems work itself was done by the Aries team at City University.

The project was divided into an initial applications survey, followed by the main analysis and implementation phase. The application survey dealt with such questions as the commercial background and motivation, setting the top-level specification for the system, and defining the target users and environment. The main phase was concerned with knowledge acquisition, building the paper model, and implementing & testing the system.

A follow-up study was also carried out, to look at the problems involved in converting the training system into an operational one. This study identified four major problems which remained to be solved before a fully operational system could be justified and built. The final reports were presented in Spring 1989, and the question of further systems work being done by the Club in life underwriting is under discussion at the time of writing.

A. APPLICATION SURVEY

Commercial Background & Motivation

Successful expansion of the British life insurance industry in recent years has meant added pressure of work for underwriters. Sums insured have increased dramatically, particularly from endowments for house purchase in a spiralling market. As a result, medical evidence more often has to be obtained and scanned, quite apart from the added precautions which have to be taken to cover risks from the AIDS epidemic. Insurance offices are increasingly risk conscious, yet senior underwriters with full experience are surprisingly thin on the ground, and much of the work has to be carried out by relatively junior staff. Given these conditions, there is adequate commercial motivation for investigating an expert system solution to the problem. The aim must be to relieve the pressure and help upgrade the effectiveness of the underwriting operation. The 1988 Aries project on life underwriting came into being with such an aim, through the enthusiastic support of 12 insurance and reinsurance offices (listed at the end of the paper).

The Life Underwriting Operation

The process of life underwriting can be envisaged as a series of filters. Proposals for life insurance are received from the public through a variety of channels: sales agents, brokers, branch offices and direct mail. The proposals pass through a series of procedures which vary a good deal from office to office. At each stage, however, office staff try to identify those proposals which are sound, and can be accepted at ordinary rates (i.e. the standard rates for healthy individuals). Other proposals which show possibly adverse features are passed on to more experienced staff for fuller assessment, and frequently medical and financial evidence of various kinds will be obtained before a decision is given.

Ultimately, as many as 95% of the original proposals are likely to be accepted at ordinary rates. The remaining 5% or so will be taken on at an increased rate to reflect the additional risk, or may be referred to a specialist reassurance office. A very few proposals, of the order of perhaps 1%, will be rejected or postponed for reassessment at a future date.

Further analysis of the underwriting process shows that its various stages condense to just two logical operations. The first of these, the vetting or pre-underwriting stage, deals with completed proposal forms as they come into the office, and is often carried out by clerical staff. An immediate acceptance may be given, or medical evidence from the proposer's GP may be called for. Additionally, a fresh medical examination by an independent doctor may be required. Those proposals needing evidence then pass into the second, or main underwriting stage. In this operation, underwriting staff assess the proposal plus the evidence (once obtained), and come to a decision on each case.

Possible Systems: Vetting System

The analysis shows that more than one expert system can potentially be built. The first type of system would be one to assist with the vetting stage. Its aim would be to push the underwriter's expertise out, so that it became available to the clerk working on the raw proposal forms. A successful system could lead to faster turn-round of business at the proposal form stage. The result would be saving of administrative costs and better sales conversion (any delay in acceptance of a proposal inevitably carries the risk of losing the business). The load on the underwriting department could be considerably reduced.

The disadvantage, for a collaborative project such as that mounted by Aries, is that the vetting stage is very company specific, and the procedures and practice used vary a good deal. Also, tight integration with the office's conventional DP systems is needed, since the basic proposal details must be input to the mainframe files. Again, a search for already-existing policies must be carried out for each proposer. Finally, there is a major data input problem to be solved, since there are many synonyms for different medical impairments and conditions. Also, a vetting system must be able to deal with faulty spellings of medical terms by clerical staff, and recognize the words nonetheless. This makes for an interesting problem, though not specifically an expert system one.

Possible Systems: Full Underwriting System

The second type of system is one which will work at the full underwriting stage, i.e. where both proposal form and medical evidence are available as inputs. The aim here will be to increase the effectiveness of junior underwriters, and improve the general consistency of underwriting in the department. There is the added advantage of quickly updatable underwriting standards, and the freeing of senior underwriters' time. Against building such a system is the fact that there is a vast domain to cover. The system must have knowledge of a wide range of medical, surgical and psychiatric impairments which can affect human lives, and be able to distinguish those which reduce life expectancy from those which have little effect. There is again a problem of data input; if this is too slow, it will not be worth using the system, since the case could be underwritten more quickly by hand. Finally, a significant part of the real skill is in scanning the medical evidence, and the Aries Club was not prepared to start building a system capable of reading doctors' handwriting. It is the remainder of the task, i.e. interpreting the key points of evidence once gleaned from the medical reports, that is the part more susceptible to expert system treatment on the computer.

Possible Systems: Training System

Faced with the obvious difficulties of building either a vetting or a full underwriting system, the Aries Club homed in on a third option. This was to build a training system, a dynamic self-help training tool to supplement the work of the underwriting training programmes which the insurance offices mount for their junior staff. Such a system could take in both the vetting and full underwriting stages, and it could build in the knowledge of top underwriters. It could be PC-based, and dispense with any need for mainframe integration. It could be built to deal with key impairments only, rather than with the whole medical range. In short, for the Club, it was the low-risk option, though not in itself offering significant cost savings. Most important, it could be seen as a good first step towards a full system. Having its own use, it would nevertheless demonstrate both the capabilities and shortcomings of expert systems in tackling the life underwriting operation.

System Scoping

The scoping decision was an important one. It was agreed the project should analyse one aspect of underwriting in depth, i.e. rather than a broader but shallower treatment of the domain as a whole. The choice was to deal with the impairment of ischaemic heart disease (IHD) only. This condition, resulting from restricted supply of blood to the heart muscle, is a very common cause of death. In spite of this, it is often insurable, and presents the knowledge engineer with an interesting and complex analysis. Cases can be divided by treatment given into surgical and medical types, and then further subdivided. Surgical cases may involve CABG (coronary artery bypass graft), left ventricular muscle excision or angioplasty; while medical cases may be classified as types of angina or myocardial infarction. (The last term here is the doctor's description for a heart attack).

Beyond the basic classification, there are many complicating factors, such as smoking, blood pressure, shortness of breath, obesity, etc. Any of these, when associated with heart disease, tend to make the prognosis rather worse, and must be taken into account. The general principle is to give a basic additional rating for heart disease itself, and then to assess extra numerical ratings for any complicating factors.

Top-level Specification

The basic mode of operation chosen for TULIP was that it should be case driven, i.e. responding to the detail of particular examples which are put through it. It was to have a number of well-identified stages:

a. Take in and analyse proposal form detail
b. Advise on the medical evidence required
c. Query the user on the medical evidence
d. Analyse for basic rating
e. Take in additional factors
f. Respond with overall case assessment

In addition, TULIP should explain key medical terms, and test the user's knowledge at critical points in the procedure. Finally, the system should instruct the user to consult the senior underwriter over any difficult points which arise in a consultation. Examples of the latter might be where there had been more than one heart attack in the past, or where ECG (electro-cardiogram) evidence needed interpretation.

Organisational Use/ Profile for User

Training in life underwriting is commonly provided by the reassurance companies. A seminar typically takes the form of a lecture on a medical topic, followed by a number of related case studies. TULIP should be aimed to supplement this type of training, but very definitely *not* to replace the trainers themselves. Its main advantage would be in showing the student what questions are important, and in what order they should be asked, in the systematic analysis of a heart disease case.

The system would not be intended for use by the absolute beginner. At least 12 months' office experience would be required, so that the user has familiarity with office procedure and the basic forms employed in the work. He or she must have the ability to learn and assimilate medical terms, and an understanding of general principles of life insurance rating. Prior underwriting experience, however, would not be essential—the system, in fact, should give a good feel for the overall procedure towards arriving at a rating, through both proposal form and medical evidence stages.

System Requirements

Initial analysis of the domain showed that it was suited to the extensive use of rules. Since a training system was being built, full help facilities were clearly needed. Although integration with conventional systems was not necessary, a database linkage might be useful, to enable standard test cases to be stored and called up. There was a certain amount of procedural manipulation to be done: rate additions, table look-up, and so on. Finally, as almost goes without saying, a screen-design capability was required.

These requirements led fairly quickly to the selection of Leonardo Level 2 (PC version) as the tool for implementing the system. The programming paradigms it offered (rules, object frames and integrated procedural language) were adequate. Further, it could be linked to a database, and had reasonable user interface design and help facilities. The price for Level 2 was acceptable to the Club, and represented good value for money. It is true that other tools might have proved equally satisfactory—however the resources for a proper evaluation of tools currently on the market were not available. The chief deciding factor was that Aries had previous experience of Leonardo in use, and knew it to be a tool of some merit.

Application Survey: General Conclusions

A number of conclusions could be drawn at the close of the application survey. There was a high level of consensus in the principles and practice of life underwriting, which appeared to apply across the whole industry in Britain. This meant that a collaborative project, drawing on underwriting expertise from a number of offices, was viable and had a good chance of success. Further the main methods were well documented, which would help to get the knowledge acquisition off to a flying start.

On the practical side, there was good commercial motivation for a system, but it was apparent that a full life underwriting system was a very ambitious project. It was sensible to choose to build a training system as a useful first step along the road. Finally, a PC/ expert system shell base was fully satisfactory as a vehicle for this first stage of the work.

B. MAIN ANALYSIS & IMPLEMENTATION

General Strategy

A principle which has been used in the Aries Club since its beginning is that there should be an intermediate stage or stages between the expertise as used by the expert and its implementation in the form of a computer system. For TULIP, two intermediate stages were used: first the expert knowledge was gathered and expressed in the form of a paper model; and second the model was converted into a series of modular design blueprints. The coding of the system was done relatively late in the day, only after a careful discipline for design had been carried through.

Knowledge Acquisition

The knowledge acquisition process was divided into three main stages: domain orientation, main acquisition, and refinement of detail. The initial orientation consisted of interviews with the project experts plus background reading to bring the knowledge engineer up to speed in life underwriting.

In the main acquisition stage, focused interviews were the main vehicle for gathering knowledge. However, verbal protocol studies were also used, with the experts thinking aloud as they solved particular proposals showing evidence of heart disease. A further technique was the simulation exercise, in which a senior underwriter (standing for the system) put a series of questions to a junior (standing for the user). The case documents were in possession of the junior, so that the senior was forced to ask for every piece of information required on the way towards giving a rating. The protocol studies and the simulation exercise were both valuable in bringing out the critical types of question asked by the senior underwriter, and in showing the sequence of sub-tasks involved in the underwriting process.

From the main acquisition work, the paper model was constructed, and discussed with the project experts. The final stage of work then consisted in refining the detail of the paper model, by asking the experts to pinpoint any errors and omissions. A number of test cases were also used for this purpose, the detail of the paper model being adequate to guide the process, i.e. without any help from a machine prototype.

Knowledge Representation

The knowledge representation, as embodied in the paper model, used a number of techniques. Of these, the central form used was the decision tree, and the two key parts of the model consisted of such trees. Apart from the trees, a domain lexicon of the principal technical terms used in life underwriting was constructed. This had particular use in classifying the symptoms, diagnoses and treatments which are either indicative of ischaemic heart disease or suggest a possible link, and in matching these with disclosures made on the proposal form.

Other parts of the representation were a rudimentary data base of drugs, classified by name and type of effect, and an extensive set of rating tables. The latter consisted of such elements as a height/ weight table, a blood pressure table and rating guides for the major classes of ischaemic heart disease, both medical and surgical.

The Paper Model

The paper model reached its final state only after 5 full drafts had been drawn up, each being revised in turn by discussion with the underwriting experts. The model itself consisted of 6 main stages:

   a. Input of details from the proposal form
   b. Decision tree for determining the medical evidence required
   c. Input of details from the medical evidence
   d. Decision tree for analysing the basic rating
   e. Comb-through of the additional factors
   f. Presentation of case assessment

Apart from functioning as the major system design document, the paper model formed an important communication role within the project. It was a representation of the team's understanding of the task at any given stage, and could be examined and discussed by experts, knowledge engineers and Project Committee representatives. It enabled errors in the reasoning to be pinpointed, and highlighted the key decision points and their overall position in the mapping of underwriting knowledge.

The main disadvantage of the paper model was its length and intricacy. By the completion of the project, it consisted of 22 pages of fine detail. It therefore presented something of a barrier to the newcomer, and threw a significant cognitive load on the experts, whose task was periodically to review it and correct its deficiencies. The paper model is a static form, and in this sense compares unfavourably with a computer prototype. It is a lot easier for an expert to review a prototype, and gain a quick impression of its performance. On the other hand, there is much detail of the modelling which may never become apparent if the expert confines himself to scanning computer screens alone. (The question of prototypes is taken up again in the section below on 'Lessons Learned').

The Software Tool—Leonardo

The software tool chosen, Leonardo, uses object frames as its main medium for coding. A frame can be of three main types: ruleset/ procedure/ screen handler. The frame is headed with a number of slots, such as Name, Type, Value, Default, etc, and then in its body contains the set of rules, the procedure or the screen description. Rules are fairly standard in that they contain a number of antecedent clauses linked by AND and OR operators, then followed by a consequent part which fires if the conditions of the antecedent hold. The consequent may consist of value assignments to objects (instantiation), and of instructions to run procedures or use particular screens.

For its inference strategy, Leonardo essentially employs backward chaining. The chaining commences in the top-level module, called the Mainruleset. Within this module, Leonardo is instructed to seek the value of a given object, which becomes the goal of the whole consultation. On the way to evaluating the goal object, Leonardo is forced to evaluate a number of subsidiary objects, which are linked together through the various rulesets built into the program by the system designer. Within the primary control strategy of backward chaining, forward chaining can also be brought into play. This is done locally, i.e. within a given ruleset, but is entirely at the discretion of the system designer.

Although Leonardo is a well thought-out shell, it does have some weak points. These can be summarised as program bugs and object/ textual limitations. The program is a lot less buggy than when first issued in 1987, but some bugs do remain. For example, it is risky to attempt to mix both AND and OR operators in the antecedent of a rule. Use of the null value to test whether or not an object has been instantiated is unreliable, and on the procedural side the testing of index variables in loops can sometimes be in error.

More serious from the Aries point of view were the object and text space limitations. The version used, Leonardo 3.15, has a text space limitation of 13K and a total space for object names of 12K. To explain further, the 13K is a text buffer set up by Leonardo in main memory, and controlled by a set of pointers. All text which is used in a program, e.g. messages on-screen to the user, text input, string values within the program, etc, is put in this 13K buffer. It does not take much imagination to see that any substantial expert system with frequent communication to the user will soon overflow the buffer.

As for object names, each of these can be up to 24 characters long. Leonardo allows for up to 1000 objects in a program, so that full-length names would require a space of 24K rather than only 12K. TULIP, in fact, has 577 objects and uses all but 200 bytes of the buffer. To extend TULIP significantly, therefore, would mean an annoying overhead in terms of shortening the existing object names, with consequent loss of readability of the program. These limits, unfortunately, are not made clear by Creative Logic, the suppliers of Leonardo. They were only discovered by the Aries team when halfway through the work, and caused a real setback in the program implementation.

Design & Implementation

This part of the work was, in essence, straightforward, and can be characterised as a disciplined top-down procedure. The process began from the paper model itself, from which a top-level structure for the program was derived. The program design was then developed in modular form, largely by cutting the paper model into pieces of workable size. Each module was then taken in isolation, and an informal schema was produced, highlighting the logical sequencing involved. The structure was matched against the programming paradigms in Leonardo, and then the module built in Leonardo code. Modules were validated in isolation, and then worked into the main structure, which was itself validated as a whole at a later stage.

The key principle in all this was to settle the inferencing pattern before starting to code. Using this discipline, most of the code worked first time, and little debugging had to be done. However, things became more difficult when the paper model was revised and the changes had then to be incorporated in the program code. It was found that on these occasions debugging was more often necessary, and that program readability tended to suffer.

A final point about the program is the tables and text files which were used. Because of the text space limitation mentioned above, the extensive tables and text lists used by TULIP had to be kept in separate files on disc, and only read into the program when needed at run-time. This was not a problem, once the need for it had been discovered, but it does make the program rather longer and slower running than it might otherwise have been.

Testing the System

During the later stages of the work, a test plan for the pilot system was drawn up. The aim was that each one of 4 project experts should produce and circulate 9 test cases, which could then be run through the system by both experts and users. In addition, the experts were asked to underwrite manually each of the 36 cases.

It was intended by this means to test and evaluate a number of aspects of TULIP and of the underwriting process itself. The particular points at issue were:

a. Consistency between experts in manual underwriting (Domain Consensus).
b. Individual expert using the system vs own manual results.
c. Cross-expert comparison of results for the 4 experts when using the system.
d. Overall validity of system in use by experts—i.e. expert + system results in relation to the domain consensus.
e. Cross-user comparison of results (users + system).
f. Overall validity of system in use—i.e. user + system results in relation to the domain consensus.

As it turns out, this was an ambitious programme, and the outcome was that relatively little of the testing was done within the timespan of the project. The results obtained, therefore, were far from conclusive. What can be stated is the initial impression, which was that the system in use was providing results generally in accord with good underwriting sense. In fact, in view of the system's intended function for training rather than a line role, the lack of quantitative data suitable for statistical analysis is not crucial. In training, the way a system presents and asks for information is as important as the veracity of its results. But it goes without saying that more stringent testing would be needed for a system intended for operational use.

System Maintenance/ Customisation

Looking ahead to TULIP as a system in use, there is the question of maintenance. The principles here are really no different than those which apply in conventional systems work. Simple types of maintenance, such as the amendment of rating tables and text-files, will require very little effort, other than to ensure that any data input parameters in the program (such as text length) are suitably modified. Where more radical changes are required, however, such as in the overall structure or the operation of given modules, it will be very important to go back to the paper model itself. The changes can then be followed through, from the paper model to the design blueprint to the code itself. The important point is not to attempt to rework the code until the changes have been properly registered at the design level.

A related point is on customisation of TULIP. The program was designed using underwriting principles which derive largely from the approach of a particular reassurer, the M&G (the market leader in Britain). However, two other reassurers were represented in the Club, namely Skandia and Victory. During the project, the differences in approach by these two offices were studied. It was found that, in main outline, the principles were the same. Consequently, the same overall system design could be used for an underwriting system on Skandia or Victory lines. But there were some differences of emphasis when it came to the classification of types of heart disease, and in the weight given to certain of the additional factors. Accordingly, sections of the paper model affected by these differences were identified, and were redrawn. It was found that only 3 of the 22 pages needed to be revised in this way, so that the overall work for customising the system from M&G to another reassurer would be relatively modest. The redrafted sections of the paper model were, however, not implemented.

Conclusions/ Lessons Learned

A great deal was learnt from the project, both by the insurance offices and by the Aries team at City University. These will be discussed under the headings of: Knowledge Acquisition, Paper Model vs Prototyping, System Implementation, Leonardo, Project Management.

Knowledge Acquisition The project was fortunate in having the services of five underwriting experts from different offices. There was strength in depth in the expertise, and many more errors and refinements were picked up along the way than might otherwise have been the case. The result was a richer, more veridical paper model, and a more robust system. However, the use of so many experts was only possible because of the strong consensus which exists on how the job of life underwriting should be done.

Paper Model vs Prototyping As stated above, the paper model was a central plank in the Aries strategy. It was good as a design tool, and useful for communication, but placed a real load on the experts. In retrospect, the team should have done more by way of exposition of the model's contents, particularly by giving the experts a higher level view of it at each stage.

Prototyping was also used in a limited sense, in that TULIP was initially implemented from the second draft of the paper model. As found by many others in the expert system field, a prototype is very useful in provoking comments from experts and others about the system design, particularly the interface. The strategy Aries will adopt in future is to make early prototypes of the user interface itself, although not of the full works behind it. Other limited aspects of the system may also be prototyped, e.g. a data-base link or an inferencing pattern, but the system as a whole will not be so implemented. The overall degree of project control and disciplined design which can be obtained through a paper model approach is too valuable to be given away.

System Implementation There is little to add here to the section above on this topic. The modular design method worked well, and the discipline of getting the inference pattern right on paper before starting to code was effective. The only real problems arose when *changes* were made to the paper model, but these were far from insuperable. It was significant, however, that the readability of the code tended to suffer at these points. The Aries experience supports the thesis that working only through computer prototypes (i.e. without proper design documentation) is a dangerous route indeed.

Leonardo The main points about Leonardo have already been covered above. One lesson, however, related to the forward chaining or 'demon' facility. The Club's experience was that, while demons are good for such tasks as screen work and data validation, they must be used with great care. It was best to avoid their use at all in the basic structure of the program, and to bring them in only as afterthoughts. The point is that demons operate rather like unstructured GO TO's in a conventional program. As a consequence, they can rapidly lead to the designer's loss of control over what is happening when the program is run.

An important plus for Leonardo is that its procedural language and screen handling are well integrated with its rulesets and inferencing strategy. The drawbacks already mentioned, in text and object limitations, are annoying, and do point to a defect which Creative Logic need to overcome. The basic question at issue is the use which Leonardo makes of main memory. Although not a memory resident system, the PC version is very much geared to the 640k limit. Now that more powerful PC's are becoming available, it is important that the better shells should start to make use of the 2, 4 or even 8 Meg memories which will soon be in common use on PS/2's and their equivalent.

Project Management The testing issue has already been mentioned. A lesson to be learnt here is that proper testing of an expert system is a complicated job, and requires considerable resources, not least from participating experts, users and their companies. It is wise, therefore, to plan the testing from the very beginning. Experts should be encouraged to generate test material from early on, and to look ahead in company schedules to see where space can be made for the work.

In terms of the general progress of the project, the work remained on target until the last stage. At this point, it was found that extra time was needed for the documentation, which emerged a few weeks overdue. As for the overall effort by the team, this was estimated at some 16 man-months' intensive effort, divided as approximately 40% for knowledge acquisition, 40% for system implementation and 20% for project management and administration. The figures exclude secretarial support and the time spent by experts and the Project Committee.

C. FOLLOW-UP STUDY

TULIP is a system which fulfils its intended function as a training system. It became clear during the project, however, that training could be regarded only as a side issue for the insurance offices. The real questions related to a full underwriting system, and the problems and benefits to be gained from implementing one. Accordingly, after TULIP was complete, the Aries team undertook a follow-up study. Its title was the 'Life Underwriting Scoping Study', since extending the scope of the system from heart disease to the full underwriting domain was originally seen as the main problem. But the work of building TULIP brought three other major questions to light, and it was imperative that these also should be tackled. They were: Integration with existing systems; Data entry of medical evidence; Dealing with inadequate or uncertain data.

The four questions represent four major obstacles which still have to be overcome if a full life underwriting expert system is to see the light of day. The obstacles also have a more universal interest, since they must stand in the way of many another would-be commercial expert system development. As concluded by the Aries follow-up, the way ahead is to mount a concerted attack on the four problems. In particular, work is needed on:

a. Further analysis to assess breadth & depth of the domain.
b. Exploration of tools for PC-mainframe integration.
c. Construction of screen-design prototype for user interface.
d. Follow-through on the system design implications of c.
e. Uncertainty study on a broad range of life insurance proposals.

It is intended that such work will be tackled by the Aries Club in the near future. However, the shape of things to come remains to be decided, and ultimately rests on the goodwill of the Club members.

Aries at City Members for the TULIP Project

Abbey Life	National Provident	Skandia Reassurance
Colonial Mutual	Norwich Union	Sun Life
Commercial Union	Scottish Equitable	TSB Trust Company
M&G Reinsurance	Scottish Widows	Victory Insurance

A KNOWLEDGE BASED APPROACH TO TELECOMMUNICATIONS NETWORK
ALARM MONITORING

Robin Khan,
IKBS Group,
Plessey Research and Technology,
Roke Manor, Romsey, Hants. SO51 0ZN.

Abstract

The development of ever more complex and sophisticated telecommunications networks is paralleled by the need for effective network management. One aspect of this is a requirement to provide automatic, comprehensive alarm monitoring and fault diagnosis capabilities. To meet this need, knowledge based techniques are being incorporated into operational systems. The paper describes work in this field, specifically with reference to a private digital circuit telecommunications network. The components of this type of network give rise to various alarm messages when problems arise. These are sent to a central collating point where they are printed out, examined and stored. The analysis of these alarm messages to find actual faults is complicated by the large number of alarm messages, the fact that faults cause many alarms through propagation effects, the fact that the alarms do not arrive in any predictable time order, and the fact that some alarms may not reach their destination. A knowledge based approach has been taken with the aim of eventually being able to process a large number of alarms, of the order of 50,000 alarms a day.

A prototype demonstrator has been implemented in Common Lisp. Alarms are generated by an object-oriented model of the network. The model uses knowledge about the behaviour of each of the entities in the network and knowledge about the way in which the connectivity of the entities allows for fault propagation effects. A diagnostic capability processes incoming alarms to determine what the faults could be.

1. Introduction

This paper reports on an initial study on the suitability of a knowledge based approach to the diagnosis of faults in an alarm-monitoring network environment. The applicability of expert systems technology for network maintenance has already received attention in other work (e.g. Callahan 1988). The work described below has been targeted at fault diagnosis on a digital private circuits network and has been divided into a number of phases. The first phase, described here, has involved the creation of a demonstrator to show feasibility. The demonstrator can identify faults entered onto a simulation of a network.

2. Background and Requirements

In the first phase of development, customer requirements for the demonstrator were, broadly, for a facility to enable simulation of a simple network scenario consisting of appropriate network information and circuits. In addition to this a mechanism was required to enable faults to be injected into these network components and to be able to examine the results of such actions, with a knowledge based system used to show that the fault injected had indeed occurred. The system would have to cater for multiple faults.

The major requirement was that the diagnostic process should be automated as far as possible since a system that can reach a diagnosis without human assistance is potentially more valuable than one that has to await a skilled operator to perform manual tests at a suspected fault site.

The demonstrator was also required to maintain an accurate model of a given network configuration since knowledge of the topology of a network is critical to diagnosis.

There was a need for a demonstrator which could reason with incomplete data. There is a relationship between problem types and the patterns of alarms generated by them across the network. Alarms normally expected when a certain problem arises may not occur and this can be due to a variety of reasons, so a diagnostic system must be able to draw some conclusions without the full set of alarms being present.

Figure 1 gives a schematic representation of the type of network configuration currently available.

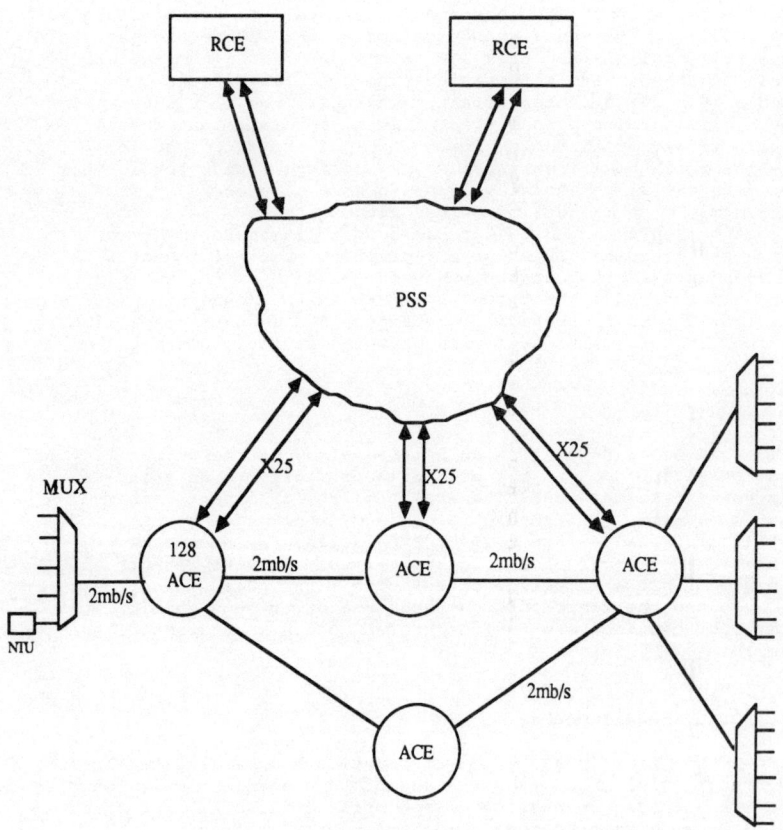

Figure 1: Current Type of Network Configuration

In terms of alarm monitoring, any faults occurring in network termination equipment (NTU), multiplexers (MUX) or automatic cross-connect switches (ACE) are directed, via the appropriate ACE, through the X25 network to an RCE (remote control equipment). Up to 50,000 alarms per day arrive at the RCE for processing. Broadly, three categories of alarms were identified: A-type at the customer side of a Mux; B-type are link alarms; and C-type are Ace alarms.

3. Modelling the Problem Domain

We have adopted a two phase approach, simulation and analysis, to modelling the domain (Coleman 1989). It is pertinent to show this separation because in the long term it is envisaged that the knowledge based system may concentrate on the analysis aspects, the simulation aspects not being necessary when the alarm monitoring work station is linked directly to appropriate equipment such as the RCE. The two major phases are now described briefly.

3.1. Simulation Phase

This involves creating a network and then overlaying it with customer circuits. In building a network the components which have to be created are the RCE, ACEs, MUXs, NTUs and links between ACEs and between MUXs and ACEs. Various restrictions are required to ensure a valid configuration of a network. For example the number of links that can be attached to an ACE is determined by the number of line cards in it. Figure 2 shows an example network fragment created graphically within the demonstrator.

3.2. Analysis Phase

This second phase of the demonstrator encompasses fault correlation and diagnosis. It involves injection of faults into network equipment, alarm propagation and the actual fault diagnosis.

Fault injection is required in our simulation so that appropriate alarms are produced and propagated through the network. The diagnostic function uses this information. Alarm generation and propagation is initiated with the injection of a fault at a network component. Alarms arriving at the RCE are then processed. Circuit information is added. Each alarm is processed in turn by the diagnostic system to try and determine what fault in the network could have caused it.

4. System Architecture

The two major stages outlined above are identified in figure 3. The simulation phase corresponds to the Functional Model of the architecture and the analysis phase corresponds to the Diagnostic Model of the system architecture. These two aspects are now detailed.

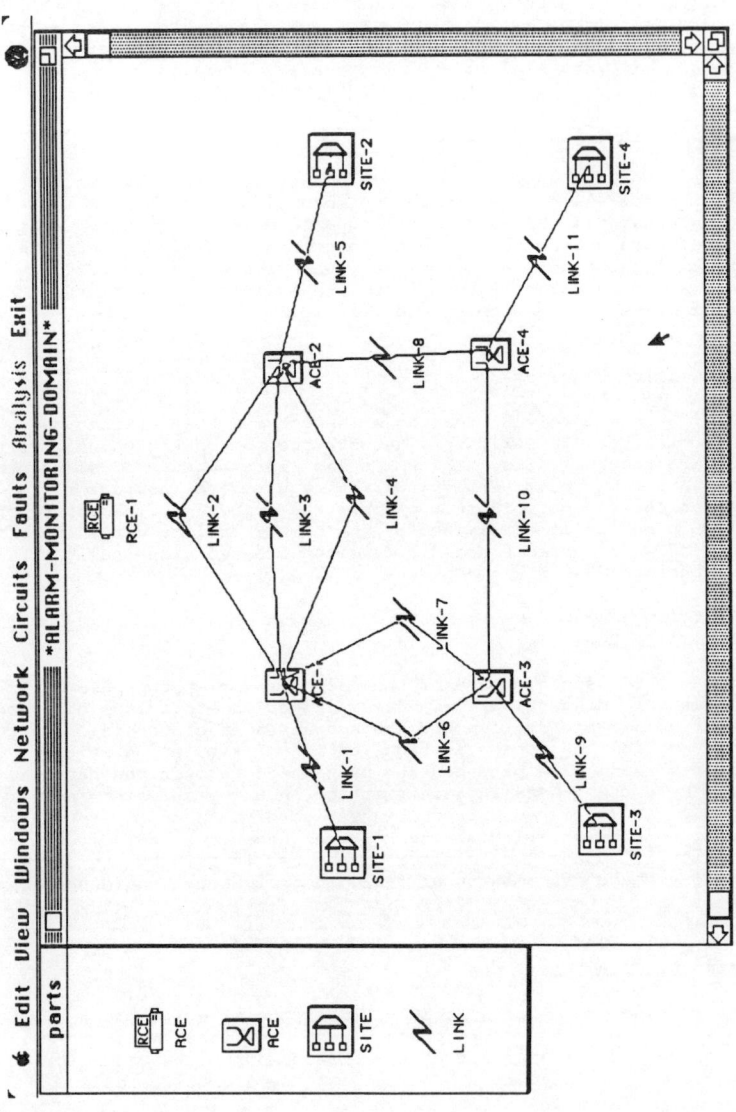

Figure 2: Sample Network Fragment

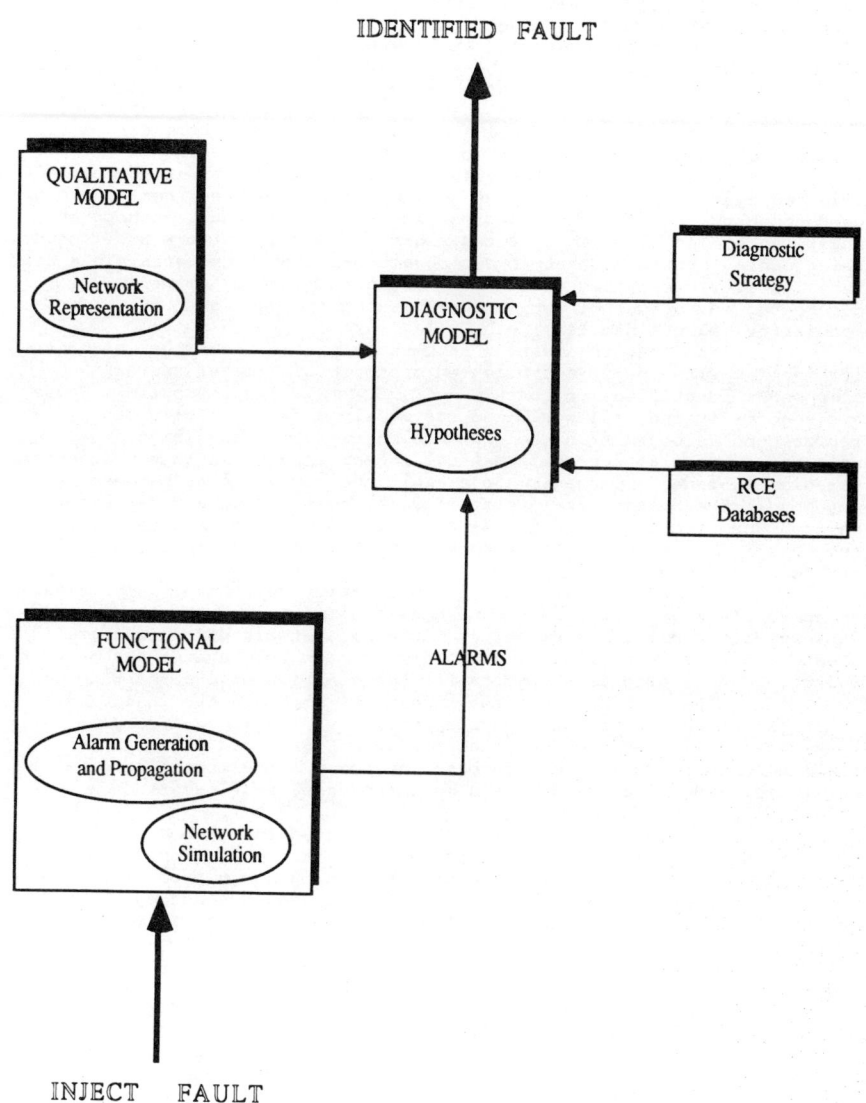

Figure 3: Architecture of Demonstrator

4.1. Functional Model

The functional model encompasses the stages of creating a network, allocating circuits, injecting a fault and propagation of the resultant alarms through the network.

It became apparent from knowledge acquisition that an object-oriented approach would be very suitable to model these stages. Since communications networks are best described in terms of the interactions of their component objects, object-oriented programming offers a convenient way to model them. In other words there is a small semantic gap between the object model and the real network.

There are fundamentally two major components in any object-oriented system; objects and the communications between them. These can be decomposed into objects, classes, instances, messages, methods and inheritance. The components of the alarm monitoring network under study have readily mapped to these basic object-oriented components. This has facilitated rapid system development along with the other well documented advantages of the object-oriented approach such as modularity, maintainability, etc.

The network creation is perhaps the most obvious in terms of its mapping with the object-oriented approach. The major network components identified are the RCE, ACE, MUX, NTU and 2mb/s link. These are objects in the real world and can easily and intuitively be represented as objects in the software model. The mechanism of inheritance is also appropriate here. Inheritance in an object-oriented paradigm provides a mechanism to exploit the similarities between objects in the domain. It is certainly the case in the alarm monitoring environment that some objects share similar properties and behaviours and this information can be factored out. This is one means of obtaining system modularity.

The first phase in the functional model, then, is to create an appropriate network. The second phase is to overlay the created network with appropriate circuits. Since all network components are treated as objects it is a straightforward task to traverse the network selecting the appropriate objects for the creation of a circuit.

The next phase in the functional model is the injection of a fault(s) and the generation and propagation of alarms as a result. This phase has again been modeled using the object-oriented paradigm, this time in conjunction with a rule-based system. In the modelling of generation and propagation of alarms the process that occurs is as follows:

An object in the network is selected and becomes faulty. In this state some initial alarm is raised. This alarm is propagated to other points in the network, each of which in turn may produce further alarms for propagation. The end point of this stage is deemed to have occurred when all alarms created as a result of this fault have arrived at the appropriate ACEs.

The information about what alarms are generated by which components and where these alarms are destined for is stored as high level rules, forming a domain knowledge base. Two example rules in the implementation language are shown in Figure 4.

These rules are translated by a rule interpreter and used in the propagation of alarms through the network. Taking the first rule as an example, the translation, in object-oriented terms, is of the form:

Given a "FAIL-NTU" message at a MUX (the message having originated at an NTU) generate two further messages. Send one of them (BIT-4&6-ON-TS0-WCF) to that MUX's associated ACE. Send the second message (AIS) to the NTU at the other end of the circuit.

In the alarm propagation stage, the rule interpreter retrieves the appropriate rule and constructs any new messages. These messages are then added to a global queue and executed in turn. The cycle of alarm propagation messages, for any given injected failure, completes when no further new messages are generated.

Appropriate propagated alarms arrive at and are stored at the appropriate ACE for future transmission to the RCE. The current mechanism of transmission to the RCE is serial and unordered. In other words only one ACE at a time transmits its buffer of alarms to the RCE, and the selection of one ACE from potentially many is non-deterministic, therefore alarms do not arrive at the RCE in any particular order.

```
(defrule
        :rule-name       MUX-1
        :doc             "a mux, receiving a fail-ntu message that
                          originated at an ntu will send out two new
                          messages"
        :source          NTU
        :recipient-type  MUX
        :message-in      FAIL-NTU
        :-->
        :message-out     BIT-4&6-ON-TS0-WCF
        :target          ACE
        :alarm-code      NONE
        :-->
        :message-out     AIS
        :target          DESTINATION-NTU
        :alarm-code      NONE
)

(defrule
        :rule-name       ACE-1
        :doc             "receiving a bit4&6wcf message at an ACE
                          causes an alarm message to be sent to the
                          RCE"
        :source          MUX
        :recipient-type  ACE
        :message-in      BIT-4&6-ON-TS0-WCF
        :-->
        :message-out     WETTING-CURRENT-FAIL
        :target          RCE
        :alarm-code      0000
)
```

Figure 4: Examples from Alarm Propagation Knowledge Base

4.2. Diagnostic and Qualitative Models

The injection of a fault into a network component generates numerous alarms across the network in accordance with the types of rule outlined in the previous section. Appropriate alarm reports eventually arrive at the RCE for processing.

The diagnostic model processes each such alarm report to try and correlate it with any existing fault hypotheses, or failing that to create a new hypothesis. The qualitative model is a model of the network representation in terms of components, attributes, links between them, etc. and is used by the diagnostic process. The basic strategy for alarm fault diagnosis used in the demonstrator is as follows:

First, the next unprocessed alarm report waiting in the RCE database is selected. Each such alarm contains information about the alarm message, the transmitting ACE, along with port and time slot information about the originating alarm. Each alarm report at the RCE also holds information about which circuit or circuits is/are affected by this alarm. This is key information needed to obtain access to all network components in any given circuit.

The alarm text portion of the alarm report is used to retrieve an appropriate diagnostic rule. A diagnostic rule is one which, given an alarm message, suggests the allocation of some level of 'blame' to certain entities in the circuit under investigation. The form of these rules is very similar to that described in the description of alarm propagation. An example rule is shown in figure 5.

```
(def-diagnosis-rule
      :rule-name        Rule-1
      :doc              "given a wetting current fail alarm, suspect the
                         following three components to different degrees"
      :alarm-message    WETTING-CURRENT-FAIL
      :-->
      :assign-blame     NTU
      :value            HIGH
      :-->
      :assign-blame     MUX
      :value            MEDIUM
      :-->
      :assign-blame     TRIB
      :value            MEDIUM
)
```

Figure 5: Example Rule from Diagnostic Knowledge Base

This can be interpreted as: given a wetting current fail alarm (associated with some circuit) assign varying degrees of 'blame' to particular entities in that circuit. Blame levels are qualitative and are translated into quantitative values by referring to the particular network object in question. In this way any network component can be specialised to have different quantitative values for the same qualitative one. Interpretation of these diagnosis rules involves accessing the qualitative model which holds the network representation.

Having retrieved the appropriate diagnosis rule for the alarm report and allocated some level of blame to appropriate network objects the next step is to analyse each object in the circuit under investigation in terms of its 'blame' levels. It is important to recognise that a particular network object can be associated with several circuits and that there are usually (if not always) several alarms under investigation. Each affected circuit is now examined to extract those component objects with the highest currently allocated blames. In other words a peak-extractor function is applied to each such circuit, and this will result in one or more entities being selected. Each such extracted object is now hypothesised as a potential fault, if it is not already one.

The final stage of diagnosis involves analysing each of the current hypotheses to see if and how the belief in them is affected by the current alarm report under investigation. This involves invoking the qualitative model again. In this model information is held such that given a faulty network component one can determine which alarms are generated and how they are propagated through the network. This knowledge can be used in the diagnosis phase, such that given a hypothesised faulty object, a set of expected alarms can be generated. The actual alarm currently under investigation is thus matched against the set of expected alarms for each hypothesised object to determine if it enhances that hypothesis.

Thus belief in some hypotheses increase as more alarms are processed. The implemented system caters for alarm clear reports as well so that when a fault is cleared appropriate messages are propagated and sent to the RCE for processing, resulting in the appropriate hypothesised objects being updated and deleted from the hypothesis set.

4.3. Summary of KBS Techniques

The implemented system uses a number of knowledge based techniques. In the functional model the representation of network components is an object-oriented one. Although this paradigm is not exclusive to knowledge based systems it is closely associated with them. Circuit allocation makes use of network constraint information such as the number of ACES allowed in any circuit.

There is a rule system for storing and interpreting domain knowledge about the generation and propagation of alarms across a network. This knowledge is stored explicitly, i.e. it is held separate from any inferential (the actual deriving of new information) or control (the strategy used to drive the inferential mechanism) knowledge. This separation of domain knowledge from how and when it is used is characteristic of knowledge based systems. There are a number of advantages to be gained from this separation, an obvious one being that since the domain knowledge is separated out into a high level form it can be readily modified by a domain expert without him having to delve into the whole system.

The interpreter for the alarm propagation domain rules is data-driven, in that there is a cycle of a) the arrival of some information (an alarm) which, b) may give rise to new information (further alarm messages). The cycle continues until no new information is generated.

The diagnosis model encompasses a mixed strategy. It is initially event driven in that it is alarm reports arriving at the RCE that are used in the formation of new hypotheses. The qualitative model, which stores a representation of the network, is accessed to determine which possible objects could be at fault. This is followed by some hypothesis-driven effort where each hypothesis is investigated to determine if the current alarm message enhances that hypothesis.

5. Implementation

The demonstrator has been written in Allegro Common Lisp with Flavors, on a Macintosh II workstation. This platform was chosen since it provides a good development environment for rapid prototyping of demonstrator software.

To comply with customer requirements the demonstrator has been designed to be used with a graphical interface. In order to accomplish this the work has made use of other research being undertaken in house. Specifically, it has used a tool called the Network Modelling Support Environment (NMSE) a lisp based tool for aiding the construction and modelling of network simulation environments (Hook 1989).

6. Evaluation and Performance Considerations

The prototype system is essentially defined by two stages, a network creation stage and a fault diagnosis stage. In the projected full system we envisage the fault diagnosis aspects of the system will run on actual network scenarios. Thus the first stage of the prototype system would be redundant, the network components would already be in place and the generation and propagation of alarms to the RCE would be taken care of by current network management practice. There would be no requirement for a performance analysis of the network build stage in the prototype. This section looks at the fault diagnosis stage to highlight the (potentially) computationally expensive sections.

The top level algorithm for the fault diagnosis stage comprises:

1. Processing the set of alarms arriving at the RCE to produce initial correlation
2. Analysing this raw correlation.

Note that these steps can be carried out independently, providing a good potential for parallelism. Each of these steps could be running its own process, with step 1 being invoked whenever there was some set of alarms waiting at the RCE for processing, and step 2 continually acting on current hypotheses, modifying and updating them in the light of incoming alarms.

6.1. Initial Alarm Correlation

For each unprocessed alarm report the system has to:

a) destructure it,
b) retrieve some appropriate diagnosis rule,
c) determine potential objects for blame in connection with that alarm,
d) note which new circuits are affected.

Determining the affected circuits retrieved from destructuring the alarm report, and accessing the appropriate rule of diagnosis are potentially constant time activities. The bulk of the processing is in step c). Here the system retrieves the objects comprising a circuit and then uses the diagnosis rule to determine which subset of these objects could be to blame and how much to blame them. Determining the objects comprising a circuit is currently expensive since this is calculated at run time. A future version could have this pre-compiled.

6.2. Analysis of Raw Correlation

The initial analysis is used to create hypotheses of faults in particular network components. The next stage comprises the following steps:

a) For each of the currently affected circuits
  i) determine the most likely object(s) to be at fault

ii) for each of i) above
      a) add it to the current set of hypotheses if it is not already a working hypothesis
      b) generate (and store) the expected alarms for this hypothesis
   b) Now, match each unprocessed alarm report in turn against each current hypothesis to determine how (if) it helps to increase the validity of that hypothesis.
   c) Order the hypotheses in terms of merit.

These steps are currently the most costly in the fault diagnosis stage and this is likely to continue to be the case in future versions. Step a) above is expensive each time it is carried out if there are a large number of currently affected circuits. Each circuit in the list will have to be examined each time to determine which of its component objects are most likely to be faulty. This is necessary on each cycle since any of the most recent alarm reports may have caused an update to any particular circuit's entities. Thus the most likely candidates in a circuit at one time frame may not be the most likely candidates at a future time frame, or at least there may be additional candidates. Expected alarm information could be pre-compiled in a full scale implementation. Both steps b) and c) above are again currently functions of the length of a list, this time the list of current hypotheses. These two steps would require most consideration in future work.

7. Summary and Further Work

The prototype implementation has successfully shown the feasibility of applying knowledge based techniques for the diagnosis of faults in private digital networks.

Two further phases have been identified and are underway. The first is creating a comprehensive set of functional and performance requirements for a large scale model and the second involves the investigation and comparison of other architectures, incorporation of CCITT standards (CCITT 1988), and design and implementation of the full scale alarm monitoring work station to be integrated with the appropriate telecommunications network management equipment.

8. Acknowledgement

The work reported here was carried out on behalf of and funded by GEC Plessey Telecommunications Limited.

9. References

Callahan, P.H. (1988).
Expert Systems for AT&T Switched Network Maintenance.
AT&T Technical Journal, Vol 67, Issue 1.

CCITT (1988).
Blue Book Recommendations.
Melbourne.

Coleman, C.S. (1989).
The Application of Knowledge Based Systems Within The Proposed TMN Environment to Support Fault Diagnosis.
In IEE Colloquium on Expert Systems for Fault Diagnosis in Engineering Applications, No. 1989/64.

Hook, M.K. (1989).
The Network Modelling Simulation Environment.
Internal Report, Plessey Research Roke Manor Ltd.

Copyright: 4 July 1989   The Plessey Company Plc

A KNOWLEDGE BASED SYSTEM FOR EXCHANGE MAINTENANCE

J Butler, W Stein, J Shepherdson & K Beard
British Telecom, RT7122, 151 Gower Street, LONDON
J Bigham
Queen Mary College, LONDON

Abstract

This paper describes a Knowledge Based System, which works mainly from switch design knowledge, developed to aid maintenance of a modern digital telephone exchange. Several aspects of the work are described including the development of a specialised knowledge representation tool built on an object oriented environment, its application, graphical presentation of information using high resolution colour screens and fault diagnosis. The demonstrator described is connected to a real exchange, used for network and exchange testing purposes, which has provided a valid development and testing environment. This work builds on the experience gained and the lessons learnt in an earlier ESPRIT project.

1. Introduction

Modern telephone exchanges are complex pieces of equipment which must be reliable. This is ensured partly by redundancy built into the design, an example of which is the use of worker/standby arrangements, and self testing capabilities. To provide required traffic handling capacity many units are replicated several times. When such systems do fail it is important that faulty units are identified and replaced quickly. Modern exchanges contain automatic diagnostic features to help locate problems, these features are contained in subsystems, which in some cases monitor actual performance or the ability to function. When some failures occur, many test reports can be generated automatically due to this self testing facility. Quick identification of the most important information from these reports can be difficult. Also, since these systems are reliable some failure types are rarely seen and use of paper manuals is necessary to understand the fault reports. On detecting some serious fault conditions an exchange itself will automatically return to a previous consistent state and restart. The cause of these "rollback and restarts" are difficult to detect because of the complexity of the exchange. Moreover, they rarely happen and so there is little opportunity for local knowledge to be acquired. When these events do occur the relevant data produced by the exchange is not in an easily readable form and detailed knowledge about the exchange, such as the switch resource dependency structure, is required.

The focus of attention in this paper is the use of Artificial Intelligence techniques to build aids, which help with maintenance activities. One activity when building conventional Expert Systems is the requirement to collect necessary heuristics. In the case of telecommunications systems, there are often many people who have elements of the information required. It is evident that such Expert Systems are valuable (Fox 1988), but they suffer from a number of disadvantages;

these include the problems of acquiring, then checking completeness and consistency of heuristics. To improve this situation the idea of using problem solving techniques that work from first principles or "deep" knowledge has been suggested, for example, qualitative reasoning techniques including: reasoning from structure to behaviour (Genesereth 1984); use of causal models, particularly for diagnosis; and use of "naive physics" to reason from general common sense knowledge. Fault identification in a water mixing process is described by Zhang, Roberts & Ellis (1988) which uses a deep knowledge approach, similar to that considered here. Characteristics of the telecommunications switch domain which can be exploited include: the availability of design information - which can be used as the base knowledge; modularity; and self testing features. Earlier research within British Telecom, in this area, has included the KRITIC project (Williamson, Butler, King & Bigham 1987) which began to exploit these characteristics. The KRITIC work also showed the need, when handling large amounts of information, for facilities to display different views of the data, the need for logical data partitioning, and the need for ways to bring together disparate information. This motivated our earlier knowledge representation work. This paper describes the Enhanced Switch Maintenance System (ESMS) project which has developed these ideas further. End users have been shown early demonstrators and made valuable comments particularly on graphical interface issues and functional requirements.

2. The Enhanced Switch Maintenance System

The Enhanced Switch Maintenance System project has concentrated on a number of key issues. These include trying to develop an efficient knowledge representation approach for the generic and instance data, how to integrate design and heuristic information for specific fault analysis (rollback and restart fault reports), and correlation of fault information potentially caused by a limited number of actual fault events. Exchange knowledge consisting of descriptions, relationships and rules has been represented using a frame-based approach to form the basis for inferencing requirements, this has also been considered by Fikes & Kehler (1985). An exchange consists of several subsystems which perform well defined functions. Development work so far has concentrated on one subsystem which is directly relevant to the difficulties described - the Processor Utility Subsystem (PUS). In order to make visible results a demonstrator has been constructed which will aid maintenance activities on the PUS. This has shown the viability of the work and provides an opportunity to experiment with the various ways Knowledge Based Systems ideas should be applied and techniques integrated to support first line maintenance.

3. Overview of Complete System

The demonstrator has been written in Lisp and Prolog on Symbolics hardware. The hardware supports multi-process working and the code has been written to take advantage of this. For example, each module is a process and several can be running continuously. In some cases a module can be running as a number of processes at the same time. The major components, see figure 1, which constitute the ESMS will now be outlined. The ESMS demonstrator is connected to a real exchange and has as its input solicited and unsolicited exchange maintenance data output. This exchange output is translated automatically by a parser into data usable by the demonstrator.

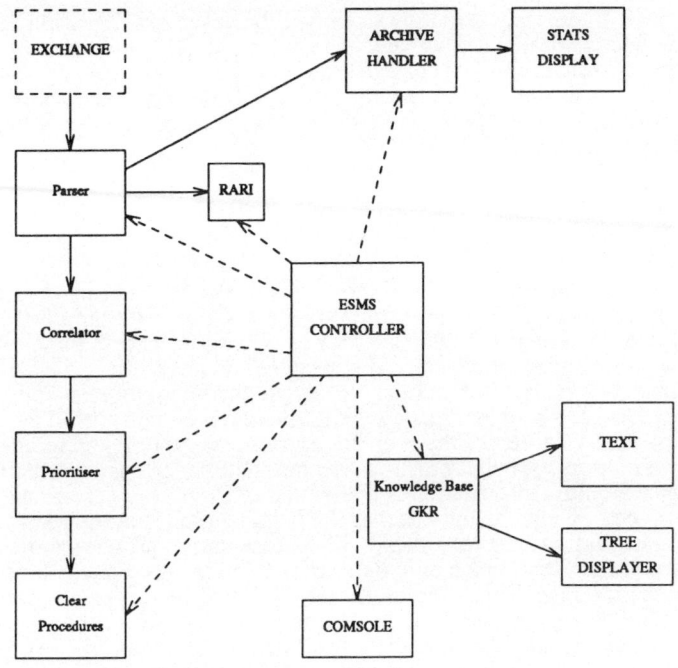

Figure 1 - ESMS Demonstrator Components

<u>KEY</u>

_____ Information
------ Control & Information

      The exchange output parser developed within the project is similar to that reported by GTE (St Jacques 1988). The ESMS Controller, which contains rules allowing various control strategies to be tried, sends this information to either the Correlator or the Rollback and Restart Interface (RARI) module. Particular fault reports which identify rollback and restart situations are dealt with by the Rollback and Restart module. This module involves the integration of design knowledge and heuristics. In order to correlate other fault information an extended Truth Maintenance System has been developed, which uses various dependency networks generated from switch design knowledge, to construct consistent lists of relevant suspect replaceable units. The identified units are then ranked by the Prioritiser, based on information such as likelihood of failure using Mean Time Between Failure (MTBF) data, possible effect on service, availability of spares, time and difficulty of repair. Once a priority suspect is identified, the appropriate replacement action is generated and displayed. A knowledge representation tool (GKR) developed to assist design knowledge capture, representation and display, provides the knowledge base. This knowledge base has also been used to support an enhanced user interface (called Comsole - Command Console) which provides facilities such as command completion and relevant parameter range identification.

Three aspects of the system will be described in greater detail. These are the knowledge base, the Rollback and Restart module, and the approach to fault information correlation. The actual operation of the demonstrator is more complicated because of the need to log activity, check repair actions and sometimes to try other suspects in an iterative fashion, these aspects and others are not described here.

4. The Knowledge Base

The demonstrator is a showcase for the application of various Artificial Intelligence techniques for building a diagnostic system, in particular, it utilises design information as the basis for its operation. This is important because when new telephone exchanges are first installed no heuristics exist for their maintenance, but there will be extensive design documentation available. The knowledge base has been built using GKR, a tool developed within the project, which specifically addresses the problem of trying to capture and represent switch design information, especially the representation of generic and specialisation information. Generic information is that which is relevant to all exchanges of a particular type. Specialisation information is that which is particular to a specific exchange installation. The tool allows the representation problem to be decomposed into Views, each of which can be used to represent different aspects of the area of interest. The tool allows information to be presented graphically which can aid data entry and checking. Further, this has been used to give engineers quick visual overviews of fault situations. For example, in one View (resource dependency) colour has been used to show the status of resources, at different levels of detail.

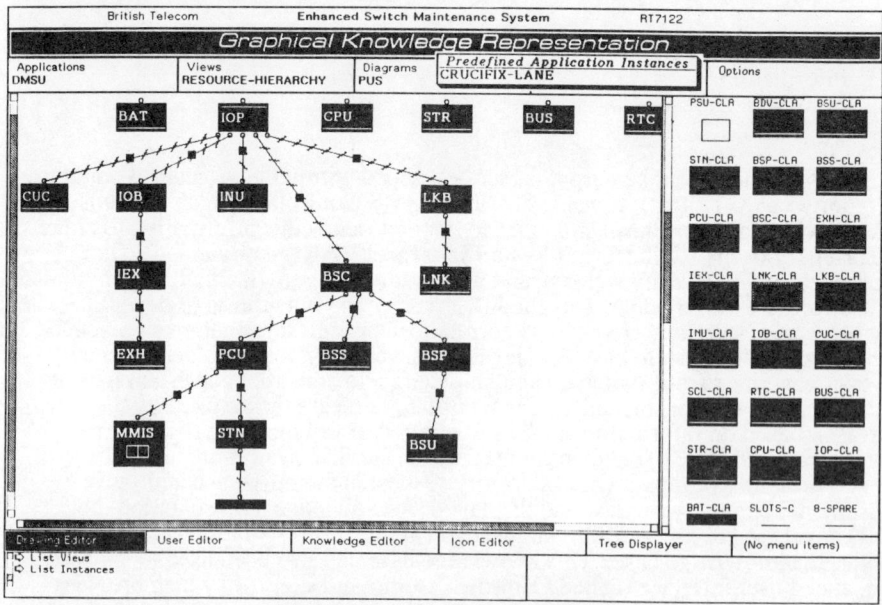

Figure 2 - GKR Drawing Editor
showing PUS Resource Dependency

Figure 2 shows part of the resource dependency hierarchy relevant to an exchange type and is termed a generic diagram. In the diagram, boxes represent generic resources and the lines between two resources indicate a designed functional dependency of the lower resource on the one above it. This relationship holds true for all exchanges of a particular type and by only displaying one of each of the resources, even when many are replicated both for security purposes and traffic handling capability, unnecessary data representation is avoided. Details about a particular installation can be added, that is the numbers of each type of resource (specialisations), to form what is termed an Application Specialisation data set. This can represent the information about all the specialisations of each resource that exists in a particular exchange. These Application Specialisation data sets can be saved and reloaded as required and many unique data sets may be constructed. In this way, the resource dependency diagram of figure 2 can be used to represent the same section of every installed exchange of a particular type.

The actual data fields associated with each generic object can be unique to each of the Views that an object appears in. Figure 3 shows the mechanism by which this is arranged. It shows a physical layout view, displayed in the Knowledge Editor interface. Intermediate data frames ("mixins") can be constructed which contain data fields which can be inherited by any objects that are made dependent upon them. In this case the intermediate data frames themselves, have been arranged so that inheritance is cascaded from floor-mixin to siu-mixin, via the intermediate ones. In this way, the class objects can be made to inherit composite data fields, thus reducing the amount of work required to associate relevant data and default values with the various objects. Figure 4 shows many of the same class objects in another view, with a simple inheritance structure dictating the different data fields that will be associated with instances of these classes in this particular View. In this way, only the data relevant to a View is displayed with a particular object in that View.

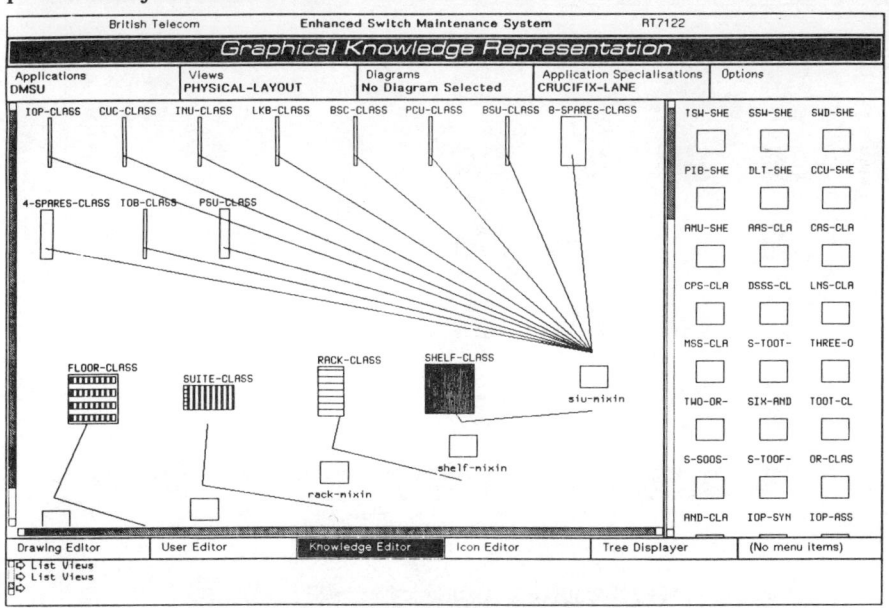

Figure 3 - GKR Knowledge Editor
showing Composition of Physical Layout Data Fields

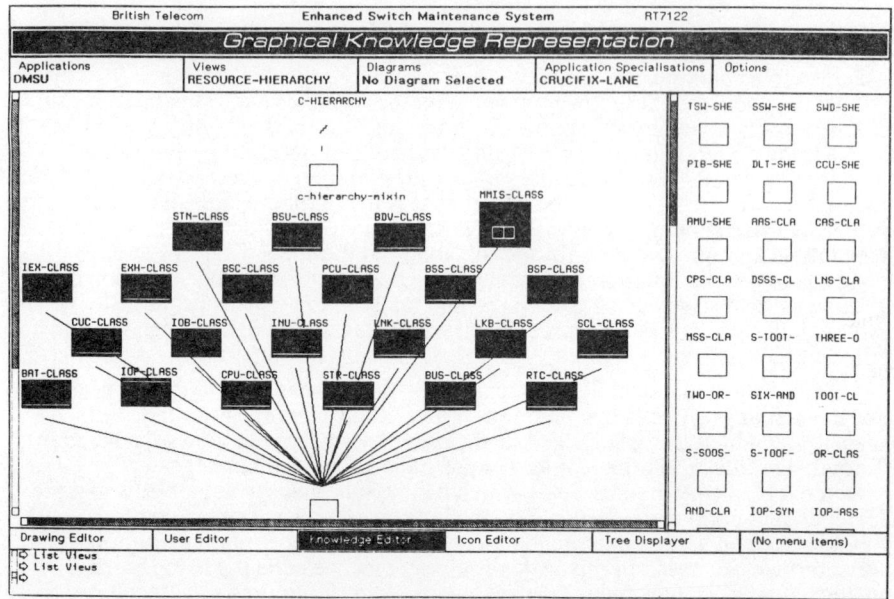

Figure 4 - GKR Knowledge Editor
showing Composition of Resource Dependency Data Fields

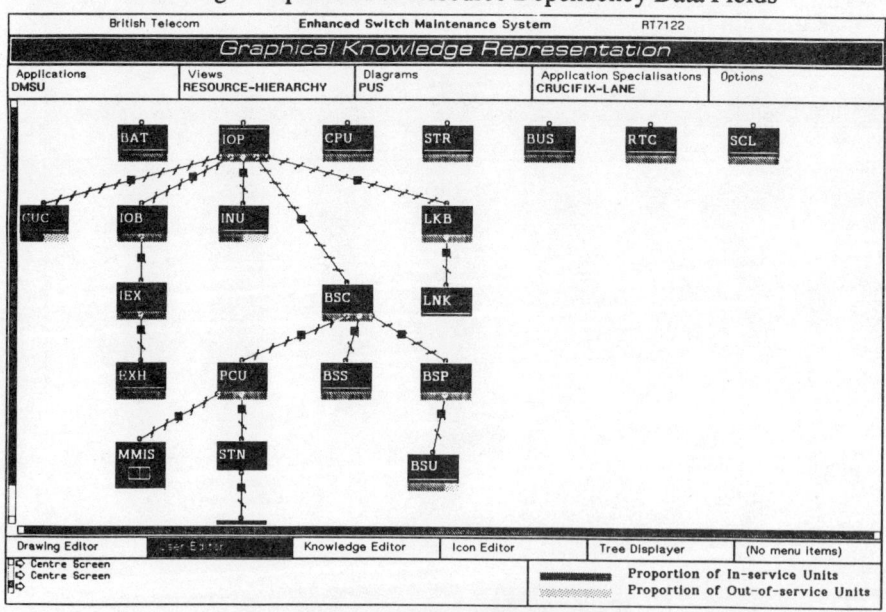

Figure 5 - GKR User Editor
showing Part of Resource Dependency with "Thermometers"

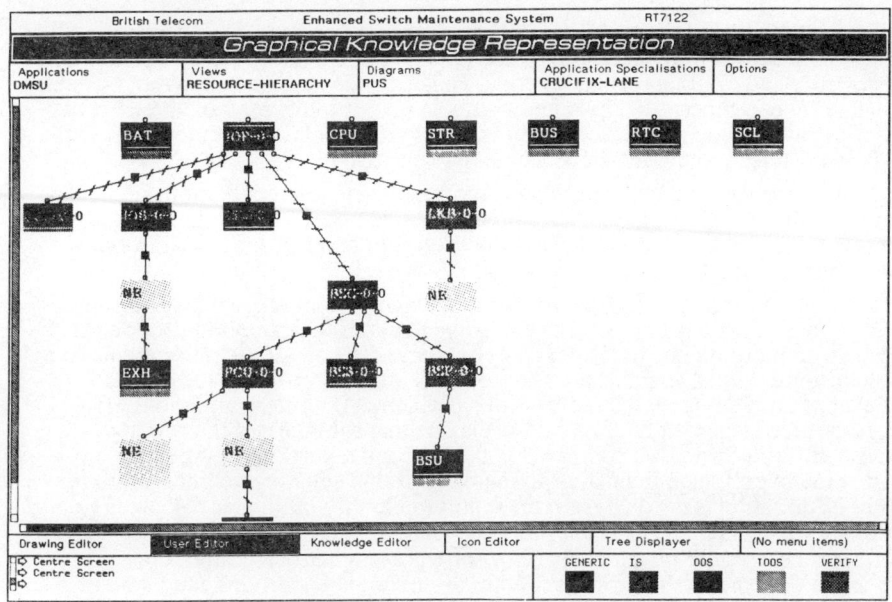

Figure 6 - GKR User Editor
showing Specialisation of Part of Resource Dependency

The Application Specialisation data for a specific exchange can be loaded and used to generate "thermometers" which appear beneath the objects. Each "thermometer" is used to indicate the proportion of specialisations in and out of service for a particular resource, an example can be seen in Figure 5 - the key for resource status is in the bottom right hand corner. Thus the maintenance engineer can see at a glance the proportions and types of resources that are faulty. Figure 6 shows the same diagram after it has been specialised. The objects now represent particular specialisations of resources belonging to one specific exchange, and each resource is colour coded according to its last known state. When a diagram is specialised more detail is displayed, the key in the bottom-right corner shows the colours and the states they denote. If the state of a displayed specialisation is updated (for example, by receipt - in a background process - of a status report from the exchange who's specialisations are being examined) then it will be immediately redisplayed in the colour that corresponds to the new state.

5. Rollback and Restart Fault Report Module

This module has been designed to deal with a set of fault situations, which are particularly involved and can require quick corrective action to be taken because of their potentially serious effect. When an exchange is operating, it continuously carries out self checks on both its hardware and software components. Detected hardware and software faults may result in initiating diagnostic and recovery procedures. These procedures, when serious, may involve a rollback process. Rollback actions are initiated to recover from automatically detected system faults (hardware or software). They involve the reloading of subsets or all of the exchange software and data. When data is thought to have been corrupted, it is replaced by an original (rollback) copy. This is to ensure that the current unstable exchange state is superseded by a known stable one. If faults remain, the level of rollback is increased and greater amounts of data reloaded. In extreme cases, such escalation can lead to the restart of a complete exchange.

In general exchanges are very reliable and these situations do not occur very often. This fact together with the relative novelty of digital exchanges means that there is little opportunity for field staff to build up knowledge of how to deal with these situations.

The task of finding the cause of these problems involves analysing dumps of exchange data, consulting exchange manuals and studying the current exchange configuration. This is not an easy task and successful identification of the problem source is not guaranteed. The Rollback and Restart Interface (RARI) module has been developed to address this problem. The inferencing in RARI occurs in three stages. In the first instance a one line summary of the restart is produced from information contained in the rollback report following steps detailed in the exchange manuals. On the basis of this generic one line summary, further information is derived from the report to identify particular resources or processes at fault. Finally when applicable, heuristics derived from engineers or information derived from the analysis of software and hardware fault reports around the time of the rollback are used to discover the underlying hardware or software faults, which caused the rollback.

Eventually the RARI module could provide a central facility, which engineers all around the country could access for advice under these special fault conditions. If a new scenario is encountered and the problem diagnosed or further heuristics identified, this new information could be added to the knowledge base and made available to others. This will require an appropriate interface and functions for checking the consistency of the rule base, when new rules are added.

RARI has been written mainly in Prolog to take advantage of its inferencing mechanism, although there are functions written in Lisp to access information concerning reports. The initial data base was built up by parsing relevant exchange documentation automatically, (which had been read using an Optical Character Reader) turning it into Prolog clauses. RARI has been tested by generating rollback situations at a test exchange, the system has responded by analysing the associated fault reports and providing the correct interpretation.

6. Fault Report Correlation

When some fault events occur in an exchange, several fault reports can be generated at the same time, in response to the same cause. Unfortunately these fault reports do not necessarily identify the underlying cause. In order to achieve this unique fault localisation, knowledge of the exchange is required and various testing procedures (which can be extracted from the exchange documentation) need to be carefully followed. The task of the Correlator is to take as input these fault reports and to generate the possible cause(s). The underlying approach taken is to use the switch design knowledge which gives various dependency information to form networks on which inferences may be made. Dependency relations of relevance include resource dependency, powering arrangements, and clock pulse supplies. The design knowledge is modularised and pre-compiled into sub-networks from the information stored in the knowledge base (GKR). The reason for this division into communicating sub-networks (modules) is because the time required for pre-compilation of entire networks would be prohibitive.

The modules communicate to maintain consistency when fault information is received. The consistent suspects from the modules are used to produce the overall suspects list. This process uses a Logical Assumption Based Truth Maintenance System (LATMS) (Bigham 1989). Generating these sub-networks is a time consuming task, but this is performed before they are required and the results are stored. The particular relationships used to generate the networks are those which can cause a fault event to produce more than one fault report. These relationships are modelled using the knowledge representation tool (GKR) to achieve the required discrimination between replaceable units. As an example, the data to build the resource dependency network is contained in GKR with each resource (object) possessing a list of its resource dependency relationships with other resources. For example, the resource BSC-0-0 (in the PUS) has an associated logical resource dependency list of: (AND PCU-0-0 BSS-0-0 BSP-0-0). In order to initially build the required networks, the LATMS module retrieves the resource dependency relationships associated with each of these three resources, then their resources dependencies and so on until termination resources are reached. From this information the LATMS then generates the network shown in Figure 7.

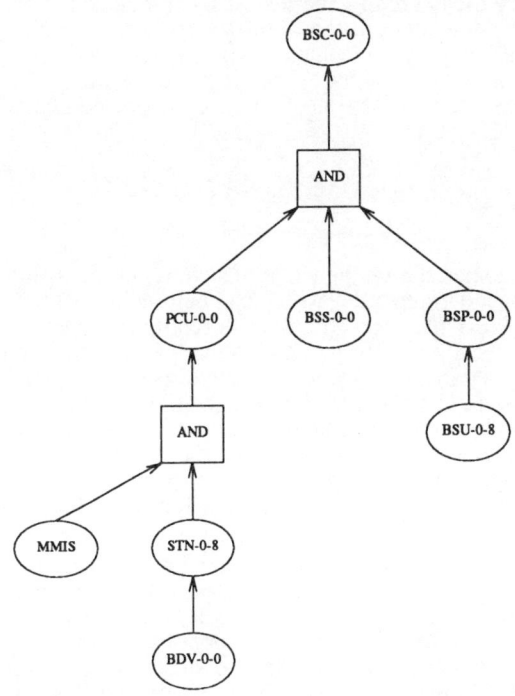

Figure 7 - Part of the Resource Dependency LATMS Network

In operation, when a group of fault reports are received they are passed to the Correlator. Several relationships are currently used for this initial phase including exchange resource dependency, powering and clocking arrangements. The results of each of these is then combined to produce a list of suspects which are passed on to the Prioritiser. In more detail, the networks remain stable until fault reports are received from the exchange. Each fault report specifies a resource and its current status. Consider part of the resource dependency relationship and assume that reports indicate "BSC-0-0" and "BSP-0-0" are both out of service. This information is propagated through the network, supersets removed and in this case the following suspect list produced "BSP-0-0 or BSU-0-8". A final suspect list is generated using this information and other suspects generated by other dependency relations and passed to the Prioritiser. The Prioritiser will order the suspects, some may be eliminated directly by running exchange tests. This particular case will result in the suggestion that the problem lies with the "BSP-0-0".

As the Correlator is in continual operation a mechanism for removing fault reports which have been accounted for is required. The current method is to restart from the base networks, regenerating suspects using only those fault reports which have not been accounted for. This is in preference to backtracking which would involve a large memory overhead. An advantage of the chosen approach is that since a known state is regularly returned to, any maloperation should not cause a serious problem.

In summary the LATMS generates suspect replaceable units given several fault reports. The advantages of this approach include: working from design knowledge so that any design changes can be incorporated into the data base and easily reflected in the Correlator operation by regenerating the effected networks, the networks can be built off-line, and the approach can handle multiple faults.

7. Conclusion

Work to date has shown the value of several Artificial Intelligence techniques by developing a demonstrator which can help field staff to handle real problems. Development work has used a rapid prototyping approach to produce demonstrations showing the applicability of a Knowledge Based System approach to diagnostic tasks. Field staff and engineers who have seen the ESMS demonstrator have considered its functionality and the use of colour graphics on high resolution screens to be valuable. The next stage of the work is the development of a full scale prototype. The system has concentrated on one subsystem of the exchange, future work will include expanding this to cover other subsystems. Meanwhile some features of this work will migrate into other maintenance aids.

In the telecommunications field the development and growing use of standards will increase the choice of equipment and services available. Several telecommunications network operators are now developing "Intelligent Networks". These will offer customers increased facilities, the opportunity to alter existing services and even allow customers to fashion their own services. In order to support this a greater separation between switching components and their control is envisaged. As new services are developed it is too inefficient to also develop individual operations and maintenance systems. It is necessary that one flexible system manage a broad range of services, with all of the infrastructure and organisation that implies. This is one of the telecommunications domains in which the use of Artificial Intelligence techniques will be essential. In order to achieve this greater use of design knowledge is required, thus removing the need for detailed heuristics. In the longer term this will require system design tools to be used for the automatic generation of the necessary knowledge bases from the design information.

The British Telecom authors acknowledge the permission of the Director of Research and Technology for permission to publish this paper. The views expressed in this paper are the personal views of the authors and do not necessarily reflect the views of British Telecom.

References

Bigham, J. (1989). Logical Assumption Based Truth Maintenance System. Technical Paper, Department of Electrical & Electronic Engineering. Queen Mary College, London.

Fikes, R. & Kehler, T. (1985). The Role of Frame-Based Representation in Reasoning. Communications of the ACM., 28, no.9.

Fox, J. & Slawsky, G. (1988). Bellcore. The Role of Expert Systems in Switch Maintenance Operations and the Generation of Switch Analysis Requirements. IEEE Journal on Selected Areas of Telecommunications, 6, no.4,

Genesereth, M.R. (1984). The Use of Design Knowledge in Automated Diagnosis. Artificial Intelligence. no. 24.

St Jacques. (1988). An Intelligent Telephone Switch Interface for a Real-Time Network Control Expert System. Artificial Intelligence in Engineering: Robotics and Processes.

Williamson, G., Butler, J., King, S., (British Telecom) & Bigham, J., (Queen Mary College). (1987). Using a KBS in Telecomms II. ESPRIT, Technical Proceedings.

Zhang, J., Roberts, P.D. & Ellis, J.E. (1988). An Application of Expert Systems Techniqes to the On-Line Control and Fault Diagnosis of a Mixing Process. Journal of Intelligent and Robotic Systems.

PROBLEMS OF DIAGNOSTIC KNOWLEDGE PROCESSING:
DESIGN AND IMPLEMENTATION OF THE SYSTEM DIGS

Gennady Agre, Danail Dochev

Institute of Engineering Cybernetics and Robotics, BAS
Acad. Bonchev str. bl. 29A, Sofia 1113
BULGARIA

Abstract

The paper presents the expert system shell DIGS intended for technical diagnosis. After a discussion of some problems of diagnostic knowledge representation the outlines of the system architecture and the fault finder strategies are described. Some conclusions obtained from experience of DIGS usage for developing particular expert systems are presented. Finally a modified version DIGS-2 - an integrated system, automating the creation, filling and verification of the knowledge base and the generation of stand-alone ES for particular applications is discussed.

1. Diagnostic knowledge representation

In a diagnostic problem a set of symptoms or "manifestations" is given and their presence must be explained by using one's knowledge about the world. At least two kinds of knowledge are used by most real-word diagnostic expert systems - structural and probabilistic. The structural knowledge specifies relations between main elements of given domain and probabilistic knowledge specifies the strengths of these relations.
Among all kinds of relations the causal relations are the most important in diagnostic problem solving.
A diagnostic problem using causal and probabilistic knowledge may be defined by a four-tuple : $< D, M, C, M^* >$ (Peng & Reggia 1987) where

$D = \{ d_1, ..., d_n \}$ - finite nonempty set of disorders,
$M = \{ m_1, ..., m_k \}$ - finite nonempty set of manifestations,
$C \subseteq D \times M$ - connections with $\text{domain}(C) = D$ and $\text{range}(C) = M$
and $<d_i, m_j> \in C$ iff "disorder d_i may cause
manifestation m_j with certainty c_{ij}".
$M^* \subseteq M$ - subset of M.

It is necessary to find out a subset of disorders $D^* \subseteq D$, which explains the existence of manifestations M^*. The existing approaches to solve this diagnostic problem can be roughly separated in two groups, depending on the representation of the connections C - pattern matching approach and sequential refinement approach.
In the first case a diagnosed system is modeled by a "black box" for which only the connections between its inputs (disorders) and outputs (observed manifestations) are known. These connections can be realized through an intermediate objects - syndromes which are associated with some subsets of the manifestations set. This approach is typical for the medical diagnosis. In this case the problem solution is reduced to con-

struction of a few most plausible hypotheses about possible disorders (illnesses) by checking for the best matching of all observed manifestations (symptoms) with given pattern (syndrome). Typical examples of this approach are the expert systems MYCIN (Buchanan & Shortliffe 1984) and INTERNIST (Pople 1985). The main disadvantage of this approach is its low effectiveness in case of many possible disorders or when multiple disorders take place.

The sequential refinement approach is more typical for the technical than for the medical diagnosis. The technical diagnosis has the following main features:
    - the number of elements of the set D containing possible disorders (faults) is very big and considerably greater than the number of observed manifestations M;
    - the more "deeper" connections between both sets are known.
Usually these connections represent the structure of the system under test (for example "part of" hierarchy) or a fault propagation net.

In this case the diagnostic problem solution is obtained by a movement in a net, localizing a fault by comparing the real behavior of the object with the expected one. A movement strategy is controlled by the test results and the strength of the net connections. Actually this approach has been used for design of the expert system DIGS.

2. Knowledge representation in the ES DIGS

The technical diagnosis process in the ES DIGS is considered as a sequence of situations, occurring during the fault search. A set of situations, linked by causal or structural connections, defines a so called diagnostic net (D-net) - a direct acyclic graph $D = <S, C>$ where the nodes represent possible situations and arcs - connections between them (Sgurev et al. 1985). The diagnostic net may be considered as a model of the concrete technical object from the diagnostic point of view.

Each situation S is described by the following three-tuple:

$$S = < N, T, A >,$$

where:

   N - a symptom, checked in the given situation;
   T - a test procedure, used to check its presence;
   A - a description of repairing action, necessary for fault
       removal (in case if the symptom is a fault).

Each arc $c_{ij} \in C$ represents a causal or structural connection between the situations S_i and S_j (S_i is manifestation of S_j) and has a certainty factor P_{ij}.

The symptoms, tested in situations without successors in the D-net (terminal nodes), correspond to possible faults.

The symptoms without ancestors in the D-net, correspond to possible initial symptoms.

The diagnostic problem solving strategy is guided by a criteria for minimizing the number of the applied tests.

3. ES DIGS architecture

The expert system DIGS consists of three main blocks - knowledge base, fault finder and interface block.

The knowledge base is a presentation of the diagnostic net reflecting the diagnostic knowledge for given technical objects.

The fault finder detects all the faults, causing the initial symptoms. This block contains the following four subblocks: monitor, block for processing of initial symptoms, inference engine and block for detection of parallel faults.

The monitor controls the overall process of faults detection, coordinates the subblocks operation and prepares statistic data about the diagnostic session.

The block for processing of initial symptoms combines the initial symptoms, entered by the user, into groups for successive faults search. More precisely, the given block tries to find out the deepest symptom in the D-net which can explain the presence of the whole group of initial symptoms. This symptom is passed as an input symptom to the inference engine.

The inference engine finds out the fault, causing the input symptom. The inference engine search strategy is based on the principle of minimizing the number of the performed tests.

The block for detection of parallel faults finds out all faults, which simultaneous existence causes the appearance of given initial symptom (or group of symptoms). The block starts after removal of the fault detected by the inference engine. In fact this block tries to detect the symptom which localizes maximally the parallel fault. This symptom is passed to the inference engine to find out the cause of the symptom appearance.

The interface block carries out communication between the user and the ES DIGS during fault finding process and supplies the user with additional information intended to increase the effectiveness of the man-machine interaction.

In the main (consultative) mode of operation the interface block shows on the screen the description and possible answers of the current test procedure and processes the answers, entered by the user. Instead of answering the test the user can also request additional information from the system. These requests are processed by the auxiliary modes of system operation.

In the "Why" mode the system explains why the test offered to the user has to be performed. The explanation is based on prediction of the possible faults if the presence of the symptom under test would be confirmed.

In the "Trace" mode the user can examine the current state of the knowledge base. This mode is used for checking the completeness of the expert knowledge.

As mentioned before the system uses a "forward" (data-driven) search strategy. The user has a possibility to reject this default strategy by means of the "Hypotheses" mode . In this mode the user may chose the most probable (in his opinion) fault which has to be tested. Thus he forces the system to use a "backward" goal-driven strategy. The combination of both strategies improves the efficiency of the system operation.

4. The underlying principles

In the next paragraph the search strategy, used by the inference engine, will be discussed in more details. For this purpose it is necessary to formulate explicitly the underlying principles of the proposed model of the diagnostic process (D-net):

1. The measurement (execution of a test procedure) does not affect the faulty device.
2. The test results are not changed during the diagnostic session.
3. The presence of a symptom, determined by the test execution, confirms the existence of all symptoms, which are its ancestors in the D-net.
4. The absence of a symptom, determined by the test execution, confirms the absence of all its successors in the D-net.

The first two principles concern the nature of faulty device. The last two ones describe the basic property of the connections, used in the D-net - their transitivity.

5. Fault finding strategy

The inference engine is designed to find out a single fault N_t, indicated by the presence of a single initial symptom N_0. The fault is searched by means of generating and testing hypotheses.
An arbitrary node N_i, for which there is a passable path, connecting N_i with N_0, will be called hypothesis H_i.
The path $L_i = \{ c_{0,1}, c_{1,2}, \ldots, c_{i-1,i} \}$ is passable iff $P_{j-1,j} > 0$ for all $j \in [1, i]$, where $P_{j-1,j}$ is a certainty factor of the arc $c_{j-1,j} \in L_i$.
The value $P(H_i)$, calculated by the following formula:

$$P(H_i) = \prod_{k=1}^{i} P_{k-1,k} \qquad (1)$$

will be called certainty of the hypothesis H_i, described by the path L_i.
We will say that the hypothesis H_i is confirmed (i.e. $P(H_i)=1$,) if the presence of the symptom S_i is determined by the execution of the test T_i, otherwise H_i is considered as rejected and the corresponding arc $c_{i-1,i}$ is defined as not passable (i.e. $P_{i-1,i} = 0$).
The hypothesis H_i is checked (the test T_i is proposed for execution), if

$$P(H_i) \leq B \qquad (2)$$

where B is the current threshold value.
The problem for detection of a single fault is considered to be solved, if there is a confirmed hypothesis H_t such that N_t is a terminal node.
It is obvious that the criteria of minimizing the number of applied tests is transformed to minimization of the number of hypotheses, which in turn depends on the certainty of the generated hypotheses and on the magnitude of a threshold value.
The formula (1) determines the direction of hypotheses generation. Let B be a given threshold value. The most probable successor N_m of N_0 is chosen as a first approximation of the most plausible hypothesis, ex-

plaining the appearance of the initial symptom N_0:

$$PO_m = \max_{k=1}^{n_0}\{PO_k\} \qquad (3)$$

where n_0 is the number of successors of N_0.

If $P(H_1) = PO_m \leq B$ (or N_m is a terminal node), then the most plausible hypothesis is built. Otherwise the most probable successor of N_m is chosen as the next candidate. The certainty of the new hypothesis is calculated according to (1). The process of hypotheses generation is terminated when the certainty of the hypothesis is equal or less than threshold value.

As can be seen, the generation of the most plausible hypothesis depends not only on the certainty factors, specified by the expert, but on the threshold value too. In most of the expert systems which use similar algorithm for hypotheses generation, the threshold value is fixed and chosen by the system developer. In the ES DIGS this value is recalculated after each test execution and determined according to the following formula:

$$B = \max_{k=1, k \neq m}^{n_0}\{PO_k\} \qquad (4)$$

where n_0 is the number of successors of N_0 and N_m - its most probable successor (see formula (3)).

In other words, in each step of hypotheses construction process the set of all possible hypotheses is reduced to the two most probable ones. The hypothesis with the greatest plausibility is used for further expansion and the certainty factor of the second one is chosen as current threshold value. This process is terminated when two hypotheses with approximately equal certainty factors occur.

If the hypothesis H_i is confirmed by the test T_i, then due to connections transitivity the problem of finding out the cause of appearance of the initial symptom N_0 comes to finding the cause of the existence of the symptom N_i. This problem is solved according to the algorithm described above by choosing a new threshold value, based on the certainty factors of the N_i successors.

If the hypothesis H_i is rejected, the corresponding arc $c_{i-1,i}$ is labeled as not passable and next to the last node N_{i-1} is chosen as a candidate to be a next hypothesis, but its certainty decreases proportionally to the certainty factor of the rejected arc:

$$P^*(H_{i-1}) = P(H_{i-1}) - P(H_i) = P(H_{i-1}) * (1 - P_{i-1,i}) \qquad (5)$$

The threshold value is not changed and the condition for applying the test (formula (3)) is checked. If it holds the most plausible hypothesis is found and the test T_{i-1} is applied. Otherwise the above-mentioned process of hypotheses construction is repeated.

The proposed algorithm may be considered as a combination of moving in depth and in breadth of the D-net, controlled only by the expert knowledge and knowledge, acquired during the diagnostic session.

6. Discussion of the chosen formalism

Two particular expert systems based on the object-independent ES DIGS have been developed - an ES for diagnosis of personal computers (Agre et al. 1985) and an ES for diagnosis of disk units. The experience acquired during the development and the use of these systems, and the cooperation with domain experts in filling the knowledge bases lead the authors to the following conclusions:
1. The experience of using ES DIGS for diagnostic of digital equipment proved the adequacy of the chosen model. The diagnostic net enables to combine surface and deep knowledge in a unified causal model, so the semantics of the different KB fragments can be defined completely by the domain experts.
2. In the case of digital equipment diagnosis the knowledge base can be easy decomposed into weakly connected parts, represented by shallow diagnostic nets. Therefore, there is no need for complicated search strategies of the inference engine.
3. The chosen fixed formalism for knowledge representation enables building of automated knowledge acquisition system, which eliminates the necessity of a knowledge engineer. This is only possible since the proposed formalism is close to the natural way of fault finding, used by human experts. So the knowledge acquisition process is also natural and the domain expert can store his own knowledge by simply following the system driven dialogue.

7. Integrated diagnostic knowledge processing system

The authors experience in building particular expert systems for technical diagnosis shows, that:
- It is recommendable to design technical diagnostic expert system which can use test equipment, enabling automatic execution of the test procedures. In the ES for diagnostic of personal computers, based on DIGS, some of the digital measurements have been automated by means of a special test equipment module. Its use considerably increased the effectiveness of the system. This approach to automate the diagnostic process can be seen as a step toward building "on-line" ES and aimed at solving diagnostic problems and monitoring and control problems as well.
- The pure consultation ES (without automation of the test procedures) can be still effective only if they provide sophisticated problem-oriented means for knowledge acquisition and updating, permitting to minimize the time, required for building a complete knowledge base for a certain technical object. Such systems can be very useful for personnel training.
- The large volume of textual information raises the requirements for the text processing facilities. It is desirable to use various functions of the general purpose text editors (screen oriented editing, accessing and copying blocks, using pattern etc.), combined with context access to the commands - depending on the current step of the process. Similar functions are useful for graphic information processing on filling the knowledge base as well.

The above-mentioned considerations have been taken into account for building a modified version of the ES DIGS - DIGS-2. It is an integrated expert system, automating all the tasks concerning the creation, filling

and verification of the knowledge base, and provide the possibility to
generate stand-alone ES for particular applications. The main features
of the DIGS-2 are the following:
    - specialized knowledge base editor, enabling the domain expert to
create and modify the knowledge bases for particular technical objects.
The situations, describing the possible paths from the initial symptoms
to the faults are successively specified by the expert by means of a
system driven dialogue. It is performed in terms of the problem domain
(symptoms, tests etc.). It is important to emphasize on the fact that at
each moment the expert works on a single KB fragment (a particular
situation of the diagnostic process) and the overall net structure is
created automatically by the system.
    - an ES shell, processing the knowledge bases, built by the specialized KB editor. The ES shell permits to test the semantics of KB
parts or incomplete knowledge bases using the standard inference and explanation mechanisms.
    - tools for configuration and generation of stand-alone expert
systems, combining the ES shell with the KB appropriately transformed in
order to increase the effectiveness of its use.
The systems DIGS and DIGS-2 are implemented in CSY-PROLOG (CSY-PROLOG
1986), a version of PROLOG with procedural interface-oriented facilities
and operate on IBM PC XT/AT computers.

Acknowledgments

   We thank Christo Dichev and Zdravko Markov for their helpful comments
on earlier drafts of this article.

References

Peng Y. and J. A. Reggia. (1987). A Probabilistic Causal Model for Diagnostic Problem Solving - Part I. IEEE Trans. Syst., Man, Cybern., vol.
SMC-17, Mar./Apr., pp. 146-162.

Buchanan B. G., E. H. Shortliffe. (1984). Rule-Based Expert   System.:
Addison-Wesley.

Pople H. (1985). Evolution of an Expert System: From INTERNIST to
CADUCEUS. In Artificial Intelligence in Medicine, eds. DeLotto and
Stefanelli, pp. 179-203.

Sgurev V., D. Dochev, C. Dichev, G. Agre and Z. Markov. (1985). A Domain
Independent Expert System for Technical Diagnostics. In Artificial Intelligence I, eds. W. Bibel and B. Petkoff, pp. 137-144.: North-Holland.

Agre, G., V. Sgurev, D. Dochev, Ch. Dichev, Z. Markov. (1985) An Implementation of the Expert System DIGS for Diagnostics, Computers & Artificial Intelligence, Bratislava, 4(1985), No 6, pp. 495-502.

CSY-PROLOG. (1986). Programming manual, IECR, Sofia.

EXPERT SYSTEMS, EXPERT TUTORS AND TRAINING IN
ELEMENTARY STATISTICS

Michael Wood
Portsmouth Polytechnic
Locksway Road, Southsea, Hants, PO4 8JF

Abstract

Elementary statistics is an area of expertise which often causes difficulties for beginners. It is also an area of considerable practical importance in a wide variety of fields (eg business, science, medicine). Traditional methods of teaching and implementing the techniques are so inadequate that success is seldom really expected. These inadequacies are described and three approaches to overcoming them are discussed: an expert tutoring system, a "pure" expert system, and an approach described by the metaphor "cognitive process engineering". Some results from an informal study of an attempt to use an expert system (written in the shell CRYSTAL) to help students learning elementary statistics are presented, and it is argued that in this domain, and others like it, expert tutoring systems and "pure" expert systems are inappropriate and that the best way forward is by means of the third approach: "cognitive process engineering". Some of the corollaries of this are explored: it is argued that it should lead to the training and implementation of disciplines like elementary statistics becoming more effective, reliable and enjoyable. In terms of research strategies: much more attention should be given to the human side of knowledge engineering, "expert" systems in this area should not try to mimic the expertise of a human expert, and the possibility of making "knowledge" itself more user friendly should be considered.

1. Introduction

The focus of this paper is the problem of teaching technical expertise to (usually reluctant) people who have to use the expertise for a practical purpose. It is thus concerned with teaching or training, learning and using knowledge, and the possibility of using expert systems, CAL, and intelligent tutoring systems to assist these endeavours.
We will take an aspect of elementary statistics as an example: the use of the normal, Poisson and binomial probability distributions. This is a standard component of many academic courses and of many training courses for specific jobs. The theory is relevant to a diversity of practical situations in, for example, business, science, social science, medicine, engineering. (It is also an essential building block for an understanding of more advanced statistical techniques, but the argument of this article only concerns its direct application in practical

situations.)

The inadequacies of this "system" are so obvious and startling that they are frequently not recognised as inadequacies but seen as inevitable. (The critique presented below is based on the writer's experience of teaching statistics to the non-mathematically inclined on short courses for industry and in higher education: I do not claim the criticisms have universal validity, but their validity is sufficiently widespread to justify taking them seriously.) There are four basic difficulties:

(i) Statistics courses of the kind we are discussing are notoriously **ineffective**. The step by step approach usually taken to teaching the subject tends to give the impression, to teachers and students, that a full, "relational" (Skemp, 1976) or "deep" understanding of the subject matter has been imparted, but this is largely an illusion. Typically, very little explanation of the origin of the normal tables, or of the assumptions underlying the normal distribution, are given, so in reality the learning process is very much on an "instrumental" (Skemp, 1976) or "surface" level which, it is generally acknowledged, is likely to lead to a lack of retention, flexibility and useful understanding (see Skemp, 1976). Even more seriously, the relative lack of attention given to the difficult task (to teach, learn, and to examine) of applying techniques to real situations, means that students are ill equipped to use their knowledge for practical purposes. In fact, typical comments from people who have attended statistics courses indicate little understanding of the techniques or their relevance immediately after the course; years later only dim memories remain.

(ii) Even when the student can apparently relate the statistical concepts to the practical situations and derive what is apparently a meaningful answer, this answer is often wrong, misleading, or inadequately understood. It is commonly accepted that a pass rate in an exam may be 40%: this presumably means that out of every 100 problems tackled it is acceptable for the student to get 60 of them wrong. A reliability of 40% would be acceptable in very few other contexts. Why is it acceptable here? Statistics courses are an **unreliable** method of training.

(iii) To non mathematical students, attending a statistics course is often a **painful** experience. This might not appear to be a serious inadequacy; after all, statistics is not meant to be pleasurable, and surely enjoyment is very low down the priority list for a technical subject area learned purely for utilitarian purposes. I would argue that this is a very short-sighted attitude even from the point of view of those utilitarian purposes. Interest and aesthetic factors are key factors in motivating people to learn something and to use it effectively. The pleasures derived from contemplating and manipulating ideas deserve to be taken seriously even by those whose only apparent motivation is productive efficiency and financial gain.

(iv) Finally, statistics courses are **time-consuming**,

which, taken in conjunction with (iii), represents a serious human problem.

Teaching and learning statistics has long been recognised as a problem, and many excellent suggestions have been made to improve the pedagogic process: eg use of simulations, more practical work, etc. In this paper I wish to consider three potential solutions each of which represents a radical departure from existing practice.

2. Use of an expert tutor

A possibility which is being increasingly canvassed as the answer to many educational problems is an intelligent knowledge based tutor. Conventional CAL, so this argument goes, is too crude and inflexible, but an expert system which incorporates a model of the learner, of his progress, of the subject matter, of tutoring skills, and of common learning problems (Yazdani, 1988) would be an automated version of a good human tutor, and so would resolve our problem.

From the point of view of the present domain (and indeed from the point of view of many other domains), there are three arguments against this perspective, any one of which, in my view, invalidates the enterprise entirely:
(i) Human tutors do not produce adequate results (see above), so why should a computer system which is essentially a copy of the traditional human approach be expected to fare any better? The attempt merely illustrates the common tendency for a new technology to be applied in ways which copy old approaches (eg cars being initially designed as copies of horse drawn carriages). Computer technology surely offers the opportunity for a radically new approach.
(ii) The suggested tutoring system involves several inter-related modules (the learner, the learner's progress, and the subject expertise, for a start). In view of the difficulties involved in building even one of these modules in isolation (see below for a discussion of the state of the art in terms of modelling statistical expertise), it seems unrealistic to expect significant progress in anything but trivial domains (eg teaching methods of subtraction, Burton, 1982).
(iii) Such an intelligent tutor could only be made for a particular domain if the problem of modelling the expertise itself has been solved. In other words, an intelligent tutor is impossible without an expert system. In which case why not let humans use the expert system directly and thus avoid the time and drudgery of submitting to a statistics training? The equivalent in terms of the evolution of the motor industry would be the proposal to use horseless carriages to train people to run faster instead of avoiding the necessity to run in the first place.

3. Using a "pure" expert system

This would entail modelling the expertise with an expert system and getting users to rely on this system instead of using their own expertise. Practically oriented statistics courses would become redundant, the problems arising from the ineffectiveness and unreliability of these courses would be resolved, the drudgery in attending them would be abolished and everyone would save a lot of time and energy. Or would they?

In practice, as with most types of expertise, implementing statistical expertise on a computer is much harder, and progress much slower, than the apparent simplicity of the subject matter to the domain expert might suggest. Gale (1987) reviewed a number of knowledge engineering applications in statistics, but emphasised that none of them "has progressed beyond the feasibility demonstration stage. They are not even prototypes...much less products..." (p.230).

This is doubtless to some extent a reflection of the current state of the art: given time and resources the situation will improve. However, there is an aspect of the problem which suggests a limit to the extent to which statistical expertise can usefully be automated in the foreseeable future. This relates to the system's interface with human beings, so it would not apply to systems which have no human interface. (For example, it is not an argument against the possibility of an expert statistical process control system in a completely automated manufacturing environment.)

The human being using the expert system and the expert system itself need to share a conceptual system to communicate. A typical dialogue might be of this form:
1   Human poses problem to expert system;
2   Expert system asks human for information;
3   Expert system gives an answer to human.

The first step requires the human being to understand the range of questions which the expert system can deal with: ie the user needs a **software model**. The second and third steps require the human to have an appropriate understanding of the concepts in terms of which the questions are posed and answers are given by the expert system: ie there must be a suitable **conceptual framework** for the human-computer interface. Obviously, if naive humans, uneducated in statistics, possess the necessary conceptual framework to understand, perhaps with a few words of explanation, what the software can achieve and the language of the dialogue and the concepts implicit in it, then no problems will arise. However, the case study presented below suggests that this is an extremely optimistic assumption: some training will be necessary so a pure expert systems resolution of the problem is very unlikely indeed.

4. Cognitive process engineering

This awkward metaphor is intended to convey the idea of designing the whole process from the creation of appropriate knowledge and techniques, the design of software and/or the training of humans and/or the writing of instruction manuals to implement these techniques, to the implementation of the expertise in the real world. "Knowledge engineering" is usually taken to refer to the design of software systems to implement knowledge elicited from human experts; this is a much more restricted concept than cognitive process engineering because it assumes that "knowledge" is unproblematic and should simply be elicited from human experts, it is purely concerned with computer knowledge bases, and it makes no explicit reference to the process of using the knowledge. As with any other holistic approach to a problem, the advantage of the metaphor of cognitive process engineering is that it provides a much more powerful and flexible perspective on a problem. The aim, of course, is to design the whole system - knowledge, training, software, other information processing systems, method of implementation, etc - to make it as effective as possible. In the present instance we would like to achieve an effective, reliable, painless and quick method of implementing statistical expertise in practical situations.

Obviously, engineering this whole process from scratch would be an extremely ambitious undertaking which the writer has certainly not attempted. However, even without attempting this, the perspective is useful in that it draws attention to several interesting possibilities.

5. Case study: use of an expert system to help students with statistics

The expert system in question, PROP, is a simple knowledge base built with the shell CRYSTAL, and the students were a statistics class for business studies in a college. The case study illustrates the problems with a "pure" expert systems approach, and leads on to a discussion of cognitive process engineering.

The original intention was that the system should cover all the "mathematical" skills listed in the relevant section of the syllabus (understanding frequency distributions, the normal, Poisson and binomial distributions and their applications to typical business situations). It was obviously not feasible to build a system which would deal with the whole problem of applying these techniques to real business situations, but a system which would cover the following topics seemed viable:
  Choosing appropriate measures of location and spread
        (eg mean, median, standard deviation);
  Calculating measures of location and spread;
  Choosing a suitable distribution to model a situation
        (eg normal, binomial);

Calculating proportions of a population in a specified
        range (using the appropriate distribution).
(Whether such a system deserves the title "expert" is
debatable. However, CRYSTAL is an excellent tool for
developing such a system.)
    The main problem with the prototype of this system
was, in retrospect, very obvious. The users (students on the
course) had no general model of what they could use the
system for, so were continually forced to ask questions like
"Will it do X?", and then "What do I press now?" (to get it
to do X). The same problem arose with single items on the
menu: students did not understand what "calculating
proportions of a population in a specified range" meant in
practice. What input was required? What did the output look
like? Who specified the range? And what is a range anyway?
Clearly students needed an image of what the system could do
for them in intuitive terms, so some teaching would be
necessary to develop the users' "software model".
    However, even when the students were led through
these hazards, their problems were not over. One of the
questions students tackled was:
    The average number of patients attending a surgery in a
    day is 156. How often would you expect more that 170
    patients to turn up?
The standard approach to this is to model the situation with
the Poisson distribution, and then use the normal
distribution as an approximation (which gives an answer of
12% of the time, or approximately once a week). PROP was
designed to lead users to this solution without the users
having any prior knowledge of the Poisson distribution or
how to implement it. Choosing the last option on the main
menu, "calculate proportion of a population in a specified
range", leads to PROP asking a series of questions to
ascertain which (if any) distribution is appropriate, and
then using this distribution to calculate the answer. For
example one rule is:
    distribution is Poisson
    IF   measure is a count
    AND   measure satisfies Poisson conditions
    AND   events are independent
    AND   events are "rare"
Thus, to find out if the distribution is Poisson, PROP will
first ask questions to determine if the measure is a count,
and then, if it concludes that the measure is a count it
will go on to find out if the count "satisfies the Poisson
conditions", and so on. (There is a certain amount of
redundancy in the above rule: the structure is designed to
facilitate a useful dialogue between system and user.) This
interaction is supported by explanations of some of these
terms, and by help screens. As is often the case, the
knowledge base needed to be considerably more complex and
extensive than I had anticipated.
    The main problem here was that of ensuring that
the users interpreted the computer's side of this dialogue
in an appropriate manner. This is partly a matter of

designing "canned" text so that it is easy to comprehend, although difficulties are inevitable when a term refers to a concept which untutored users are not likely to share. In the above rule, "count" was understood easily (with the aid of a screen of explanation), but, not surprisingly, "rare" was not, so this condition was broken down into a further set of more detailed rules and questions which could be phrased in terms which can be understood by untutored, "common" sense. The concepts in terms of which the dialogue is actually conducted form the conceptual framework for the human-computer interface. In the present version of PROP this process of breaking down concepts into their common sense constituents has not been taken very far, but there seems no reason, in principle, why it should not be taken as far as is required.

However, there is one aspect of the dialogue which is not amenable to this process in any obvious way. This is the establishment of a "frame of reference" for PROP's analysis of the situation. PROP communicates with the user by means of the concepts of "population", "object" and "measurement". The user needs to relate these concepts to the particular situation in question if PROP is to be helpful. In the present case the "objects" are days, the "population" is a population of days, and the "measurement" is the number of patients coming to the surgery on a particular day. PROP can then calculate the proportion of days when more than 170 patients turn up. In practice none of the students realised this: they all assumed that the "objects" were people and were then unsure what the "measurement" was; they could not make the Gestalt switch to a more useful interpretation. The problem is that of relating the semi-formal language of PROP to the practical situation as understood by the user.

Once they had been helped over this hurdle most of the students managed to answer a series of questions enabling PROP to determine that the Poisson distribution was appropriate and to give them an answer. However, the real significance of the answer eluded them because they did not appreciate the importance of the assumptions underlying the answer: for example that patients arrive independently and randomly (so that, for example, a major accident leading to 100 patients arriving would be outside the scope of the model), that there are no weekly cycles or long term trends in the number of arrivals, and so on. The answer was correct, because it was produced by the computer, but mysterious, because they had no idea of the rationale behind it. It is difficult to see how these assumptions could be really appreciated without a clear feeling for mathematical modelling - which these users did not possess.

On the positive side, there was another problem which caused many fewer difficulties:
What percentage of 16-20 year-olds take size 1 shoes, what percentage take size 2, size 3, etc?
Having realized that they had to conduct a small survey, PROP then helped them to analyse their results by means of

the normal distribution. The interpretation of "objects" and "measurement" (people, shoe size) caused no difficulties here, and the sequence of questions used by PROP to ascertain that the normal distribution was appropriate, that the data came from a suitable sample, and that the measurement was a discrete one going up in steps of one, was relatively straightforward. The interpretation of the answers was also satisfactory as the technique employed by PROP involved little more than a smoothing out of the empirical data.

To summarise, there were two main problems in the use of PROP and other similar systems:
(1)   Users need a **software model** to see what PROP can do for them. This is easier if the software has one function instead of several, so the revised version of PROP only "calculates proportions in a specified range". However, as illustrated above, this does not solve the problem entirely, so some training is necessary to provide users with a suitable software model.
(2)   Users need an adequate grasp of the **conceptual framework** used by PROP in its dialogue with the user and in its presentation of conclusions. This applies especially to the concepts necessary to establish a frame of reference for the dialogue, and to the concepts underlying the meaning and significance of the answers presented by PROP. Again, this implies, that some training or education is necessary; and therefore an expert system is not sufficient by itself.

6. Implications of the case study

The above case study demonstrates both the potential for expert systems to assist in this area (the shoe size problem was solved without the human side of the partnership getting involved in the implementation of the normal distribution, the calculation of standard deviations and the correction for the variable being discrete: these processes represent a substantial and troublesome element of a typical statistics course), and the main difficulties, which relate to the interface between the system and the human user. This forces us to the rather obvious conclusion that the best way forward is to split the work between the human being and the computer. Computers are better at some aspects (given the current state of hardware and software technology); humans at others.

The main thesis of this paper is that this division of labour should be carried out in a deliberate and considered manner. The whole cognitive process, from the design of the "knowledge", the software, the training given to the human partners, and the final implementation of the techniques should be carefully engineered bearing in mind:
(a)   the properties of human beings,
(b)   the properties of computer systems,
(c)   the properties of the human-computer interface,
(d)   the nature of the end processes (eg are we

concerned with business, science, or with a wider domain encompassing both?)

There is an extensive literature on (a), (b) and (c), but (d) perhaps calls for explanation. If we were designing a training course in statistical process control for a manufacturing firm, the end process would be the application of statistical techniques in the manufacturing process. We would need to decide how the techniques were to be implemented, what computers would do, and what people would do. Furthermore we should also decide whether the people are to rely on their memory, or whether they should have pictures, diagrams or books to assist them. We should also try to assess how reliable the system is: are people likely to make mistakes or is the system likely to be reliable? And finally, are they likely to enjoy operating the system or is it likely to become a chore which is not given the attention it needs? If our concern was with more general training in, say, a college course, then the above questions would still be relevant, but they would apply to a range of potential situations, many of them as yet unknown. The critical feature here would be the flexibility of the (human and computer) system.

All this would clearly represent a very considerable investment in time and research effort. Such an investment would only be justified if the approach does make a significant difference to actual practice, and yield real benefits. What difference is cognitive process engineering likely to make in practice? (This of course depends on the engineers, and the suggestions here can only be speculative.)

We argued above that the human side of the partnership would need training to grasp the meaning of interface concepts such as "population", "measurement", "mathematical model", "sample", random", and also to develop a suitable model of the software itself. The precise list of concepts would be based on a careful analysis of the whole situation, and would represent the key concepts which must be grasped in intuitive terms: ie they must be related to "common sense" and associated with a fringe of tacit meaning or imagery if they are to be understood and handled successfully. Then the computer can safely be left to handle the rules and algorithms built into its knowledge base.

A training to achieve these ends would be very different from a conventional statistics course: it would probably concentrate on conceptual analysis, open ended problem solving and "philosophising". All the usual rules about when to use this formula and when to use that formula, and the actual implementation of the algorithms, could be omitted from the course because they are all on the computer's side of the division of labour.

This division of labour, provided it is carefully designed, has a number of potential advantages. It would enable the power of the computer to be harnessed whilst freeing the human partner of a lot of tedious effort. It would probably entail more emphasis on the intuitive aspect than is at present normal in statistics courses, which would lead to greater enjoyment of statistics among people (the majority?) who enjoy the "philosophical" aspects of the subject more than the algebraic aspects, and this in turn may lead to enhanced effectiveness. Moreover, the reliability of the results may be improved if humans are kept out of the arithmetical and rule based aspects and encouraged to concentrate on getting the conceptual aspects right. To summarise, the system should be quicker, more effective and reliable, and less painful.

7. User friendly knowledge

Another consequence of the cognitive process engineering perspective is a loosening of the concept of "knowledge", from something fixed once the expert has "discovered" it, to something rather more flexible. Some aspects of what is traditonally taught may be firmly on the computer side of the partnership so there is no reason for the human to know anything about them. For example, the idea of a standardised normal variable, the use of standard normal tables, and even the concept of "standard deviation" might be entirely on the computer side of the demarcation line. From the human's point of view this may represent a radical simplification of the subject matter, making it easier to learn and handle.

There are also situations where it may be possible to redesign concepts to make them easier for humans to deal with: in the currently fashionable phrase, to make them more user friendly. The concept of significance is very widely misunderstood; the obvious solution to the problem is to redesign the concept (Wood, 1984).

In a similar vein, the conventional measure of spread for a normally distributed variable is the standard deviation. In some contexts this would need to be part of the human conceptual framework, but it is in origin a mathematician's concept which is difficult to explain and justify in everyday terms. A more intuitively accessible concept is the interquartile-range which has the further advantage of applying to non normal distributions as well. Traditionally students are taught about the standard deviation and about the inter-quartile range (or equivalent), and told that the former is to be used for normal distributions and the latter for other distributions. Why not delete the standard deviation from the human conceptual framework and replace it with the inter-quartile range? The computer would be given the rule for converting from the standard deviation of a normal distribution to the interquartile range (iqr = 1.35 x sd), and vice versa, so its access to aspects of statistical theory which depend on the standard deviation would be unaffected. The human would have a simpler, but equally powerful, conceptual framework to handle.

8. Counter arguments to these suggestions

There are a number of obvious objections to the proposals put forward in this paper:

If the human does not "understand" the algorithm used by the computer, misinterpretations will occur and mistakes will be made.

An ability to use an algorithm does not necessarily imply an understanding of the algorithm; in practice it would seem very unlikely that, for example, students using the normal or Poisson distributions in the traditonal way would have sufficient understanding of the mathematical rationale behind the techniques to enable them to avoid mistakes and misinterpretations.

Knowledge and truth are absolutes: they should not be tampered with for short term utilitarian ends. It is dishonest and patronising to teach a cut-down or doctored version of an academic discipline.

There is a strong tradition in the philosophy of science which maintains that knowledge is not an absolute but is very much the product of particular social and historical circumstances (Kuhn, 1970). A traditional statistics training does not involve teaching the whole truth either (eg the mathematics of the normal distribution is usually ignored), and what students actually learn may be still further from the "whole truth". The suggestion here is simply that, as the process of tailoring human knowledge for specific ends is inevitable, it should be done in a considered manner.

Who will do the engineering? Isn't there a danger of manipulation by big brother?

Any system can manipulate people. The best defence is that the aims and methods should be openly declared.

What happens if someone is trained to interact with a particular computer system, which turns out to be unavailable when they want to use it? Or if someone who has been taught about interquartile ranges has to operate in a situation where a knowledge of standard deviations is required?

This is a problem. Introducing such systems in a piecemeal way may create difficulties.

9. Conclusions

In the domain of elementary statistics, we have argued that traditional training methods are woefully inadequate, that neither expert tutors, nor expert systems alone, can provide a complete and satisfactory solution, and that a more fruitful perspective is provided by the metaphor of "cognitive process engineering". The aim would be to facilitate a quicker and more enjoyable training, leading to a more effective and reliable implementation of the techniques.

Similar conclusions may apply to similar domains:

for example linear programming and calculus (commonly taught to non-mathematicians with very dubious benefits).

There are two implications for research strategies which deserve mention. First, the role of human beings in cognitive processes is likely to change, so the human side of knowledge engineering deserves more emphasis than it currently receives. (For example, **what** should be taught in statistics courses?) Second, designers of expert systems in these domains should not simply elicit knowledge from human experts and put it into their systems: instead they should concentrate their attentions on designing software to complement the skills and aptitudes of humans, which may involve rethinking the nature of the knowledge itself.

References

Burton, R. (1982). Diagnosing bugs in simple procedural skills. In Intelligent tutoring systems, ed D. Sleeman and J. Brown. Academic Press.

Gale, W. A. (1987). Statistical applications of artificial intelligence and knowledge engineering. Knowledge Engineering Review 2, no 4, 227-247.

Kuhn, T. S. (1970). The structure of scientific revolutions, 2nd edition. University of Chicago Press.

Skemp, R. (1976). Relational understanding and instrumental understanding. Mathematics Teaching. 77, 20-26.

Wood, M. (1984). Making the idea of significance easier to understand. Teaching Statistics, 6, no 2, 57-59.

Yazdani, M. (1988). Expert tutoring systems. Expert Systems, 5, no 4, 270-272.

MEEPLES - AN EXPERT SYSTEM FOR SCHEDULING MEETINGS

C N Cadas
Rolls-Royce and Associates Limited
PO Box 31
Raynesway
Derby UK

Abstract

Scheduling meetings in a large or medium-sized company which, like RRA, is heavily project-orientated is a difficult and time-consuming task. MEEPLES (MEEtings PLanner Expert System) has been developed to generate meeting schedules that optimise attendance and flow of information. Plan repair, a varied degree of automation, user help and query facilities are all considered to be important features of MEEPLES. In addition, a suite of output and summary routines are available, together with reporting mechanisms.

1. Introduction

1.1 Background

Traditionally at RRA, the yearly schedule of meetings has been produced by hand. The number of meetings on this schedule is usually very large with some Managers having as much as 20% of their available time during the forthcoming year taken up by scheduled meetings. The plan is generally of a hierarchical nature in that meetings lower down the hierarchy feed in and out of others further up the hierarchy. It has generally been a task that has been difficult to do well and was rarely completed on time due to a number of factors (eg. co-ordination of data input). There was also little scope for effective plan repair.
The aim of the MEEPLES project was to produce a yearly schedule of meetings on time at reduced cost which was of a better quality than would have been produced by hand. MEEPLES was also to allow plan repair to be effected economically.

1.2 Nature of problem

The problem is characterised by 2 factors:-

a) The availability of resources - in this case, personnel and conference rooms.

b) The imposed constraints or preferences for meetings (as declared by Chairmen).

The problem is exacerbated in that these can often be conflicting requirements.

In generating a yearly plan of meetings, meetings are scheduled with the aim of maximising attendance, whilst ensuring that the correct flow of information is established. Essentially this means that links between meetings must be maintained. (A link is defined as the dependency of one meeting on another eg. Meeting A is 5-10 working days before Meeting B).

Constraints generally are of 2 types - rigid constraints and preferences. Rigid constraints include such things as not scheduling a meeting over weekends, Bank Holidays and any dates for which the Chairman has declared personal unavailability. Preferences (such as day and time of day for the meeting) are also taken account of when scheduling.

1.3 Project goals

1.3.1 Short term

The project was conceived during a feasibility study in May 1988. The particular history of the scheduling task had led to there being no single rich source of knowledge. Indeed, this was one reason why many previous schedules had been disappointing. One of the first goals was, then, to assimilate knowledge from a wide range of sources, in order to discover the sorts of scheduling requirements and preferences that might be needed. It was also necessary to produce a concise questionnaire for issue to meeting Chairmen which would elicit the various requests and information necessary.

The information contained on the questionnaire would need to be reflected in the structure of the eventual system. MEEPLES was, as a second short term goal, required to produce the 1989 calendar of meetings.

As a third and less tangible short term goal, the high profile of the project was to be used in promoting awareness of expert system capabilities within the company.

1.3.2 Long term

A delivery version of the system, which could be handed over to a user in the company projects area, was identified as a long term project goal.

As well as performing a useful task for RRA it was considered that the system could usefully perform the same or a similar task for other establishments and therefore a second long term goal has been identified which was to assess the commercial possibilities for the system.

1.4 Meeting requirements and desired preferences

Following the process of acquiring knowledge about the nature of company meetings in general, a questionnaire was drawn up which, when completed by the Chairman, would establish the requirements and desired preferences for his meetings. The information needed to schedule the meeting is as below:

Venue	–	Town and, where applicable, room.
Attendees	–	Essential and representative. Essential attendees are those without whom the meeting should not take place. Representatives are those whose attendance is desired but substitutes would be accepted if necessary. Associated with this is a maximum number of substitutes acceptable.
Link	–	Any meetings to which the one in question should be linked eg. Meeting A 3-5 working days before Meeting B.
Number	–	Number of meetings in the year. This is not needed if defined totally by a link.
Approximate Interval	–	Approximate spacing between meetings, specified in one of a number of different ways.
Preferred Day and Time	–	eg. Tuesday 1300 - 1700
Not-Day	–	eg. Monday 9-12 would mean that the meeting could not take place on Monday between 9 and 12 o'clock.
Not-Weeks and Not-Months	–	Weeks and months of the year when the meeting cannot take place.
Chairman Unavailability	–	Calendar dates when the Chairman is unavailable for holiday or other reasons. Also, times during the week when he should be made unavailable eg. Monday 9-12.

Note that links can be quite complex, with meetings linking to others with a different frequency and sometimes with an additional preference to link to other meetings where possible.

2. Choice of environment

Such a large and complex problem requires a considerable amount of computing power. The hierarchical structure of the meetings calendar and the large number of attributes common to all meetings make it suitable for a frame-based tool. In addition, requirements for the inference mechanism to handle rules and perform what was anticipated to be a large amount of list manipulation led to the conclusion that KEE[1] and LISP operating on a SUN platform were suitable development tools.

---

[1] KEE is a registered trademark of Intellicorp

3. Development of prototype and the chosen approach

Three prototypes were developed before the chosen approach was adopted. These are outlined briefly below:-

3.1 A goal-directed depth - first search with unlimited backtracking

This prototype assumed that a solution existed such that meeting attendance would be complete ie. at all meetings all nominated attendees would be able to attend. To find this solution the prototype could backtrack up the meetings hierarchy as far as necessary to resolve a clash lower down ie. the entire search space was open to it.

This prototype was rejected for two reasons:-

a) Calculations showed that a fullscale system was likely to run too slowly, if at all.

b) The hierarchical structure of the meetings calendar meant that often backtracking was not desirable. This is so where resolving a constraint at one level of the hierarchy results in a slight loss in preference at some higher level in the hierarchy.

3.2 A three-level approach with comparative worlds

In this approach each level in the hierarchy is considered in turn. All satisfactory dates for meetings at this level are evaluated. None of these dates are as yet made concrete in the plan but a set of worlds, or contexts, are created in which these meetings assume one or other of those dates evaluated.

Each world is then considered in turn and a plan generated for two further levels in the hierarchy (with no backtracking). A set of criteria for assessing each world was implemented and the world which contained the most satisfactory solution chosen. The resulting plan for the two further levels would be retracted and the solution for the hierarchical level under scrutiny adopted. The process would then be repeated for the next level in the hierarchy and so on until a complete plan was produced.

Again there were two problems with this approach:-

a) Generation of worlds in this manner is combinatorially explosive. For a fullscale system, it would be necessary to selectively generate worlds with no guarantee that the worlds chosen were any better than any others.

b) As the system develops, the set of criteria for assessing each world becomes increasingly complex and open to debate. Generating this set of criteria can become a serious problem in itself.

3.3 An opportunistic approach with forward planning and limited backtracking

In this approach a flawed, or draft, plan is created regardless of any conflicts which the plan may contain. The plan is created with a degree of forward planning which takes consideration of the inter-dependencies of meetings to prevent the appearance of potential bottle-necks in the plan. The plan is then corrected and any conflicts resolved in a top-down fashion. It is generally assumed that conflicts at any particular level in the meetings hierarchy cannot be resolved by moving a meeting which is at a higher level in the hierarchy. This means that conflict resolution is relatively easy for meetings occupying a high position in the hierarchy, but not for those occupying a lowly position. Hence the need for forward planning.

Backtracking is allowed, but is limited to those occasions where forward planning has not been sufficient to prevent all bottle-necks. Backtracking is not fully automatic, but is directed by the user in response to warnings from the system.

This approach is unlikely to produce the best possible schedule, but should produce one which is at least adequate, and which is certainly superior to that which would be produced by conventional methods. In addition, this would be done in a much reduced time.

Unlike the previous two prototypes, calculations showed that a system of this type would probably be able to cope with a full-specification of meetings. For this reason, of the three prototypes considered it was decided to pursue this option at least as far as a large scale test. Further development of MEEPLES using this approach would depend on the results of this test (Section 8).

4. Constraints

Attendees are divided into two categories:-
<u>Essential</u> - those without whom the meeting should not take place.
<u>Representative</u> - those attendees whose presence is preferred but who could be substituted if necessary. Associated with this category, each meeting has a maximum number of substitutes allowed.

Any one attendee can be unavailable for a particular meeting on a particular day for a number of reasons:-

a) He is required to attend a meeting of higher standing at the same time.

b) He is to attend a meeting of higher standing at a different time but at a venue which makes it difficult to move to the new meeting location in the available time.

c) Travel constraints make it possible for personnel at certain locations to attend meetings at other locations only on certain days (eg. RRA personnel in North Scotland are constrained to attend meetings in Derby by the twice-weekly flights).

d) An attendee of the meeting is on holiday or is unavailable for some unspecified reason on that date.

e)   An attendee of the meeting is generally unavailable on that day and at that time eg. always unavailable on Monday from 9-12.

Constraints are generally represented by values in slots of KEE units. For example, each person is represented by a unit which inherits characteristics from the class unit "PERSONS". The slots held in this class include "essential-meetings", "representative-meetings", "unavailable-dates" and "unavailable-days". If a person, say "jim", has (thursday 900 1200) as a value in his slot "unavailable-days", MEEPLES will recognise this as a constraint and will try to avoid scheduling meetings involving "jim" on a Thursday between 9 a.m. and 12 noon.
In assessing some constraints such as b) above, MEEPLES needs to access the "venue" slot of meetings which are less than two days apart and also a table which indicates the minimum reasonable journey time for a person travelling between the two venues eg. if "jim" attends a meeting at Dounreay on one day, then he cannot attend a meeting in Derby on the next.
Apart from constraints relating to personnel, other conflicts are covered by:-

a)   A meeting of higher standing at the same venue at the same time.

b)   The date of the meeting being a week-end, Bank Holiday, a not-day (a day of the week when the meeting is not allowed to take place eg. Monday 9-12) or occurs during a not-week or not-month (weeks or months of the year when the meeting is not allowed to take place).

c)   The date conflicts with its requirements to link to another meeting.

5.   Input

A large amount of data is required for MEEPLES to generate a calendar. The type of interface necessary for a fast and efficient input can be seen in Fig.1. Values are entered for attendees in the appropriate places and input is menu-driven where convenient, else values are typed in. Any invalid values are rejected and error messages are displayed in the explanation window. On completion of data entry for a generic meeting, warnings of missing information are displayed, particularly those omissions which would make it impossible to schedule the meetings.

6.   Plan Generation

In generating a plan, MEEPLES first produces a draft schedule which may contain many conflicts. In this schedule each meeting is given a preferred date. This will depend on whether the chairman has requested the meeting to be set up in a specific month or week of the year, or for example, 13 meetings separated by approximately 4 weeks. MEEPLES will identify any links between meetings and use this information to create a dependency network - a tree-like representation in which a high-level meeting may have several others linking to it, which, in turn, may have others linking to them. MEEPLES examines each branch of the dependency

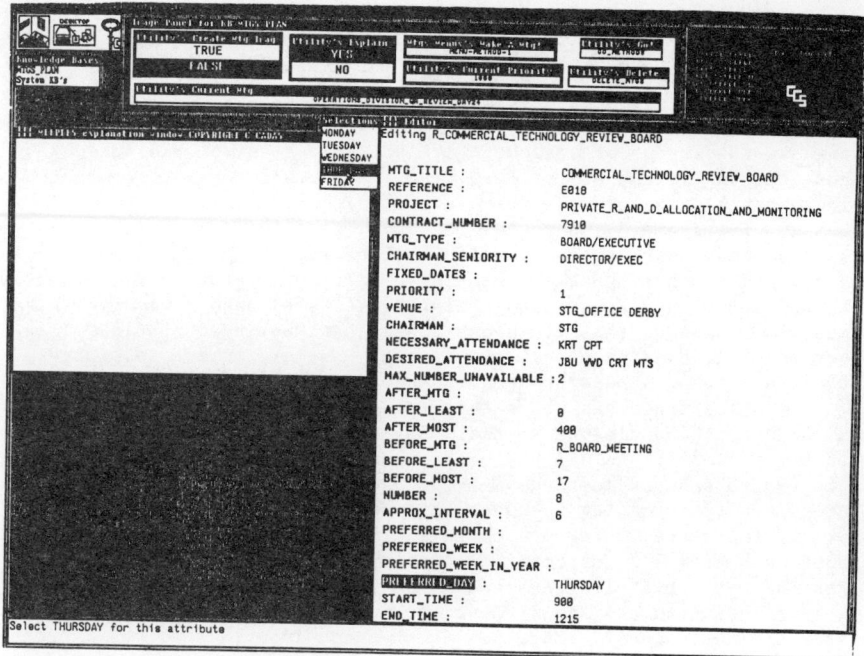

Figure 1 Typical KEE Screen During Input

network in turn and will modify the draft plan when it recognises a potential bottleneck.

Conflicts in the draft plan are resolved in a top down fashion and control of the conflict resolution stage is performed with various degrees of automation which also allows the user to check on progress.

Initially in its conflict resolution, MEEPLES does not distinguish between types of attendees and simply attempts to ensure full attendance.

If a meeting clash occurs, MEEPLES will try a date which is as close to the preferred date of the meeting as possible. If all reasonable dates have been tried, and failed, MEEPLES will relax the preferences gradually to allocate a date for the meeting. For example, the simplified rule

IF   The minimum number of substitutes required is greater
         than the maximum allowed.

THEN   Alter the start time of the meeting.

indicates that the time of day is less important than a full attendance. This relative importance of preferences can be altered if, for example, the time of day is more important.

6.1   Degree of automation

A degree of user-interaction was introduced to MEEPLES when it was discovered that some of the linking requirements were quite complex. It is useful if the user can check on the resolution of certain meetings as they occur or at some other suitable stage of the scheduling process (such as at the end of resolving conflicts for a whole batch of meetings at the same level in the hierarchy).

For example, suppose a meeting with 11 occurrences, Meeting 8, is to precede another meeting with 5 occurrences (Meeting 6) by between 2 and 10 working days. Meeting 8 is to be approximately 5-weekly and is preferred on a Wednesday. MEEPLES will set these up as in Fig.2a. Suppose, in addition, that it is desirable that Meeting 8 should follow another meeting, Meeting 5, by approximately a week, (where possible) and that no meeting should be held in August.

Experience has shown that this type of scenario is difficult for a computer to handle unassisted. Any unevenness in the spread of meetings as a result of fully automatic analysis can cause knock-on effects for subsequent meetings linked to Meeting 8 and can worsen the end product. By involving the user to a small degree and with the aid of a suitable interface, a few mouseclicks will reveal the scheduled dates for Meeting 5 (Fig.2b), attempt various improved arrangements (Fig.2c) and respond appropriately when resolution is satisfactory (Fig.2d - note a '+' here indicated the requirement for substitutes for one or more non-essential attendees). MEEPLES can then continue in whatever degree of automation is required.

7.   Plan repair

Plan repair can broadly be divided into two main parts - small and large scale. The former deals with small changes, such as minor additions, deletions or where an individual changes responsibilities. The second category deals with large scale changes, such as when the company undergoes complete re-organisation with new jobs, new meetings and different attendance lists for meetings.

In both cases the repair is mouse-and-menu driven, often by the use of one or more unit-editor windows (eg. Figure 1) by which values in various slots can be accessed or changed. KEE active values attached to these slots ensure that any typed values are in the correct format.

7.1   Small scale repairs

These are performed interactively with a minimum disruption policy. An editor window with a subset of the slots used for the input editor window (only those slots which affect scheduling) is exposed (Fig.3a) and the user can try to fix the meeting within a window of dates. He can change the meeting time, relax linking constraints and attendance constraints if necessary to schedule the meeting.

Suitable and unsuitable dates alike are commented upon in the explanation window (Fig.3b) and any iteration around the repair is menu-driven.

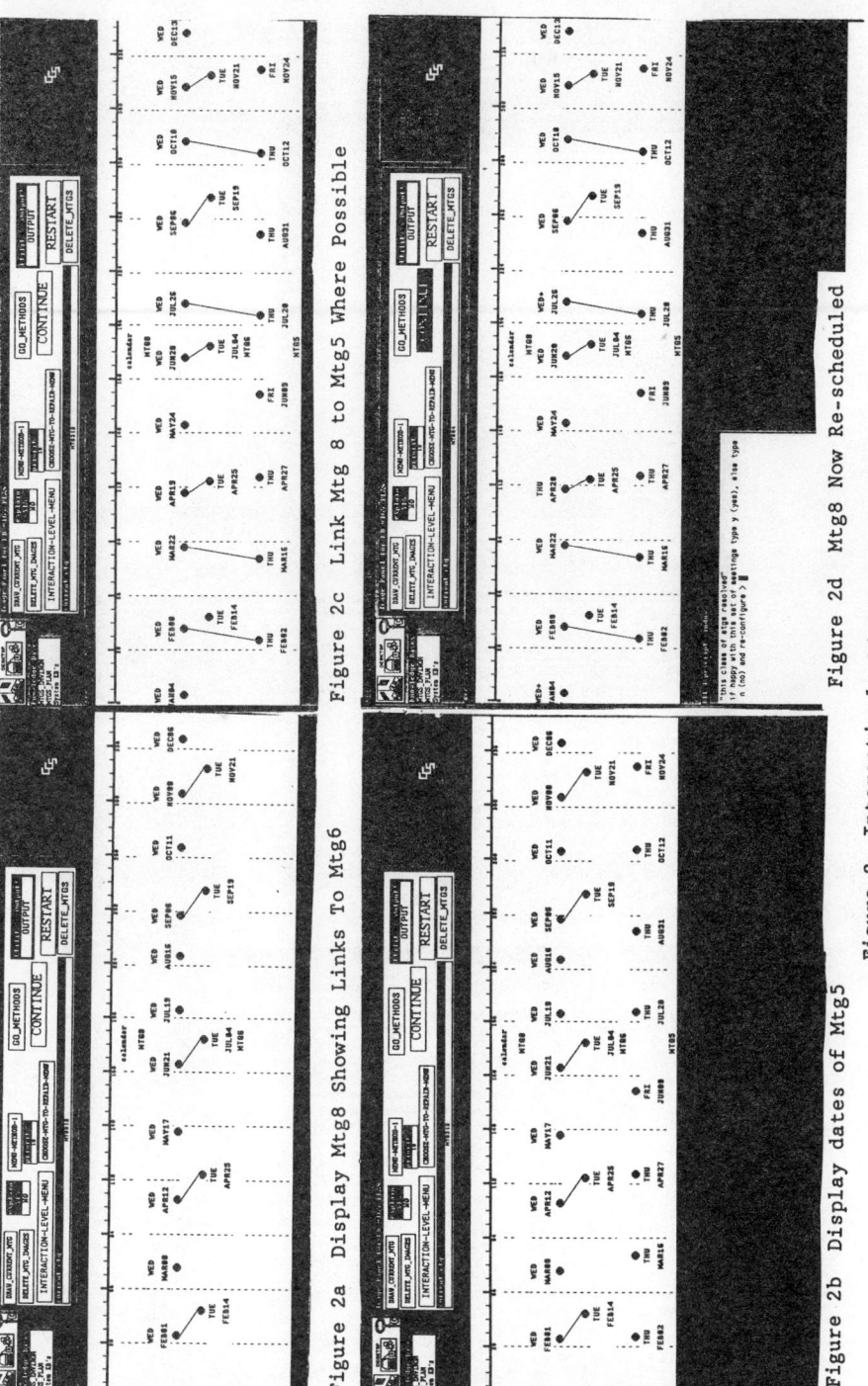

Figure 2a Display dates of Mtg5

Figure 2b Display Mtg8 Showing Links To Mtg6

Figure 2c Link Mtg 8 to Mtg5 Where Possible

Figure 2d Mtg8 Now Re-scheduled

Figure 2 Interactively Linking Meetings

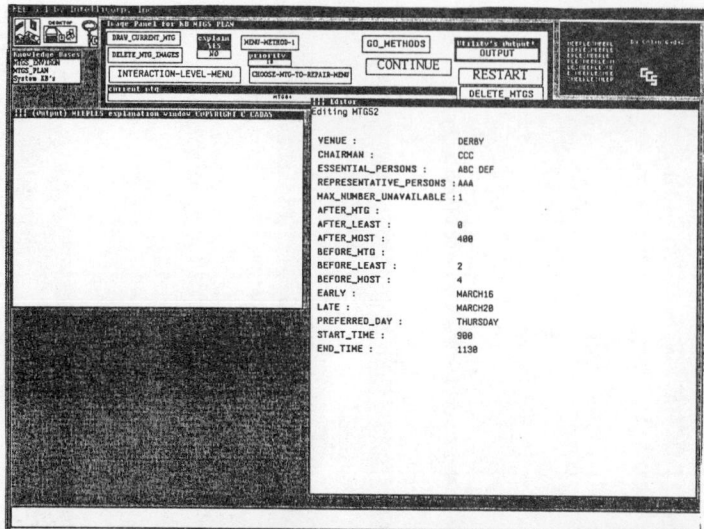

Figure 3a   Edit Requirements For an Individual Meeting

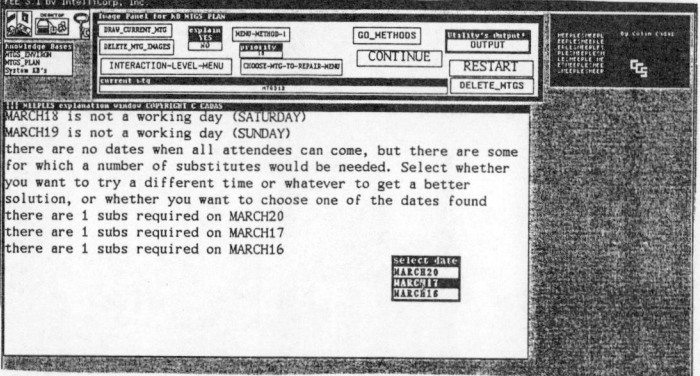

Figure 3b (i)   Select Suitable Date From Menu

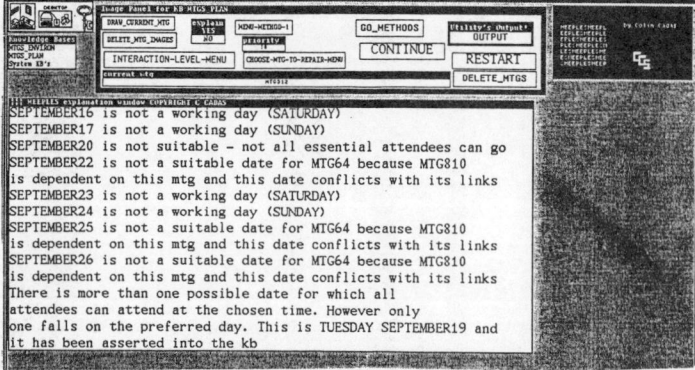

Figure 3b (ii)   Suitable Date Selected By MEEPLES

Any resulting enforced disruption to the calendar is traced through the schedule and also resolved interactively.

7.2   Large scale repairs

In this mode of plan repair, whole generic meetings are deleted, new ones created, titles, attendees and Chairmen changed and preferences altered (such as preferred day and preferred time). Data for new meetings are input as previously and the "draft" plan for these meetings superimposed on the existing one. Changes to be made to meetings are input via a mouse-menu interface and stored in a file to be loaded as calls to various LISP functions. Plan repair is subsequently carried out via the same conflict resolution strategy used in the original plan generation. The resulting degree of plan disruption depends entirely on the number of changes taking place.

8.   Test programme

One of the major problems associated with expert systems is that, often, small prototypes do not scale up easily into a full working system.

With timescales for producing the 1989 calendar being quite short, it was essential to run a full-scale test to ensure that MEEPLES could process a large KB. In addition, the validation and verification of the various modules in MEEPLES was another consideration.

Using a previous years' calendar, information was extracted and from this, typical requirements were estimated. All the information was fed into MEEPLES which was set into plan generation mode. Initially running too slowly, measures were taken to improve efficiency/speed until a complete schedule of around 1600 meetings was completed in approximately 3 hours.

At that stage of development, MEEPLES produced a calendar which was not perfect in terms of the spacing of meetings, but was very successful in terms of maximising attendance. The test therefore appeared to justify the adopted prototype as an approach likely to succeed.

9.   Data acquisition

Data acquisition is currently performed by means of a questionnaire. Detailed data can only be provided via a complex questionnaire which could run to several pages in order to cater for all foreseeable preferences and requests. Deciding which preferences to allow on the questionnaire and how to specify them proved to be an unexpectedly difficult task. There were a surprising number of options, both in terms of the actual information on the questionnaire and the way it was to be presented.

The questionnaire goes hand-in-hand with data input and also must reflect the way knowledge is represented in MEEPLES. This, in some ways, effectively restricts the development of the system since it is of no value to program features which cannot be utilised because the information necessary to those features cannot be extracted.

Most of the problems encountered so far in the project have been related in one way or another to data acquisition. In addition, having decided on the format of the questionnaire and having issued it to the Chairmen, there was no guarantee that all the questionnaires would be correctly filled out and returned on time.

In general it was found that the Chairmen responded favourably to requests for data but some problems were encountered:

a) Some forms were received late - and some were never returned.

b) Some forms were only partially completed.

c) Illegible handwriting.

d) Incorrect or ambiguous titles of meetings in the linking arrangements.

It is possible that the data acquisition bottleneck encountered could be overcome by using some medium other than a questionnaire for this process. In response to a questionnaire in January 1989, some Chairmen reacted favourably to the idea that information could be gathered by means of a short interview, but just as many did not like the idea, thinking that it would mean a greater time commitment on their behalf. An alternative could be the production of an 'intelligent' front end to be mounted on office terminals.

It is unlikely that this would cure a), (above), but should help with b), c) and d) and would remove the need for manual input to MEEPLES which would save user-time.

10. Help facilities and general ease of use

At the time of writing, use of the system has been confined to the programmer. The system has been built with delivery to a user area in mind, and it is intended that it will be handed over during the latter half of 1989. Although explanation facilities exist at present, help facilities and the degree of user-friendliness required for a delivery version are not adequate. The requirements for such have been outlined in a specification of further work which is to be carried out before handover takes place.

11. Meeples in action

The short term goal of using MEEPLES to produce the 1989 RRA calendar of meetings was met by December 1988. Actual constraints imposed by Chairmen proved to be greater and more complex than those generated for the large scale test. As a result, 4% of meetings scheduled required substitutes, although very few required more than one. Eleven meetings out of the 1200 scheduled had to be scheduled interactively using the small-scale plan repair feature.

Following the production of the plan, a questionnaire regarding its effectiveness indicated that most Chairmen agreed that it was the best calendar ever produced at RRA.

In addition to an improvement in the quality of the calendar, the information stored in MEEPLES is more flexibly available. All personnel involved in meetings received personal calendars - something that had previously been impossible. Furthermore various pieces of statistical information, such as the distribution of meetings throughout the week or year and costs of meetings have been made available.

12. Estimated savings and benefits

All expert systems have to be justified on some basis - often on cost. Although MEEPLES will only be used in its entirety yearly, it is estimated that investment will be recouped within 2 or 3 years. Apart from savings in user-time to produce the calendar, the ability to download a file automatically into the company mainframe diary system also represents a substantial saving in typing effort.

The necessity for rapid repair was graphically illustrated when there was some degree of company re-organisation part way through the calendar year. It is unlikely on the given timescales, that anything of real use could have been done manually to repair the calendar and MEEPLES was used to produce the new meetings schedule.

An additional saving which cannot easily be estimated comes as a result of the improved company efficiency which is effected by an organised calendar where a full and correct set of people attend the scheduled meetings. Although this cannot be quantified it is undoubtedly true that an optimised meetings plan has been of significant value to the company.

13. Summary

MEEPLES is a knowledge-based system for scheduling meetings. It has been programmed in KEE and LISP and runs on a SUN workstation. The system has produced a meetings schedule of better quality than that which could have been achieved by conventional methods and on much reduced timescales. Plan repair facilities exist when modifications (due to personnel changes etc.) are required. A wide variety of information regarding the plan can also be easily extracted from MEEPLES.

A PARALLEL EXPERT SYSTEM FOR REAL-TIME APPLICATIONS

Haihong Dai, Terry J. Anderson and Fabian C. Monds
Dept. of Information Systems
University of Ulster at Jordanstown
Newtownabbey
Co. Antrim BT37 0QB
N. Ireland, U.K.

Abstract

In recent years, AI applications in the engineering field, especially expert systems, have received much attention from researchers. Some expert systems have been developed for areas ranging from process control, fault diagnosis to signal interpretation. They have shown that AI techniques are potentially of great value to applications in the engineering field. On the other hand, however, expert systems also face many difficulties when applied to the engineering field because the field has its own special characteristics which make it different from other fields. These characteristics make special requirements of expert systems used in the engineering field. In this paper, we overview characteristics of engineering applications of AI, and two of them are discussed in detail, i.e., real-time requirements and task complexity. The requirements of expert systems for real-time signal processing and interpretation (SPI) applications are presented and discussed. A parallel expert system, called HOPES (Hierarchically Organized Parallel Expert System) is proposed for real-time applications. Unlike other traditional expert systems, the HOPES system consists of a few knowledge sources (KS) which are hierarchically organized and capable of parallel execution. Some important features of the HOPES system are discussed in the paper, such as hierarchical structure of the system, multi-blackboard architecture and communication strategies. A prototype HOPES system is also presented which is for radar SPI.

1. Introduction

In recent years, AI has received much attention from researchers in the engineering field. Great research effort has been focused on AI techniques and their applications, especially expert systems which is arguably the most important category of AI applications (Riese 1986). Some expert systems have been developed for areas ranging from process control, fault diagnosis to signal interpretation (Moore & Kramer 1986; Waterman 1986; Cleary & Kramer 1986; Campbell & Olson 1986; Daku & Grant 1988; Nii & Feigenbaum 1982), and they have proven to be successful. On the other hand, however, since the engineering field has its own characteristics which differ from those of other fields, it presents difficult problems to expert systems for engineering applications. Among these characteristics, we believe that the *real-time requirement* and *task complexity* are the most important, and are common to many areas in the engineering field.

By real-time, firstly, we mean that the expert system used must operate on-line with other systems, rather than working in an off-line advisory mode. Secondly, we mean that the expert system must be able to achieve a goal or obtain a result in a limited time period. For instance, an expert system for real-time SPI (signal processing and interpretation) must be able to co-operate with some other signal processing systems, and interpret the signals without ignoring the on-going process. As signals may vary with time very quickly, the expert system used must be fast enough to give the responses required.

By task complexity, we mean that all engineering problems are always very complex and can not usually be solved in the question-answer manner popular in some traditional expert systems. The knowledge base will be very big, and the inference engine will be very complicated. In many cases, the tasks will need to be accomplished at many levels of analysis such as numerical processing level and symbolic analysis level. This characteristic makes expert systems for engineering applications more complicated than expert systems for other fields.

For example, unlike other applications, such as medical diagnosis, domains of engineering applications are not usually well structured and not much heuristic knowledge is available. Inference processes tend to be very complicated and therefore more sophisticated inference strategies are needed in order to deal with such situations. Explanation facilities is another difficult problem. Because the inference processes are very complicated, it is infeasible to simply use back-tracking to explain the results obtained. More effective method needs to be found. Furthermore, it is typical that data used by the expert systems are input from sensors. These raw sensor data sometimes contain noise, and this presents additional difficulties for the expert systems. In order to be able to cope with such difficult situations, many different kinds of knowledge are needed, and co-operation among them is essential. The knowledge must be organized and used effectively and efficiently.

The two characteristics described above are not independent of each other. The real-time requirement limits the complexity of a task that can be accomplished by an expert system working in a real-time environment. On the other hand, the task complexity makes it very difficult to build a real-time expert system. They make expert systems for engineering applications different from other expert systems. Many special requirements need to be accommodated in the expert systems for engineering problems.

As high task complexity is in the nature of the engineering applications, it can not be avoided or simplified in the real world. Therefore, the key problem has become how to build real-time expert systems capable of accomplishing very complicated tasks. Currently, research effort is being focused on all aspects of real-time expert systems such as system structure, inference strategies and knowledge representation, and some real-time expert systems have been developed (Morgan 1988; Bailey & Kraft 1987; Hawkinson & Levin 1985; Leinweber & Gidwani 1986; Wright 1986; Mathonet & Cotthem 1987; Cartwright & Ruskin 1986). Compared with other application areas, however, relatively little effort has been applied to the real-time area. To date this has restricted the expert system applications in the engineering field.

In this paper, we propose a real-time expert system called HOPES (Hierarchically Organized Parallel Expert System) which will be used for SPI applications. Firstly, we discuss requirements of expert systems for real-time SPI applications. Then we propose the HOPES system and discuss some important aspects of the system. Finally, a prototype HOPES system is described.

2. Requirements of expert systems for real-time SPI applications

As mentioned in the last section, two important characteristics of engineering applications are the real-time requirement and task complexity. In this section, we discuss them in detail in order to sort out the requirements of expert systems for real-time SPI applications, which will be used to guide the design of a real-time expert system.

2.1. Real-time requirement

What does "real-time" mean? People with different backgrounds will explain it in different ways. Here, we adopt the following definition of "real-time": a strictly limited time period in which the system must produce a response to environmental stimuli, no matter what kind of algorithms it employs. Hence, the key feature of a real-time expert system is its ability to guarantee a response after a fixed time has elapsed, where that fixed time is provided as a part of the problem statement (O'Reilly & Cromarty 1985).

Furthermore, "real-time" has another meaning concerned with an expert system for SPI. It requires that the expert system should work continuously with time, as in most cases the signals are continuous. Therefore the real-time expert system must be able to focus its attention on the relevant parts of the domain without ignoring on-going processes. It should be able to keep acquiring signal data while doing interpretation. Thus, data acquisition should ideally be done in parallel with the operation of the inference engine to accommodate this requirement. In the HOPES system proposed, the signal data acquisition part is separated from other parts of the system, and they will run concurrently, as depicted in Figure 1.

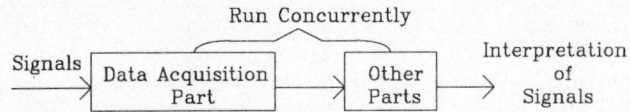

Figure 1. Concurrency between data acquisition & other processing in HOPES

2.2. Task complexity

We have briefly explained the term "task complexity" in section 1. It also makes some special requirements of the expert system for SPI. Here we discuss two aspects of the task complexity of SPI.

2.2.1. Complicated nature of SPI task

The task of SPI is to uncover meanings of signals. Given a set of signals, the goal is to find an interpretation consisting of an event or events that would yield the set of signals. The interpretation process is so complex that a lot of work needs to be done by the system before a final interpretation can be obtained. This presents a serious problem to the real-time system, as the system may not be fast enough to meet the real-time requirement.

Currently, there are three solutions to this problem: 1) Use a very powerful uni-processor computer system. 2) Use certain kinds of computer language to program the system so that it can execute very fast. 3) Use parallel techniques.

Among these, we think that use of parallel techniques is the most promising, although it needs to be supported by both hardware and software.

Some work has already been done by other researchers in the area of applying parallel techniques to AI (or DAI: Distributed Artificial Intelligence) (Talukdar & Cardozo 1986; Lessor & Erman 1980; Smith & Davis 1981; Lessor & Corkill 1982; Fennell & Lessor 1977; Gupta 1985; Fox 1981). The prime goals of using parallel techniques are speed, reliability, co-operation, and extensibility. Here, we are mainly concerned with using parallel techniques to provide the expert system with the real-time ability. Discussions of other aspects are beyond the scope of this paper.

Use of the parallel techniques will be able to speed up the inference process of the expert system, and therefore response time may be reduced. The basis of this idea is that if a task can be divided into several sub-tasks, then it will be possible to accomplish these sub-tasks concurrently. Thus, the time needed to complete the task may be reduced. (Figure 2). On the other hand, however, if the task is undividable, then concurrent processing will not be very useful. Fortunately, most SPI tasks are dividable, and therefore parallel techniques are applicable. This forms the essential basis on which our HOPES system is constructed.

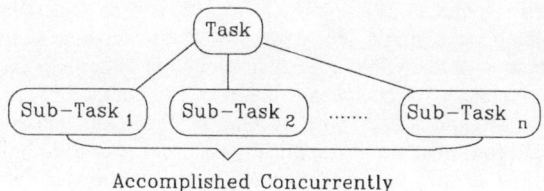

Figure 2. Concurrent accomplishing of a task

2.2.2. Multi-level processing

The SPI task is so complicated that it needs to use many aspects of the domain knowledge. From raw sensor data to final interpretation, it is accomplished at various levels of analysis.

In radar SPI area, for example, most signal processing algorithms for filtering and FFT use data in numerical form (Kane 1983; Kamén 1987). They belong to the numerical processing level, and are usually called *low level processing*. On the other hand, information used by the inference engine is in symbolic form. The analyses at this level are symbolic in nature, and are usually called *high level analysis*.

Obviously, the knowledge used is hybrid and must be very extensive in order to complete a real world task. Thus, it is infeasible simply to put them in a single knowledge base. The normal way to organize the knowledge is to arrange them into several knowledge sources (KS). A KS may be viewed as an agent that embodies the knowledge of a particular aspect of the problem domain and is useful in solving a problem from that domain by taking actions based on its knowledge so as to make a contribution to the overall solution. This method was first used by Erman et al. in their Hearsay-II system (Erman & Hayes-Roth 1980.

As different levels of analysis need to exist and co-operate in the same system, they are not usually independent. Relationships among them are very important. Firstly, data transformation among the levels is necessary because data at different levels may be in different representation forms. Secondly, information exchange among KSs at different levels is essential for co-operation because each KS may only accomplish part of the task.

Therefore, all the KSs must have some way to communicate with each other. If this can not be handled properly, it will cause problems.

As described by Nii & Feigenbaum (1982), for example, signal-to-symbol transformation is an essential operation in the expert system for SPI. Because the low level analysis uses numerical data while the information used by the high level analysis is in symbolic form, a partial result obtained at the low level must be transferred before it can be used by the high level. If the problem of signal-to-symbol transformation can not be solved properly, the performance of the system will be seriously degraded.

In next two sections, we present a parallel expert system (HOPES) for SPI. The structure of the system and strategies for communication among KSs are discussed in order to accommodate the special requirements described above.

3. Structure of HOPES system

Most traditional expert systems for engineering applications, such as HASP/SIAP (Nii & Feigenbaum 1982) and RESCU (Bailey & Kraft 1987), were designed and used for running on a single processor, thus their real-time abilities may be seriously limited. In these systems, while a KS is in execution, other KSs have to wait until the KS finishes and the processor becomes available. This method is not very suitable for real-time purposes. Structures and some working strategies of such systems can not be completely adopted for real-time SPI applications. In order to accommodate the issues raised in the SPI field, some technical changes to the traditional systems are needed, and accordingly new structures and strategies need to be explored.

Motivated by the observation described above, we proposed a parallel expert system called HOPES which is able to provide concurrent reasoning. The initial purpose of HOPES is for real-time SPI. Therefore, the design of the system has been guided by the considerations presented in section 2.

3.1. Basic structure of the system

As the name HOPES implies, the KSs in this system are hierarchically organized and capable of concurrent inferencing. Its basic structure is depicted in Figure 3.

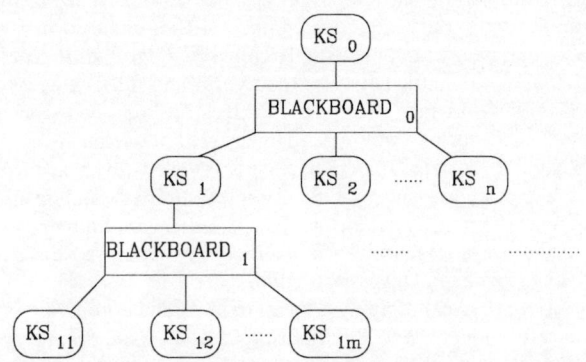

Figure 3. Basic structure of HOPES

As can be seen from the figure, a tree structure is adopted, because such a structure has several advantages for real-time SPI applications.

Firstly, all the KSs, which have been developed to perform a variety of functions, are arranged at different layers of the "tree". This hierarchical organization of the KSs naturally corresponds to the multi-level analysis. Each layer represents an analysis level and those KSs that perform the same level processing are organized at the same layer. As shown in Figure 3, for example, KS_0 is at the root of the "tree", and performs the highest level of analysis. It collects and summarizes those intermediate results presented by low level KSs such as KS_1, KS_2, ..., KS_n, and gives out final results (i.e., final interpretation of signals). KS_1, KS_2, ..., KS_n are at a lower layer than KS_0. They perform lower level analysis as indicated in Figure 2.

Secondly, a system with this "tree" structure can be easily extended as necessary. As described before, a SPI task can be very complicated. Although the task has been divided into several sub-tasks, a sub-task may still be too complicated and in need of further division. Accordingly, HOPES provides for any KS to be extended when necessary. It can be seen from Figure 3 that KS_1 is expanded to contain other KSs such as KS_{11}, KS_{12}, ..., KS_{1m} which are at an even lower level.

Finally, all the KSs are loosely coupled in the system and capable of running concurrently. A multi-blackboard architecture is proposed to provide communication channels among the KSs. (The multi-blackboard architecture will be discussed more fully in the next section). As a result, reasoning processes of the system can be speeded up.

3.2. Constitution of a KS

According to the structure proposed, a KS of HOPES consists mainly of three kinds of knowledge: 1) knowledge about information exchange; 2) knowledge about the problem domain; 3) knowledge about data transformation (Figure 4).

Figure 4. Constitution of a KS

The information exchange knowledge and data transformation knowledge are two kinds of meta-knowledge, i.e., knowledge about knowledge. During the execution, a KS always needs to exchange information with other KSs at the same level in order to cooperate. Also it needs to present its reasoning results to a KS at a higher level so that it can contribute to the complete solution of the problem. When and how to do this are entirely determined by using information exchange knowledge. If information is needed from a KS at the lower level, data transformation knowledge is used to "interpret" the information. Then the information can be "understood" and used. Domain knowledge is the main body of the knowledge that a KS possesses. It represents the domain knowledge necessary to accomplish the SPI task.

If the KS is at the highest level, i.e., at the root of the "tree" structure, the information exchange knowledge may include interface to a human operator or other systems which can take some further actions according to the interpretation of signals. If the KS is at the lowest level, i.e., a leaf of the "tree", the data transformation knowledge may include interface to sensors by which signals are detected.

3.3 Hardware support

As presented above, the KSs in the HOPES system are organized hierarchically in a tree structure. They are capable of parallel execution, and the multi-blackboard architecture provides communication channels among them. In order to implement such an expert system, a computer system with a multi-processor architecture will be adopted. This computer system consists of several processors, each of which has its own instruction set and is capable of independent action. In the system, a common memory is shared by the processors. The structure of such a system is shown in Figure 5 (Perrott 1987).

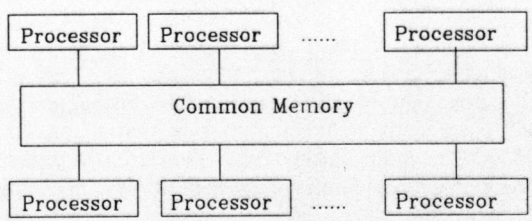

Figure 5. Multi-processor architecture with shared memory

In such a system, different parts of an application program, e.g., KSs of HOPES, could be assigned to different processors for execution with the result that the time for executing the complete program would be substantially reduced. Several experiments were performed on the system and it was found that such a multi-processor system can provide a linear speed-up factor (Perrott 1987). That is, N processors, at best, can perform the same task as a single processor in 1/Nth of the time.

On the other hand, however, there are some factors that can affect the performance of the system, such as: 1) *Synchronization*: Some of the processors may be idle waiting on other processors to catch up; 2) *Contention*: If several processors require the same resource, they must take turns in using it.

The first problem can be avoided if all the KSs are carefully organized, and properly assigned to the processors. The second problem occurs in an expert system mainly because different KSs will probably contend for information while accomplishing a task. In order to solve this problem, in the HOPES system we use the multi-blackboard architecture for communications among the KSs, and some corresponding strategies are adopted. These are discussed in the next section.

4. Multi-blackboard architecture and communication strategies

Communication channels and strategies play a very important role in a parallel expert system. As a task is usually complex, close co-ordination of all agents (e.g. KSs) in the system is needed. Large amount of information will be transferred among these agents. The performance of the parallel system thus depends strongly on communication methods and strategies. If this problem can not be solved properly, the communication will be a bottleneck in the parallel system, and the performance of the system will be seriously degraded.

4.1. Brief overview of different communication methods

The communication methods and strategies of parallel expert systems have always been an important research area of DAI. Many methods and strategies have been proposed and used in constructing expert systems. All these methods and strategies may be classified according to the ways in which information is exchanged. Basically, there are three kind of methods. 1) *Centrally controlled information exchange*: By using this method, all the information that needs to be exchanged is collected by a control unit first (This control unit could be an expert system or just a KS). Then this control unit will decide when, how and to where the information should be sent (Gerstenfeld & Gosling 1987). 2) *Decentralized exchange of information*: By using this method, all the information that needs to be exchanged is put in a place (e.g., a blackboard) which can be accessed by all agents working in the system. From that place, an agent may obtain the information necessary for its task (Ensor & Gabbe 1985; Velthuijsen & Lippolt 1987). 3) *Direct message passing*: By using this method, when an agent has some information to exchange, it directly sends this information to another agent or agents which the sender "thinks" will need the information (Green 1987; Smith 1980).

Among these three methods, the first one seems less suitable for real-time SPI task than the other two because of the bottleneck problem. The second method is used in many current expert systems (Engelmore & Morgan 1988), and if proper communication strategies are incorporated in the method, it can be used for real-time applications. The third method may provide a quick way for information exchange in some cases. However, it tends to make an agent (e.g.,KS) complex because the agent has to have knowledge about all other agents in the system. As a result, the execution of such an agent may be quite slow, and the overall system is more difficult to modify.

4.2. Multi-blackboard architecture

We are in favour of using the blackboard method. In the HOPES system, however, instead of using a single blackboard, we adopt a multi-blackboard architecture to provide communication channels among KSs at different levels (Figure 3). The reasons for this are set out below.

Firstly, the multi-blackboard architecture is the most suitable model for the hierarchical structure of HOPES and parallel processing. Secondly, if a single blackboard is used, then it may become a bottleneck when the number of KSs increases. Thirdly, as a task may be very complex, the information used may be very complex too. The use of the multi-blackboard architecture will be able to reduce the information complexity. Fourthly, as such an architecture distributes information over several blackboards, each blackboard contains relatively small amount of information. This makes the system efficient. Finally, managing the multi-blackboard architecture is easier than managing a big, single blackboard, because the management can be spread over several KSs.

From Figure 3, it can be seen that there is a blackboard shared among KSs at any level, such as $BLACKBOARD_0$ and $BLACKBOARD_1$. The blackboards provide communication channels among KSs at the same level, and they are also "bridges" between different levels of analysis.

For example, KS_{11}, KS_{12}, ..., KS_{1m} exchange information through BLACKBOARD$_1$, so that they can co-ordinate with each other. After they obtain some results, KS_1 will collect them from BLACKBOARD$_1$. If these results are useful for other high level KSs such as KS_2, ..., KS_n, they will be transferred to BLACKBOARD$_0$ for exchanging at a higher level. Finally, KS_0 summarizes results on BLACKBOARD$_0$ and will give out the final interpretation of signals.

From this paradigm, it can be seen that all intermediate results from certain level KSs are stored on the blackboard at that level. Only those intermediate results which may be useful for high level analysis will be transferred by a high level KS to the blackboard at the higher level. Irrelevant information can never appear on the higher level blackboard. The level of data abstraction increases gradually from low level blackboards to high level blackboards.

4.3. Communication strategies in HOPES

The multi-blackboard architecture has been adopted in HOPES. Correspondingly, there are some communication strategies. The prime goals of these strategies are to keep effective communications in HOPES and make the system efficient.

By *effective communication*, we mean that the blackboards should be unimpeded communication channels rather than bottlenecks. All interference of concurrent KSs should be avoided. By *system efficiency*, we mean that all irrelevant information may not be exchanged or transferred. If this is unavoidable, the amount of the irrelevant information exchanged should be kept as small as possible.

Interference of KSs occurs due to the parallel execution abilities of the KSs. There always exists the possibility that more than one KS wants to operate on the blackboard at the same time, and even on the same data. In order to prevent this happening, a normal way is to use a blackboard handler or manager to process requests from KSs for operating on the blackboard (Velthuijsen & Lippolt 1987). While a KS is operating on the blackboard, other access requests are refused. However, if too many KSs request access to the blackboard at the same time, the blackboard will be a bottleneck because only one KS can get access and others have to wait. On the other hand, once a new piece of information is put on the blackboard by a KS, other KSs have to apply for access in order to check the new information. In fact, some of the KSs do not need to do so because the information may not be relevant to them. This makes the system inefficient.

In order to overcome the shortcomings of using a blackboard handler, new strategies are proposed for using in HOPES.

4.3.1. Constitution of a blackboard

Each blackboard in HOPES is divided into areas, among which there is a *common area* and several *private areas*. The number of private areas depends on the number of KSs at that level. Each private area corresponds to a KS as shown in Figure 6a

A private area may be sub-divided into two sections: *local section* and *global section*, as shown in Figure 6b. Such a structure forms the base of the communication strategies used in HOPES.

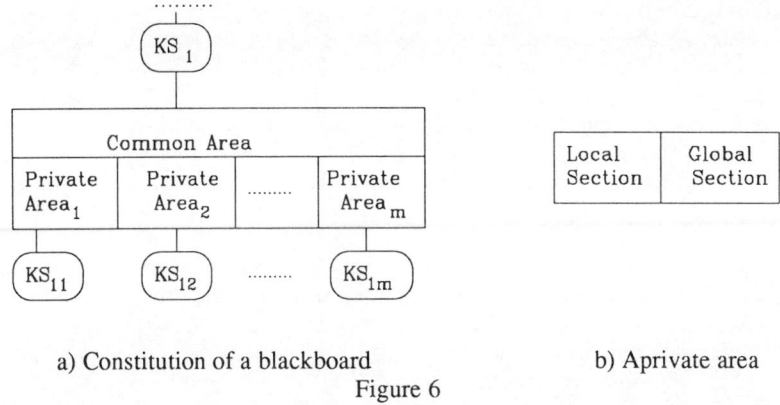

a) Constitution of a blackboard b) A private area

Figure 6

4.3.2. Communication strategies

Each KS uses its own private area as working memory. All intermediate results it obtained are put in the area, either in the local section or in the global section. The information in the global section may be read by other KSs, conversely, information in the local section can not. If a KS "thinks", by using its information exchange knowledge (see section 3.2), that an intermediate result may be useful for other KSs, then it will put the result in the global section. Otherwise, the result will be put in the local section, and can only be used by that KS. This hides irrelevant information from other KSs. This method is similar to the concept of data hiding in software engineering.

All writing operations of KSs are limited in their private areas and in the common area. For example, as shown in Figure 6a, KS_{11} may only write data to its private area$_1$ or the common area. It can not perform any writing operation to any other area.

The common area is a special area on the blackboard. Any KS can read information from it or write data to it. It acts as an *announce board*. When a KS find an intermediate result which is useful for some other KSs, the KS will "inform" those KSs by putting an announcement in the common area. The contents of the announcement include an abstract of the result, name of the announcer, and name(s) of the potential "beneficiaries", i.e., those KSs that may find the information helpful.

During execution, a KS checks the announce board when it needs help from other KSs. Firstly, it has to find an announcement in which it is one of the potential beneficiaries. Then it should check the abstract of the information to see whether or not it is really useful. In fact, the abstract is another guard for preventing redundant information exchange. Finally, if the information is helpful to it, the KS may use the abstract and the name of the announcer as an index to find the information. If it is a high level KS that gets the information provided by a KS at lower level, it may put the information in its global section or local section depending on whether or not the information is useful for other high level KSs. If two KSs are at the same level, the receiver must put the information in its local section of the private area.

After a KS reads an announcement, it deletes its name from the name list of the beneficiaries. A KS which is the last one to read the announcement will delete it after it finishes reading, as no KS needs it any more.

Here, we give a simple example to show how these strategies work (Figure 6a). Suppose at certain time of execution, KS_{11} obtains a result which it thinks is useful for KS_1 and KS_{12}, and KS_{12} obtains a result useful for KS_{11} and KS_{1m}. Then KS_{11} and KS_{12} will put their announcements in the common area. The announcements will be:

$$announce(abstract_{11}, KS_{11}, (KS_1, KS_{12})),$$
$$announce(abstract_{12}, KS_{12}, (KS_{11}, KS_{1m})).$$

Assume that at this time, KS_1, KS_{12} and KS_{1m} need help from other KSs. Then they may read these announcements at the same time without interfering with each other. KS_1 and KS_{1m} find the information is helpful, then they will get access to the private areas of KS_{11} and KS_{12} to read the information, also without affecting each other. After reading, KS_1 deletes its name from the announcement, and so does KS_{1m}. At this stage, the information in the common area is:

$$announce(abstract_{11}, KS_{11}, (KS_{12})),$$
$$announce(abstract_{12}, KS_{12}, (KS_{11})).$$

According to the $abstract_{11}$, KS_{12} may find that the information provided by KS_{11} is not really useful. Then it will not read the information, and just delete its name from the announcement. After deleting, it finds that there is no more beneficiary of the announcement, thus it deletes the announcement. Finally, there is only one announcement left on the announce board. But KS_{11} does not need help from other KSs at that time, therefore, it has to remain there until KS_{11} reads it and deletes it.

From the descriptions above, it can be seen that interference among KSs may only occur in the common area. There is, however, no possibility that more than one KS is simultaneously operating on the same data (although more than one writing operations can be performed on the same announcement at the same time, it will not affect the correctness of the announcement.). Therefore, *multi-access* to a blackboard may become possible, and this can reduce the possibility of the contention of the KSs. This makes the system more efficient.

5. A prototype system of HOPES

Currently, a range-measuring intruder alarm system has been chosen as the application area for the HOPES system. This system uses diplex-doppler radar techniques to detect the presence of a moving target, and measure its velocity and distance to the radar receiver. According to the measurements obtained, it will determine whether or not the target is a human intruder (Kane 1983; Winter 1979). As the diplex-doppler radar system faces difficulties in dealing with problems presented by a human target, it is proposed to use the HOPES system to improve the performance of the alarm system.

A prototype system of HOPES is under development at the present time. A simulation approach on a uni-processor has been adopted in order to test the architectural design before moving to a more expensive multi-processor configuration. This prototype system is used to interpret the simulated diplex-doppler radar signals reflected from a moving target. According to the information provided in the signals, the system will determine whether the moving target is a human being.

The prototype system consists of eight KSs arranged at three levels. There are three blackboards used as communication channels among the KSs. The basic organization of the system is shown in Figure 7.

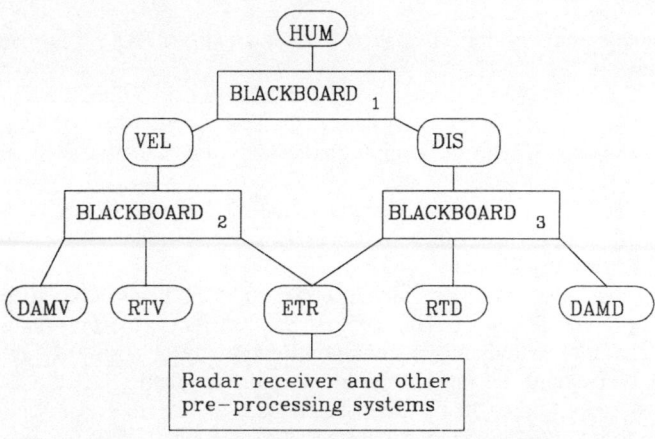

Figure 7. Organization of prototype HOPES system

Following is a brief summary of the eight KSs (the names are indicated in Brackets): 1) Extract relevant information from sampled signals (ETR). 2) Manage sampled data which will be used to calculate the target's velocity ($DAMV$). 3) Find the target's velocity in real-time (RTV). 4) Monitor velocities of the moving target in a certain time period (VEL). 5) Manage sampled data which will be used to calculate the target's distance ($DAMD$). 6) Find the target's distance in real-time (RTD). 7) Monitor distances between the target and the radar receiver over a time period (DIS). 8) Summarize the changes of the target's velocity and distance, and accordingly determine whether or not the target is a human being (HUM).

The radar signals are taken from a model alarm system (Kane 1983) and compiled into several data files. The pre-processing systems are implemented by using signal processing algorithms such as FFT. The Modula-2 language has been chosen to implement the prototype system because it has several advantages for the simulation of the real-time parallel systems (Sale 1986). The parallel processing activities are simulated by using a VAX-11 computer under the operating system VMS. The KSs that need to run concurrently are executed in a time sharing environment.

6. Conclusions

In this paper, we overviewed important characteristics of the engineering applications of AI, such as the real-time requirement and task complexity which have been discussed in detail. It can been seen that these characteristics have much influence over expert systems used. Traditional expert system structures and inference strategies are not fully adequate for this class of tasks. Some technical changes are needed in order to accommodate the special requirements of the expert systems for engineering applications.

The HOPES system, which is a parallel expert system, has been proposed for real-time SPI applications. This system consists of several KSs which are hierarchically organized and capable of parallel processing. A multi-blackboard architecture and corresponding communication strategies are used in the HOPES system to provide communication channels among different KSs. The advantages of the HOPES system are summarized as follows:

1) Different kinds of knowledge are arranged in different KSs. All KSs are hierarchically organized in the tree structure. Data abstractions are divided into several levels. This corresponds with the complicated nature of SPI applications, such as multi-level processing and analysis.

2) Each KS is capable of running concurrently with other KSs. Thus, the time needed for completing a task can be reduced. This accommodates the real-time requirement of engineering applications.

3) Instead of using a single blackboard, a multi-blackboard architecture is adopted in the HOPES system. This architecture distributes the information used over several blackboards, so reducing information complexity and simplifying the management of each blackboard. This makes the system more efficient.

4) Corresponding to the multi-blackboard architecture, some communication strategies are proposed. They reduce the possibility of contention of the parallel KSs, and should result in enhanced system performance.

5) The HOPES system may be readily implemented on the hardware configuration as described in section 3.3.

The HOPES system provides a general model of real-time expert systems. It may be used not only for SPI, but also for some other engineering applications such as real-time process control and image processing.

[References]

Bailey, M.G. & Kraft, R., et al. (1987): "RESCU - A Real-Time Expert System", *Proc. of Int. Conf. on Control and Industrial Processes*, Milan, pp.485-502

Campbell, S.D. & Olson, S.H. (1986): "WX1 - An Expert System for Weather Radar Interpretation", *Coupling Symbolic and Numerical Computing in Expert Systems*, J. S. Kowalik (Ed.), North-Holland, pp.329-348

Cartwright, C. & Ruskin, P. (1986): "Musing on the Needs of Real Time AI Toolkits", *Expert Systems User*, December, pp.30-31

Cleary, J.G. & Kramer, L.L., et al. (1986): "Knowledge-Based Systems for the Interpretation of Seismic Data", *Coupling Symbolic and Numerical Computing in Expert Systems*, J. S. Kowalik (Ed.), North-Holland, pp.231-246

Daku, B.L.F. & Grant, P.M., et al. (1988): "Intelligent Techniques for Spectral Estimation", *J. of the Institution of Electronic and Radio Engineers*, Vol.58, No.6, pp.275-283

Engelmore, R. & Morgan, T. (Eds.) (1988): "Blackboard Systems", Addison-Wesley

Ensor, J.R. & Gabbe, J.D. (1985): "Transactional Blackboards", *Proc. of 9th IJCAI*, pp.340-344

Erman, L.D. & Hayes-Roth, F. et al. (1980): "The Hearsay-II Speech-Understanding System: Integrating Knowledge to Resolve Uncertainty", *Computing Surveys*, Vol.12, No.2, Jun., pp.213-253

Fennell, R.D. & Lessor, V.R. (1977): "Parallelism in Artificial Intelligence Problem Solving: A Case Study of Hearsay-II", *IEEE Transactions on Computers*, Vol.C-26, No.2, Feb., pp.98-111

Fox, M.S. (1981): "An Organizational View of Distributed Systems", *IEEE Transactions on Systems, Man, and Cybernetics*, Vol.SMC-11, No.1, Jan., pp.70-80

Gerstenfeld, A. & Gosling, G., et al. (1987): "An Expert System for Managing Co-operating Expert Systems", *Artificial Intelligence in Engineering: Tools and Techniques*, UK: Comput. Mech. Publications, pp219-244

Green, P.E. (1987): "AF: A Framework for Real-Time Distributed Co-operative Problem Solving", *Distributed Artificial Intelligence*, M. N. Huhns (Ed.), Pitman, pp.153-175

Gupta, A. (1985): "Parallelism in Production Systems: The Sources and the Expected Speed-Up", *5th Int. Workshop: Expert Systems and Their Applications*, France, Vol.1, pp.25-57

Hawkinson, L.B. & Levin, M.E., et al. (1985): "A Paradigm for Real-Time Inference", *Proc. of AI and Advanced Computer Technology*, pp.51-56

Kamen, E. (1987): "Introduction to Signals and Systems", Collier Macmillan

Kane, R.A. (1983): "Signal-Processing in Short-Range Radar Systems", *Ph.D Thesis*, The Queen's University of Belfast

Leinweber, D. & Gidwani, K. (1986): "Real-Time Expert System Development Techniques and Applications", *Proc. IEEE WESTEX-86*, USA, pp.69-77

Lessor, V.R. & Corkill, D. et al. (1982): "A High-Level Simulation Testbed for Co-operative Distributed Problem Solving", *Proc. 3rd Int. Conf. Dist. Computer Systems*, pp.341-349

Lessor, V.R. & Erman, L.D. (1980): "Distributed Interpretation: A Model and Experiment", *IEEE Transactions on Computers*, Vol.C-29, No.12, Dec., pp.1144-1163

Mathonet, R. & Cotthem, H.V., et al. (1987): "DANTES: An Expert System for Real-Time Network Troubleshooting", *Proc. of 10th IJCAI*, pp.527-530

Moore, R.L. & Kramer, M.A. (1986): "Expert Systems in ON-Line Process Control", *Proc. 3rd CPC Conference*, California, pp.839-867

Morgan, A. (1988): "Real-Time Expert Systems for Industrial Applications", *Proc. of the 4th Int. Expert Systems Conf.*, London, pp.149-157

Nii, H.P. & Feigenbaum, E.A., et al. (1982): "Signal-to-Symbol Transformation: HASP/SIAP Case Study", *The AI Magazine*, Spring, pp.23-35

O'Reilly, C.A. & Cromarty, A.S. (1985): ""Fast" is not "Real-Time": Designing Effective Real-Time AI Systems", *Proc. of SPIE*, Vol.548: *Applications of Artificial Intelligence II*, pp.249-257

Perrott, R.H. (1987): "Parallel Programming", Addison-Wesley

Riese, C.E. (1986): "Expert Systems in Engineering: Some Issues", *Proc. IEEE WESTEX-86*, USA, pp.147-154

Sale, A. (1986): "Modula-2: Discipline & Design", Addison-Wesley

Smith, R.G. (1980): "The Contract Net Protocol: High-Level Communication and Control in a Distributed Problem Solver", *IEEE Transactions on Computers*, Vol.C-29, No.12, Dec., pp.1104-1113

Smith, R.G. & Davis, R. (1981): "Frameworks for Co-operation in Distributed Problem Solving", *IEEE Transactions on Systems, Man, and Cybernetics*, Vol.SMC-11, No.1, Jan., pp.61-70

Talukdar, S.N. & Cardozo, E., et al. (1986): " A System for Distributed Problem Solving", *Coupling Symbolic and Numerical Computing in Expert Systems*, J. S. Kowalik (Ed.), North-Holland, pp.59-67

Velthuijsen, H. & Lippolt, B.J., et al. (1987): "A Parallel Blackboard System for Robert Control", *Proc. of 10th IJCAI*, pp.1157-1159

Waterman, D.A. (1986): "A Guide to Expert Systems", Addison-Wesley

Winter, D.A. (1979): "Biomechanics of Human Movement", John Wiley & Sons

Wright, M.L. (1986): "HEXSCON: A Hybrid Microcomputer-Based Expert System for Real-Time Control Applications", *Proc. IEEE WESTEX-86*, USA, pp.49-54

CONCURRENT REFINEMENT OF STRUCTURED OBJECTS: A
LANGUAGE FOR DISTRIBUTED KNOWLEDGE PROGRAMMING USING
SPECIFICATIONS AND ANNOTATIONS[**]

M. BARBUCEANU [*]
S. TRAUSAN-MATU [*]
B. MOLNAR

Central Research Institute for Physics H1525
Budapest 114. P.O.B. 49, Hungary

[*] Institute for Computer and Information Sciences
8-10 Miciurin, 71316 Bucharest 1, ROMANIA

1. The objects model

Structured objects are a simple, uniform and intuitively appealing mechanism for modelling application domains through objects with specific structure and behaviour. We shall assume a fairly conventional model of a structured object language with the following features:

(1) Structured objects (also called units) are composed of slots, each slot being filled with a value description and also possessing a slot description. The slot description is given in terms of another object with slots specifying various information pertaining to the described slot such as its domain and range, its cardinality, its default value, various sorts of book-keeping information. Objects also have associated object descriptions. These are specified in terms of other objects which have slots for the various kinds of information relevant to the described object, including inheritance specifications.

(2) Objects have associated behaviours which can be activated through message passing. The specification of the attachment of methods to objects is done by devoting a slot description for every message type (selector) the object and slot responds to and by filling this slot with the name of the method to be executed in response to the message. Our language, which we call XRL, allows methods to be specified as structured objects and provides for many method combination possibilities whose description is outside the scope of this paper.

(3) In our XRL language objects are of a prototypical nature in that a given object can at the same time be both an instance of another and a generic object with instances of its own. Instances inherit all the slots, values and descriptions of the parent object except for those which are explicitly overridden by the instance.

2. Refinement

If objects are interpreted as partial specifications which leave an amount of incertitude, then a natural task of a problem solving

---

[**] This is an extended abstract. Due to the production schedule, a full translated paper was not available.

system employing such objects is that of incrementally removing this incertitude by producing more and more specific objects.

The informal definition of incremental refinement is of a process which incrementally reduces the ambiguity of generic objects by producing more and more specific versions of these objects. The problem solving language to be discussed provides organizations of computational processes which carry out this sort of incremental refinement.

We have implemented the language in the form of two architectures in order to allow flexibility in usage. The first architecture, called Concurrent Refinement, provides an organization whereby objects are refined by associated processes which run concurrently. The architecture allows the specification of diverse features of the concurrent refinement process to be declaratively specified by a special annotation language. Annotations are slot descriptions which direct the development of the refinement process associated with the annotated unit or slot. For example, a basic choice in concurrent refinement is between refining an object by creating a new process for each of its non terminal (refinable) slots or by executing some computation which will return the whole refined object. The former variant is called "expanding" the object while the latter is referred to as "anchoring" the object. The Concurrent Refinement architecture provides an encompassing annotation language which directs all aspects of the refinement process. The architecture is agenda based and employs a structured blackboard as the working space for producing networks of refined objects. It provides special primitives for communication and synchronization of the concurrent refinement processes, a special event handling scheme, as well as several built-in control regimes including refinement replay.

The second architecure, built on top of Concurrent Refinement and named Set Oriented Refinement, advances the formalization of refinement by using set theoretic mechanisms.

3. Concurrent Refinement

The concurrent refinement architecture interprets structured objects as specifications of concurrently executing processes which produce refined instances of themselves as the results of execution. The object-as-process interpretation promoted by this architecture is complementary to the usual object-as-active-data interpretation common to structured object languages.

3.1 Task Processing

Each activity which is part of the refinement process is assigned a task. Examples of tasks include; the refinement of structured objects, the evaluation of arbitrary expressions, carrying out synchronization and communication. Besides these, the architecture also uses a fourth kind of task, event handling tasks, these tasks handle events generated by other tasks in the system.

The task is the concurrent unit of the architecture. There

exists a well defined set of activities related to all aspects of task processing and whose execution can be programmed through annotations. These include activities to be executed before, after, or at certain moments during the lifetime of the task, task activation preconditions, priority setting actions, event description and handling and others.

The task-subtask relation structures the collection of tasks associated with the refinement of a given object into a tree.

3.2 The annotation language

Much of the convenience of using the architecture stems from the manner in which it can be programmed through the declarative annotation language. Annotations appear as selectors whose values are those returned by sending the corresponding message to the annotated object. The method specified for the selector is an evaluable expression. This implementation of annotations was selected because it allows dynamically determined values and the use of method combinations. In our XRL implementation, method combination also allows combining methods in the lexical context of an object nesting (called context sensitive combination). This is useful for sensitizing the annotations vocabulary to the particular context in which objects appear.

The annotations employed by concurrent refinement are grouped in to several classes.

3.3 Communication and synchronization

Concurrent refinement processes synchronize themselves and communicate data by means of the primitives <u>path</u> and <u>using</u>. Thus, when a refinement process needs a value computed by another parallel refinement process, the former process attempts to access the data it needs by following a sequence of slots and objects starting from a known instance and leading to the desired value. The dependencies between instances created by paths or by direct references to slot names in expressions are recorded by the architecture and used to support the replay regime.

In our implementation of concurrent refinement we have introduced a special recursive language for path definition. This language has constructs for navigating in the instance network built by the refinement process and for automated backtracking when exploring several tentative paths in this network.

3.4 Refinement systems

Concurrent refinement processes are globally defined and controlled by means of the refinement systems mechanism. Refinement systems are objects which specify the structure and overall behaviour of refinement processes. The structural part of the specification comprises the following aspects: (1) the agendas associated with the process and (2), the spaces on the blackboard controlled by the refinement process and the units to be refined on each of these spaces.

The behavioural part of the specification refers to: (1) the possible states of the refinement process and the state transition network which defines the overall behaviour of the process (2) the events which can occur during refinement and the associated handlers provided by the refinement system and (3), the settings of the various parameters controlling the instrumentation of the refinement process - including the level of tracing, the interruption moments or conditions, etc.

The state transition mechanism describes the behaviour of the refinement system in a classic manner. The system can be in one state at a given moment and will pass to another state when an event occurs. The event handlers, being specified as rule interpreters, can condition the transitions in any way. The state transition mechanism serves in fact three distinct purposes relevant to refinement system behaviour specification. The first is that of establishing a focus of attention by forcing refinement to deal only with the objects held on the named spaces or processed through the named agendas. Second, it serves as a serialisation mechanism as only one state can be active at any moment. Third, it allows specification of different instrumentation regimes in the development stages.

Refinement systems cooperate by sharing the blackboard. Access paths employed by one system can look anywhere on the blackboard. A user can have any number of refinement systems run in parallel. An interactive interface allows these systems to be monitored from associated windows, including dynamic changes of slots of the refinement system.

3.5 Set Oriented Refinement

Concurrent refinement provides a mechanism for interpreting objects as specifications of concurrent refinement process. The semantics of refinement in this architecture are operationally specified. Refining an object means doing what the refinement annotations say should be done. The set oriented refinement architecture takes the further step of giving a formal definition to refinement. It is based on the introduction of a new set oriented description language. The expressions of this language can be used to describe the possible slot values of objects. The new structured object language which results from allowing set oriented descriptions as slot value descriptions has a formal definition of refinement which can be mechanically verified and operationalized. As a knowledge processing language, this architecture provides two major advantages. First, the extension of the structured object language turns it into a high level declarative specification language which allows knowledge processing to be specified in more abstract, mathematically oriented terms. The declarative specification language has a clearly defined semantics. This makes the language more powerful, allowing specification of complex computational processes and makes programs more understandable. Second, programs written in terms of this language make the factorisation into the description of the specification (what should the program compute) and the description of the implementation (how should the program do the computation) clearer than in the underlying concurrent refinement layer. The specification part is formulated in terms of the extended structured object language including set oriented descriptions while the implementation part is formulated through the same annotation mechanism employed for concurrent refinement, with new annotations introduced for the set oriented concepts. This factorisation leads us further along the direction of declarative specification programming in structured object environments.

3.6 The set oriented description language

Concurrent refinement allowed any construct of the underlying structured object level to fill a refinable slot. It also added a few constructs of its own (path, using). Set oriented refinement also allows any construct to engage in refinement. Moreover, it adds the expressions which can be formed with the special set oriented description language (SODL). SODL builds upon the interpretation of a generic structured object as representing a class of terminal objects. The semantics of SODL defines the meaning of SODL constructs in terms of associated classes of terminal objects. On this basis the refinement notion is also defined. Annotations provide the means for attaching to set oriented descriptions their operationalization mechanism, that is the computational process which will actually carry out the retrieval and/or construction of the refined objects.

3.7 Expert systems

The refinement language was used for implementing a number of medium scale expert systems in several domains. Some of these were delivered to customers and are in current use. One class of systems was in the configuration domain and we have built systems for configuring computer systems and distributed controllers for industrial process. Another system was built for homeopathy diagnosis and treatment. Finally, a larger system has been built for the civil domain, more precisely for designing industrial halls.

The experience with these systems has shown that concurrent refinement gives us a useful way of thinking when modelling application domains. The declarative style of programming using incomplete specifications is a powerful programming concept which helps in rapid prototyping, program understanding and modification.

4. Conclusion

The epistemological commitments of XRL make the language level higher than most currently used languages, yet preserving its domain independence. We believe that knowledge based programs should be written in terms that reflect as close as possible the patterns of thinking in the domain. High level languages like this one provide a better basis for modelling certain types of expert problem solving. The ease of programming some recently investigaged problem solving types as well as the ease with which several systems have been built and modified justify this claim.

A Graphical Expert System for Microfossil Identification

P. A. Swaby

BP Research International,
Chertsey Road, Sunbury-on-Thames,
Middlesex, TW16 7LN, UK.

Abstract

This paper describes the design and development of a graphical expert system for the identification of objects which are arranged in a hierarchy. The main components of the system are a graphical expert system shell and a set of knowledge bases. The knowledge for each group of objects was elicited from an expert and was stored in a specially designed knowledge metafile, the corresponding images were also stored in a special image metafile. A knowledge base building tool was developed to generate knowledge bases automatically, which include rules, frames and graphical interface, from the metafiles. The graphical expert system shell was designed so that users can enter information about an object, on a generic picture of the object group by selecting parts of the picture in turn and choosing the most appropriate description in each case. The expert system uses the rules and frames to make inferences with information that is entered. The combination of an expert system with extensive domain knowledge, in the form of rules and frames, and an easy-to-use graphical interface makes the system powerful, flexible and very effective. The system has already been successfully applied to the domain of microfossil identification.

1 Introduction

The work reported here was concerned with the design and development of a graphical approach to the identification of fossils in the phylum Conodonta down to the species level. It was realised that there were significant advantages to be gained from the application of computer workstations in the field of fossil identification, for example, reduced cost of identification, increased speed, multiple copies of the system spread worldwide and the permanent capture of expert knowledge. Previous expert systems for fossil identification have been purely text-based, see Wiley (1987), or have made only limited use of the graphical nature of the problem, see Conrad & Beightol (1988) and Brough & Alexander (1986). This system was designed to take full advantage of the graphical nature of the problem and used high quality images at each stage of the identification process. The functional interaction of the system is shown in Figure 1. The following sections describe the work done in the areas of knowledge elicitation, expert systems and graphical interface design; a sample session is described; and finally, a discussion of the work and conclusions are presented.

2 Knowledge Elicitation

One of the major problems encountered during the building of this expert system was that of acquisition of knowledge. Initial attempts were very time consuming, but many refinements were made to the techniques used which have led to quite efficient methods. The stages in this development process and the current techniques used are described below.

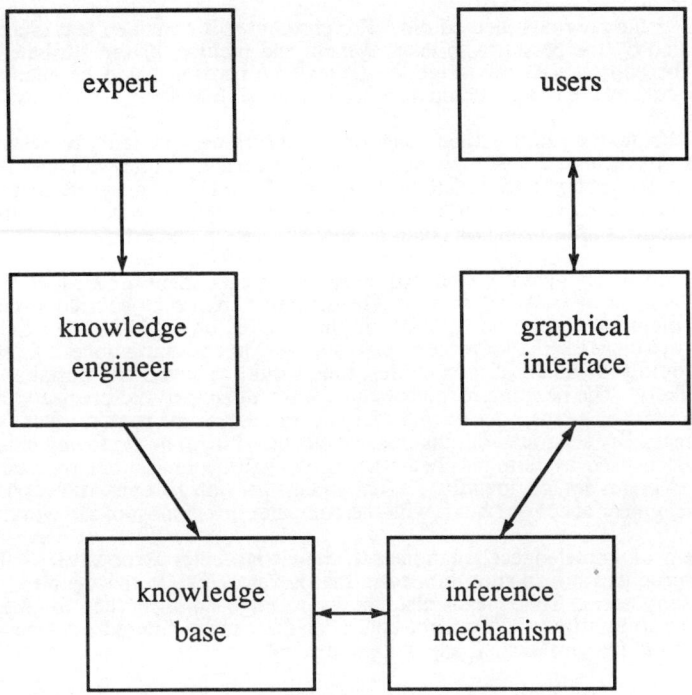

Figure 1 Functional Interaction of the System.

Initially, the expert described how fifteen species within the genus *Gnathodus* could be distinguished. The identification process was filmed and notes were taken. The expert drew pictures of each of the species within the genus and these were scanned in using a frame store connected to a camera; this took two people approximately one hour. From a careful review of the film and notes it was possible to gain some understanding of how the expert solved the problem. However, several more sessions were necessary to clarify certain points and correct certain mistakes that were made by the knowledge engineers. This process proved to be quite lengthy and time consuming. Once the information had been verified it was entered into the computer manually. This often proved unsatisfactory since pictures of the attribute values were selected by whoever entered the information and several inappropriate pictures were chosen since that person was not familiar with the terminology.

The next stage adopted the same procedure as before for the genus *Scaliognathus* with the exception that photographs of the species were used instead of poor quality sketches. They provided much better images; however, they weren't of perfect quality because the size of the fossils, typically less than a millimetre, caused ordinary light photography to lose some resolution. One solution to this would have been to use electron micrographs, but these are not always available.

A pattern began to emerge from the experience gained with the first two genera. What was needed was simply a table of species, attributes and attribute values, a description and a picture for each genus. The expert was able to write down such a table and provide pictures for the genus and species. The textual information was entered manually as before. However, the pictures now provided were high quality drawings and were scanned in using an image scanner; this required only one person and not two as the previous method did. The problem still remained that images had to be separated by the person who entered them and pictures of the attribute values still had to be chosen. At this stage the textual information could be entered in a couple of hours and the images could be entered in about one day.

Entering the textual information was time consuming, particularly when long descriptions of species etc., were given. The next refinement came with the use of an optical character recognition (OCR) system which could read typed text into a computer. This meant that the time taken to enter descriptions was cut significantly and large quantities of information could be entered quickly and efficiently.

The problems of image entry were still present and accounted for most of the time taken in the process of knowledge entry. The greatest bottleneck occurred in selecting appropriate pictures of attribute values from the pictures provided by the expert; this was due to the fact that the knowledge engineer was not a stratigrapher. Clearly, if the expert could provide all of the pictures, time would be saved and mistakes would be far less likely. The next improvement came when the expert did precisely this and provided pictures of genus, species and attribute values. Some routines were written which automatically separated out the images, enhanced them by removing small dots such as those caused by dust on photocopiers, named the images appropriately and placed them in an image metafile. The process of image entry now takes the knowledge engineer about one hour, with the computer doing most of the work.

The system of knowledge elicitation and knowledge entry is now very efficient. The expert produces information in a form that is very close to that required by the knowledge engineer. This means that the knowledge engineer has to make few modifications to this information and, hence, that it can be entered into the system very quickly and few mistakes, if any, will be made.

3 Expert System

An expert system is used to try to match the description of the fossil entered by the user to a subset of objects, such as species from within a genus. It consists of two main parts which are described below.

3.1 knowledge base

One of the essential components of an expert system is the knowledge that it contains. Any representation of this knowledge should consider the following requirements. Firstly, the knowledge must be contained in manageable units. It would not practical to store it all in one file or data structure; location and modification of individual pieces of information would be very difficult. Also, it would not be practical to store the information in many individual files or data structures. It would be very difficult to keep track of so many data items. One solution to this problem is to choose a representation that is somewhere in between such as the knowledge and image metafile structures used in this system. Secondly, the knowledge representation structures should be kept as simple as possible, in order to facilitate the modification and addition of knowledge. Thirdly, knowledge should be in a homogeneous form so that the inference mechanism and other parts of the system can be altered more easily and thus extended more readily.

The choice of an appropriate size and format for the structures that hold the information supplied by the expert was influenced by the way in which stratigraphers classify and identify fossils manually. Fossil groups are classified in a tree structure from the phylum level at the top, down to the species level at the bottom. At each level there are usually five to fifteen branches. This is a manageable number; any more and it would be too difficult to distinguish between them; any less and there would be too many taxa in the hierarchy. It therefore seemed that the choice of knowledge representation structures should take advantage of the experience gained by stratigraphers and contain all of the information for one taxon within the hierarchy. Hence, the knowledge and image metafile structures have been defined. A knowledge metafile contains all of the textual information and an image metafile contains all of the images for one node.

The generic structure for a knowledge metafile is shown below:

```
genus name
    attribute name
        description
        attribute value
            description
            .
            .
        .
        .
    species name
        author
        description
        attribute
            value
            .
            .
        .
        .
        range
        basin
        environment
        detailed catalogue description
        .
        .
    rule
        .
        .
```

The generic structure for an image metafile is shown below:

```
main image

species image
    .
    .

attribute value image
    .
    .
```

Knowledge bases are generated by the **knowledge base building tool** from the knowledge and image metafiles. Within these knowledge bases the knowledge is held in two forms, frames and rules.

Frames are used to hold information that is common to all objects within a group, i.e. attributes that have values defined for each object within the group. An example frame for the species *Gnathodus delicatus* is shown below:

```
name                Delicatus
range               Upper Typicus to Lower Commutatus
carina              unexpanded
inner parapet       long
outer parapet       absent
outer cup           noded
```

Rules are used to hold information that is not common to all objects within a group, i.e. attributes that have values defined for only a subset of objects within the group. An example rule to distinguish between *Gnathodus bollandensis* and *Gnathodus simplex* is shown below:

```
If the outer side of the cup is subrectangular
        Then conclude bollandensis
If the posterior half of the outer side of the cup is elongate
        Then conclude simplex
If the outer side of the cup is any other shape
        Then conclude other
```

3.2 inference mechanism

The inference mechanism is the part of the system that tries to identify fossils using the information that the user has supplied and the knowledge within its knowledge base. The knowledge that the inference mechanism uses is held in the form of rules and frames; the attributes associated with a frame, which are used to describe a fossil, can take a finite range of values. The design of the inference mechanism was influenced by the following problems which are often encountered during the process of fossil identification:

- Fossils are often broken and it may not be possible for palaeontologists to identify all the necessary features required to make a single conclusion possible.

- In some cases it may be possible to distinguish between fossils using only a subset of attribute values i.e. it may not always be necessary to enter a value for each attribute used to describe a fossil.

- A paleaontologist may not be certain of the particular attribute value which describes a feature, but may know that it could be one of a subset of values.

The inference mechanism is quite simple in its operation and has been designed to work using both missing and multi-valued information. When no information is available about a particular attribute the inference mechanism assumes all its possible values are true; hence, the system is able to work if a fossil is broken and an attribute cannot be observed clearly. When a subset of the possible values is entered for a particular attribute the inference mechanism selects all fossils for which those values may be true; using the rules and frames. This subset may be a singleton, indicating the user's certainty concerning the attribute, or may contain several values, indicating that the user is unsure of the precise value, possibly due to damage.

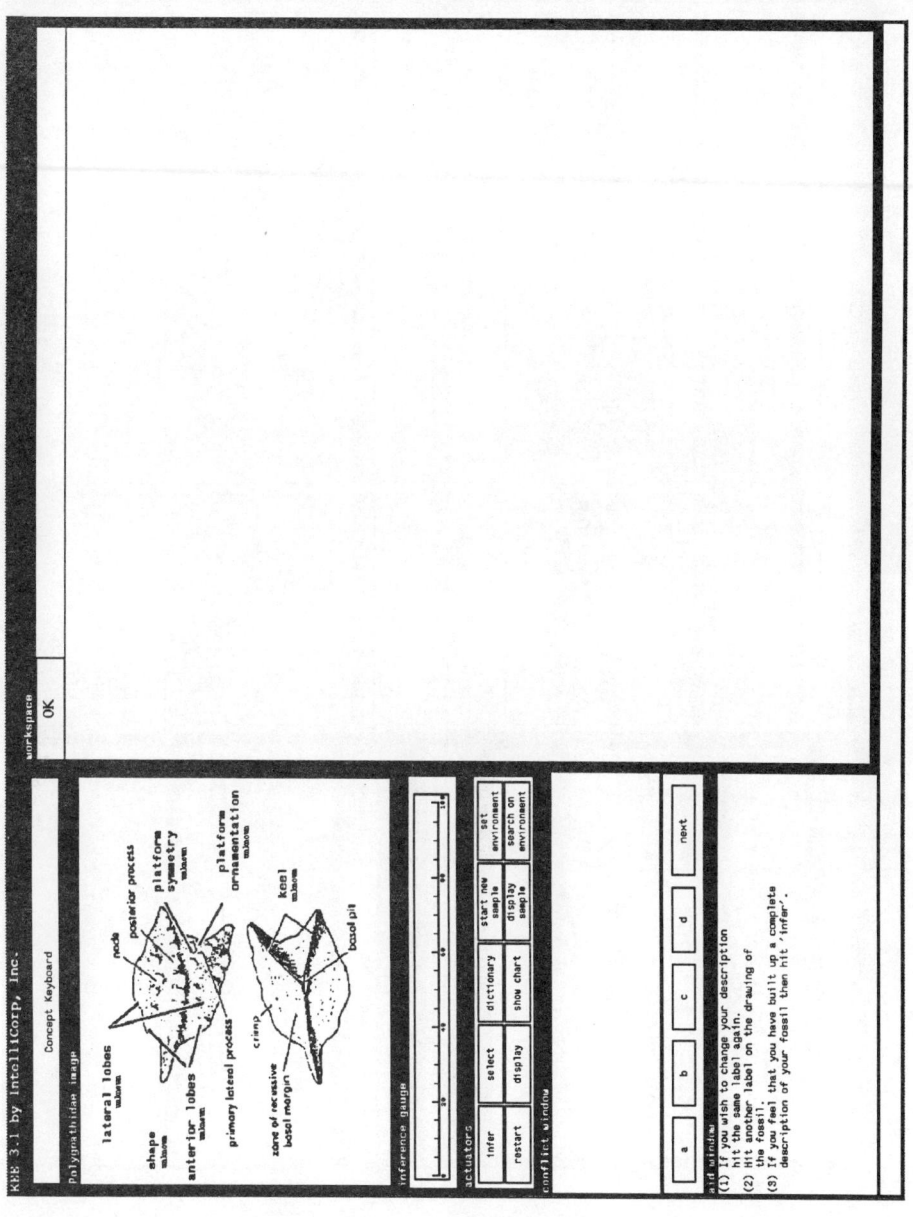

Plate 1 The Initial Screen Layout.

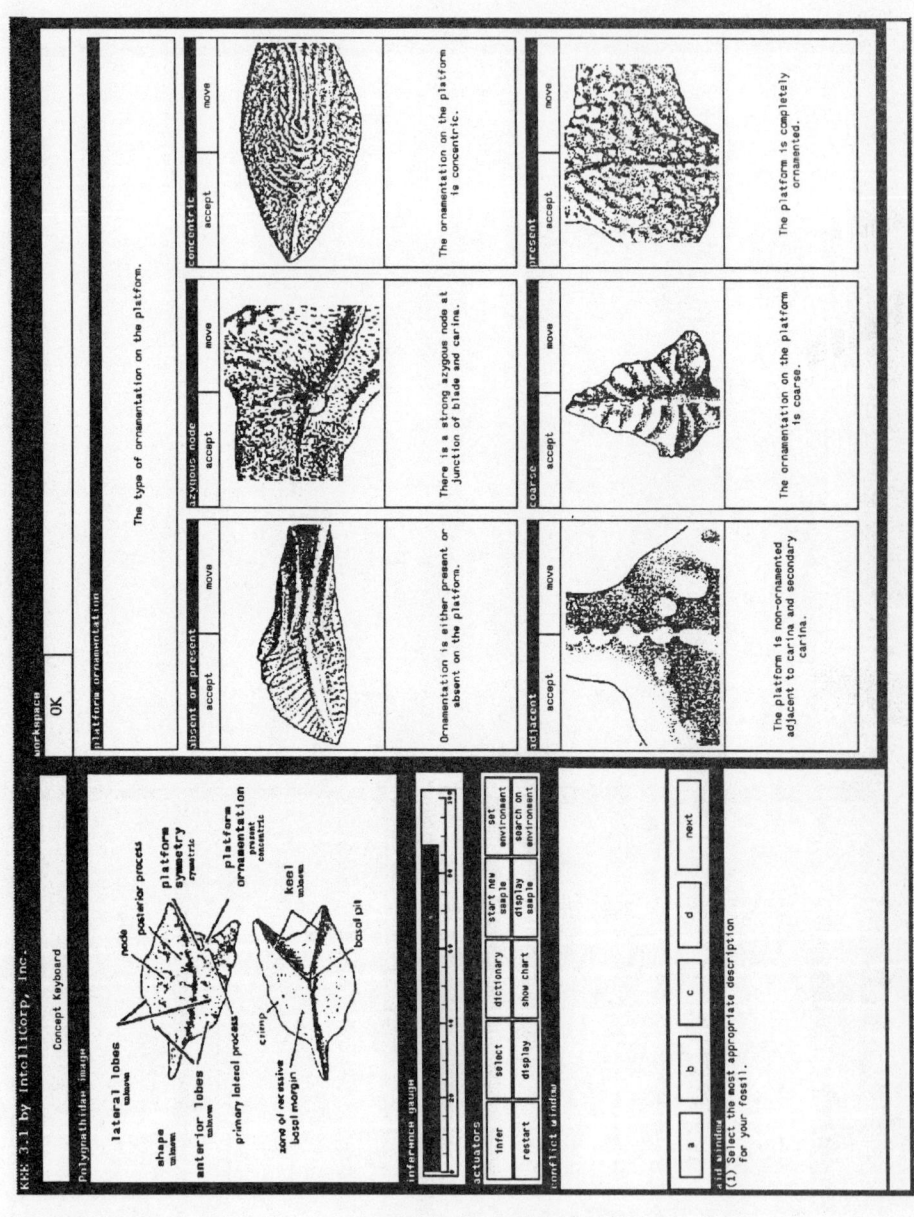

Plate 2 Selecting an Attribute.

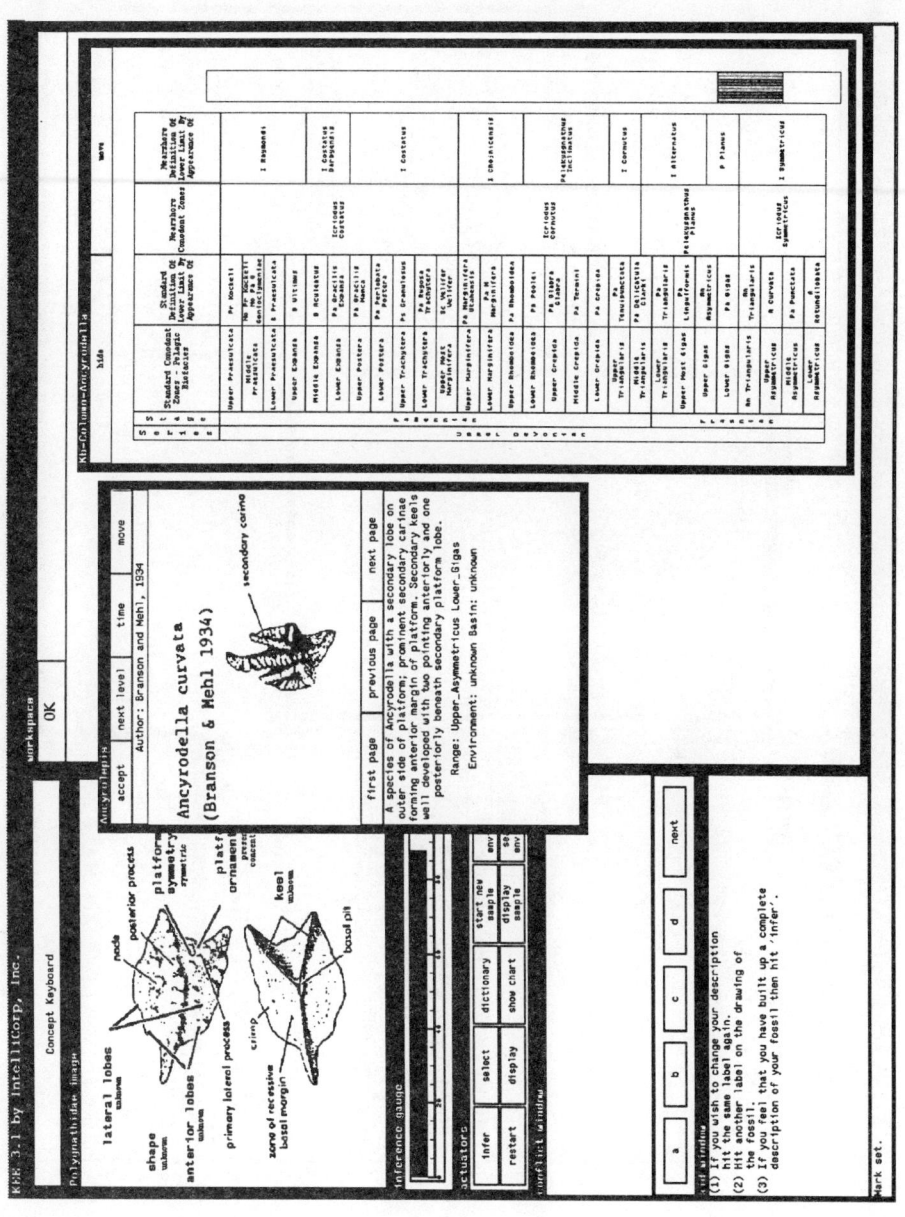

Plate 3 Looking at a Species.

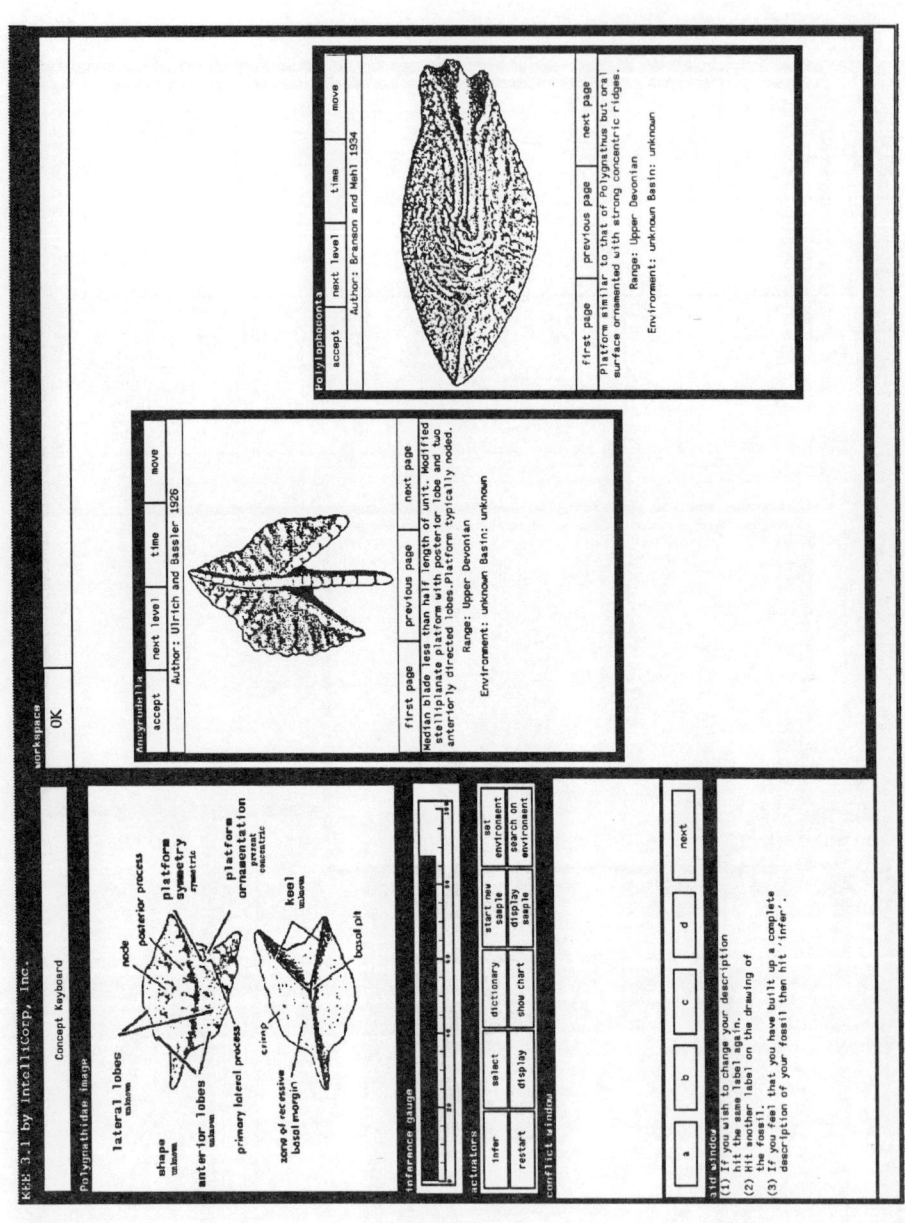

Plate 4 Using the Inference Mechanism.

4 Graphical Interface

Users interact with the system through the graphical interface (see Plates 1 to 4) using a mouse. The interface was designed to be used by people, such as stratigraphers, who do not normally use computers in their daily work. The function and purpose of each of the windows in the graphical interface are described below.

The **aid window** contains relevant guidance to the user at each point during the interaction. The information given is designed to be brief but helpful and consists of a list of the main options at each stage.

The **image window** contains a diagram, such as that of a genus, with all of the important features labelled. Those features that are used to identify species have attribute values entered below them. Initially these values are unknown, but during an identification session they are changed to reflect entered values. The user can enter attribute values by selecting the relevant attribute with the mouse and choosing the most appropriate values from the cards that appear.

The **actuator panel** contains several buttons including:
- The **infer** button, which causes the system to display the species within the genus which match the description entered so far, and may also cause further questioning of the user to help resolve conflict.
- The **select** button, which allows the user to select a particular genus to work with.
- The **display** button, which allows the user to select one of the species within the current genus and display it in the workspace window.
- The **dictionary** button, which allows the user to select a card containing a picture and description of a term and display it in the workspace window.

The **conflict window** contains the questions, derived from the rules, used to resolve conflicts within the expert system when it does not have enough information to decide on one particular species from the attributes values entered.

The **workspace window** is a general work area and is used to display the species, attributes and values, dictionary cards and stratigraphic column.

The **inference gauge** gauge gives a measure of the current degree of discrimination as a percentage, shown graphically as a proportional-length shaded bar. Zero percent means that the system cannot select any species as being more likely to fit the information given at that point. One hundred percent means that the system is certain that the information matches only one species.

5 A Sample Session

This section describes how the user builds a description of a fossil within the system and asks the system to decide which species most closely match it. It also shows how the user may alter this description and finally accept the decision of the system.

5.1 entering a fossil description

Initially the system knows nothing of the fossil that the user wants to identify; the initial screen display is shown in Plate 1. A partial description of the specimen is given to the system by mousing one of the labels on the drawing in the image window. When this is done a series of 'cards' appears in the workspace window as shown in Plate 2. The first card contains a general description of the attribute. The other cards show a picture of each attribute value and give a description of it. The user may look at these and select the most appropriate ones using the mouse. The values are recorded on the diagram and the inference gauge is updated. At any point the user may look at any of the species contained in the current genus and its time range as shown in Plate 3.

5.2 displaying the result and conflict resolution

The inferred species are displayed by mousing the **infer** button. However, it may not always be possible for the system to decide that the solution is one species, and typically two or three will be chosen and displayed in the workspace window. This is shown in Plate 4.

If several species are inferred as being possible matches, the user may then refine the description entered so far. There are three ways to do this:

- The user may enter more attribute values in the image window.

- In some cases the system will ask some questions in the conflict window to try to resolve the conflict.

- The user may look at each of the cards shown in the workspace window and select the species whose picture and description is most similar.

6 Discussion

The task that this project faced was to develop a graphical identification system. There were many problems that had to be overcome in order to achieve this goal. The initial problems involved choice of hardware and software. It was decided that the hardware should be a Sun 3/160 because this machine was quite powerful and had a high resolution graphics screen. This proved to be a good choice for several reasons. Firstly, there was a lot of software already available for Sun workstations and Unix-based computers in general; some of this was used in the production of the system and in particular in the development of the image metafiles. Secondly, it was fast enough to make identifications in a very short time, typically several seconds were all that was required. Thirdly, the high resolution screen meant that high quality images could be displayed. Finally, the power of the computer and the fact that it had a multiprocessing environment meant that a lot of work during development, such as image processing and compression, could be done in parallel allowing several tasks to be performed at the same time. The software chosen was Intellicorp's Knowledge Engineering Environment (KEE) and the Lisp programming language. Lisp, which is described by Steele (1984) and Charniak et al. (1979), has a proven track record for Artificial Intelligence applications such as those reported by Shortliffe (1976) and Moses (1971). KEE, which is described by Fraser (1987), also proved to be a good choice allowing the system to be developed to a high standard in a short period of time. This was possible because both Lisp and KEE contained a large number of high level programming primitives that would have taken a long time to reproduce in other programming languages and environments. KEE, in particular, had a large number of graphical primitives which made the development of the interface far easier than would have been possible with simpler graphics packages; for example, it had the ability to handle images and display them on the computer screen.

The most important consideration throughout this project was that the system should be acceptable to the users when it was fully developed, because if it was not usable it would be rejected. Every effort was made from the start to design the system with these people in mind; for instance, it was decided that the main way of interacting with the system should be via a mouse and not a keyboard, since novice users can learn to use a mouse much more quickly than they can learn to type. At each stage of development we asked stratigraphers, when possible, what they would like to see displayed on the screen at each stage of the interaction.

One of the main components of any expert system is the expert's knowledge that is contained within it. The biggest problem here was eliciting the knowledge from an expert and reproducing it in a form that could be used by an inference mechanism. Experience gained over a period of time showed that the best results were obtained when the expert produced knowledge in a form that was as close as possible to the form of the machine representation. This meant that the person entering the information had to make few decisions about it and hence that it was less likely to be incorrectly interpreted. Information in this form about a particular group, such as a family or genus, could be entered into the system in one or two hours. Also, it was found that the knowledge stored in the knowledge and image metafiles could be automatically converted into knowledge bases of the form required by the system; hence a program called the **knowledge base building tool** was written. It generates the code and data structures that the expert system needs, and produces all of the graphical windows complete with pictures and descriptions which are used in the interface.

At present approximately 25% of all of the knowledge required for the phylum Conodonta is in the system. Future work will include completing this knowledge base and producing others for different fossil groups, as well as looking into other application areas. Other research will be concerned with evaluating the usability of the system, investigating the problems of uncertainty and conflict resolution, and producing and maintaining large knowledge bases.

7 Conclusions

The implementation of the Conodont Identification Expert System has shown that it is possible and practical to build a graphical expert system for microfossil identification in less than a year. The small group of stratigraphers who have evaluated the system so far built have given favourable responses. Several lessons have been learned from this work:

- The use of Lisp and KEE can allow a prototype system to be developed quickly and modified easily.

- The methods of knowledge elicitation which were developed for this system can reduce the time taken for the knowledge elicitation process significantly. This can in turn reduce the cost of the development of large knowledge bases.

- The use of a high-level well-structured knowledge representation which is close to the structure of the data presented by the expert combined with automatic translation of this to a machine-readable form, enables the system to be developed with minimal effort from the knowledge engineer, and reduces the chances of errors.

References

Brough, D. R., and Alexander, I. F., The Fossil Expert System, Expert Systems, Vol. 3, No. 2, p76-83, April 1986.

Charniak, E., Riesbeck, C., and McDermott, D. V., Artificial Intelligence Programming, Hillsdale, Erlbaum, New Jersey, 1979.

Conrad, M. A., and Beightol D. S., Expert Systems Identify Fossils and Manage Large Palaeontological Databases, Geobyte, p42-46, February 1988.

Fraser, J., Some Aspects of Programming in KEE, Airing, AIAI, University of Endinburgh, 1987.

Moses, J., A MACSYMA Primer, Mathlab Memo No. 2, Computer Science Laboratory, Massachusetts Institute of Technology, 1971.

Shortliffe, E. H., Computer-based Medical Consultations:MYCIN, American Elsevier, New York, 1976.

Steele Jr., G. L., Common Lisp: The Language, Digital Press, New Jersey, 1984.

Wiley, P. A., To Evaluate the use of the Expert System Builder 'CRYSTAL' for use in Conodont Identification, unpublished information technology MSc thesis, Kingston Polytechnic, 1987.

Acknowledgments

The author would like to thank Dr. Richard Howarth of BPRI, Sunbury, for his support and encouragement and also Dr. Alan Higgins of BPRI, Sunbury, for his expertise and help, during this project.

FADES : A Tool for Automated Fault Analysis of Complex Systems

C. L. Wood
Rolls Royce and Associates Limited,
PO Box 31
Raynesway
Derby
UK.

Abstract.

FADES is an Expert System for performing fault analyses on complex connected systems. By using a graphical editor to draw components and link them together the *FADES* system allows the analyst to describe a given system. The knowledge base created is used to qualitatively simulate the system behaviour. By inducing all possible component failures in the system and determining their effects, a set of facts is built up. These facts are then used to create Fault Trees, or FMEA tables. The facts may also be used for explanation of effects, and to generate diagnostic rules allowing system instrumentation to be optimised.

The prototype system has been built and tested and is presently undergoing testing by users. All comments from these trials will be used to tailor the system to the requirements of the user so that the end product performs the exact task required.

1. Introduction

The *FADES* project (Fault Analysis and Diagnosis Expert System) has been developed as a tool for use in the design and analysis of complex connected systems. These systems may take many forms; at present *FADES* will analyse fluid systems, but the potential exists for electrical or electronic systems or manufacturing processes to be modelled and analysed.

Development of the project began as a Journeyman project at the Turing Institute, Glasgow (Wood & Clark 1987). The development effort expended so far is 2 man years. The present state of the project is that a prototype system is working and has been tested. It has now been passed to a user area for a more rigorous examination of its performance.

FADES consists of three basic parts. The *Picture Editor* allows the analyst to draw the system to be analysed. Using a library of symbols, system diagrams may be quickly and easily built up, whilst at the same time creating a knowledge base with all the component behaviour and connectivity descriptions. The knowledge base so constructed is then analysed using the *Analysis* part of *FADES* which looks at the effects on the system of the failures of all components or combinations of components. A set of facts is produced from this analysis, which are then used by the *Output* part of *FADES*. Output may be in a number of forms including Fault Trees and Failure Mode and Effect Analysis (FMEA) tables which are the most common manually created output. A diagnostics output is also provided where diagnosis rules may be induced from the facts and used to determine the sufficiency of the system instrumentation.

The *FADES* system has been constructed using IntelliCorp's KEE (Knowledge Engineering Environment) toolkit, and Common LISP. The system is frame-based, providing a structured information storage and retrieval environment and allowing inheritance of properties from parent component types to the component instances. The graphics facilities within KEE are used in the *Picture Editor* and allow facilities such as zoom and pan.

2. The Fault Analysis Problem.

The present manual methods of fault analysis are very time consuming, and often are not as comprehensive as they could be. In general the designer of the system is the very person who performs the bulk of the failure analysis purely because he is the only person who knows and understands the system in detail. The analysis is generally performed by an examination of the system and allowing a decision to be made on which fault effects are worth analysing. These are then investigated in more detail to determine the fault sequences, failure rates, consequences, etc. This method is prone to errors in that some faults may be dismissed as insignificant at an early stage, and not investigated further. This may allow the effects of some failures or failure combinations to be over-looked, resulting in a false impression of system operation under various fault scenarios.

In order to analyse the effects of a component failure on the system, the system behaviour needs to be modelled in some way. The simulation and analysis of complex processes is one of the most powerful and useful applications of computing technology. However, computational resources constrain the complexity of simulation which is possible. Above a certain level of size and detail, simulation becomes computationally intractable. In addition, the use of numerical modelling is often constrained or prevented. The necessary mathematics and knowledge of initial conditions needed for simulation may be unknown or only approximate the real-world system.

3. System Modelling.

One way of easing these constraints is through the use of qualitative modelling, where the process to be simulated is modelled at a level of abstraction, in a behavioural rather than analytical manner. Specifically, numerical parameters and calculations are removed from the model in preference to more coarse-grained, discrete parameters. For example a numeric value of voltage can be replaced with a parameter taking values of high or low. This eases the computations necessary to perform a simulation, thus increasing the size of model which may be simulated, as well as relaxing the requirement for mathematical models. In addition, there are large benefits to be gained from the observation that qualitative views often model the language and reasoning of an expert closer than a mathematical model would. A behavioural, rather than analytical, model often aids system comprehension by an expert, and allows the automatic generation of useful explanation facilities.

Recently, methodologies of qualitative modelling have been formulated, for example by Kuipers (1984), Forbus's qualitative process theory (Forbus, 1984), DeKleer and Brown's work on qualitative physics (DeKleer & Brown, 1984), and Bratko et als. work on the KARDIO system (Bratko et al., 1985, 1986).

FADES mimics the human analyst in that it uses a system diagram, (with all inferred information) as the starting point for a fault analysis. These system diagrams are the most common form of system information used by designers and therefore by the analysts. It is prudent to use the same representation as the information source for *FADES*, as this will be the most readily understood by the designer and analyst alike.

A graphics *Picture Editor* is provided within *FADES* so that the analyst can describe the system in much the same way as it might be described or drawn on a CAD machine. However the major difference between the *FADES Picture Editor* and a typical CAD machine is that *FADES* registers further information about the components such as their immediate neighbours, present state, etc. As components are created in the *Picture Editor*, they appear in the graphics window, so that they can be seen and then positioned. At the same time units are created in a separate knowledge base, and they are made members of a parent class which contains further knowledge about that type of component. The created unit which represents the component's behaviour will inherit various attributes from the parent such as failure rate, failure mode, etc.

The *Picture Editor* consists of two parts. One is a library of components available for inclusion in the system. The other is a picture (window) where the diagram itself is drawn. The *Picture Editor* Library allows the user to select a component and its pictorial rotation, and to position the component on the picture. Functions available on the picture allow components to be connected together, moved, deleted, aligned, etc. A horizontal menu bar is situated above the picture and allows access to further functions such as the plotting of the picture. An 'Information' button allows the user to retrieve information on individual components or the system as a whole, such as which components are connected, what the isolation boundaries of a component are, etc.

Typical fluid systems are large and complex in nature, and these are the sort of system for which *FADES* is most suited. Most systems are divided into small sub-systems in order that they may be more easily understood and followed, and so that they may be drawn onto a single piece of paper. In the same way it is posssible to draw sub-systems in the *FADES Picture Editor*, and then join them together in order to perform a complete fault analysis. The connections between sub-systems are represented by the use of link components, which do not have any behaviour associated with them, but act purely as place holders. When two or more sub-systems are merged together, these link components are connected together by the analyst, using a *Link Editor*, and the components either side of two connected links become connected. The links are then removed, thus creating a joined system. When the sub-systems are merged together they may be analysed as a whole determining how a fault in one sub-system may affect other sub-systems.

4. FADES Model Description.

It should be noted that *FADES* is designed to be a general fault analysis and diagnosis tool. It has been designed for any application where the effects of some change may propagate through a connected system. This may include manufacturing processes, and electrical or electronic circuit analysis.

The *FADES* model uses both path and behaviour rule modelling paradigms to form the deep knowledge representation of the connected system. All that is required to enable *FADES* to analyse these different systems is a new path classification algorithm and behaviour rule set. This paper describes the *FADES* system as applied to the domain of fluid system analysis.

The basic data required by a human fault analyst, or system diagnostician, is contained on a fluid system diagram. From this he can see each component, where it fits into the whole system, what state it is normally in, etc. He may also infer what each component contains, and what function it performs within the system. *FADES* also requires this data, and it too retrieves the relevant information from a system diagram which is drawn using the *Picture Editor* described above. Information available directly from a system diagram describes the physical construction of the system, eg. for a valve it will show its type, neighbours, state etc. The information about components which is not explicitly shown on a system diagram, such as the failure modes of a component or what it contains is inferred by *FADES* from its position and type. The inferred information describes the component's behaviour.

The *FADES* model is qualitative in the sense that it does not deal with parameters represented numerically, such as pressure rise with time, but with parameters represented by symbolic descriptions that specify qualitative features of the parameters. Such a qualitative modelling approach has several advantages over conventional numerical modelling.

The effects of failures may only propagate through a system along paths. Paths are defined as the collection of components in the system which lie between a source and a sink component (linear path) or which appear in a circuit (circular path). Source components are those from which a flow of some medium may originate. In the case of fluid systems these may be gas bottles or tanks. Sinks may be considered to be the opposite, a component where flow may end up, such as a drain. Paths between the sink and source pairs may take many routes, all of which must be found for completeness. A particular path will have various attributes to describe what kind of path it is. If for instance flow may originate from a tank via a dip leg, then the flow method of that path will be 'forced', meaning that in order for flow to exist, some mechanism must force the fluid from the tank. This path attribute will determine whether a pump or other flow inducing component is required to empty the tank along this path. A path in the example system (Figure 1) might be (reservoir storage_tank pump storage_tank) with the flow method = forced.

Another attribute of a path is its resistance to flow. This determines whether flow along the path is possible. If the resistance of the path is shut then under no circumstance is it possible to get flow along it. On the other hand, if resistance is open then flow will depend on the flow method of the path and whether flow is being forced. For the path described above the path resistance is open, the flow-method is forced, and the pump is running, therefore the path has flow.

In addition to the path model, another model is required to determine the effects of the paths on the individual components. This model may best be described with an example. If at least one path, which has the storage_tank as its source, has flow then the storage_tank level will fall. This behaviour may be written generally in the form of a rule such as:

If   Path has flow
 and source of Path is Source
 and Source has attribute Attribute
then the Attribute of Source will decrease.

These rules hold true for all fluid systems, as they describe the general behaviour of fluids. It might appear at first sight that there would be a large number of different rules in the set in order to model all eventualities, but if organised appropriately there is only a need for some twenty or thirty such rules. It should be noted however that the flow of fluid from one component to another is handled using the path model. Therefore the behaviour rules only react to the effects of flow changes on other fluid system parameters.

5. System Analysis.

Fault analyses may be performed in two ways, both using a common looping function. The two analysis methods are;

1. A 'Set Failures' analysis, where the analyst may select which components in the system to fail. The effects of these failures are then displayed to the analyst as the fault sequence progresses through the system. This method of analysis would be useful to a novice analyst who could use the simulation to discover how a failure propagates from one component to the next. It could also be used by an experienced analyst looking at a novel or new system, where the component interaction is complex or unknown.

2. A 'Complete' analysis, where *FADES* selects all components (and combinations of components to a given level) to fail and works through these one at a time, analysing its effect on the system. During this method of analysis, facts describing the behaviour of the system under these conditions are created and collected together for further use. By analysing all possible component faults, the set of facts created is guaranteed complete, with no failure mode being overlooked.

This is an improvement over the present manual analysis method, where an analyst may decide not to investigate a failure mode because he thinks it is insignificant, but in reality may become very serious when combined with other failures. *FADES* ensures that all such failure modes are analysed and are used to create the required form of output.

In the 'Complete' analysis, the combination of simultaneous failures must obviously be limited by some factor as the number of separate analyses to be performed will increase combinatorially. For example if a system contains 20 failable components, and two simultaneous failures are considered, then 210 separate analyses are performed, but if 3 simultaneous failures are considered then 1350 analyses are performed.

Two forms of combination limiting strategies are allowed by *FADES*. The first allows the user to specify the maximum number of simultaneous failures to consider. All combinations of length up to and including this limit are then created and analysed. The other limit strategy is to allow the user to specify the maximum combined failure rate for the failed components. This cut-off point is often used in the manual analysis process.

Following a 'Complete Analysis' a set of facts will have been created. There are two types of facts. One is used for forward chaining to show the system reaction to some failures without having to redo that analysis. The other form of fact is used for backward chaining to produce explanation, and the required output.

The facts take the following form;

Forward Chain Facts : (List of initial failures, List of affected components)
Backward Chain Facts : (System effect, Reason, Cause)

The common analysis algorithm is basically a loop, which takes items to look at next from an 'Investigate List', it then determines the knock-on effects, and puts those effects on to the end of this 'Investigate List'. Analysis stops when the list is empty.

Initially, the failed component (or components) is put into its failed state, according to the failure mode information, and the 'Investigate List' is initialised to contain only this component. Other lists called the components-to-be-updated list and the paths-to-be-updated list are cleared.

The modelling now proceeds as follows;

1. Remove the first component from the 'Investigate List'.

2. If this component operates others (such as a switch) then ;

    2.1 Find all components which are directly operated by this component, and put them onto the components-to-be-updated list.

Otherwise;

    2.2 Find all the paths this component is in, and put them
    onto the paths-to-be-updated list.

3. Goto 1 until the 'Investigate List' is empty.

4. Update all the paths on the paths-to-be-updated list, by checking for a change in the path flow. If the flow is affected then put all components on that path with a flow attribute onto the component-to-be-updated list.

5. Fire the Rules, (described previously).

6. Update all the components on the component-to-be-updated list. Put all these components onto the now empty 'Investigate List'. It is at this stage that facts are created for use in the output modules.

7. If something exists on the 'Investigate List' then goto 1, otherwise stop.

A typical analysis for the example system shown in Figure 1 might be the failure of house_stop_1 valve.
The valve is set to a failed state : eg. shut,
Find all its paths : path-1 (storage_tank, main_stop_valve, road_stop_1, house_stop_1, house_supply_1).
Update the paths : valve is shut therefore path-1 becomes shut, and flow in path-1 stops.
Fire the rules : storage_tank has flow out via other paths therefore no effect, but
    house_supply_1 has no flow.
Investigate the effect of house_supply_1 having no flow : nothing.

The facts created by this analysis might be ;
Forward chain : ((house_stop_1 state shut)) (house_supply_1 flow no-flow), and
Backward chain : (house_supply_1 flow no-flow)
"it is isolated from storage_tank by house_stop_1"
(house_stop_1 state shut).

6. Output.

Fault analyses performed manually usually result in the production of a set of fault trees, or an FMEA table. Fault trees consist of a top-event which is the particular system effect to be investigated. Under this is a tree depicting, via logic gates, how component failures interact to produce the top-event. A sample fault tree is given in Figure 2. An FMEA (Failure Mode and Effects Analysis) table shows similar information in tabular text form. The first column indicates the system effect, and other columns show what component failures may cause this effect, together with the probability of this effect occurring. An example of an FMEA is given in Figure 3.

FADES will produce whatever form of output is required by the user. Both fault trees and FMEAs can be produced from the appropriate set of facts created during a 'Complete Analysis'. By selecting the top-event (or system effect), a function then looks at all the facts and collects those which have this top-event as the system-effect (Backward Chain Rules). The causes of all these facts are then extracted, and they are then used to collect further facts which have these causes as the system-effect. By chaining through the set of facts in this manner a tree is produced from the selected top-event through to base-events (component failures). The failure rate of the top-event is then calculated from this chain of events using the individual component failure rates.

As an alternative to the *FADES* produced output, the facts may be re-arranged and used as input to a commercially available reliability analysis package. These packages normally analyse the fault tree descriptions supplied manually and produce plotted fault trees and all the relevant calculations. The *FADES* link may easily be constructed to allow an analyst to provide input files to these packages automatically.

6.1 Explanation.

When a 'Set Analysis' is performed, a description of the fault propagation is given to the user. This shows which components have been affected, as the effects of the fault moves from one component to the next (the 'Fault Wave'). A novice analyst may not understand a particular system response, or a new or novel system may exhibit apparently strange behaviour, in which case a more detailed description of the 'Fault Wave' is required. By selecting the effect in question from a menu, an explanation of how that effect occurred due to the initial failures will be generated. The explanation algorithm uses the Backward Chain facts, and starting at the effect to be explained, it chains through the facts back to the initial fault. At each step in the chain, a portion of 'canned text' is displayed explaining how the particular effect causes the previous one. The resultant display shows a detailed route through the system from effect to fault with detailed explanation text.

6.2 Diagnosis.

The set of facts produced from the 'Complete Analysis' of a system contain a useful description of the behaviour of the system under all failure situations. By giving this set of behaviour descriptions to a simple rule induction package, a set of diagnostic rules may be produced. The rule induction algorithm required is very simple because factors such as incomplete information, which make induction difficult, do not exist. The set of facts produced by *FADES* is complete and free from any noise. Thus all the rule induction algorithm does is to group or categorise the failures according to the attributes.

The most useful categorisation is to use the instrumentation available on the system. This is all that the operator of such a system has to determine the cause of a particular system fault. In general when a system fault occurs the operator will rely on a set of instrumentation to diagnose the fault. The set of instrumentation is decided upon by the system designer, who is usually required to use the minimum number of instruments to detect the maximum number of faults. Again this process is currently performed manually and is open to error. *FADES* uses the system instrumentation as attributes for the rule induction, and the sets of facts for the examples. The resulting output from the rule induction algorithm is a set of 'If ... Then ...' rules. These are written in such a way as to allow the analyst to look down the rules and determine ;

1. Which instruments are redundant, (precisely those which do not appear in any of the rule premises). *FADES* helps in this situation by noting all these parameters separately.

2. Which system faults cannot be detected. These show up in the same rule conclusion as the 'Normal State' fault.

3. Which system faults are indistinguishable from one another. These show up in the rules as multiple rule conclusions.

From the set of rules produced, the analyst may see what changes are required to the instrumentation suite in order to optimise its fault detection capabilities.

The diagnosis rules may also be used in a simple diagnosis package, where the actual system indications are pattern matched against the diagnosis rules. When a match is found, the rule conclusion determines the fault in the system, if any.

7. Summary.

The use of simple qualitative modelling techniques to provide a simulation of the system to be analysed allows flexibility in the behavioural descriptions of component types. Many component types have been modelled and no component is thought to be impossible to model. The drawback of such a model is that quantitative measures such as the time taken to empty a tank are not available. However the output produced by *FADES* gives the analyst a rguide as to the system behaviour and from this he will be able to evaluate the effects of quantitative behaviours.

The prototype system developed so far has correctly analysed several complex systems. The analysis time, including some user familiarisation, may be measured in terms of days rather than the weeks required for manual analyses. The manual process may take between 6 and 20 weeks depending on the level of expertise of the analyst and the familiarity of the system being analysed. This time will include drawing the fault trees etc. to the required standards. *FADES* however may produce the same output in 2/3 days. *FADES* allows the designer to make minor changes to the design and to re-analyse the system quickly and consistently. This allows the system to be analysed during the design stage which is not possible with the present methods. The major benefit of *FADES* is a great saving in time (and hence money) for the Company.

The inclusion of the *Picture Editor* greatly eased the user's worries over the interface, which previously used a text editor. By using the analysts common information media (pictures) they can communicate with the system much more freely. An attached laser printer is used to produce high quality diagrams from those entered, together with fault trees and FMEA tables to the required report standard. This eliminates the need for the user to have the information drawn up by a specialist.

The present system is fragile at the edges, and requires feedback from the users on problems experienced. Stray mousing, for instance, needs to be trapped to prevent spurious input. As more systems are modelled by users, an increasing number of component types will become modelled making the library of component classes more complete. To date, no analysis problems have been encountered due to incomplete behaviour rules. This suggests that the rules are abstract enough to cover all possibilities.

The system has been passed to the users and it is hoped that a fully supported version will be used 'in anger' by the end of this year.

8. References.

Bratko L., Mozetic I., Lavrac N. (1986) Automated synthesis and compression of cardiological knowledge. *Machine Intelligence 11.*

Bratko L., Mozetic I., Lavrac N., Cercek B., Horvat M., Grad A. (1985) KARDIO-E An expert system for electrocardiographic diagnosis of cardiac arrythmias. *Expert Systems 2* (1) pp.46-50.

DeKleer J., Brown J.S. (1984) A qualitative physics based on confluences *Artificial Intelligence 24.*

Forbus K. (1984) Qualitative process theory *Artificial Intelligence 24.*

Kuipers B. (1984) Common sense reasoning about causality *Artificial Intelligence 24.*

Wood C., Clark P. (1987). FADES - An Expert System for Fault Analysis and Diagnosis. *TIRM-87-024.*

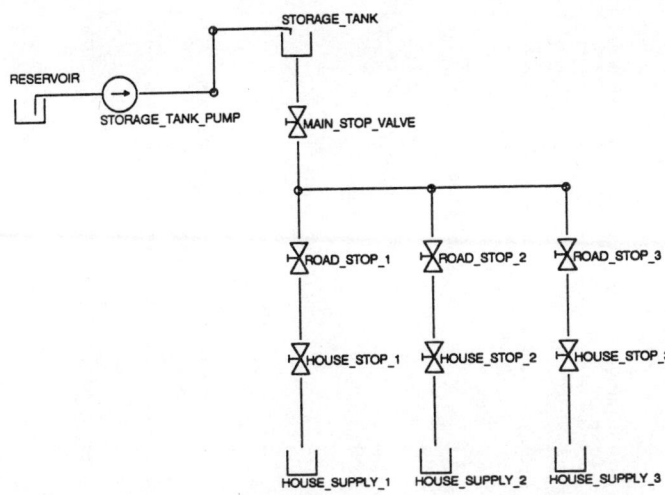

Figure 1. A simple household water supply system.

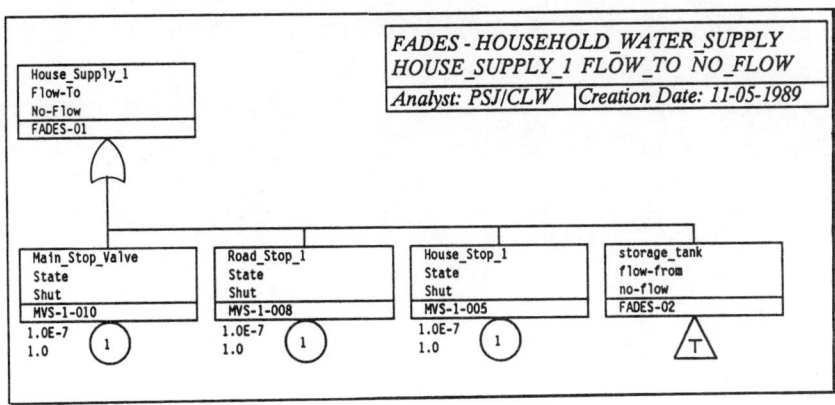

Figure 2. A sample fault tree with 'No flow to house_supply_1' as the top event.

FADES by C.L.Wood

F.M.E.A. for HOUSEHOLD_WATER_SUPPLY   8:32:8   11/5/1989   Maximum simultaneous failures = 1   Page 1

Failure Mode	Possible Causes of Failure Mode	System Effects due to Failure Mode	Existing Mitigating Features	Probability (per Year)	Probability Ranking	Consequence Ranking
STORAGE_TANK LEVEL DECREASE	STORAGE_TANK flow-to no-flow	No system effect		5.0E-3	HIGH	
STORAGE_TANK FLOW-TO NO-FLOW	STORAGE_TANK_PUMP state stopped	STORAGE_TANK level decrease RESERVOIR flow-from no-flow		5.0E-3	HIGH	
STORAGE_TANK LEVEL INCREASE	STORAGE_TANK flow-from no-flow	DANGER storage_tank overflow		1.0E-7	LOW	
STORAGE_TANK FLOW-FROM NO-FLOW	MAIN_STOP_VALVE state shut	STORAGE_TANK level increase DANGER storage_tank overflow HOUSE_SUPPLY_1 flow-to no-flow HOUSE_SUPPLY_2 flow-to no-flow HOUSE_SUPPLY_3 flow-to no-flow		1.0E-7	LOW	
RESERVOIR FLOW-FROM NO-FLOW	STORAGE_TANK_PUMP state stopped	STORAGE_TANK flow-to no-flow		5.0E-3	HIGH	
HOUSE_SUPPLY_3 FLOW-TO NO-FLOW	MAIN_STOP_VALVE state shut ROAD_STOP_3 state shut HOUSE_STOP_3 state shut	No system effect		3.0E-7	LOW	
HOUSE_SUPPLY_2 FLOW-TO NO-FLOW	MAIN_STOP_VALVE state shut ROAD_STOP_2 state shut HOUSE_STOP_2 state shut	No system effect		3.0E-7	LOW	
HOUSE_SUPPLY_1 FLOW-TO NO-FLOW	MAIN_STOP_VALVE state shut ROAD_STOP_1 state shut HOUSE_STOP_1 state shut	No system effect		3.0E-7	LOW	

Figure 3. A Sample Failure Modes and Effects Analysis table.

A KBS APPROACH TO THE SYNTHESIS OF DISTILLATION SEQUENCES

Vijay Vadhwana
BP Research International
Chertsey Road
Sunbury-on-Thames
Middlesex

ABSTRACT

Certain classes of optimisation problems require excessive computational time for a solution. However, a domain expert can readily solve the problem using heuristic knowledge. The problem of synthesis of distillation trains, which is combinatorial in nature, is used as a test-bed for the investigation of optimisation using heuristics. The heuristic rules used by experts to solve this problem are encoded in a KBS system developed in KEE. The system is used to solve a number of synthesis problems and is found to approximate well the results obtained by rigorous optimisation. A system for heuristic optimisation offers the possibility of accelerating the process of solving a certain class of optimisation problems. These types of system will enable design engineers to carry out extensive sensitivity analysis over a relatively short period of time. Additionally, they will reduce the excessive demand on the computational resources.

1. INTRODUCTION

A certain class of engineering design problems are combinatorial in nature and even the fastest computer cannot solve them in "reasonable" time. However, these problems are readily solved by engineers using heuristic knowledge. Although the solutions found are not guaranteed to be optimal, they are usually found to be within a few percent of the optimum.

The problem chosen for this study is the optimum synthesis of the process for separation of hydrocarbon mixtures by simple distillation. The selection of the optimal (least expensive) separation sequence of multicomponent mixtures into desired products has been long recognised as an important design problem. The penalty for selecting a non-optimal sequence can be an increase in the final cost of as much as 25%. The combinatorial nature of the problem can be illustrated by considering the following example: to separate a mixture of six components into six products streams, there are 42 different sequences, however for a seven component system, the number of sequences increases to 132. To cost a sequence, information on complete mass and heat balances, design of column including number of trays, energy consumption, etc., is required. Costing a sequence is a time consuming and a non-trivial exercise. The engineer's solution to the problem would reduce the vast number of alternatives, by using heuristics, to a manageable two or three sequences.

In this paper, the solution obtained by a KBS system for optimisation is compared with that from a mathematically rigorous *Implicit Enumeration* algorithm. Implicit Enumeration is guaranteed to generate the optimum solution.

2. IMPLICIT ENUMERATION

The implicit enumeration procedure is used to generate the optimal solution of a set of example problems.

The implicit enumeration procedure for optimisation centres around an efficient method for solving the following recursive equation:

$$Q(a) = \text{Min } [P_i(a) + Q(b_i) + Q(c_i)]$$

For distillation, **a** defines the feed stream to a column, $P_i(a)$ is the discounted cost of the *ith* way of designing a column to process **a** and **bi** and **ci** are the corresponding top and bottom product streams. $Q(a)$ is the most economic method of processing **a** to acceptable process outputs.

For enumeration procedure, the distillation sequence is represented by a sequence of numbers which correspond to the subproblems involved; e.g. for the mixture ABC, the sequence:

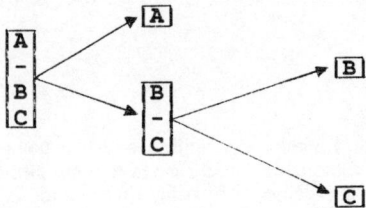

is represented by [3;2]

where subproblem 1 represents the separation A/B
subproblem 2 represents the separation B/C
subproblem 3 represents the separation A/BC
subproblem 4 represents the separation AB/C

The cost correlations employed are based on the methods in (Rathore 1974; Haven 1969; Marcopoulos 1984)

3. SYNTHESIS PROBLEM

The purpose of synthesis is to determine a sequence of distillation columns which separate a component mixture into individual components. Each distillation column separates its feed streams into two fractions, whereby each component in the feed appears exclusively in one of the fractions. This separation is termed a split. In the simple distillation synthesis problem, the target is to find the economic optimum split of a mixture into two fractions. Thus, for the simple distillation of an "n" component mixture, (n-1) sharp splits are necessary, requiring (n-1) distillation columns.

Thus, to separate a three component mixture (ABC) into individual components, there are two alternative sequences, each requiring two distillation columns:

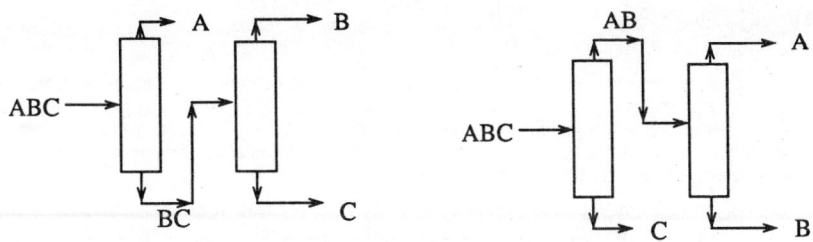

By using heuristics, it is possible to determine which of two sequences is economical.

4. RULES

The primary heuristic rules widely used in distillation train design, as found in (Westerberg 1980), have been used in process industry for over 30 years. The rules are as follows:

1. Favour "easy" separation first.
   Easy separation is defined by the magnitude of the ratio of relative volatility of a split. Thus, a ratio of 1 means the split is impossible and a ratio of 100 means the separation is extremely easy.

2. Favour 50/50 balanced splits.
   A balanced split is defined by the ratio of flowrates of the two streams produced by splitting the feed stream. This ratio lies in the range 0 to 1, thus a ratio of 1 indicates that the split is perfectly balanced.

3. Favour taking one component from the top of the column.
   One component from the top gives the required single product and reduces the cost of further processing in subsequent distillation.

4. Favour removing major components early in the separation sequence.
   By removing major components early, the cost of further processing is reduced.

5. Reject splitting components that are acceptable as mixed products.
   It is pointless to split a stream that is acceptable as a mixed probuct stream.

The reason why heuristic procedures produce near-optimal solutions is they are based on long engineering experience and insights into the physical and chemical nature of the system. For distillation sequence synthesis, there is a sound theoretical basis for these rules, in that, under certain simplifying assumptions, they tend to minimise total vapour rates in the system. Vapour rates determine both reboiler and condenser duties and also column diameters, and hence the cost.

To achieve the target of finding the most desirable split, a form of targetting on a pass/fail basis is used. Each decision rule is assigned a weighting factor in accordance with its importance, i.e. rule 1 is more important than rule 3, rule 5 is more important than rule 3, etc. The weighting factors are tuned against a set of examples.

The implicit enumeration is used to generate optimal solutions of a set of example problems. These solutions are used to tune the weighting factors for the five rules. Basically, the weights are manipulated until there is close agreement between the optimal solutions and those generated by the KBS system.

5. TUNING RULES

The training examples used to tune the rules consisted of 4 components streams with varying composition. The training set consisted of thirty examples. The weights for the rules were manipulated until the average deviation between all the KBS generated solutions and the training set was less than 3%. This criterion was arbitrarily chosen. The training examples were divided into groups of five, thus:

- Group 1 examples had components with a wide range of volatilies and where other parameters were similar, i.e. the composition of each component in the feed was kept almost identical. This group was used to derive the initial weight for the first rule *favour easy separation first*.

- Group 2 consisted of examples with varying degree of 'balanced splits'. This group was used to derive the initial weight for the second rule *favour 50/50 balanced split*.

- Groups 3, 4 and 5 consisted of examples which were used to derive the initial weight for the third, forth and fifth rules respectively.

- Group 6 examples had interactions in terms of varying compositions and volatilities. This group was used to fine tunes the weights for all the rules.

Once tuned, the knowledge based system performance is good and could be applied to larger problems which have more components. For example, the system is applied to six component feed and gives an answer which is 1% more costly than optimal solution.

Although only five rules are used in this system, there are many tuning variables. There are five weighting parameters for the rules, but there are also decisions on the many interpretations and use of the individual heuristic rules. For example, what is meant by a balanced split?. The split ratio of 1:1 is perfectly balanced but when does the split become unbalanced? is it at ratios 1:15, 1:2, or 1:5 ? These decisions are rather subjective and quite difficult to quantify. Once again, arbitrary criteria were chosen to define *easy split, balanced split* and *major component* used in the rules.

6. TREE REPRESENTATION

A possible separation sequence may be:

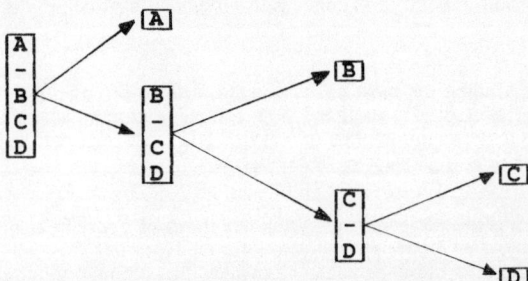

The streams, (ABCD), (BCD) etc., in the sequence may be represented as nodes and the sequence list as a tree structure. A multicomponent stream to be split is the parent node and the product streams generated by separation are child nodes. The pure component product stream are the goals or terminal nodes.

From the tree representation, the development of a sequence may be viewed as the problem of finding a solution path in an AND/OR tree. The property of the AND/OR graph is that it represents the solution of problems that can be solved by decomposing them into a set of smaller problems, all of which must be solved. An example of this decomposition is given below:

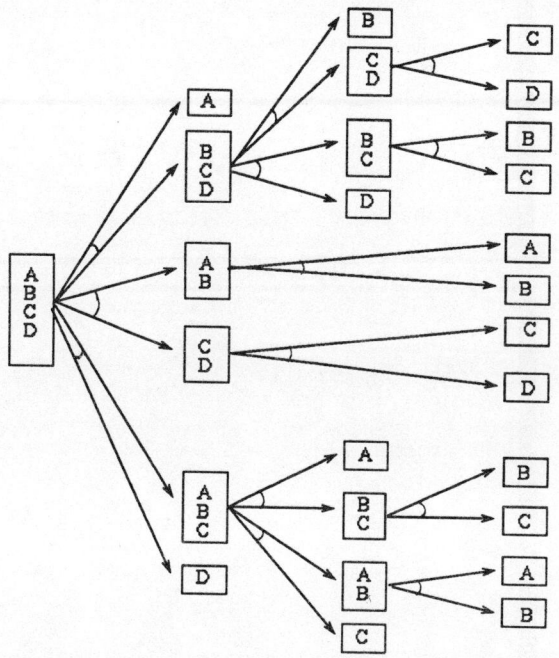

The decomposition generates AND arcs which may point to any number of successive nodes, all of which are solved in order for the arc to point to a solution. There are a variety of ways in which the original problem may be solved, that is a single node may give rise to several arcs. For example, the stream (ABCD) may be split into (A/BCD),(AB/CD) or (ABC/D), which represents three OR arcs.

7. SEARCH STRATEGY

A distillation sequence may be determined by starting at the process feed node and making a path decision at an OR node until the terminal nodes are reached. From the OR nodes, only one path is selected and from the AND node, both paths are selected for further treatment. The algorithm used for the solution is *best first search*, which combines the advantages of both depth-first and breadth-first search (Rich 1983; Nilsson 1982). At each step of the search process, nodes representing all possible splits are generated and, the most promising of the nodes generated is selected. This is achieved by applying the five heuristic rules to each of them. To illustrate how the heuristic rules are applied in practice, consider the problem of separation of a mixture of five components, ABCDE, into five product streams. There are a total of 14 sequences for this problem, see Figure 1.1. To determine the first level of split, the rules are applied to initial OR nodes ([A],[BCDE]) ([AB],[CDE]) ([ABC],[DE]) and ([ABCD],[E]). If a split satisfies the conditions of a rule, it is awarded a number of points. The node which scores the highest points is selected as the optimum split and the others are rejected, thus reducing the search space of 14 sequences to a subset of 3, see Figure 1.2. The

Figure 1.1 Search space for a 5 component system

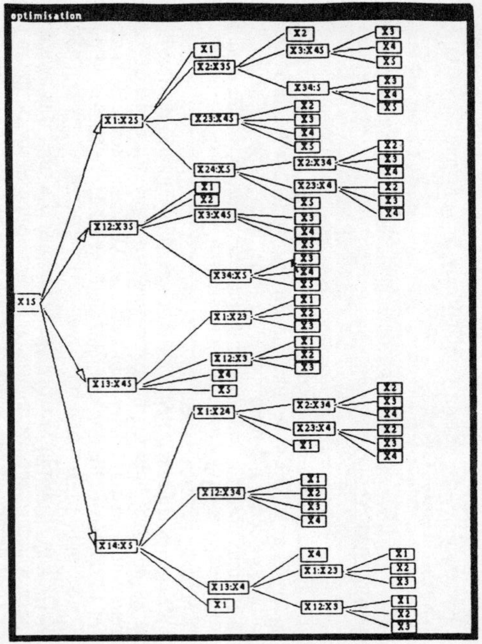

Figure 1.2 Search space for a 5 component system - after first level evaluation

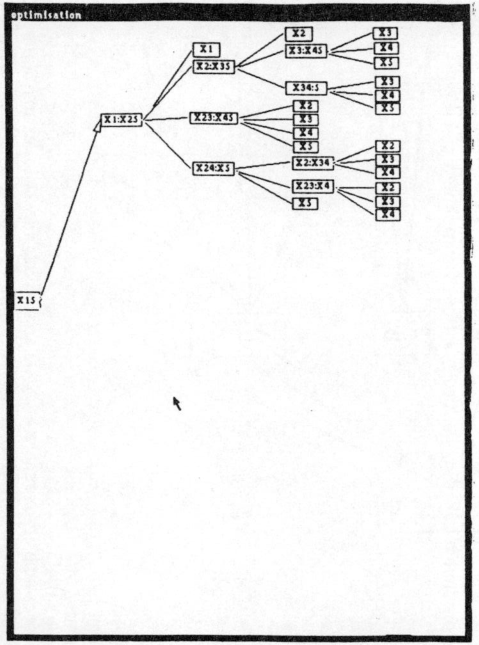

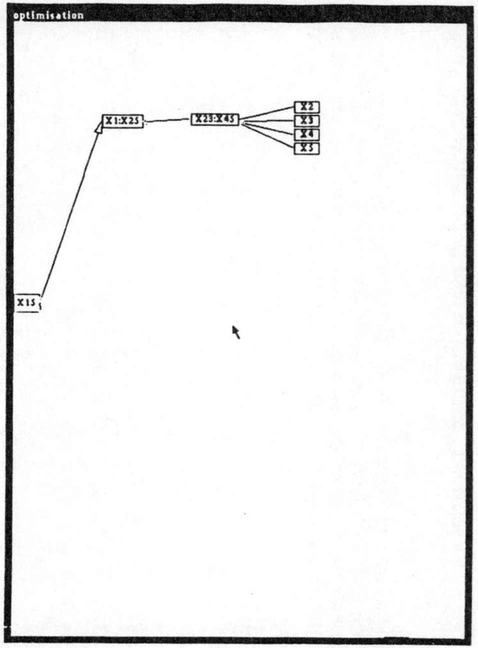

Figure 1.3 Search space for a 5 component system - after second level evaluation

rules are now applied to split-set ([B],[CDE]) ([BC],[DE]) ([BCD],[E]) and the best split determined. In this case, there are no other alternatives to consider and the analysis is terminated, see Figure 1.3. However, for larger problems, the above procedure would be repeatedly applied until the number of sequences reduced to just one.

8. IMPLEMENTATION

The knowledge based system for heuristic optimisation has been developed in a KBS system development environment, KEE (Intellicorp 1986), on a Symbolics workstation. The complete system comprises:

- The problem database.
- A set of heuristic rules.
- An inference engine to interpret the rules.

The problem database is defined in terms of **component class** with slots for *feed composition, feed flow, volatility* and *component number*. The actual components are defined as subclass members of **component class**, thus inheriting the predefined slots, which hold "local values". The problem database initially consists of the raw facts known about the problem. For the separation system chosen, this comprises:

- The composition of the initial feed.
- The relative volatilities of the individual components.
- The flow rates of the individual components.

The heuristic rules and the inference engine for the rule interpreter are written in LISP.

The interface to the system makes extensive use of the graphic facilities in KEE. *Active Values* and *Active Images* are used to control the problem analysis, which can be carried out in a stepwise or one-pass mode. In stepwise mode, the user can observe the split analysed, which rules are fired, how many points are scored and the 'closeness' of the decisions.

9. USER INTERACTION

The system has been designed so that the user may add extra rules to the set of five in the rulebase. For example, a user may deem it necessary to add a rule to 'deal' with heat-sensitive components in the feed, for instance :

> Remove a component early in the process if that component
> is likely to degrade under high temperature or pressure.

The facility to enter this rule is fairly easy to use. Secondly, he can assign a large weighting factor to the new rule so that it overrides the other rules. When new rules are added, the system stores these in a working space separate from the internal rules. When the consultation is over, these new rules are discarded. If the user is allowed to keep new rules within the system then the validation of the system becomes redundant. As an alternative to adding rules into the system, the user has a facility to force the system to select a particular split in preference to the system choice. This interaction takes place at runtime.

The question is which of the two facilities is more appropriate for the users? The first facility, where rules are added to the system, is relatively easy to use but a user may not be computer literate and may find it very difficult to use the system. It is a non-trivial task to design a system which would suit all the end-users. It is advocated that the end-users' active

Figure 2.1 Relative cost distribution of the sequences for Example 2

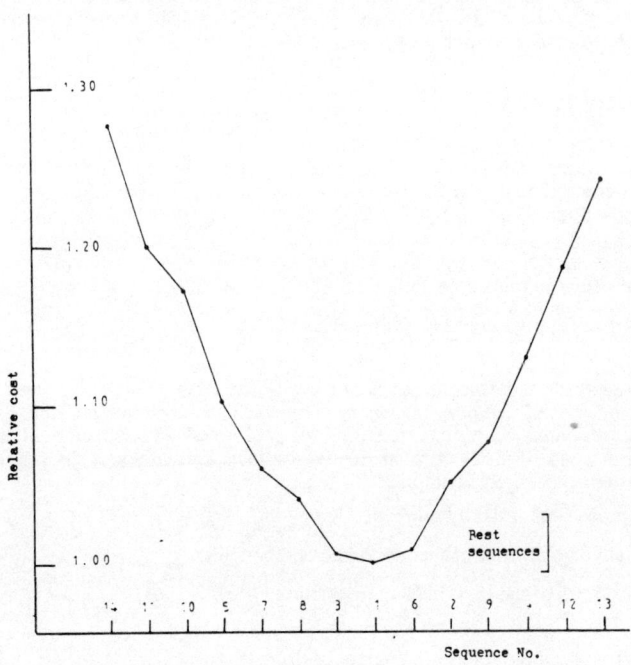

FIGURE 2.2   OPTIMAL SEQUENCES GENERATED FOR EXAMPLE 2

Sequence generated by Implicit Enumeration Algorithm

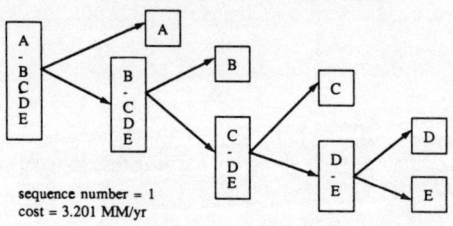

sequence number = 1
cost = 3.201 MM/yr

Sequence generated by KBS

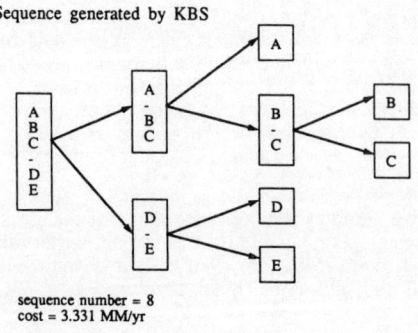

sequence number = 8
cost = 3.331 MM/yr

Relative Cost = 3.331/3.201 = 1.04

participation in the design of the application is a particular necessity (Fawcett 1987) but this is not always practical due to lack of time, resources, off-site operations, etc. No matter how carefully tailored, design environments are simply not identical to user environments. They differ with respect to the problem mix, how familar the users are with the program, and a range of other factors (Davis 1982).

The interactive approach fits well in the methodology proposed by Gillies and Hart (Gillies & Hart 1988) where the computer and user jointly solve the problem. This requires the computer's strategy to be compatible with that of the user. In this particular application, the computer emulates the decision making process of the expert and therfore the strategies are compatible. This philosophy is advantageous as it keeps the user involved in the 'problem solving' phase of the computer system and therefore he can appreciate, learn (if a novice) and feel confident about the final solution. The user should be able to explain how the computer derived a particular solution rather than say 'it's computer solution, I did not determine the sequence'! If the user is discouraged from interaction, the benefits of a transparent system are lost and the approach becomes more like a conventional 'blackbox' approach.

10. RESULTS

The knowledge based optimisation system was applied to determine the best sequence for separation of the range of typical mixtures shown below.

example 1

Component		Mole Fraction
propane	(A)	0.050
i-butane	(B)	0.150
n-butane	(C)	0.250
i-pentane	(D)	0.200
n-pentane	(E)	0.350

The mixture in this example contained 5 components. There are 14 sequences for splitting the mixture into pure component streams. The approximate costs for all the sequences were determined and it was found that the KBS generated sequence is identical to the optimal sequence.

example 2

Component		Mole Fraction
i-butane	(A)	0.200
neo-pentane	(B)	0.175
n-pentane	(C)	0.200
2-methylpentane	(D)	0.250
cyclohexane	(E)	0.175

This example is similar to the 5 component system in example 1, but the components and feed composition are different. The approximate costs for all the sequences are plotted in Figure 2.1. The sequence generated by the KBS is 4% more expensive than the optimal sequence, (see Figure 2.2), whereas the global worst sequence is nearly 30% more costly.

Vadhwana : Synthesis of distillation sequences

Figure 3.1 Relative cost distribution of the sequences for Example 3

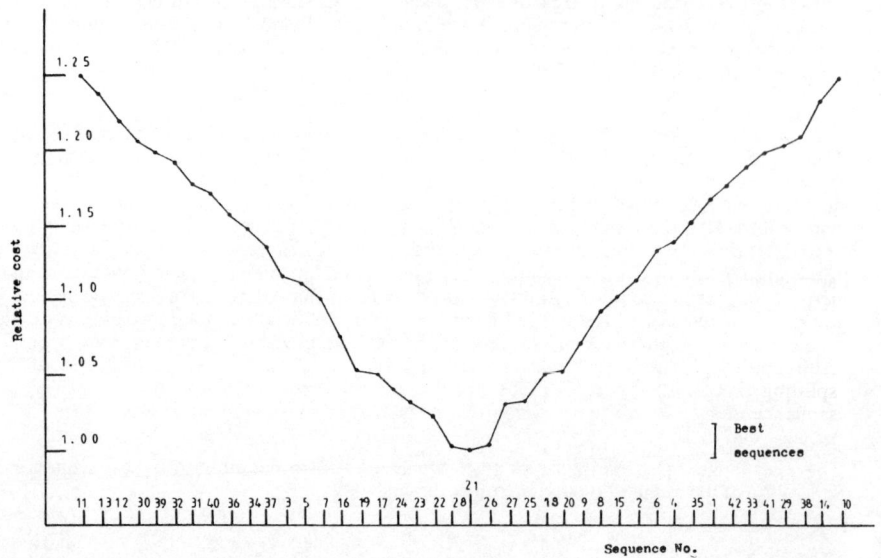

FIGURE 3.2   OPTIMAL SEQUENCES GENERATED FOR EXAMPLE 3

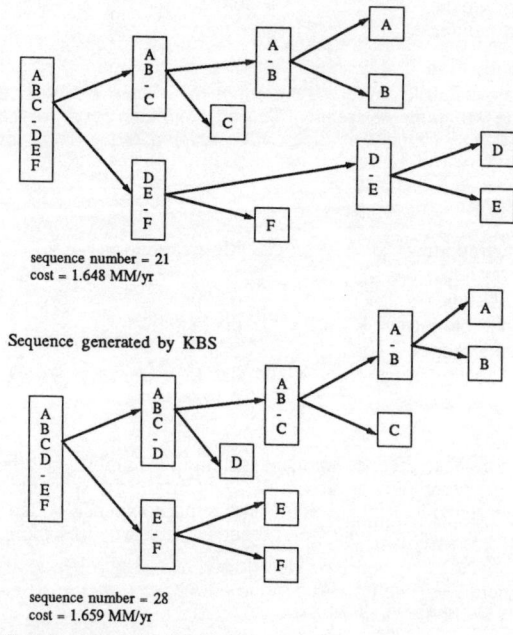

Relative Cost = 1.659/1.648 = 1.01

example 3

Component		Mole Fraction
i-butane	(A)	0.050
n-pentane	(B)	0.050
neo-pentane	(C)	0.100
n-pentane	(D)	0.150
n-hexane	(E)	0.250
n-heptane	(F)	0.400

This example tackles a 6 component system, giving rise to 42 alternative sequences. The approximate costs for the sequences are plotted in Figure 3.1. The cost associated with the KBS generated sequence is approximately 1% higher than the optimal (see Figure 3.2).

Although only three example are presented here, the KBS was tested against 25 different splitting problems. The KBS procedure did succeed, in all cases studied, in generating a sequence quite close to the optimum. The results are considered to be good since the cost penalty of 1% and 4%, in examples 3 and 2 respectively, is insignificant compared to the worst global sequences with up to 30% penalties.

11. DISCUSSION

The close agreement between the results generated by the KBS system and the rigorous procedures indicates that where good heuristics are available, a KBS approach provides a means by which a certain type of complex problems can be tackled. However, it should be noted that rules required considerable 'tuning', against a set of training examples, in order to get the degree of agreement exhibited in the results.

An interactive facility has been incorporated into the system whereby the user can give guidance to the system where the choice between two decisions is too close for confident automatic discrimination. For instance, when two OR arcs (splits) are similar (i.e. there is little to choose between the two), the user may have a preference and can make the system select the desired split. This facility is considered to be useful as it keeps the user involved in the decision process. The user can, for safety reasons, force the system to avoid a particular split that may give rise to explosive mixtures. In other instance, a particular component may be highly corrosive and therefore it has to be separated early in the sequence inspite of other rules, and this can be achieved using the interactive facility. This 'specific' knowledge would be difficult to incorporate in a conventional system.

An interactive approach is preferable to an approach which gives a final answer without an explanation. In the KBS systems approach, the user can see why a certain split was selected and which rules were instrumental in selection of a particular split.

Whilst, for the problems studied to date, computer run times are negligible, the KBS approach has the advantage of having run times less sensitive to problem size for very large problems. If the number of components in a feed stream increases, the run time for KBS approach will increase linearly whereas the run time for implicit enumeration would increase exponentially (see Figure 4). Against this advantage should be weighed the fact that KBS decision rules contain many adjustable parameters. The greatest advantage will be obtained from knowledge based systems if known physical relationships and mathematical optimisation procedures are incorporated alongside the heuristic decision rules. In this way the number of arbitrary adjustable parameters will be kept to a minimum and the ability to generate completely novel solutions reliably will be radically improved.

Figure 4 Expected CPU time vs Size of problem for KBS and mathematical method

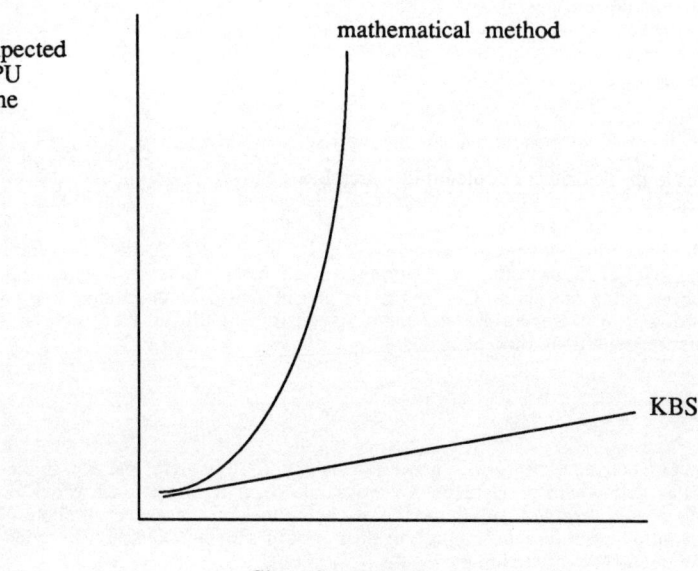

12. CONCLUDING REMARKS

Knowledge based heuristic optimisation techniques have the potential to provide a powerful tool which will enable designers to quickly perform extensive sensitivity analysis. In the cases studied, KBS approach synthesised process flowsheets that are closely similar to those developed by mathematical programming. KBS procedures do, however, need tuning against reliable yardsticks before they can be employed with confidence. They should, at least in a Process Engineering context, be used with caution where such yardsticks are not available.

Acknowledgements

The author wishes to thank British Petroleum Research International for permission to publish this paper and the members of ITRU for the useful suggestions in the preparation of this paper.

REFERENCES

Davis R., 'Expert system: where are we? and where do we go from here?', The AI magazine, Vol 3 (2), 3-21, 1982.

Fawcett N., 'The cognitive engineering of commercial expert system', Expert Systems and their Applications, Avignon 1987.

Gillies A.C. Hart A., 'Using KBS ideas in image processing - a case study in human computer interaction', Proc ES '88, Res and Dev in ES V, Brighton 1988.

Haven, D L, 'Optimum Sequencing of Distillation Columns in Multi-Component Fractionation', MS Thesis, University of California, Berkeley, 1969.

Intellicorp, 'KEE Reference Manuals', 1986.

Marcopoulos, N, 'Energy Integration of Distillation Systems', Ph.D Thesis, University of London, London, 1984.

Nilsson, N J, 'Principles of Artificial Intelligence', Springer-Verlag, 1982.

Rathore, R S, Wormer, K A V and Powers, G J, 'Synthesis of Distillation Systems with Energy Integration', AIChEJ, 20, (No 5), p 940, 1974.

Rich, E, 'Artificial Intelligence', McGraw Hill, 1983.

Westerberg A.W., 'Process Synthesis', ACS Symposium Series, Computer Applications to Chem Engineering, 1980.

An Expert System for the Control of the Activated Sludge Process.

R.Williams, B.Knight, P.Watts and J.Burns[*]
Thames Polytechnic, Woolwich, London SE18 6PF, U.K.
[*]Water Research Centre, Swindon, Wilts. SN5 8YR, U.K.

Abstract

This paper describes an expert system to assist in the control of the Activated Sludge Process used in sewage treatment. The process is a highly complex biological one, subject to many changing environmental factors, which needs control over long time scales. The expert system deals with a combination of faults in the treatment system and errors of control due to changing conditions.

The fault diagnosis system is an example of causal reasoning based on heuristic knowledge of plant behaviour. It employs meta-rules to resolve conflicts, and to control the beam search of a causal link tree.

The control advice system is an example of a qualitative state based planner. It utilises a state transition network to produce a timed sequence of control actions to serve as a recovery plan. The network is stored as a logic program, with database elements and rules, i.e. a deductive database. The systems communicate with each other and the user via a blackboard.

A prototype system has been constructed and the diagnostic system is currently undergoing field trials.

1.Introduction

1.1 Genesis of project

This paper describes the work done on a project to design and implement co-operating expert systems to form part of an intelligent decision support system for management of the activated sludge process (ASP). The project was set up by the Water Research centre (WRc) and Thames Polytechnic in 1986, with WRc and SERC funding. The overall objectives of the project are the design, implementation and evaluation of a system to advise both on day-to-day operation, and on long term control strategies for the ASP.

1.2 The Activated Sludge Process.

The basis of the sewage treatment process consists of the removal of large objects by screening and settlement followed by biological treatment and a final settlement stage. One of the main biological treatment methods currently in use is the Activated Sludge Process (ASP). The ASP uses bacteria and other micro-organisms in a liquid suspension known as activated sludge. In the process, the activated sludge is continuously mixed with the sewage and the resultant mixed liquor stirred and aerated, allowing the sludge to grow and consume the organic debris in the sewage. When the effluent is released the sludge is settled out and a fraction recycled to be mixed with more sewage.

The ASP allows a high degree of control over the treatment, giving the potential for recovery from abnormal conditions and for optimisation of the treatment. The process may be altered in many ways such as a change in the rate of aeration, a change in the rate at which the activated sludge is recycled or the number of tanks through which the mixed liquor is passed and aerated. These changes can be made for a specific purpose e.g. to increase the speed of the process, or to prevent rising sludge at the secondary settlement stage. The ASP is also easier to observe and measure than other biological systems because it is more open and accessible allowing sight observations and easy installation and maintenance of instruments.

However, the benefits that extended control brings to the ASP are accompanied by several drawbacks. The ASP is not only subject to effects induced by variations in the quality of the incoming sewage but also by variations in control, which take place over a very long time scale. Any excursion (i.e. a variation from normal) can have an effect on the ability of the bacteria to consume the sewage which in turn affects effluent quality. Operation of the ASP is constrained both by the consent standards for effluent quality and by the operating costs of the process. When the process is operating at maximum efficiency very slight excursions can cause severe falls in effluent quality, perhaps leading to total failure to achieve the consent standards. The prime requirement when this occurs is the restoration of effluent quality to within the consent standards; a secondary consideration is the re-optimisation of the process.

Operator and management experience as well as archived examples form the basis of many ASP control decisions. Approaches based on this expertise have the advantage of being dependent only on readily available data but, being unformalised, suffer from inconsistency and incompleteness in application. For instance, recovery from an excursion may have been the result of the recommended control action or it may have happened coincidentally due to the changing of some other factor. The long time scales involved in the ASP, typically taking weeks to show an effect, allow such inconsistencies to occur. Archived examples may also be insufficient for control purposes as they may be inappropriate for the plant configuration or for the current environmental conditions.

Experience and example are often augmented by simulation of the ASP using a mathematical model such as that of Jones (1978). This forecasts the state of the ASP given a set of initial conditions. Such models are limited in two respects: firstly they work forwards to derive effects from causes and cannot easily be used to find the causes of a given effect; secondly, the factors that the models use are a subset of the factors that affect the ASP and thus there are areas that lie outside the model's active domain (e.g. fault conditions). Another drawback is that a great deal of care is needed in setting up the model and in interpreting the results.

1.3 Overview of system

The problem to be addressed in this project is that of determining a course of action which will lead to recovery from a situation which is abnormal in some way. These abnormal situations can be divided into two separate classes, although recognition of the class for a given situation is not always immediately obvious. One class consists of situations in which the ASP plant and control system are functioning as designed, but in unusual areas for which recovery actions are not well established. This class is termed 'fault-free'.

The other class consists of situations arising from faults which have occurred in some part of the system as designed. A characteristic of this second class of situation is that recovery may involve user action in checking and correcting suspected faults, whereupon the recovery proceeds as for the fault-free case. The top level architecture for a system to assist in these decisions as suggested by this classification is shown in the data flow diagram of figure 1.

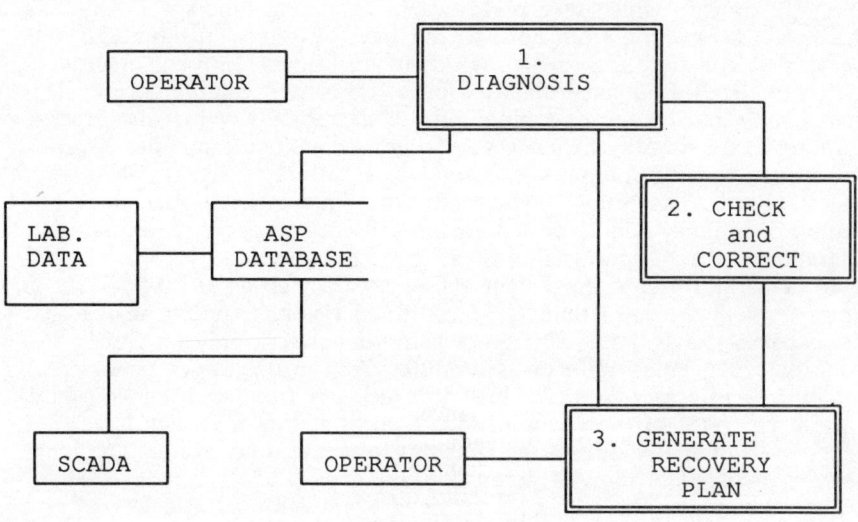

Figure 1
Top Level System Architecture Diagram

This diagram shows an initial process of diagnosis, which operates on the available situation data to classify it according to possible fault conditions, or as fault-free. The user action, in process 2, is to check physically for certain suggested malfunctions and possibly to make a decision on the basis of several suggested possibilities. Process 3 represents a planner which generates recovery plans for the correctly functioning system.

The principal features of the system are those of a blackboard architecture (Erman and Lesser, 1975; Hayes-Roth, 1985). Communication between the various sources of knowledge is through a partitioned global data structure, i.e. the blackboard. The knowledge sources for the complete system will include the diagnostic and planning systems, the current control system (SCADA), the quantitative model, and the system giving immediate advice on treatment (see section 2.4).

2. The Diagnosis Process

2.1 Knowledge representation.

In formalising the knowledge, an approach was adopted, centred on the compilation of a qualitative "data dictionary", with the object of simplifying the handling of uncertainty of user input by restricting factors to a small number of discrete values.There were several other benefits from this data definition approach including:

(i) definition of the problem domain;

(ii) provision of a focus for experts in identifying relevant factors that affect the ASP;

(iii) formation of a basis for the construction of the rules.

```
Effluent ammonia
Description   :  Ammoniacal nitrogen (ammonia)
                 Nitrogen as ammonia (NH₃) or the
                 ammonium ion  (NH₄⁺). This the
                 normal measure of 'ammonia' in
                 sewage treatment, and does not
                 include organic  nitrogen.
Units         :  mg/l
Abbreviation  :  Eff NH₃-N
Bands         :  Low         {0   ..  1}
                 Medium      {1   ..  5}
                 High        {5   .. 10}
                 Very high  {10   .. 40}
```

Figure 2
Effluent ammonia

Figure 2 shows the definition of the factor, "Effluent Ammonia", a typical data dictionary entry. The "bands" referred to above are essentially a device used to restrict the values that the factor can take to a small but sufficient set. This effectively discretises the normally potentially infinite range of numeric values to a finite set of meaningful qualitative descriptors. As well as these normally numeric factors there are factors that are naturally discrete.

2.2 Diagnosis Knowledge

Knowledge about the diagnosis of faults may be expressed in terms of the tree structure illustrated in the example of figure 3. Here the leaves of a tree represent possible diagnoses, and the root represents an initially identified problem. We may interpret the tree shown as a causal model by working from leaf to root:

Discharge of a toxic substance (1.1.4.1) -- causes -- decrease in bacterial activity (1.1.4)

Decrease in bacterial activity (1.1.4) -- causes -- problems with aeration tanks (1.1)

Problems with aeration tanks (1.1) -- causes -- effluent problems (1)

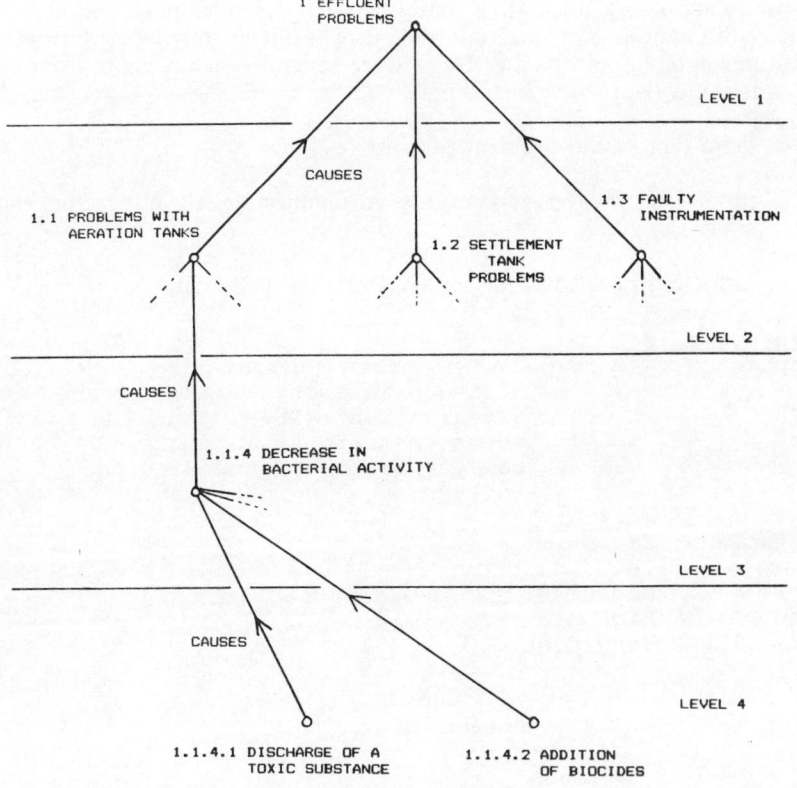

Figure 3
Diagnosis knowledge tree

This is an interpretation of the knowledge as a causal model akin to the existing quantitative model; i.e. it predicts the future behaviour of the system given a present set of circumstances.

It is different from the quantitative model in two respects:
   It deals with both classes of situation: fault and fault-free.
   It operates on a finite and discrete set of leaves, whereas the quantitative model uses real numbers as inputs.

The problems of control addressed by this project require the use of such qualitative models, not to predict effects knowing the cause, but inversely, to establish the cause knowing some of the effects. For instance, to solve the problem of diagnosis we must start at the root of the tree (e.g. effluent problems) and attempt to find the right path to a leaf (e.g. discharge of a toxic substance).

To help in this process there exists a great deal of experiential knowledge relating observable and measured data on the system state to the likelihood of the links in the causal tree. This knowledge has been formulated as rules, examples of which are shown below.

R39.IF "Is DO controlled ?" is "Yes" AND
   "DO in the first zone" is "medium" OR "high" OR "very high" AND
   "Proportion of the aerator capacity being used in the first zone" is "low"   THEN Causal_link(1.1,1.1.4) is "probable"

R40.IF "Is DO controlled ?" is "No" AND
   "DO in the first zone" is "high" OR "very high"
   THEN Causal_link(1.1,1.1.4) is "probable"

R41.IF "Is DO controlled ?" is "No" AND
   "DO generally in zones after the first" is "very high"
   THEN Causal_link(1.1,1.1.4) is "probable"

R42.IF "Alkalinity [mg/l CaCO3]" is "low"
   THEN Causal_link(1.1,1.1.4) is "possible"

R43.IF "Is this a soft water area ?" is "Yes"
   THEN Causal_link(1.1,1.1.4) is "possible"

R44.IF "Settled sewage nitrogen to carbon ratio" is "low" OR "very low"
   THEN Causal_link(1.1,1.1.4) is "possible"

R45.DEFAULT Causal_link(1.1,1.1.4) is "probably_not"

   Rules such as these, together with default likelihoods allow us to establish the likelihood of any complete path between root and leaf, based upon all available data. As in the qualitative assessment of data, the likelihoods are restricted to five broad bands for simplicity and clarity i.e."certainly not", "probably not", "possible", "probable", "certain".
This process of establishing causal links can be thought of as a combination of the abductive and deductive phases of the diagnostic task as stated by Peirce (1878) and later expanded by Johnson (1986). The rules themselves embody the deductive phase in that we expect a set of facts to hold certain values if a causal link is to be established. It is abductive because the causal links established may lead to further hypotheses to be examined.

2.3 Inference Mechanism

The design of an inference mechanism to operate on the rule base so as to output appropriate diagnoses must deal with a number of problems:

1. Much of the data is to be entered manually by the operator. Hence it is necessary for operational reasons to confine the searching to a minimum of causal paths, by some type of beam search.

2. Conflicts occur between the rules, requiring a flexible method of conflict resolution.

3. Some sets of evidence are in themselves 'harder' than other sets. e.g. Of the three evidence sets below, the first is much more important to the causal link between nodes 1.1.4 and 1.1.

   evidence set (1)
   "Is DO controlled ?"
   "DO in the first zone"
   "Proportion of the aerator capacity being used in the first zone"
   "DO generally in zones after the first"

   evidence set (2)
   "Alkalinity [mg/l CaCO3]"
   "Settled sewage nitrogen to carbon ratio"
   evidence set (3)
   "Is this a soft water area ?"
   This must be reflected by the conflict resolution method.

4. Some causal links must be investigated even if their likelihood is low. The causes involved may be considered important enough because of their potential effects not to be disregarded at an early stage. This problem entails the addition of an attribute "level of importance" to each node in the causal tree.

In the current implementation these problems have been solved by means of an inference engine which conducts a beam search of the tree, with meta-rules that govern the width of the beam at each level, and which assist in the resolution of conflicts between rules. The mechanism for the beam search is to start with a root node, which is effectively user defined, as the level 1 beam set, and derive likelihoods for all links to nodes on level 2. The beam set for level 2 (and later for levels 3 and 4) is then constructed by meta-rules such as:

   MR1. Include all nodes that are "certain" or "probable" causes of other nodes.

   MR2. If the highest available node at the current level is not "certain", include "important" nodes that are "possible".

MR3 If the highest available node at the current level is "possible" and the number of nodes in the beam set is less than a prescribed minimum, then include "unimportant" nodes which are "possible".

Rules such as these provide an explicit statement of the control strategy for the beam search. The flexibility of this approach has been found to be important in practice as changes in the control strategy can be easily implemented and the mechanism of the control itself is apparent to the user. In the present implementation the meta-rules operate on the likelihood and importance of nodes; they may also need to operate on other attributes such as the cost of acquiring the data needed to establish likelihoods.

A feature of the search mechanism is its dynamic treatment of the beam set. At any stage in the consultation the beam may be widened on any level of the causal tree. By this means, the system is able to 'think again' about its line of enquiry, and possibly explore other paths in the light of new data.

Conflict resolution is also explicitly defined by meta-rules. The most important of these in the current implementation are :

CR1. Choose the rule based on the harder evidence set.
e.g. If DO is controlled and is very high generally in zones after the first, then rules 41 and 43 (see example rules above) could fire, and would conflict. However, firmer conclusions can be drawn from measured laboratory factors, such as dissolved oxygen, than from general observations, such as the area being a soft water area, so that rule 41 is to be preferred.

CR2. If a general and a more specific rule fire, choose the more specific one.
e.g. If effluent ammonia is very high and the works is supposed to nitrify then the following rules will fire :

R5. IF "Effluent ammonia" is "very high"
    THEN Causal_link(1,1.1) is "possible"

R7. IF "Is the works supposed to nitrify?" is "Yes" AND
    "Effluent ammonia" is "high" OR "very high"
    THEN Causal_link(1,1.1) is "certain"

However, rule 7 is more specific than rule 5, so rule 7 is preferred.

When the inference mechanism has completed a search - i.e. when all the links between nodes in the beam sets are assigned likelihoods - the final problem is to decide on the set of leaves to output to the user. This diagnosis set is a function of the likelihoods and again is set by meta-rules based on path-likelihood.

In the current implementation a path-likelihood is defined for each leaf as the minimum likelihood of the links from the root to the leaf.

The diagnosis set is then taken as the set with the maximum path-likelihoods.

2.4 Operator Interaction.

Process 2 in the data flow diagram of figure 1 represents essential operator participation in the decision process. The suggested faults diagnosed are to be checked and corrected to the satisfaction of the operator, so that the recovery plan can be generated for a fault-free system. However, it may not be possible for the operator to correct the fault immediately, for example when checks need to be made or parts need to be ordered. Many of the checks take time to complete, involving perhaps remote equipment or laboratory analyses. In such cases, interim emergency actions need to be specified which temporarily hold the plant in an acceptable state. Advice on such immediate actions is provided by means of a 'treatment advice' system which volunteers a list of recommended holding actions, depending upon the diagnoses.

3. The Planning Module

The problem of recovery of plant condition is to decide on a sequence of control actions over time, so that the condition of the AS will evolve over a time period into a 'normal' condition, i.e. a condition where routine run-time control procedures apply. Although the existing quantitative model may be used for plan confirmation, the long run time involved makes it impractical for plan formulation.

For this purpose an alternative model has been developed by using the data dictionary definitions to define qualitative states of the process, which may then be viewed as a finite state process. The process model which results may be illustrated by the weighted directed graph of figure 4. In this diagram the weights represent the expected time in weeks for the process to evolve into its next elementary state. The parameters defining the system states may be classified as:

(i) process variables, which evolve with time according to the biological process.

(ii) fixed parameters, which may be taken as constant during the recovery.

(iii) control parameters, which are constants but may be changed by control actions during a recovery.

Changes of state due to control actions have been represented on the diagram by double barred arrows. An elementary path of the directed graph represents a sequence of timed control actions.

The planner searches for optimal paths from initial to target state according to cost and time. It also takes account of possible constraints, such as on the length of time that flow may be reduced.

The planning system resolves into three separate recovery problems corresponding to the effluent quality factors: ammonia, biochemical oxygen demand (BOD) and solids. Although the initial values of quality are usually known, the bacterial factors (e.g. nitrifiers and heterotrophs) are not directly measurable, and must be inferred from the diagnosis. This sets the initial state, and the user controls the desired final state.

The prototype system operates on a set of 96 stored state transitions. The states take the form of compound Prolog predicates:

state(variable(_,_,...),control(_,...),fixed(_,...)),

and transitions are stored both as database items and rules, i.e. as a deductive database.

The rules contain heuristic knowledge about the affect of fixed parameter settings, and reduce greatly the size of the database.

For example, for ranges of values for the other fixed parameters, temperature affects only the time for transitions. Hence, the following rule for interpolation allows the deduction of intermediate transitions from two stored transitions:

Transition(X,Y,...,Temp,Time):-
    Transition(X,Y,...,Temp1,Time1),
    Transition(X,Y,...,Temp2,Time2),
    Temp1 < Temp < Temp2,
    Next(Temp1,Temp2),
    Time = Time1 + (Time2-Time1)(Temp-Temp1)/(Temp2-Temp1).

Example

From the example diagnosis : " Industrial discharge of a toxic waste", the planning system infers that for a plant which is intended to nitrify, ammonia recovery is the primary problem. It also infers from the diagnosis that nitrifying bacteria have been destroyed, and sets the nitrifiers as 'low' in the initial state for the recovery plan.

Example fixed factors are:

Temperature 7 C,   Number of aeration tanks 6, Anoxic zone, DO setpoint 2.0, MLSS setpoint 4000.

For these values, a set of transitions may be derived from the deductive database. An illustrative subset of these is shown in figure 4. Here the states have been labelled : (ammonia level, nitrifier level), and the objective is to reach a state with low ammonia level.

The diagram shows the effect of the control action to use an extra tank. We see that, if this is the only available control action, (in fact there are several others not shown here), then it must be performed at some time in order to reach the low ammonia state. The minimum time route is to use the extra tank immediately, whereupon the recovery takes 10 weeks. The minimum cost solution is to use an extra tank after 14 weeks, giving a duration of 15 weeks for total recovery.

In fact the system also has to take account of practical constraints. For example, if an extra tank is only allowed for a total of 4 weeks, the minimum time solution is to use the extra tank after 9 weeks , giving a recovery time of 13 weeks.

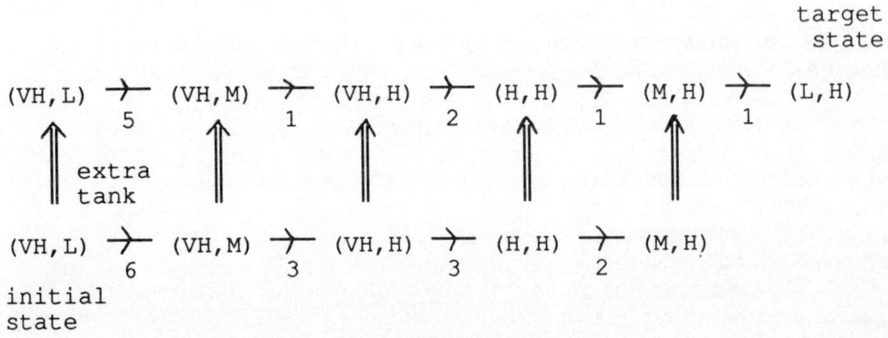

```
                                                                    target
                                                                    state
(VH,L)  →—  (VH,M)  →—  (VH,H)  →—  (H,H)  →—  (M,H)  →—  (L,H)
          5          1          2         1          1
   ↑                ↑          ↑         ↑          ↑
 extra
 tank

(VH,L)  →—  (VH,M)  →—  (VH,H)  →—  (H,H)  →—  (M,H)
          6          3          3         2
initial
state
```

Figure 4
Qualitative State Transition Diagram

4. Future Developments

The progress towards the solution of a problem is not a simple sequential one. In the example, the diagnosis and plan selected appear to be leading to a satisfactory solution, but the diagnosis and plan selection are not always fool-proof. Diagnoses and plans may be wrong, and the recovery may not proceed as planned. In this case, diagnostic and planning phases must be re-scheduled.

A Scheduler, i.e. an intelligent control mechanism which decides which task is performed next, is an integral component of blackboard systems. At this stage in the project, no attempt has been made to automate scheduling, which is dealt with entirely by the operator, viewing the blackboard via the screen. It is felt that the feasibility of intelligent scheduling will be assessable only when experience has been gained with operator scheduling.

The potential of the qualitative state-transition model lies in its capability for various types of query. In the prototype system, it is assumed that the initial conditions are known and the model is then queried to determine the control actions necessary to achieve the desired recovery path. In practice, there are situations where the initial conditions are not known with precision and thus the control actions given by the planner may cause the ASP to move to a state different from that predicted by the model. In this case, the model can be queried using the known current state and control actions to give a more accurate assessment of the initial conditions. The planner will then be able to produce a better recovery plan.

Acknowledgements

The authors would like to acknowledge the contributions of colleagues at the Water Research Centre and at Thames Polytechnic, and to thank SERC and the Water Research Centre for funding the project.

References

Jones, G.L. A mathematical model for bacterial growth and substrate utilisation in the activated sludge process. In Water Pollution Control, ed. A. James. pp 265-279. Wylie, Chichester.

Johnson, L.(1986). Analysis of the diagnostic task. International Journal of Systems Research and Information Science 1 225-236.

Hayes-Roth, B. (1985) A Blackboard Architecture for Control. Artificial Intelligence no. 26 237-246.

Erman, L.D. and Lesser, V.R. (1975) A multi-level organisation for problem solving using many diverse, cooperating sources of knowledge. In Advanced papers from the International Joint Conference on Artificial Intelligence 483-490.

Peirce, C.S. (1878) Illustrations of the logic of Science, sixth paper - deduction, induction, hypothesis. The Popular Science Monthly 1 470-482

FUTURE DIRECTIONS IN KNOWLEDGE ACQUISITION*

Bob Wielinga
Guus Schreiber

Department of Social Science Informatics,
University of Amsterdam
Herengracht 196, NL-1016 BS Amsterdam, The Netherlands
Tel. +31 20 525 2160/2073
Electronic mail: wielinga@swivax.UUCP

Abstract

In this paper knowledge acquisition for the development of knowledge-based systems is viewed as essentially a modeling activity [Hayward et al., 1987]. A KBS is not a container filled with knowledge extracted from an expert, but an operational model that exhibits some desired behavior observed or specified in terms of real-world phenomena. Several types of models relevant to knowledge acquisition are discussed. The use of models in the knowledge acquisition process is a means of coping with the complexity of the development process. Modeling at the knowledge level is considered to be an essential intermediate step in the development process for KBS. Some of the consequences and potential of the modeling approach for knowledge acquisition are discussed.

1 Viewpoints on Knowledge Acquisition

In the knowledge acquisition process the knowledge that a knowledge-based system (KBS) needs to perform a task, is defined in such a way that a computer program can represent and adequately use that knowledge. Knowledge acquisition involves at least the following activities: *eliciting* the knowledge in an informal — usually verbal — form, *interpreting* the elicited data using some conceptual framework, and *formalising* the conceptualisations in such way that the program can use the knowledge. In this paper we will mainly focus on the interpretation and formalisation activities in knowledge acquisition. Elicitation techniques have been the subject of a number of recent papers and their role in the knowledge acquisition process is reasonably well understood [Neale, 1988; Wielinga et al., 1988].

Traditionally the knowledge acquisition process has been viewed as a process of extracting knowledge from a human expert and transferring the extracted knowledge into the KBS. In practice this often means that the expert is asked what rules are applicable in a certain problem situation and the knowledge engineer translates the natural language formulation of that rule into the appropriate format. Several authors [Hayward

---

*The research reported here was partially supported by a
research project funded by the Esprit Programme of the Commission of the
European Communities as project number 1098. The partners in the latter
project are STC Technology Ltd., SD-SCICON Ltd., KBSC of TRMC (all UK),
NTE Neutech (W-G), Cap Sogeti Innovation (F), and the University of
Amsterdam (NL).

et al., 1987; Morik, 1989] have pointed out that the transfer-view of knowledge acquisition is only applicable in very few cases. The expert, the knowledge engineer and the KBS should share a common view on the problem solving process and a common vocabulary in order to make knowledge transfer a viable way of knowledge acquisition. If the expert has a different way of looking at the problem or the domain, asking for rules or similar knowledge structures and translating them into the knowledge representation formalism of the system, simply will not work.

A different view on knowledge acquisition is that of a modeling activity. Constructing a KBS is seen as the construction of a computational model of some observed or desired behaviour. For example if we observe a physician asking questions about a patient and drawing conclusions about the patient's disease, we cannot directly observe the problem solving process that goes on in the head of the doctor, but we can specify the behaviour that we want an expert system to display in terms of the observed actions. From the observed/desired behaviour we have to construct a model of the reasoning process that will display that desired behaviour. So, knowledge acquisition essentially is a constructive process in which the knowledge engineer can use all sorts of data about the behaviour of the expert, but in which the ultimate design decisions have to be made by the knowledge engineer in a constructive way. In this sense knowledge engineering is similar to other design tasks: the real world only provides certain constraints on what the artifact should provide in terms of functionality, the designer will have to aggregate the bits and pieces into a coherent system.

In this paper we will adopt the modeling perspective on knowledge acquisition and investigate the consequences and potential of the modeling approach. In the next sections we will address the following questions:

1. what should be modeled?

2. how should be modeled?

3. what is the relation between the models and the actual KBS?

Subsequently we will discuss how the modeling approach can support the knowledge acquisition process.

2 Models of What?

Adopting the modeling view, we take a closer look at the question what has to be modeled.

2.1 Task Model

Traditionally the emphasis in knowledge acquisition has been on modeling the performance of the expert. In research on expert systems over the last decade, however, it has become clear [Roth & Woods, 1989] that just mimicing the expert's behaviour is not always the most optimal solution for a problem that an organisation wants to be solved. A KBS may be able to perform certain additional tasks that the expert in a current situation is not able to perform, or the KBS may integrate tasks of several different experts.

So, a first requirement in knowledge acquisition is to model the task that the system will have to perform, i.e. a task model has to be constructed. A task model specifies what has to be done, what the different subtasks are and what the constraints that the task environment poses are. For example, consider a task such as medical therapy selection. The MYCIN approach to this task has been to first determine the identity of the organism that causes a disease and on the basis of that identity select the optimal combination of drugs to administer to the patient. In real life hospital practice, determining the identity of the organism is, however, usually not a major goal, it is the recovery of the patient that is the primary concern. So, if identification of the organism proves difficult, e.g. because no laboratory data are available, a therapy will be selected on heuristic grounds. In fact some doctors show little interest in the identity of the organism causing a disease as long as the therapy works. Stated in more general terms: given a goal that a system should achieve, there may be several alternative ways in which that goal can be achieved. Which alternatives are appropriate in a given problem situation depends on characteristics of that problem situation, on availability of knowledge and data, and on requirements imposed by the user or external factors, e.g. juridical factors.

Modeling the task environment involves a number of issues. First, the task analysis has to determine what the expected result of task performance will be. Although this seems rather obvious, it is not always so in practice. Several experiments [Pollack et al., 1982; Alty & Coombs, 1980; Belkin et al., 1987] have shown that tasks which are seemingly straight forward advice giving tasks, involve much more than providing advice: they involve negotiating the problem space, cooperative problem solving and strategic deliberations.

Even for a simple task such as diagnosis, it is not always clear what a diagnosis of a faulty system means. A diagnosis could be the identification of a subsystem (component) that malfunctions, or it could be a full causal model of how a malfunction came about. Similarly the result of a design task could be a detailed description of the structure of a system (e.g. a device for monitoring patients in an intensive care unit) or it could be a description of the functionality, structure and use of the device.

If we take the broad view on knowledge acquisition as being the first stage of defining the functionality of a KBS as well as the knowledge that will be needed to achieve that functionality, knowledge acquisition should encompass the analysis of the task environment as well as the analysis of the knowledge required for that functionality.

2.2 Model of Cooperation

The model of the task and task environment is the input for the next step in knowledge acquisition: modeling the user-system cooperation at the global level. The task model consists of a decomposition of the top-level goal into a number of sub-goals. Some of these subgoals will be achieved by the system, others may be realised by the user. For example, in a diagnostic task the system may suggest certain tests to be performed by the user, while the user will actually perform the tests and will report the observed results back to the system. Alternatively, the user may want to volunteer a solution to the diagnostic problem while the system will critique that solution by comparing it with its own solutions. So, given the goal decomposition in the task model the knowledge engineer has to decide what subtasks to assign to the system and what tasks to the user. These decisions are essentially a cognitive engineering problem [Roth & Woods, 1989]: they should be made on the basis of an analysis of the user requirements and expectations, the knowledge and skills that the user has, and the potential capabilities and limitations of the system. The result is a model of cooperative problem solving in which the user and the system together achieve a goal in a way that satisfies the various constraints posed by the task environment, the user and the state of the art of KBS technology [deGreef, 1988; deGreef, 1989].

2.3 Model of Expertise vs. Model of Artifact

Given a task division between user and system, the knowledge acquisition process can focus on the reasoning processes that the system should perform. One can take two different perspectives on modeling the reasoning that is required from a system. A first perspective -the one that is usually taken in AI- is to focus on the problem solving methods and the knowledge structures that will be the basis of the systems behaviour. A second perspective focusses on the behaviour that the system should display and on the types of knowledge that are involved in generating such behaviour, abstracting from the details of how the reasoning is actually realised in the implementation.

The models created from the second perspective are similar to what are called conceptual models in conventional database application development. Conceptual models are abstract descriptions of the objects and operations that a system should know about, formulated in such a way that they capture the intuitions that humans have of the required behaviour. The language in which conceptual models are expressed is not the formal language of AI constructs and methods, but is the language that relates real world phenomena to the cognitive framework of the observer. In this sense conceptual models are subjective, they are relative to the cognitive vocabulary and framework of the human modeler. A good example of such a conceptual framework is the heuristic classification model for analytic tasks developed by Clancey [Clancey, 1985]. The framework distinguishes between different types of reasoning steps: abstraction, association and refinement. Steps in a problem solving process can be classified in terms of these categories of inferences, and thus give rise to a conceptual model of how a particular problem is solved. The conceptual model classifies different types of knowledge, their relations and types of inferences that give rise to new information about a problem, but it does not model the actual technique that will be used in a system to derive the inferences. The abstraction step in a heuristic classification system can be achieved by using abstraction rules and a forward chaining rule interpreter, but could also be achieved by searching a hierarchical structure of problem features.

So, the actual problem solving methods that a system will embodied are not modeled in the conceptual model, they are part of the model that focusses on the reasoning in the system itself. The two viewpoints on modeling reasoning processes are summarised in figure 1. The real-world viewpoint corresponds to modeling expertise as it is empirically observed, these observations being embodied in actual elicitation data. The artifact viewpoint, in contrast, models the structure of the knowledge base of a computational system.

Given this distinction in viewpoints, the knowledge engineering process can be seen as going through a number of phases, not dissimilar to the phases in conventional data modeling. In figure 1 these phases are shown in relation to the two levels (*knowledge* and *symbol level*) as defined by Newell [Newell, 1982]). *Raw data* in this figure refers to the input data from the real world: text books, interviews, thinking aloud protocols, etcetera. The *conceptual model* is a knowledge-level model of the domain expertise. The conceptual model is real-world oriented in the sense that it only describes the

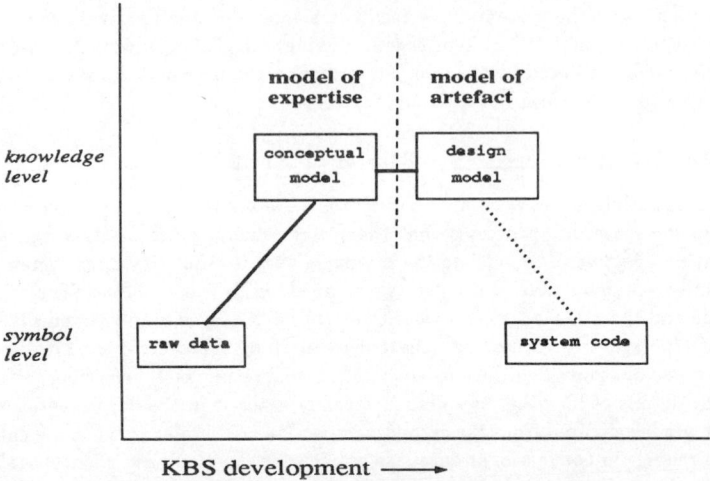

Figure 1: Viewpoints on Modeling

competence in expert problem solving, and has a cognitive flavour. In particular, it does not take into account constraints with regard to the artifact, *i.e.*, it is completely neutral with respect to implementation formalisms. The *design model* is a model at the same level of abstraction, but of the artifact rather than of the real world. It is, in fact, a high-level (logic) system design. The idea is that the design model can be transformed into a detailed system design and subsequently into actual *system code* without further major decisions having to be made.

The conceptual model is a competence model of the problem solving as observed in, for example, domain experts. The major difference between the conceptual model and the design model thus is that the design model takes into account external requirements (*e.g.*, speed, software) and user requirements (*e.g.*, a natural language interface). These requirements may limit in certain instances the scope of the conceptual model, but they usually do not change the contents of this model. We have experienced that building a conceptual model model without having to worry about system requirements makes life easier for the knowledge engineer. The distinction between the two knowledge-level models is also useful, if one opts for another problem-solving method in the artifact than the one used by the domain expert. For example, if the domain expert uses heuristics to find a particular solution, one may choose to use a *generate and test* method in the KBS, because its computational resources are larger. An explicit representation of both models can in that case be used to explain the differences in behaviour between the system and the expert to a user.

With respect to the design model, two different viewpoints are again applicable: the functional and the physical viewpoint. The functional viewpoint emphasises what functions the system should perform, while the physical viewpoint focuses on how these functions will be realised in the physical system. The relation between functional model and physical model is made by the actual problem solving and representation methods that the system embodies [Schreiber *et al.*, 1988].

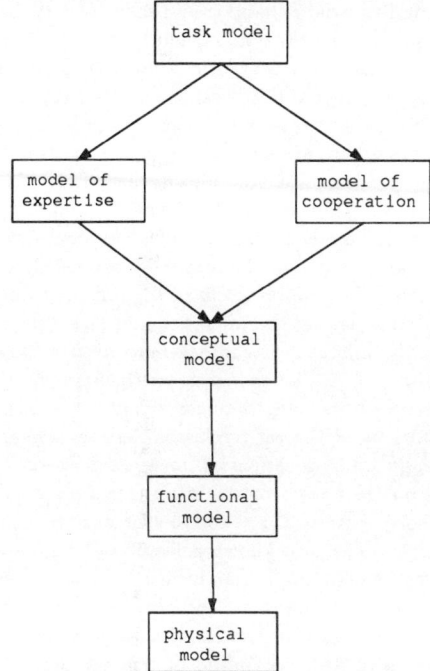

Figure 2: Models in KBS Development

Figure 2 summarises the various types of models that are constructed during the knowledge acquisition process. In summary we can say that the modeling view of knowledge acquisition gives rise to a methodology that involves the construction of a variety of models in the course of the knowledge acquisition process. Knowledge acquisition involves much more than just building a reasoning model.

3 How to model expertise?

The construction of each of the models introduced in the previous section requires its own methodology. In the KADS project [Hayward et al., 1987; Schreiber et al., 1988] the different modeling frameworks and techniques are being developed. In this paper we will focus on the conceptual modeling of expertise.

In earlier work [Wielinga & Breuker, 1984; Wielinga & Breuker, 1986] we proposed a framework for modeling expertise, based on a categorisation of knowledge according to the role that it plays in a reasoning process. In this framework four categories of knowledge are distinguished.

The first category of knowledge concerns *static domain knowledge*. The static domain knowledge consists of the domain concepts and their attributes, domain facts, structures representing complex relations etc. The static knowledge can be viewed as the layer of knowledge representing a declarative theory of the domain. In fact, adding a simple deductive capability would enable a system in theory, but not in practice, to solve all problems solvable by the theory. The static domain knowledge is considered to be largely task neutral, i.e. represented in a form that is independent of its use. There is ample evidence [Wielinga & Bredeweg, 1988] that experts are able to use their domain knowledge in a variety of ways, e.g. for problem solving, explanation, teaching etc. Separating static domain knowledge embodying the theory of the domain from its use in a problem solving process, is a first step towards flexible use and reusability of domain knowledge.

A second type of knowledge concerns canonical inference steps. An inference is considered to be an elementary step in the reasoning process deriving new information from existing information. An important characteristic of an inference is the type of information that is used in making the inference and the type of information that it produces. In addition, the inference is characterised by the type of domain concepts and relations it uses. For example, an elementary classification inference takes as input a bundle of features of an object and produces as output a class to which the object can belong, using definitions of the set of classes that the system knows about. The information used or produced by a canonical inference is described by a *metaclass*. In the terminology of the KADS 4-layer model inferences are named *knowledge sources*.

With respect to the question of a taxonomy of canonical inferences there is no consensus in the literature. The best known collection of canonical inference steps can be found in Clancey's model of heuristic classification [Clancey, 1985]. In this model the inferences are: *abstraction*, *association* and *refinement*. Within our model we assume a somewhat larger set of canonical inferences. Example additions are *transformation*, *selection* and *computation* (a full description of this set can be found in [Breuker et al., 1987a]). If one views canonical inferences as functions, then the metaclasses are the types of the *formal* arguments of these functions. A metaclass describes the role a group of domain concepts can play in the reasoning process (e.g. datum, feature, hypothesis, solution).

The third category contains knowledge about how elementary inferences can be combined to reach a certain goal. The prime knowledge type in this category is the *task*. A task can be defined statically (a control structure with the usual control primitives) or dynamically (as a planner function which interprets descriptions of the second category). Tasks satisfy a particular *goal*. The relations between tasks and goals are in principle many-to-many. Knowledge at the task level is usually characterised by a vocabulary of control terms, for instance indicating that a finding has been processed or a hypothesis has been verified.

The fourth category of knowledge is the *strategic knowledge*. Strategic knowledge determines what goals are relevant to solve a particular problem. How each goal is achieved is determined by the knowledge at the task layer. Knowledge at the strategic layer will also have to deal with situations where the lower layers fail to produce a partial solution. For example, the problem solving process may reach an impasse because information is not available or because contradictory information arises. In such cases the strategic reasoning should suggest new lines of approach or attempt to introduce new information e.g., through assumptions [Jansweijer, 1988].

The categories can be seen as knowledge *layers* in the sense that each successive layer interprets the description at the lower layer. In figure 3 the four categories and their interrelations are summarised. The four-layer framework for knowledge modeling has been successfully used as a basis for structured acquisition and description of

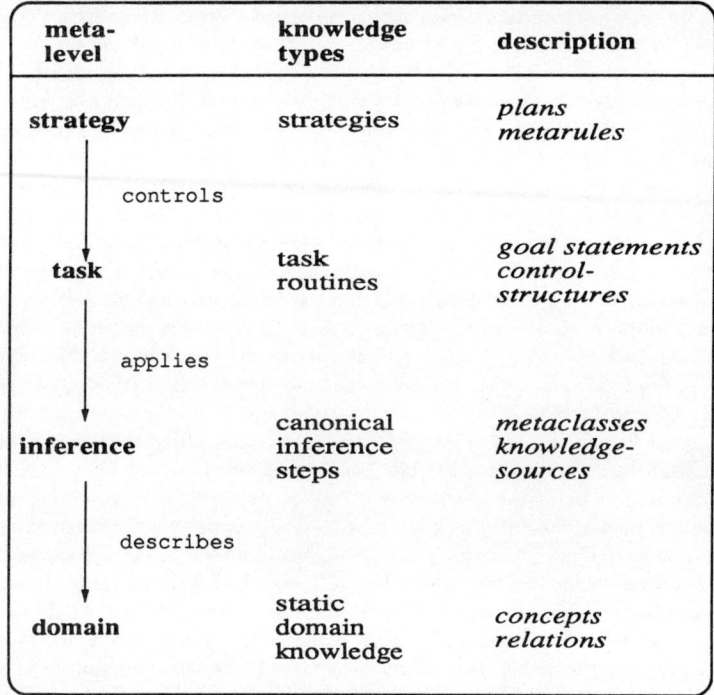

Figure 3: The KADS four-layer model

knowledge at an intermediate level between the verbal data obtained from experts and the knowledge representation in an implemented system [deGreef & Breuker, 1985].

From the point of view of knowledge models, the four-layer model captures all knowledge types that occur in other models, even though differences exist about where to situate a particular type of knowledge. For instance, in NEOMYCIN task knowledge and strategic knowledge are merged into one level. In Steels' proposal [Steels, 1988] heuristic annotations are part of the domain knowledge, while we would place that type of knowledge in the inference layer. In spite of these differences it appears that a coherent framework for conceptual modeling is emerging.

4 Knowledge Models in Perspective

One major objection to the use of knowledge-level models in the KBS development process is the potential computational inadequacy of such models. Since knowledge-level models do not specify the control regime in full detail they are apt to potential combinatorial explosion behaviour. Although it is true in principle that this problem may occur, the structure of the models proposed here provides important safeguards against the computational inadequacy. The knowledge that is specified in a KADS four-layer model cannot be used in arbitrary ways, it has to fulfill certain typing requirements and can only be applied within the constraints specified by the model. For instance, a logical implication of a certain type can only be used for abstraction inferences, not for all types of inference steps. Our introduction of knowledge sources and task structures generally yields the possibility of selecting specific rules or theories needed to produce a certain inference. In this way the knowledge-level model provides a *role-limiting* [McDermott, 1989] constraint to knowledge, and hence constrains the combinatorial explosion.

Some recent approaches to knowledge-based system development take a similar viewpoint as KADS. However the terminology and classification of knowledge types differ. Alexander [Alexander *et al.*, 1988] for example, defines the static ontology as one of the essential parts of a knowledge level model. A static ontology defines the wellformed sentences that can be formulated in a particular domain. The static ontology is in many respects similar to the KADS domain layer, albeit that KADS limits the conceptual primitives at the domain layer largely to concepts and relations.

The work of Clancey [Clancey, 1985] on heuristic classification is clearly a precursor of the KADS four-layer model. Clancey argues that many classification tasks can be described at the knowledge level in terms of *abstraction* steps, abstracting data to abstract problem features, *association* steps between abstracted data and abstract solutions, and *refinement* steps of the abstract solution to a specific solution. The heuristic-classification model does not, however, specify the nature of the domain knowledge that is needed to support the inferences. In addition to the inference structure Clancey defines problem solving behaviour in terms of *tasks* which are procedures to achieve a particular goal. In a similar spirit, Steels [Steels, 1988] distinguishes the following types of knowledge underlying expertise: domain models, describing what form domain concepts and facts can take; heuristic annotations, describing what role domain knowledge can or should play; task knowledge, describing the structure of the problem-solving task; problem-solving methods, indicating how a task may be performed; and strategic knowledge.

Although terminology is different, a common view appears to be emerging based on the idea that different types of knowledge constitute the knowledge level and that these different types of knowledge play different roles in the reasoning process and have inherently different structuring principles. One salient characteristic is that all approaches distinguish between static knowledge and control knowledge. Moreover, control knowledge has two aspects: basic control of how to go about the task, and specific control knowledge specifying how and/or when to apply certain actions.

The KADS four-layer model and our notion of interpretation models (inference structures that are typical for certain classes of problems [Breuker *et al.*, 1987a]) provides a framework to further investigate the notion of *generic task*. Chandrasekaran [Chandrasekaran, 1988] defines a generic task as building blocks of reasoning strategies that are generic and can be used as components for complex reasoning tasks. It appears that generic tasks are very similar to the interpretation models used in KADS.

Similarly, MOLE [Eshelman *et al.*, 1988] exploits the generic method *cover and differentiate* for diagnosis in terms of the following steps:

1. Determine events that potentially explain symptoms.

2. Identify information that can differentiate between candidate explanations by ruling out, providing support for candidates, providing preferences.

3. Get this differentiating information and apply it.

4. If new symptoms become available, go to step 1.

In this example, several types of knowledge are specified in an informal way. First, the domain should provide concepts like: event, symptom, explanation link, preference, rule-out relations etc. Second, a number of basic inference types (similar to knowledge sources) are defined: generating a hypothesis, matching an hypothesis to the available data, selection or ordering, compute preferences. Figure 4 shows a somewhat simplified version of the cover-and-differentiate method. Our example discussed in Sec. 5 gives a full formal specification of this generic inference structure and shows how it applies to a simple medical domain.

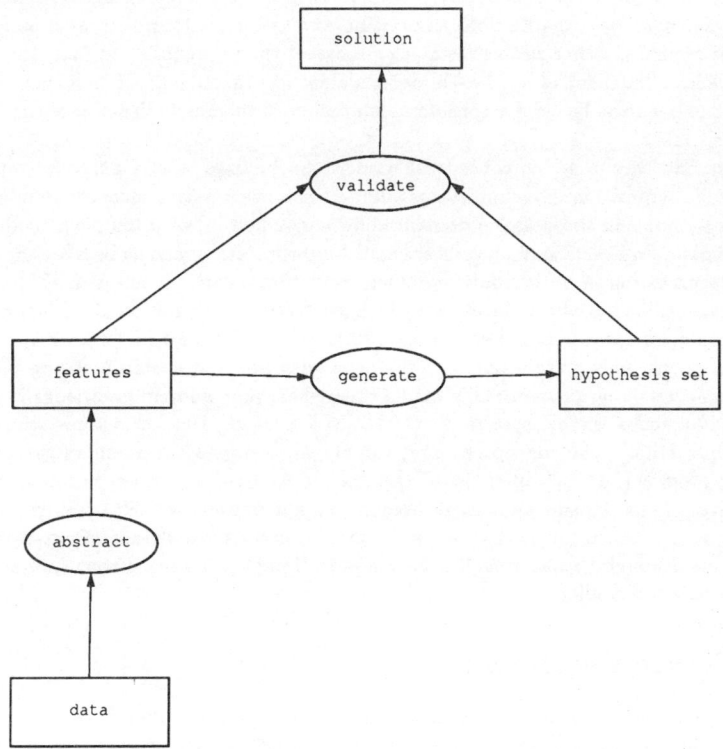

Figure 4: Inference structure for cover-and-differentiate

In addition there is control knowledge that indicates that all possible candidates are generated given a set of symptoms, and that differentiating information is obtained in a backward manner. These types of knowledge would be located in the task layer of KADS.

There is no doubt that generic models of classes of tasks can be of great help in knowledge acquisition, as systems like MOLE show, but there is little consensus in the literature about what constitutes a generic model. The KADS framework provides a handle on some of the issues that arise from the current literature on generic tasks.

5 The Use of Conceptual Modeling in Knowledge Acquisition

There are several ways in which conceptual models can be used in the knowledge acquisition process. The first way in which the knowledge engineer can make use of the notion of conceptual modeling is as an intermediate specification of the functionality of a KBS and as a specification of the knowledge types relevant to a particular task and domain. Such an intermediate specification is useful not only as a means to cope with the complexity of the knowledge acquisition process, but also as a means to identify building blocks of models of reasoning processes independent of their actual implementation. For example the elementary problem solving steps that constitute the heuristic classification model (abstraction, association and refinement) can be used as ingredients for modeling other problem solving processes than diagnosis. In fact, the KADS methodology [Breuker et al., 1987b] defines a set of primitive problem solving actions which has been the basis of a considerable amount of models both for analytic and for synthesis tasks.

A second way in which conceptual models can be used is as a guide for top-down knowledge acquisition. The knowledge engineer can use partial conceptual models (e.g. models without all the detailed domain knowledge filled in) as a template model for a new domain. In KADS such models are called interpretation models because they guide the interpretation of verbal data obtained from the expert. A number of knowledge acquisition tools have been developed which are based on the notion of a generic model of the problem solving task. For example, ROGET, MOLE and BURN, are all systems that drive the knowledge acquisition dialogue with an expert from a strong model of the problem solving process. This model prescribes what domain knowledge is needed to build an actual expert system. In OPAL [Musen et al., 1988] this approach is taken one step further. The conceptual model in OPAL is not just a model of the problem solving process (i.e. the upper three layers in the KADS framework) but also contains templates of the domain knowledge needed. As a consequence OPAL can present the expert with detailed forms that he or she can fill in with the details of an application domain. Although this approach is very powerful indeed, its has strong limitations in scope and applicability.

6 Future Developments

In this paper we have taken the position that knowledge acquisition is to a large extent a constructive activity: models of several aspects of the task and domain have to be build before implementing a knowledge based system.

Looking at the future of knowledge acquisition from this point of view, raises the obvious question of how AI and knowledge based systems themselves can support the various modeling processes. Recent developments in the area of knowledge acquisition tools provide some directions in how this could be done.

Given the modeling approach to knowledge acquisition it is of vital importance that a knowledge engineer has some language in which the various models can be formulated. Such a language is not only important for the knowledge acquisition process itself, but also for communicating models and comparing models for different tasks. A comparative analysis of models of human expertise and of expertise embodied in KBS's will advance the knowledge acquisition activity from an art to a proper engineering discipline. Although there is currently little consensus on what the ingredients and vocabulary of such a modeling language should be, the various ideas appear to converge. The framework developed in KADS enhanced with relations between the knowledge types in different layers may be a starting point for such a language. In our view, it is worthwhile to investigate the different types of knowledge and their relationships from a more formal point of view. A first attempt has been made in this direction [Akkermans *et al.*, 1989; Wielinga *et al.*, 1989]. Such a formal account of knowledge models clarifies at least some of the notions that have been used in a rather informal way so far.

If a common language for defining conceptual models of problem solving processes became accepted, it would be of great interest to study the large collection of problem solving models that currently exist. A consolidation and integration of the models in the KADS interpretation model library [Breuker *et al.*, 1987b], the generic problem solving models of Chandrasekaran and co-workers [Chandrasekaran, 1988], the models underlying the various model-driven knowledge acquisition tools [McDermott, 1989], and various other models in the literature, could provide the knowledge engineering community with an invaluable tool for knowledge acquisition. Also, such a collection of generic models could be the basis of a powerful knowledge acquisition tool that could both communicate with experts and with knowledge engineers.

Looking beyond the traditional knowledge engineering paradigm where the knowledge engineer does most of the work, we envisage an important role for knowledge about models in knowledge acquisition tools that integrate traditional knowledge acquisition techniques and automated learning techniques. One of the major problems in this area is that of integrating knowledge of various sources. A system that has knowledge about the kinds of knowledge that it needs to acquire can exercise much more focused control on the acquisition process and hence solve at least part of the integration problems.

In summary, the notion of knowledge acquisition as a modeling activity has proved to be fruitful both as a basis of methodology development and as a starting point for the development of powerful tools to support and partially automate the KBS development process.

References

H. Akkermans, B. Wielinga, G. Schreiber, and J. Balder. *Towards a Formal Specification of Knowledge Models.* Restricted Distribution Report ECN-89-006, ECN, Petten, The Netherlands, 1989.

J.H. Alexander, M.J. Freling, S.J. Shulman, S. Rehfuss, and S.L. Messick. Ontological analysis: an ongoing experiment. In J. Boose and B. Gaines, editors, *Knowledge-Based Systems, Volume 2: Knowledge Acquisition Tools for Expert Systems*, pages 25–37, Academic Press, London, 1988.

J.L. Alty and M.J. Coombs. Face-to-face guidance of university computer users-i: a study of advisory services. *International Journal of Man-Machine Studies*, 12:390–406, 1980.

J. Breuker, B. Wielinga, M. van Someren, R. de Hoog, G. Schreiber, P. de Greef, B.

Bredeweg, J. Wielemaker, J-P Billault, M. Davoodi, and S. Hayward. *Model Driven Knowledge Acquisition: Interpretation Models*. Esprit Project P1098, Deliverable D1 (task A1), University of Amsterdam and STL Ltd,, 1987.

J. Breuker, R. Winkels, and J. Sandberg. A shell for intelligent help systems. In *Proceedings of the 10th IJCAI*, pages 167–173, Milano, 1987.

H.M. Brooks and N.J. Belkin and P.J. Daniels. Knowledge elicitation using discourse analysis. *International Journal of Man-Machine Studies*, 27(2):127–144, 1987.

B. Chandrasekaran. Generic tasks as building blocks for knowledge-based systems: the diagnosis and routine design examples. *Knowledge Engineering Review*, 1988. to appear.

W.J. Clancey. Heuristic classification. *Artificial Intelligence*, 27:289–350, 1985.

P. de Greef and J. Breuker. A case study in structured knowledge acquisition,. In *Proceedings of the 9th IJCAI*, pages 390–392, Los Angeles, 1985.

P. de Greef. *Cooperative Statistical Problem Solving*. Paper presented at the Second International Workshop on AI and Statistics, SWI, University of Amsterdam, 1988.

P. de Greef. *Control of Cooperation*. Working Paper UvA-B4.2, University of Amsterdam, June 1989.

L. Eshelman, D. Ehret, J. McDermott, and M. Tan. MOLE: a tenacious knowledge acquisition tool. In J.H. Boose and B.R. Gaines, editors, *Knowledge Based Systems, Volume 2: Knowledge Acquisition Tools for Exoert Systems*, pages 95–108, Academic Press, London, 1988.

S.A. Hayward, B.J. Wielinga, and J.A. Breuker. Structured analysis of knowledge. *International Journal of Man-Machine Studies*, 26:487–498, 1987.

W. Jansweijer. *PDP*. PhD thesis, University of Amsterdam, 1988.

J. McDermott. Preliminary steps towards a taxonomy of problem-solving methods. In S. Marcus, editor, *Automating Knowledge Acquisition for Expert Systems*, pages 225–255, Kluwer Academic Publishers, The Netherlands, 1989.

K. Morik. Sloppy modelling. In K. Morik, editor, *Knowledge Representation and Organisation in Machine Learning*, Springer Verlag, 1989.

M.A. Musen, L.M. Fagan, D.M. Combs, and E.H. Shortliffe. Use of a domain model to drive an interactive knowledge editing tool. In J. Boose and B. Gaines, editors, *Knowledge-Based Systems, Volume 2: Knowledge Acquisition Tools for Expert Systems*, pages 257–273, Academic Press, London, 1988.

I.M. Neale. First generation expert systems: a review of knowledge acquisition methodologies. *The Knowledge Engineering Review*, (2):105–145, 1988.

A. Newell. The knowledge level. *Artificial Intelligence*, 1982:87–127, 1982.

M. E. Pollack, J. Hirschberg, and B. Webber. User participation in the reasoning process of an expert system. In *Proceedings of the AAAI 1982*, pages 286–291, Morgan Kaufman, 1982.

E. M. Roth and D.D. Woods. Cognitive task analysis: an approach to knowledge acquisition for intelligent system design. In P. Guida and G. Tasso, editors, *Topics in Expert System Design*, pages 233–264, North Holland, Amsterdam, 1989.

G. Schreiber, J. Breuker, B. Bredeweg, and B. Wielinga. Modelling in KBS development. In *Proc. 2th European Knowledge Acquisition Workshop, Bonn*, 1988.

L. Steels. *Components of Expertise*. AI Memo 88-16, AI Lab, Vrije Universiteit Brussel, 1988.

B.J. Wielinga and B. Bredeweg. Knowledge and expertise in expert systems. In G.C. van der Veer an G. Mulder, editor, *Human-Computer Interaction: Psychonomics Aspects*, pages 290–297, Springer-Verlag, Berlin, 1988.

B. Wielinga and J. Breuker. Interpretation of verbal data for knowledge acquisition. In T. O'Shea, editor, *Advances in Artificial Intelligence*, pages 41–50, ECAI, Elsevier Science publishers, Amsterdam, 1984.

B. Wielinga and J. Breuker. Models of expertise. In *Proceedings ECAI'86*, pages 306–318, 1986.

B.J. Wielinga, B. Bredeweg, and J.A. Breuker. Knowledge acquisition for expert systems. In R.T. Nossum, editor, *Advanced Topics in Artificial Intelligence (ACAI-87)*, pages 96–124, Spinger-Verlag, Berlin Heidelberg, 1988.

B. Wielinga, H. Akkermans, G. Schreiber, and J. Balder. A knowledge acquisition perspective on knowledge-level models. In *Proceedings Knowledge Acquisition Worksop KAW'89, Bannf*, 1989. To Appear.